Serving
Gifted Students
in **Rural** Settings

Serving Gifted Students in Rural Settings

A Framework for Bridging Gifted Education and Rural Classrooms

Edited by Tamra Stambaugh, Ph.D., and Susannah M. Wood, Ph.D.

Copublished With the

NEW YORK AND LONDON

Library of Congress Cataloging-in-Publication Data

Serving gifted students in rural settings / edited by Tamra Stambaugh, Ph.D., and Susannah M. Wood, Ph.D.
   pages cm
 ISBN 978-1-61821-429-4 (pbk.)
 1. Gifted children--Education--United States. 2. Children with social disabilities--Education--United States. 3. Minorities--Education--United States. 4. Education, Rural--United States. 5. Rural poor--United States. 6. United States--Rural conditions. I. Stambaugh, Tamra. II. Wood, Susannah M.
 LC3993.9.S44 2015
 371.95--dc23
                             2015010360

First published in 2015 by Prufrock Press Inc.

Published in 2021 by Routledge
605 Third Avenue, New York, NY 10017
2 Park Square, Milton Park, Abingdon, Oxon OX14 4RN

Routledge is an imprint of the Taylor & Francis Group, an informa business

Copyright © 2015 Taylor & Francis Group

Cover design by Raquel Trevino and layout design by Allegra Denbo

All rights reserved. No part of this book may be reprinted or reproduced or utilised in any form or by any electronic, mechanical, or other means, now known or hereafter invented, including photocopying and recording, or in any information storage or retrieval system, without permission in writing from the publishers.

Notice:
Product or corporate names may be trademarks or registered trademarks, and are used only for identification and explanation without intent to infringe.

ISBN: 9781032144771 (hbk)
ISBN: 9781618214294 (pbk)

DOI: 10.4324/9781003237938

TABLE OF CONTENTS

FOREWORD by Nicholas Colangelo, Ph.D. — vii

Part I: The Rural Life

CHAPTER 1 — National Context of Rural Schools — 1
Zachary J. Richards and Tamra Stambaugh, Ph.D.

CHAPTER 2 — Leaving or Staying Home — 23
Belief Systems and Paradigms
Craig Howley, Ed.D., Aimee Howley, Ph.D., and Daniel Showalter, Ph.D.

CHAPTER 3 — Education in Rural America — 53
Challenges and Opportunities
Marybeth J. Mattingly, Ph.D., and Andrew Schaefer

CHAPTER 4 — Like Finding a Needle in a Haystack — 71
Gifted Black and Hispanic Students in Rural Settings
Donna Y. Ford, Ph.D.

PART I SUMMARY — 91

Part II: Identification, Curriculum, and Instruction for Rural Gifted Learners

CHAPTER 5 — Celebrating Talent — 97
Identification of Rural Gifted Students
Tamra Stambaugh, Ph.D.

CHAPTER 6 — Grouping and Instructional Management Strategies — 111
Kristen Seward and Marcia Gentry, Ph.D.

CHAPTER 7 — Challenges and Solutions for Serving Rural Gifted Students — 135
Accelerative Strategies
Susan G. Assouline, Ph.D., Kristin Flanary, and Megan Foley-Nicpon, Ph.D.

CHAPTER 8 — Serving the Rural Gifted Child Through Advanced Curriculum — 155
Joyce VanTassel-Baska, Ph.D. and Gail Fischer Hubbard

CHAPTER 9	Programming and Rural Gifted Learners *A Review of Models and Applications* Joan D. Lewis, Ph.D.	179
CHAPTER 10	Best of Both Worlds *Technology as a Pathway for Meaningful Choice* Brian C. Housand, Ph.D., and Angela M. Housand, Ph.D.	219
CHAPTER 11	Serving Rural Gifted Students Through Supplemental and Out-of-School Programming Paula Olszewski-Kubilius, Ph.D., Susan Corwith, Ph.D, and Eric Calvert, Ph.D.	239

PART II SUMMARY   257

Part III: Affecting Change for Gifted Learners in Rural Communities

CHAPTER 12	Counseling and the Rural Gifted Susannah M. Wood, Ph.D., and Erin Lane, M.A.	263
CHAPTER 13	"Mommy, I'm Bored" *School-Family-Community Approaches to Working With Gifted, Rural Black Males* Dana Griffin, Ph.D., and Susannah M. Wood, Ph.D.	289
CHAPTER 14	Leading Policy, Advocacy, and Relationship Building in Rural Schools Elissa F. Brown, Ph.D.	317
CHAPTER 15	Rural Teachers of the Gifted *The Importance of Professional Development* Laurie Croft, Ph.D.	341
CHAPTER 16	Concluding Thoughts and Voices From Gifted Individuals in Rural Areas Tamra Stambaugh, Ph.D.	363

ABOUT THE EDITORS   381

ABOUT THE AUTHORS   383

Foreword

How to identify the academic and social needs of gifted students has been a major challenge in education for the past 50 years. Unlike other areas of special focus, gifted education carries the added burden of fighting political and philosophical battles regarding elitism and relevance in times of resource shortages in education.

I have been involved in gifted education for more than 40 years and I have seen a number of trends in the field. There have been times when gifted education oscillated between being "in" regarding a national agenda and when it was "out." Over the decades gifted education has survived and changed based on research and practice. The challenges remain, as they do in all aspects of education, yet gifted education is vibrant and clearly focuses on an important and fascinating group of students, those we identify as gifted and talented.

One area within gifted education that has not received due attention has been gifted students in rural settings. Although there is understandably considerable attention to education issues in urban settings, there are still a large number of America's students who attend rural schools. These students reflect the fabric of our society.

When we speak of gifted students we invariably are speaking of a minority in terms of numbers and in terms of special needs. The needs for differentiated curricula, acceleration, and grouping for peer group experiences become more challenging in rural settings not only because of smaller numbers in schools but also because of distance from resources such as museums, libraries, and centers that can enrich the K–12 experience. Although technology has minimized some of these issues, we still have much to understand and respond to in terms of providing a fair and appropriate educational experience to gifted students in rural areas.

This book focusing on rural issues has been needed and I am confident will make its contribution to the field. It is comprehensive in that it covers an array of important topics from philosophies, to identification, to acceleration, to technology, to diversity, to poverty, to counseling, to advocacy. The chapters are written by a number of highly respected scholars and practitioners in the field.

I am familiar with the work of Drs. Stambaugh and Wood. They are intelligent, productive, and dedicated scholars in gifted education. They will continue to be strong, forward thinkers in the field, and I believe this book will be a benchmark contribution in their careers.

Serving Gifted Students in Rural Settings is a bridge to past work in gifted education as well as future issues and trends. We have been provided a valuable resource.

Nicholas Colangelo, Ph.D., Dean,
College of Education, University of Iowa
Myron and Jacqueline Blank Professor of Gifted Education

PART I
The Rural Life

CHAPTER 1

National Context of Rural Schools

Zachary J. Richards and Tamra Stambaugh, Ph.D.

What Is Rural?

When presented with the term rural, one is likely to conjure clichéd images of idyllic landscapes, from rolling green hills and abundant pastures to winding roads and fenced in farmland. There is much more to the concept of ruralness than these rustic images provide. For one, Duncan (2012) discussed the implications for these communities when we move beyond such idealized fantasies. Not all rural spaces are the same, nor are these spaces created equal. Where some areas like the Upper Peninsula of Michigan or the Rocky Mountain West benefit from the touristic and retirement allure that their natural beauty and resources generate, regions like the South, Midwest, and Appalachia do not find themselves in such a fortunate situation. In these circumstances, markets are not as strong and there do not exist such beneficial factors enticing others to spend their time and money in these communities (Duncan, 2012).

Also important to understanding the essence of rural communities is how their far-flung physical locations from urban centers situate them in a position where accessibility to many modern conveniences is hard-found. Difficulties in obtaining broadband connectivity, developing basic frameworks for services like water and sewage access, and meeting transportation needs complicate the rural landscape (Battelle for Kids, 2014). Instead of public transit services, everyone relies on cars and trucks for getting around. These remote communities lack the infrastructural necessities to support economic growth, and because of this shortcoming in commercial viability, the institutions that make up rural areas are much less diverse than their urban counterparts (Duncan, 2010).

Nailing down what rural means is no simple task. Should a community be labeled as rural based on its geographic location, or by the number of people living there? Do agricultural economies or the way land is used determine that a community is a rural one? When do urban areas end and rural ones begin? Federal agencies use more than two dozen definitions to characterize a community as rural depending on the issues at hand, emphasizing the multifaceted considerations needed to capture this complicated idea. Generally speaking, rural communities are defined as not urban. In addition to using purely jurisdictional boundaries to delineate the rural from the urban, examinations of settlement density and cities' influence on labor, trade, and media also matter for drawing this line. Residents in rural areas are not as concentrated as those of their urban counterparts, and they do not find themselves within a reasonable commuting distance to urban cores for employment and other necessities. Population size also matters, although ascertaining an appropriate threshold for characterizing a community as rural is subject to ongoing debate. With technological developments in the 20th century organizing economic and social activities around cities and large towns, recalibrations were necessary to take suburban development into account. Where a rural population was once defined as those communities with less than 2,500 people in 1910, this definition is now more fluid. A rural characterization is applied to areas with populations between 2,500 and 50,000 people, depending on the situation (Cromartie & Bucholtz, 2008).

But these answers do not wholly capture the essence of rural communities. They are more than being outside the city limits. They are more than communities with fewer than 50,000 people. Rural communities are more than "not urban." People are rural, too. Tight bonds are forged in these small environments that foster neighborliness and communal cooperation. With this it may seem paradoxical, but there is also a great deal of respect for independence and hard work (Howley, 2009). Such an irony speaks to the difficulties one encounters when trying to discuss the rural. Rural communities consist of individuals of differing values, belief systems, and characteristics. No two rural areas are the same, but there exist patterns—patterns we now discuss as "the essence of rural."

The Essence of Rural

Although one rural community may differ drastically from the next, embedded in these rustic landscapes and the people who inhabit them are common themes that permit a discussion of a rural essence. A sense of place is especially strong where the individuals are tied to the lands in which they were born and raised. Home and personal histories are valued for the powerfully informative role they have on one's self—past, present, and future. Concern for tradition is prominent as well, and requires reconciling a committal to the way things have always been done in the face of an always-advancing world that necessitates adjustments in response to developing technologies and emerging markets. Along with neighborliness and communal cooperation, it is no surprise that rural communities find ways to organize themselves in meaningful ways around nexuses like family and religion. Success is measured in ways ranging from assessments of self-worth, to recently developed standards of material possessions and financial gain. Although the term *rural* is difficult to encapsulate, considering these themes as they relate to the rural experience opens the door for a focused and relevant discussion of a rural essence.

Sense of Place

Consisting of pastures and farmlands, agriculture also makes up a big part of what it means to be rural, both for the place and its people. In his essay, "A Native Hill," Berry (2002) discussed the role farming had on developing his character. Born during the Great Depression, Berry remarked on how working with his grandfather and father on their farm in a setting not yet affected by the developments of industrialized farming forged a bond more strongly held to the history of his home community than to his generation. Berry believes this strong sense of place tied to working the land was crucial in the development of his character (Berry, 2002). Recent developments, however, threaten such traditional ties to rural places where fewer than 2% of rural workers now work in agricultural occupations (Duncan, 2010).

Given the pull of sense of place and the emphasis on family and community for many rural individuals, the decision to move to an urban area for education or employment is a difficult one. The pull to return "home" is strong and the rural area is always likely to be referred to as "home," regardless of how long the individual has been living elsewhere (Jones, 1994). The feeling rural people often exhibit toward their rustic homes speaks to the importance that ought to be placed on understanding a rural sense of place. When individuals bear a special connection to the land they inhabit, they perceive themselves embedded in that place and its history, all its dilemmas, and the possibilities inherent within it. Indeed, fostering such a perception proves promising for the benefit of rural communities.

Berry's (2002) discussion of his home in Port Royal, KY, speaks to the profound effect a rural sense of place may have on individuals and the compelling mindset they may develop toward their rustic homes. He traced multiple generations of his family back through his community and recalled how although he achieved the (presumed) highest status within his literary career, for him, his home and its history were inseparable from him. In discussing his early years, he wrote, "It entered my imagination, and gave its substance and tone to my mind. It fashioned in me possibilities and limits, desires and frustrations, that I do not expect to live to the end of" (p. 4).

After leaving New York University to return to his old Kentucky home, Berry's fears that he would be unfulfilled were wrong, and instead, he felt more alive and conscious of himself than before. Berry saw his home with not only with positive fervor, but a poignant scrutiny as well. Where he could occupy the role of outsider and critic while living in New York, as both a native and a citizen in Kentucky, Berry enjoyed no such immunity. In entwining himself with Port Royal and his predecessors, he became aware of how their treatment of the place narrowed its future, forcing him to be cognizant of how his actions would influence what of his community he will leave behind (Berry, 2002). A heightened sense of place, then, undoubtedly has great potential to impact rural communities for the better. When citizens see themselves as part of a communal tradition, they are obliged to have its best interests in mind and cultivate in that place a set of values, traditions, and opportunities in the best interests of all its people.

Value of Tradition

Another definitive feature of rural communities that helps to explain the static tendencies of rustic economies is a commitment to the way things have always been done. This tradition coincides with some rural communities being seen as "back woods" or not embracing change. In an age where adjustment is required to keep pace with advances in technology and global markets, the tradition of assuming the same occupation as one's parents is not always a viable option (Duncan, 2010). Where government and policy do not lend themselves to moving beyond nostalgia, rural communities suffer in that a limited range of employment options, and a lack of a diversified local economy discourages individuals from seeking to live and work in rural communities (Huang et al., 2002). In these situations, the economies of rural communities remain stagnant.

With a lack of a foundation for economic growth also come challenges in attracting jobs to rural communities, thereby creating a situation where capital is unequally distributed to urban areas over rural ones. High-paying service jobs in finance, law, medicine, and technology are typically reserved for urban centers, where unskilled careers like work in factories are the norm for rural employment (Duncan, 1999). Also, recent economic restructuring of a declining goods-producing industry can be attributed to exacerbating the inequality between urban and rural communities. This situation also creates problems when rural individuals hold multiple jobs over their lifetimes, never develop a traditional career, and prevent them from forging beneficial professional connections (Howley, 2009).

Adhering to tradition may also have benefits for rural youth. Although they might fear openly identifying with their rural heritage because of the potential for negative stereotyping, second-generation Appalachian students are nevertheless more forward and direct in communication and open to hearing other values and worldviews. With a stronger orientation toward family, a dominant work ethic, and a practical approach to education, Appalachian students are positioned to success in community-oriented work at home (Helton, 2010). Complying with rural traditions, then, has the capacity to set rural youth up for success within their communities. Abandoning the country lifestyle and its accompanying tenets for the overbearing values of the metropolitan mainstream is not necessary to equip rural youth with the tools to sustain their communities.

Role of Family

Delving into the institutions of family and religion illuminate the ways in which rural youth organize themselves within their communities. From 2008 through 2018, the Carsey Institute at the University of New Hampshire is conducting a study on education and job opportunity decisions of young people in rural Coös County in northern New Hampshire. The Coös Study, as it is known, seeks to understand trends of how rural youth approach realizing their life goals. Students' findings from the first half of this study show the impact of family on rural aspirations and students' perception of their rustic homes.

For rural youth, mentorships play an informative role in developing ambition where they instill in rural students the idea that they can realize their achievements with dedication and hard work. Where family members comprise 68% of these relationships for Coös County youth, a positive experience with relatives in professional spheres encourages students to have more faith in bringing their goals to fruition. Rural students' understanding of their relatives' professional lives also has the potential to place strain on familial relationships. The study found that when families face economic pressure, rural students are more likely develop negative opinions of their parents and siblings. But that is not to say that these feelings necessarily deter rural youth in Coös County from considering family as an important factor in deciding where to make their lives. Although 76% of study participants said leaving Coös County was important, 93% said that living close to family was meaningful as well. These findings speak to the tenuous threshold and conflicting priorities in which rural students largely find themselves (Staunton & Jaffee, 2014).

What can be done, then, to reconcile these conflicting interests? From their findings, the Carsey Institute recommends expanding educational opportunities and strengthening professional mentorship bonds to alleviate the difficulties rural students face in realizing their goals. They encourage teaching youth money management skills to reduce the anxiety rural students of poverty might face in light of their families' financial strain. Lastly, they urge for programs that provide assistance for families with fiscal issues that develop problem solving, communication, and conflict resolution skills (Staunton & Jaffee, 2014). Where familial relationships constitute a key thread in the rural fabric, investing in rural families is not only an investment in rural students, but their communities as well.

Role of Religion

Church is the hub of many rural areas and is relied upon as a foundation for shaping the culture, beliefs, and traditions of several rural communities. The church is a place for families to gather and for a sense of community to be established. According to Jones (1994), a leading expert on rural Appalachia studies, social reformers criticize the idea of rural individuals holding to strong religious beliefs as it is viewed as impeding progress, although, as he explained, one cannot understand rural Appalachian families without understanding the importance of the church in their lives. Strong beliefs in God helped rural Appalachians make it through difficult times and find meaning and purpose.

Even if rural individuals do not go to church, faith and a strong reliance on and trust in God is an integral part of many rural communities.

Dillon and Savage (2006) compared the religious beliefs and voting patterns of those from urban, suburban, and rural areas. The study divided rural areas into four regions: South, West, Midwest, and Northeast America. They found significant differences in belief systems among rural individuals in each locale, with the rural South being the most religious, followed by the rural Midwest, Northeast, and then the West. They also found that rural areas, in general, are more conservative in their voting patterns and religious beliefs than their nonrural counterparts, regardless of the region in which they live. As church is the foundation of many rural communities, it serves an integral role in rural culture and influence across the lifespan.

Commercialism and Definitions of Success

The definitions of success for urban and rural families differ. Berry's experiences in early 20th-century rural America, previously discussed, speak to the traditional characteristics associated with rural communities, particularly those found in Appalachia. In 1994, Jones wrote of 10 beliefs that make up Appalachian values. These included principles of independence, self-reliance, and pride; community sociability; strong ties to family; personability; religion; modesty; love of place; patriotism; and senses of beauty and humor (Jones, 1994). These characteristics are valued above all else. As Jones (1994) explained, rural Appalachians are more concerned with who you are instead of what you do, what you have attained, or how much money you have.

Although these aspects once captured the social landscape of rural communities, recent materialistic ethics jeopardizes this beneficially collectivistic disposition. The philosopher, bell hooks, who grew up lower class and Black in rural Hopkinsville, KY, offered us a personal example of how rural individuals may be changing the priorities of their ancestors, leaving a wholesome, simple life for that of a consumer-dominated culture. She recalled how handmade quilts decorated her grandmother's house and how her grandmother's hand-picked and hang-dried peppers in windowsills provided hooks with insight into her identity and ancestry as a Black agrarian, but her own house did not feature such cultural objects. Her mother did not adorn their homes with objects that reflected the people who lived there, but instead subscribed to satisfying material expectations: Imagine always striving for the newest television, the most luxurious furniture, and bearing the burden of a high price tag to satisfy these wants (hooks, 1995).

This obsession with the material is problematic for hooks, as it obscures the experiences of one's people by recalibrating the measurement of worth in terms of possessions. Where the issues facing rural communities are already unpronounced, abandoning such traditions in favor of material possessions contributes to a lack of an identifiably rural aesthetic, metaphorically voiding rural communities of a readily recognizable culture. Instead, hooks (1995) urged for the cultivation of a cultural aesthetic, like that found in her grandmother's house, that heightens awareness and understanding of one's communal history and present status. This cultural expression of circumstance, for hooks, was an important step in bridging the gap between the haves and have-nots. To address the problems facing rural communities in light of this lack of a cultural atmosphere raises the question of who will take the initiative to vocalize rural issues, a question complicated by present orientations of educational institutions that will be discussed later.

Education, Success, and the Rural Essence

An overemphasis on commercialism is not the only way rural communities may be changing. The definitions of success are also called into question through an overemphasis on national policies related to schooling—many of which do not favor or consider rural schools. Recent developments in what it means to achieve academic success seem only to burden the prospects of righting the wrongs rural students, schools, and communities encounter. Later trends show that the United States' education policies have reoriented schooling to be a tool for training students to be future employees of corporations so that the nation can be an effective competitor in the global economy. With this, any potential for education is thought of in terms of employment prospects (Howley, 2009).

Where such corporate concerns are devastating for rural communities is in how they discredit the traditional values associated with a rural way of life—like self-provisioning, neighborliness, and diverse farming—in favor of the cosmopolitan mainstream. This disposition has misinformed rural students, particularly those who strive to be academically successful, that the middle-class professional trajectory is the only successful way to live. Such commoditization

National Context of Rural Schools

of education has managed to find its way into the relationships between individuals in rural communities as well, where those who subscribe to the terms of corporate success are more compelled to act in line with global demands than local ones (Howley, 2009). Much like bell hooks' own account of the differences between her grandmother's and her own houses, when success is abstracted from the realities of one's immediate environment, important aspects of one's identity are prone to being lost. With this, rural communities are debilitated in their relationship with urban communities and the autocratic notions of success bound to corporate interests. Craig Howley (2009) was not exaggerating when he said, "Rural places are relatively powerless in political, economic, and cultural terms" (p. 540).

But these corporate priorities of education do not always coincide with the characteristic features of rural students, and where these differences clash, much work is to be done in making known the different fabric of the cloth from which rural students are cut. For one, qualitative studies conducted by observing Appalachian students in classroom settings saw more informal manners of communication and a lack of typically good writing skills. Although they usually were not college ready in terms of verbal or math ability, these rural students were nevertheless described as sincere and motivated in obtaining an education. Interestingly, this motivation coincides with the fact that many are working class and approached life as a struggle (Helton, 2010).

Even within the group of observed students, differences were found between first- and second-generation Appalachians. First-generation students were more committed to Appalachian customs and valued education as a privilege, believing that they would take what they learned back home and share their successes within their culture. Second-generation Appalachians, however, fit more into the effects of the aforementioned commoditization of education. These students had better literacy skills and were less bound to Appalachian customs. They avoided identifying too strongly with Appalachian culture as to avoid being negatively stereotyped. Second-generation Appalachians were described as more forward and direct, more inclined to pursue graduate or professional degrees, and more liberal and flexible in their values. Adding weight to arguments for obsessions of achieving corporate success away from one's rural home, an observer remarked, "It's as if second generation Appalachian students grow up with a strong expectation for success, the motivation to do better than their parents have done, educationally and economically" (Helton, 2010, p. 69).

In relation to their urban counterparts, Appalachian students were observed to be more reflective and take more time to digest what they learned. Many held part-time work in addition to their studies, likely as a result of the concern for the economic pressures that their families face. Because of this, many cut corners on completing assignments and showed more interest in practical application of material rather than theoretical concepts. Urban students were also observed as being more verbal, asking more questions in class, showing more initiative, and more prone to employing critical thinking to understand concepts than their rural peers (Helton, 2010).

The Relationship Between Poverty and Education in Rural Areas

Another factor to consider is the role of poverty in many rural areas. The socio-economic circumstances to be expressed for rural communities are not presently favorable. The more than 50 million adults and 12 million rural children face a greater likelihood of lower incomes, higher poverty rates, declining health outcomes, and lower educational attainment than those individuals hailing from suburban and urban regions (Battelle for Kids, 2014). Statistically speaking, 85.4% of rural adults have a high school diploma and 6.6% are unemployed; 46.6% of rural students are eligible for free or reduced school lunch, and 19.3% of rural students are eligible for Title I funds (Johnson et al., 2014).

It should be noted, however, that rural areas in certain regions feature more exaggerated challenges associated with impoverishment. Rural areas in states in Central Appalachia, the Southeast, and the Mid-South Delta have higher unemployment rates than others elsewhere, and states in these same regions feature lower median incomes as well (Johnson et al., 2014). Nonmetropolitan areas with the most severe persistence of child poverty rates are also regionalized, clustered in the Appalachian states of Kentucky and West Virginia and banded from east to west across the southern United States from Virginia and North Carolina to New Mexico and Arizona (Duncan, 2010).

Given the ties between education and job-preparedness, it is unsurprising that those communities facing the greatest struggles associated with poverty are also the ones with lower rates of adults with high school diplomas. This factor compounds itself where a lack of an educated adult population diminishes the capacity to support public schools in these rural localities (Johnson et al., 2014). Parents lacking an education perpetuate this educational shortcoming for future generations by approaching the subject of education beyond high school as impractical for their children (Helton, 1995; Reck & Reck, 1980;

Wilson et al., 1997). They seek to direct their children toward staying in the community and taking general labor at home, and particularly for women, Appalachian families discourage the pursuit of education beyond high school (Wallace & Diekroger, 2000). Further complicating the educational situation in rural America is the lack of knowledge where parents who do indeed desire to have their children to seek higher education do not understand how these goals can be realized (Battelle for Kids, 2014).

Regarding the policy decisions that impact rural public schools, there is a wide host of intersecting factors that have bearing on student outcomes. Fiscal concerns like spending per pupil and for transportation, as well as concerns of obtaining funding from outside sources, strap rural schools for resources to use for serving students. Also at play are more abstract elements like expectations for and implications of achieving academic success and the often unacknowledged and particular characteristics of rural students themselves.

The rate at which rural schools spend money per pupil does not keep up with their urban and suburban counterparts. The national average expenditure for each student is $5,826, but states with very small rural districts, or those in the Mid-Atlantic and Northeast spend upwards of twice this amount. Sixteen states, many of which are found in the same previously discussed impoverished regions in the South and Southwest, spend less than half as much as states like New York in those more privileged areas (Johnson et al., 2014).

The ratio at which school districts spend money on transporting students to instructing them also complicates the issues surrounding rural educational policy. Unavoidable issues of geographic isolation, cumbersome terrain, and dispersed residential zones require that some rural districts devote more funds to getting students to and from school. When money is spent on fueling buses and hiring drivers, it is necessarily diverted away from beneficial programs that benefit student learning. Rural districts find themselves spending an average of $11.71 for instructional purposes per dollar devoted to transportation costs. Although spending can vary even between areas with similar geographies, school size and area serve as better correlations to higher spending. When a single school system serves many people living in dispersed and isolated communities, this increases costs. Having many school districts serve small, isolated population clusters and large, sparsely populated geographic areas can sidestep decreases in instructional spending. Large schools and school districts also have been shown to be problematic for successful student outcomes, especially for impoverished and minority students. States in the Southeast, Appalachia, and neighboring areas in the Mid-Atlantic are prone to suffering from these size problems as a result of typical countywide districting and regional high schools (Johnson et al., 2014).

The ratio at which local and state governments contribute money to rural schools has resounding consequences where impoverished communities cannot make up the difference of underfunded districts. Many states leave expenses of transportation, capital investments, teacher pay supplements, and sometimes even benefits to the responsibility of local governments (Battelle for Kids, 2014). Where rural communities have low income, low property values, and low income taxes, they are at an obvious disadvantage in this respect (Williams, 2013). Exaggerating this problem is that states have begun funding schools less since the recession that hit in the late 2000s. Even in the 2013–2014 year, 34 states decreased their support to rural schools, with 13 states cutting funding by 10% or more (Leachman & Mai, 2013).

Federal funding disparities also disadvantage rural schools and students. Title I funds are allocated on considerations of high concentrations of poverty, which are determined either by a high number of poor students or a high percentage of poor students in a particular area. But with these considerations taken into account, the higher number typically has more sway. Due to the present Title I distribution formula, an overall wealthier suburban district with a higher headcount of poor students, for example, will usually receive greater funding from this federal program than rural communities with a higher percentage of students living in poverty (Strange, 2011).

Financial problems of rural education policy also carry over into the wages that can be paid to teachers. Rural educators earn on average 13.4% less than their urban and suburban counterparts, leaving rural schools with detrimental prospects of attracting highly qualified teachers of advanced subjects and STEM courses (Jimerson, 2005). Without the financial means to attract these desirable candidates or take advantage of professional development opportunities to better their own teacher's practices, rural districts will continue to underserve their students, and the rural-urban achievement gap will continue to widen (Battelle for Kids, 2014).

As a result of their educational hardships, rural students also fall behind their urban and suburban peers in educational outcomes. Data gathered through the National Assessment of Educational Progress by the United States Department of Education compares the testing outcomes between regions within and across states. In the states where overall scores were the highest, rural students consistently performed more poorly on grade-level and subject area assessments than their nonrural peers. Additionally, when comparing performance across state lines, those states previously mentioned to suffer most from rural impoverishment—states in the Appalachian, Southeastern, and Southwestern United States—score lower than states in the Northeast, Mid-Atlantic, and near the Great Lakes (Johnson et al., 2014). Clearly, then, if these assessments are to be trusted, a lack of funding has had a consistently adverse affect on the success rates of rural students.

Overcoming these funding disparities remains a difficult task for rural communities where such districts lack the people, resources, and experience to vie for federal funding in the form of grants against better funded, more seasoned districts. Instead of grant writers, rural districts often rely upon principals and superintendents for completing grant applications (Ayers, 2011). As a result of these unpromising prospects, some have argued that more provisions ought to be set aside for funding rural schools and communities, and more efforts initiated for equipping rural educational officials with the technical schools to be more competitive for future grants (Battelle for Kids, 2014).

Out-Migration and Brain Drain

Another consequence of a lack of investment in high-quality education in rural areas and investments in community development is the phenomenon of brain drain, also referred to as out-migration. This concept alludes to the values that have come to define rural communities in spite of traditional perceptions of neighborliness and hospitality typically associated with this population. Brain drain, which describes the mass exodus of young and educated individuals from their rural homes in favor of education and employment opportunities in urban communities, may be seen as a direct response to the economic problems facing rural regions. Brain drain has far-reaching implications. For one, it perpetuates the widening gap found between rural and urban incomes by luring college-educated youngsters away from their homes to work in the suburbs and metropolises (Artz, 2003). This causes concern for rural areas where population loss is feared to diminish the possibility of providing public services like police and fire departments, qualified teachers, and access to healthcare. On such a slippery slope, rural communities have the potential to be too small and their populations so underqualified that they can no longer sustain themselves (Huang et al., 2002).

The present situation in rural communities fails its gifted youth in their ability to realize their aspirations, but much remains to be done in terms of investing in terms of opportunities. Parents lacking an education perpetuate an underfunding of human capital that threatens to dissolve the potential future of rural communities. Investing in future generations to have a greater prevalence of professions in teaching, medicine, law, and the sciences benefits not only rural communities immediately, but in the future as well. A diversified economy is a more stable economy, and where mentor relationships have been shown to improve rural youth's desire to remain in the communities, this diversification better provides the rural gifted with the opportunity to realize their aspirations at home. Being from close-knit communities, gifted rural youth would certainly benefit from solidifying their relationships to their fellow rural citizens. To sustain rural communities and ways of life, then, it is necessary to invest in those individuals who make up such places and provide for their future.

The Rural Gifted Student and Rural Essence

Now that we have considered the broad and complicated characteristics associated with what it means to be rural, implications of these characteristics for education, and the features that differentiate rural students from their nonrural peers, we may consider what all this has in store for gifted and talented students from rural areas. First, even knowing which students are gifted in rural environments proves to be a difficult task requiring unconventional methods of identification. Geography limits access for gifted students to enriching activities that have otherwise been proven to benefit this population. Economic problems plaguing rural communities have implications for gifted rural students as well, especially in terms of providing them with academic and professional resources to meet their needs. Expectations from families, schools, and future employers also have resounding consequences for developing these students' identities.

Less than 8% of students identified as gifted and talented come from backgrounds of impoverishment, significantly below the statistics of students identified from the middle and upper classes. This unequal distribution is likely the result of measures like standardized testing, teacher recommendations, and grades, all of which more frequently screen out students of poverty because of the discrepancies found between these students' lower quality of education and fewer academic opportunities. Although students of poverty might have great potential, they are unable to compete against the enriched backgrounds of their more fortunate counterparts. When circumstantial factors are left out of the equation of identifying gifted students, what is selected is not talent, but rather access to opportunities that allow gifted students the choice to further their education and to be prepared to do so (Slocumb & Payne, 2000).

Belief systems and geographic isolation serve as obstacles for rural students in gaining access to enriching activities. Rural parents are more likely to take their children to athletic events rather than to visit museums, zoos, aquariums, and libraries (Provasnik et al., 2007). Although a simple lack of access might serve as one explanation to this situation, the priorities of parents and communities are reflected in the attitudes of students as well, where despite being unsatisfied with the conditions of their rural schools and educational opportunities, they view their athletics departments as points of pride (Herzog and Pittman, 1995). Clearly, then, where gifted students can benefit from enriching academic activities, they have been told that sports are more important to their communities than their scholastic achievements.

In their study of beliefs and values of individuals from a rural county in the mid-South, Deggs and Miller (2011) noted contradictory opinions between the value of continued education and the rural identity. Families were in favor of higher education opportunities but also highly valued the rural quality of life, community identity, and loyalty—which are compromised when postsecondary educational opportunities are sought.

When rural communities do not have the infrastructure to support higher educational attainment, both the communities and the individuals suffer. When individuals from rural communities do leave, it is generally because of economic conditions more than a desire to leave (Petrin, Schafft, & Meece, 2012). Contrary to popular belief, the desire to remain in the rural area is true for many gifted students from rural communities as well (Howley, 2009). However, when rural communities do not have the jobs or support networks to keep gifted individuals in the local community, they are forced to leave if they want to follow their passion.

Quality of available education also has implications for rural gifted and talented students. Where it was previously discussed how rural school districts have difficulty attracting highly qualified teachers, this means less access to advanced materials and courses like Advanced Placement and International Baccalaureate programs in comparison to urban and suburban students. The lack of access to rigorous academics is also a result of the classroom dynamics at play in these communities. Concerning math courses, rural gifted students are subjected to repetitive, lower level basic skills instead of being presented with advanced materials (Howley et al., 2005).

These students described school as mundane and not as challenging in contrast to the perspectives of their urban and suburban peers (Gentry et al., 2001). Without the resources to challenge these students and make them more competitive with their advanced, nonrural peers, rural gifted students skate through school easily, unchallenged until the rude awakenings of a more rigorous college experience (Colangelo et al., 1999). To compensate for the lack of available academic challenges, rural gifted students might consider looking outside of the classroom, but in light of earlier considerations of the overall lack of professional employment in rural communities, content experts for some fields are in short supply (Provasnik et al., 2007).

This is truly problematic for prospects of talent development where studies have shown mentor relationships to be essential in this pursuit for rural gifted students, especially those from impoverished backgrounds (Payne, 1996). These relationships equip students with perspectives to better deal with issues of poverty, help them set appropriate goals for their futures, and allow them to recognize and develop desirable skills they see in someone they can emulate. These benefits are not reserved to the immediate student at hand, but families can learn what skills to cultivate in their children as well, and thereby become more involved in developing their talent (Montgomery, 2001; Olszewski-Kubulius, 2007; VanTassel-Baska & Stambaugh, 2007).

Where rural communities lack outlets for gifted students to explore their interests or understand their unique abilities, intensities, and passions, these students are likely to feel out of place and without similar peers who "get" them. For those rural gifted students who do succeed in achieving academic success in spite of feeling out of place, they are often encouraged to look beyond their home communities for professional success (Colangelo et al., 1999). Work still remains to be done in attracting rural gifted students to return in high numbers to their rural homes and impact their communities for the better in spite of the magnetic pull exerted on these students to flock to cities to satisfy normative goals of corporate success (Howley, 2009). As we have seen, however, rural students and their upbringings and values do not neatly coincide with those of their nonrural counterparts. With this dual incompatibility facing rural gifted students in whichever environment they find themselves, it is important to consider how occupying this threshold between their anomalously rural homes and the allure (or push for some) to the cosmopolitan urban spaces affects how they understand and project themselves.

Wendell Berry is one such person who finds himself in this threshold, and he tries to make sense of his conflicting experiences growing up in rural Kentucky and serving as a professor at New York University. When Berry moved from the farm to the city, he noticed how the new setting conflicted with his rurally informed identity insofar as he was detached from the contexts in which his character was developed. In living in the metropolis of New York, Berry realized the problems facing this environment were not his to be responsible for, and while there, he had no authentic investment in critiquing or attempting to solve issues facing his new community. Likewise, the situation is reversed where he feels urban issues take precedence over rural ones, continually comprising the issues that are seen to truly matter. Berry (2002) nevertheless must come to terms with the unique situation he found himself, writing, "In my acceptance of twentieth-century realities there has had to be a certain deliberateness, whereas most of my contemporaries had them simply by being born to them" (p. 4). Here, Berry finds himself in the tenuous threshold of recalling the informative experiences complicating his rural upbringing in light of an alien surrounding that neither recognizes nor accommodates these issues.

In my (first author) own experiences as someone who left the farm for the city, I can attest to the realities of this concept of deliberateness and its impact on how the rural gifted conceptualize and project their identities. In class discussions at college, I perfected my pronunciation of the letter "I" and abandoned my vernacular of conversational "ain't nevers" in order to avoid sounding ignorant to my professors and peers. As discussed earlier with second-generation Appalachian students, there is a desire to avoid being too publicly entrenched in a rural native culture as to avoid being negatively stereotyped. This awareness and self-manipulation does not end for rural gifted students when they finish school, but carries on throughout the course of their lives in how they relate to nonrural friends and coworkers and how they decide to cultivate their own families. For rural gifted students who achieve success away from their rural homes, then, there exist problematic situations of abandoning informative experiences and undervaluing the rural aspects of the self that have made them who they are.

Conclusion

Reasons for investigating the broad definitions of rural communities, how poverty affects these regions, the conditions of rural education and students, and the implications of these features for rural gifted and talented students are not limited to concerns rural communities have for themselves, however. Instead, healthy, prosperous, and spirited rural regions are in the best interests of America at large. More than 44% of the men and women who serve in our country's military come from rural areas, despite only comprising 17% of the national population. Most American-born NASA engineers in the revolutionary era of the 1950s and 1960s hailed from rural communities, and today, advancements in ecologically sound technologies are coming from those rural areas where people have always lived closer to the land and have been more apt to make due with scarcer resources. Rural communities, although employing fewer people in the fields, still lead the country in agricultural production and in making food safer, more nutritious, and less expensive. The natural resources found in rural areas are key to continuing to drive our national economy and require deft oversight (Battelle for Kids, 2014). It goes without saying that investing efforts in rural communities is worthwhile, yet we must also maintain the integrity of the community values and beliefs that make rural part of the American quilt that is a necessary juxtaposition to the urban and suburban ways of life. Discussions of the issues of rural regions cannot afford to fall upon deaf ears.

References

Artz, G. (2003). Rural area brain drain: Is it a reality? *Choices: A Publication of the American Agricultural Economics Association*, 11–16.

Ayers, J. (2011). Make rural schools a priority: Considerations for reauthorizing the elementary and secondary education act. Retrieved from http://www.americanprogress.org/issues/education/report/2011/08/04/10216/make-rural-schools-a-priority/

Battelle for Kids (2014). *Making rural education work for our children and our future*. Columbus, OH: Author.

Berry, W. (2002). *The art of the common-place: The agrarian essays of Wendell Berry*. Washington, D.C.: Counterpoint.

Colangelo, N., Assouline, S. G., & New, J. K. (1999). *Gifted education in rural schools: A national assessment*. Iowa: The University of Iowa, The Connie Belin & Jacqueline N. Blank International Center for Gifted Education and Talent Development.

Cromartie, J., & Bucholtz, S. (2008) *Defining the "rural" in rural America*. Washington, D.C.: United States Department of Agriculture. Retrieved from http://www.ers.usda.gov/amber-waves/2008-june/defining-the-%E2%80%9Crural%E2%80%9D-in-rural-america.aspx#.VPxmMWR4pbc

Deggs, D. M., & Miller, M. T. (2011). Beliefs and values among rural citizens: Shared expectations for educational attainment? *Planning and Changing, 42,* 302–315.

Dillon, M., & Savage, S. (2006). Values and religion in rural America: Attitudes toward abortion and same-sex relations. *The Carsey School of Public Policy at the Scholars' Repository*, Paper 12. Retrieved from http://scholars.unh.edu/carsey/12

Duncan, C. (1999). *World's apart: Why poverty persists in rural America.* New Haven, CT: Yale University Press.

Duncan, C. (2010). Demographic trends and challenges in rural America. Meridian IFAP roundtable from the Carsey Institute. Durham: University of New Hampshire. Retrieved from https://carsey.unh.edu/sites/carsey.unh.edu/files/media/pdf/Duncan-Meridian-Roundtable-12-2010.pdf

Duncan, C. (2012). Community development in rural America: Collaborative, regional, and comprehensive. San Francisco, CA: Federal Reserve Bank of San Francisco. Retrieved from http://www.whatworksforamerica.org/ideas/community-development-in-rural-america-collaborative-regional-and-comprehensive/#.VG5slFfF-c_

Gentry, M., Rizza, M. G., & Gable, R. K. (2001). Gifted students' perceptions of their class activities: Differences among rural, urban, and suburban student attitudes. *Gifted Child Quarterly, 45,* 115–129.

Helton, L. R. (1995). Intervention with Appalachians: Strategies for a cultural specific practice. *Journal of Cultural Diversity, 2*(1), 20–26.

Helton, L. R. (2010). Faculty perceptions of differences between teaching rural Appalachian and urban social work students. *Contemporary Rural Social Work, 2,* 66–74.

Herzog, M. J., & Pittman, R. (1995). Home, family, and community: Ingredients in the rural education equation. *Phi Delta Kappan, 77*(2), 113–118.

hooks, b. (1995). An aesthetic of blackness: Strange and oppositional. *Lenox Avenue: A Journal of Interarts Inquiry, 1,* 65–72.

Howley, A., Pendarvis, E., & Gholson, M. (2005). How talented students in a rural school district experience mathematics. *Journal for the Education of the Gifted, 29,* 123–160.

Howley, C. B. (2009). The meaning of rural difference for bright rednecks. *Journal for the Education of the Gifted 32*(4), 537–564.

Huang, T., Orazem, P., & Wohlgemuth (2002). Rural population growth, 1950–1990: The roles of human capital, industry structure, and government policy. *American Journal of Agricultural Economics 84*(3). 615–627.

Jimerson, L. (2005). Placism in NCLB—How rural children are left behind. *Equity & Excellence in Education, 38,* 211–219.

Johnson, J., Showalter, D., Klein, R., & Lester, C. (2014, May). *Why rural matters 2013–2014: The condition of rural education in the 50 states.* Retrieved from http://www.ruraledu.org/user_uploads/file/2013-14-Why-Rural-Matters.pdf

Jones, L. (1994). *Appalachian values.* Ashland, KY: Jesse Stuart Foundation.

Leachman, M., & Mai, C. (2013, Sept.). *Most states funding schools less than before the recession.* Retrieved from http://www.cbpp.org/cms/?fa=view&id=4011

Montgomery, D. (2001). Increasing Native American Indian involvement in gifted programs in rural schools. *Psychology in the Schools, 38,* 467–475.

Olszewski-Kubilius, P. (2007). Working with promising learners from poverty. In J. VanTassel-Baska & T. Stambaugh (Eds.) *Overlooked gems: A national perspective on low-income promising learners* (pp. 43–460). Washington, D.C.: National Association for Gifted Children.

Payne, R. K. (1996). *A framework for understanding poverty.* Highlands, TX: Aha! Process.

Petrin, R., Schafft, K., & Meece, J. (2012). Educational sorting and residential aspirations among rural high school students: What are the contributions of schools and educators to the rural brain drain? Paper presented at the American Educational Research Association annual meeting, April 2012, Vancouver, BC.

Provasnik, S., KewalRamani, A., Coleman, M. M., Gilbertson, L., Herring, W., & Xie, Q. (2007). *Status of education in rural America* (NCES 2007-040). Washington, D.C.: National center for Education Statistics, Institute of Education Sciences, U.S. Department of Education.

Reck, V. M., & Reck, G. G. (1980). Living is more important than schooling: Schools and self-concept in Appalachia. *Appalachian Journal, 8,* 19–25.

Slocumb P. D., & Payne, R. (2000). Identifying and nurturing the gifted poor. *Principal: The New Diversity, 79*(5), 28–32.

Staunton, M. S., & Jafee E. M. (2014). Key findings and recommendations from the Coös youth study: Research from the first half of the study. *Carsey Research, Regional Issue Brief 41,* 1–8.

Strange, M. (2011). Finding fairness for rural students. *Phi Delta Kappan Magazine, 89*(6). 8–15.

VanTassel-Baska, J., & Stambaugh, T. (Eds.) 2007). *Overlooked gems: A national perspective on low-income promising learners.* Washington, D.C.: National Association for Gifted Children.

Wallace, L. A., & Diekroger, D. K. (2000). The ABC's in Appalachia: A descriptive view of perceptions of higher education in Appalachian culture. Paper presented at the Women of Appalachia Conference, Ohio University, Zanesville, OH.

Williams, D. (2013). Rural students and communities. Compendium: Independently Authored Materials by Equity and Excellence Commission Members.

Wilson, S. M., Henry, C. S., & Peterson, G. W. (1997). Life satisfaction among low-income rural youth from Appalachia. *Journal of Adolescence, 20,* 443–459.

CHAPTER 2

Leaving or Staying Home
Belief Systems and Paradigms

Craig Howley, Ed.D., Aimee Howley, Ph.D.,
and Daniel Showalter, Ph.D.

Introduction

This chapter considers three standpoints on rural giftedness. By "standpoint" we indicate a grounded way of reading the world: based on a place in it and, in our case, an articulated position (i.e., writing the world) about being there. Our particular standpoint for writing the world—given previously in many venues—is that *rural* is best understood as a set of meanings related to the land, to family, to rural sorts of work, and to local communities (see Howley, Howley, & Pendarvis, 2003; Howley, Showalter, Howley, Howley, Klein, & Johnson, 2011; Howley, Showalter, Klein, Sturgill, & Smith, 2013). Such meanings as these inform our overall position (i.e., on what should be) *as rural educators*: that rural schooling *should* encourage, support, and actively facilitate rural adulthoods for rural students.

The dominant position, however, suggests instead that most rural children, especially bright ones, should abandon their home places for opportunities elsewhere (see Carr & Kefalas, 2009; Corbett, 2007; Gibbs & Cromartie, 1994; Haller & Monk, 1992; Hektner, 1995; Huang, Weng, Zhang, & Cohen, 1997). In any case, academic ability, aspirations for higher education, and academic track placement are strong predictors of rural outmigration (Huang et al., 1997). As Carr and Kefalas (2009) tellingly observed, students who leave to pursue college, medical school, and metropolitan careers, and who abandon rural places altogether, are viewed as *successful* among not only rural school professionals, but among influential rural community members—and indeed, by everyone else. They appear to have escaped an unworthy and parochial fate.

In national culture, and therefore from the perspective of many educators (even rural ones), rural attachments are usually subsidiary to dominant positions and purposes (Corbett, 2007; Scott, 1998; Theobald, 1997). However, we want to explain a contrary and largely disparaged position (a position *unusually* appreciative of the educational potential of rural cultures and places); that is, rural life is not limiting and restrictive, but is instead inclusive and generative. In articulating this position, though, we often—almost always—encounter bafflement among education faculty.[1] To be clear: We are not opposed to any individual leaving or, indeed, arriving anywhere. Instead, we ask why the American culture is disparaging of rural locality. At this juncture in American history, the disparagement should strike those concerned for the American future as especially troubling, because of the role of locality in fostering popular rule ("democracy"). This role for locality in American democracy has been argued for generations, with the classic treatment provided by Alexis De Tocqueville (1848; but for recent iterations, see for example Berry, 1970, 2010; Scott, 1998, 2012; Theobald & Campbell, 2014; Walzer, 1988). It's quite true that America is no longer a popular democracy, nor a rural nation, but rather an urbanized oligarchic plutocracy (Blacker, 2013; Lévy, 2007). It is a plutocracy, however, in which accumulation of wealth is illogically held to be an opportunity democratically open to everyone, even as the distribution of wealth becomes more and more lopsided. The cultural, political, and economic marginality of rural places, indeed, increases as the distribution of wealth becomes more unequal (Berry, 2010; Theobald & Campbell, 2014). First, cities remain the economic, political, and cultural center in developed and developing nations (see, e.g., Jacobs, 1986; Williams, 1973), a fact that explains their appeal as destinations for gifted minds everywhere and over many centuries (Corbett, 2007; Hobsbawm, 1962). Second, wealth signals power, and as the power becomes more lopsided with the wealth, rural places not only become comparatively poorer, their political marginalization increases (see, e.g., Corbett, 2007; Howley, Howley, & Eppley, 2013; Theobald & Campbell, 2014).

---

1   P–12 teachers and administrators in rural schools are more receptive, but they all confront regimes of accountability (changeable standards and testing regimes) that propagate not simply reluctance to engage local options (Theobald, 1997), but the same cultures of fear that afflict nearly all schools and districts (see, e.g., Blacker, 2013; Olsen & Sexton, 2009).

The rural pathways explained (or *essayed*) in this chapter are a mighty alternative to typical thinking, in our view. Atypical thinking about such issues seems critically important at a time of global insecurity about the viability of progress as an inevitable improvement: It seems that "progress" could be responsible for an ultimate dystopian reality (see, e.g., Conkin, 2009; Mathez, 2009; Solomon, 2010). We want, here, to help open eyes. What one will see after opening one's eyes, though, is inevitably difficult and disturbing. We think that *writing the world* should serve exactly this purpose.

The Three Standpoints: STEM, the Aesthetic Dimension, and Practical Knowledge

In this chapter, then, we want to consider three additional standpoints beyond our own writing of the world that relate to giftedness in particular in order to develop rural options within them. Two of these standpoints will be quite familiar with respect to the gifted: first, "STEM", which is an acronym for science, technology, engineering, and mathematics—a concatenation deployed to cultivate mathematical and scientific talent broadly, and second, what we will call "the aesthetic dimension." The aesthetic dimension takes up the other half of academic concern: literature, art, and music—the realm (loosely) of "the beautiful."[2] We delimit the academic world like this in order to develop contrast and to generate tension about educational purpose: Science and art—what could seem more different in themselves, and yet what could be more familiar (as in "The College of Arts and Sciences")? The final standpoint considers practical knowledge encompassing the unusual aptitude for making things go in the *ordinary real rural world* and realization of such aptitude: practical engineering and invention, construction and manufacture, repair, and maintenance (Crawford, 2009; Rose, 2004).

This third standpoint of practical knowledge, however, may not be as familiar in gifted education in the United States as the other two. Unusual aptitudes exist in these practical realms, but they are roundly ignored in American discussions of gifted education (Crawford, 2009; Rose, 2004); in Europe though,

---

2   Art (e.g., music, fine art, literature) may be very difficult and even simultaneously ugly, of course, as with much 20th-century music and painting. The concept is confusing because anything unfamiliar may seem difficult and ugly—even when sublimely beautiful.

where apprenticeship programs are seriously part of the educational system, the situation is different (see, e.g., Stamm & Niederhauser, 2008). Note that our conception of aptitude for "making things go in the ordinary real world" is grounded more in an appreciation of working-class employment common in rural areas than in elite applications in engineering and cutting-edge science. Our vantage, then, is more sociological than psychological, more about culture (rural) and class (lower-middle) than about adjusting curriculum and pedagogy to newly valued psychological constructs. We are, in short, less concerned with engineering as a profession than with plumbing as a vocation open to "the gifted." Contemporary psychological theorists (e.g., Gagné, 1998; Gardner, 1983; Sternberg, 1985) certainly value engineering sorts of talent, but we have always found their appreciation more expedient than innovative because multiple talents have always been recognized in psychology (see, e.g., Pendarvis, Howley, & Howley, 1990). By contrast, gifted education has hardly ever exhibited appreciation of ordinary, as compared to eminent, occupations; that is, we have never encountered any such examples.

With the following sections we seek to describe rural paths in our three realms. In science (STEM) and art, these rural paths *already exist* within typical versions of gifted education. But the consideration of low-status employment as rurally relevant for gifted students marks the third pathway as very different. The reason, of course, is that mainstream versions of gifted education seek to open access to high-status employment because such employment is considered to define success in America (Berry, 1970). As Wendell Berry argued, this view is inherently antirural but, more importantly, is culturally and intellectually self-destructive (see also Crawford, 2009; Rose, 2004; Theobald, 1997).

The STEM Standpoint

STEM talents are featured in virtually all national reports (see, e.g., National Science Board, 2010) as underwriting the nation's future economic well-being. The truth of the claim, however, is less important than the nearly universal belief in it. Widespread assent to the claim makes math and science talent—as it figured during the Cold War—an issue of national security (see, e.g., Conant, 1959; Glass, 2007; Gross & MacLaury, 2003). And as an issue of national security in a well-urbanized nation, any rural connections to the issue are footnotes: the economic, political, and cultural margin is by definition nearly powerless (under ordinary circumstances). Larger proportions of conscripts or volunteers may come from rural areas (Scott, 1998), but they are still a minority, and all foot soldiers obey orders rather than give them. Quite salient footnotes in times of war, of course, may include policies regulating such rurally generated commodities as food and fuel. Rural is not irrelevant; it is instead subservient (Berry, 2010; Jacobs, 1986; Scott, 1998).

In the following discussion, we characterize the familiar metropolitan pathway, and then describe how national ideology obscures rural STEM talent. Next, we explain the rural STEM path, and we conclude the section with a cultural contrast (Thailand) in order to suggest an extant parallel in the U.S. easily accessible in rural communities.

The Metropolitan Pathway

The upshot of this circumstance is that the economic powerhouse of nations—cities—is understood as the natural home of and for STEM talent. Metropolitan locale is where STEM happens because cities house the great research universities, the great laboratories, the great corporate headquarters, and, in fact, most of the people in whom STEM talent might be cultivated: 80% of the national population, after all, lives in metropolitan areas (Bureau of Census, 2007; Jacobs, 1986).

The metropolitan pathway to developing and deploying STEM talent has been very clear for a long time: excellent K–12 schools, elite universities, and corporate or academic recruitment into an urban-based profession (see, e.g., Lowell, Salzman, Bernstein, & Henderson, 2009). Of course, many metropolitan residents (disproportionately African American or Hispanic) do not actually have clear access to this pathway (see e.g., Cogan, Schmidt, & Wiley, 2001). But with good fortune, metropolitan students enjoy a comparatively straightforward path toward lucrative STEM employment. Because the U.S. is an urbanized nation, it is also clear that equalized access overall would mean that 80% of STEM workers would come from metropolitan areas, and just 20% from rural places. But access is far from equal precisely because of the metropolitan location of high-status scientific and academic jobs (Carr & Kefalas, 2009). In studying this issue, we have repeatedly heard from high school math teachers that rural areas offer almost no opportunities for the application of "advanced" math skills (Howley, Howley, & Yahn, 2014).

Ideology Trumps Rural STEM Talent.

A recent report jointly undertaken by three leading federal agencies—the National Science Board, National Science Foundation, and the U.S. Department of Education (National Science Board, 2010)—gives an authoritative national view of how, in the name of national economic defense, to find and educate the most talented youth for STEM fields. The word "rural" appears just four times in the report: in the phrases "rural and low-income areas" (pp. 3 and 18) and "economically disadvantaged urban and rural areas" (pp. 3 and 21).

This prominent usage illustrates that, from a national metro-centric vantage, rural places are considered deficient: deficient in the national imaginary for STEM education (see, e.g., Howley, Howley, & Huber, 2005) and, in fact, in the national culture generally (see, e.g., Herzog & Pittman, 1995). The silence and construction of deficiency are not accidental: rural places figure as the hinterlands whose resources must be appropriated by the national centers (see, e.g., Berry, 2010; Jacobs, 1986; Scott, 1998).[3] Imprecations of deficiency are national cultural "necessities" in the view of the thinkers just cited, and this linkage represents both cultural and economic moves that proceed ideologically, as they see it. With respect to recruitment to STEM fields in the national corporate interest, recruitment in rural places is not efficient—that is, given the population proportions.[4]

In recent decades gifted education as a scholarly field has devoted some attention to the dilemmas of talented students in rural schools (see, e.g., Colangelo, Assouline, & New, 1999; Howley, Harmon, & Leopold, 1996). The comprehensive review by Colangelo and colleagues (1999), however, demonstrated clearly how little attention gifted education scholarship had directed toward rural schools—let alone the issues of rural students—prior to the turn of the 21st century. As a field of *practice*, however, gifted education continues to regard rural places, cultures, and people similarly—that is, as probably deficient. Less surprisingly, the general constructions of cultural, political, economic, and intellectual deficiency predictably apply to the actual schooling of the gifted.

---

3   As we were working on revisions to this chapter, the *New York Times* published a story (Healy, 2015) about rural towns that had adopted local statutes to ban hydraulic facturing ("fracking"). The industry response was to sue, arguing that only states had the authority to impose such bans. The corporations regard local action as *illegal*. We have often written that rurally located natural resources are by no means the property of those who live atop or near them. Every resource has its price, and rural places where such resources exist are often impoverished. Alas, the boom-and-bust economies of resource extraction make matters worse (see, e.g., Douglas & Walker, 2013).

4   That is, approximately 80% of the U.S. population lives in metropolitan areas, and 50% lives in metropolitan areas of one million or more. See Lichter and Brown (2011) for a recent review of rural trends and a useful characterization of competing interpretations of what such trends mean.

After all, gifted education takes place in schools that operate under the guiding state and corporate ideology (Blacker, 2013; White & Corbett, 2014; Donehower, Hogg, & Schell, 2012). Ample evidence exists. For instance, Lewis and Hafer (2007, para. 8) advised educators of talented STEM students in rural areas to seek out "specialized counseling . . . from adults who succeeded in pursuing their dreams despite growing up in a rural environment."

Succeeded *despite growing up rural*? One must observe that such language—language that manifestly treats rural places as deficient—is nearly ubiquitous in scholarship that focuses on rural schools; see our recent review of nearly 200 rurally focused studies in curriculum and instruction (Howley, Howley, & Yahn, 2014), which found rampant imputations of deficiency. This outlook is, in fact, historically common in school reform (Kannapel & DeYoung, 1999). Its prevalence in gifted education is not particularly notable, just predictable (see, e.g., Howley, Howley, & Pendarvis, 2003).

A Pathway for Rural STEM Talent or Vice-Versa?

By "vice-versa," we indicate a *rural* pathway for STEM talent, instead of simply a pathway *out* for rural talent. In other words, we suggest that STEM training programs might well cultivate rural STEM talent for explicit use in rural communities, not for export elsewhere. Because of the predictable shortage of physicians in rural areas in a market-based system of healthcare allocation, medical schools in some parts of the nation have already established programs to recruit rural young people into rural medical employment.[5]

However, in most instances, for high-status jobs rural STEM talent must go where the STEM opportunities lie—to the metropolis. Of course, the American cultural template for *what rural is*[6] cultivates the unseeing (cf. Miéville, 2009) that renders a rural alternative almost unimaginable: rural places are understood as *so* deficient that STEM talent is obliged—actually obligated in the name of national security—to leave. The operation of the ideology that keeps talented youth moving out of rural places is well documented (see, e.g., Carr & Kefalas, 2009; Corbett, 2007; Hektner, 1995; Howley, Harmon, & Leopold, 1996; Jamieson, 2000).

---

5   In West Virginia, Marshall University operates such a program (see http://crh.marshall.edu/), as does the University of Alabama (see http://cchs.ua.edu/education/rural-programs/). Both institutions call their efforts "pipeline" programs.

6   Or, rather what it is understood to be: a cultural, political, economic, and intellectual backwater that, rather inconveniently, harbors natural resources that the cultural, political, economic, and intellectual center requires to sustain itself as the center (see, e.g., Theobald & Campbell, 2014; Scott, 1998).

Talented students are, nonetheless, *more* attached to their local communities than other students according to empirical studies (Hektner, 1995; Howley et al., 1996; Petrin, Schafft, & Meece, 2014): their conflict about having to leave to pursue their passion is sharp. Attachment to place is a storied feature of rural existence rather well documented in the studies just cited. The difficulty of attachment, on American national terms, is that opportunities for conventional, high-status rural success are comparatively meager. So although the best and brightest (as in Corbett, 2007; Hektner, 1995; and Howley et al., 1996) would like to stay put, they are led by national ideological purpose—inculcated always in the national media but also very frequently in rural schooling[7]—to "higher aspirations" that necessitate moving away permanently. Indeed, rural schooling does not typically offer alternatives, as Burnell (2003) discovered in her study of college-ready students who actually exercised their option to stay. Burnell's study remains the only such study of the logic and courage of such students, although Carr and Kefalas (2009) reached a conclusion similar to Burnell's. At least in these two rural districts and communities, no one was listening to students or asking themselves the relevant questions. These were both case studies, but our own professional and personal experience across the country suggests the findings are widely transferrable.

To be clear: We are not opposing anyone's freedom of movement or suggesting confinement. To the contrary, we see the operation of just such a restriction of freedom in the ideology that promotes—powerfully enforces—movement *out*. Because of the nature of employment opportunities, conventionally understood, rural STEM talent is seen to deserve removal to someplace *better* (see, e.g., Lowell et al., 2009; National Science Board, 2010).

Thus, when national entities fund projects they announce as rural, the projects must conform (in order to be become competitive) to program designs based on erroneous assumptions about the deficiency of rural places. We once examined the discourse of mathematics education reform projects (many proceeding from National Science Foundation projects) with a rural focus. The rationale for funding, in most cases, and the recommendations given by funded projects (with a few exceptions) framed rural issues as shortcomings in comparison to the metropolitan norm. The solution was for rural places to ape the practices of the "best" metropolitan schooling (Howley et al., 2005), which were understood, of course, as universally best. As Kannapel and DeYoung (1999)

---

7   Again, one must note that rural schools may sustain strong connections to local communities, but that the press of accountability concerns, the ideology of national defense, and the American cultural misconstruction of "success" work systematically to weaken local ties and impose national and corporate ones according to many observers (see, e.g., DeYoung, 1995; Theobald & Campbell, 2014; Scott, 1998).

found, this sequence of events has typified the national professional outlook on rural schools for at least a century.

If the criterion for a happy life is money, and more money means greater happiness, then anyone who could leave a rural place would do so. Developed STEM talent is well paid; rural places offer lower salaries and comparably meager employment opportunities, although these circumstances are somewhat offset by lower costs of living (see, e.g., Carr & Kefalas, 2009; Howley, Howley, & Johnson, 2014). Treating money as the marker of a happy or good life, though, has been judged corrupt by centuries of philosophy (Deresiewicz, 2014). There is much more to leading a meaningful life, and astute rural writers (e.g., Berry, 1970) have always told urban Americans that community, family, land, and rural occupations offer abundant opportunity to lead a fulfilled life in league with others. These assets are largely inaccessible via other pathways (wherever one lives). What one needs to imagine the alternative is a bit of cultural dissonance. We offer one such alternative, in conclusion.

Gaining Cultural Perspective: Thailand

When travelling in Thailand, one of the authors (Dan) was impressed with the reception given local Buddhist monks. At the appointed time, residents lined the streets, holding an impressive array of culinary delights. Soon afterwards, the local monks filed silently by, bowls humbly extended to receive what the residents offered. The tradition is supported, in part, by the communal understanding that the monks have devoted their lives to promoting the well-being of the local place and, indeed, of all beings everywhere. Part of the monastic vow, moreover, is to eat only what is freely offered to them. For an American the oddest feature is that the monks, neither well off nor impoverished, clearly seem to thrive: They lead purposeful lives remarkably free of worry about money.

An American parallel exists, however. Lay pastors in rural places serve their communities in a similar way. They counsel parishioners about personal issues, organize events for the common good of the congregation and the entire community, and they do not expect to become rich. Many are not even paid (see, e.g., Dewalt, 2006). Their role functions dramatically outside the prevalent American norm. They exhibit a commonplace—but ignored and even disparaged—rural alternative. Pastors claim to serve a "higher power," but their actions are not entirely, or even mostly, "spiritual." The devotion of rural pastors, however, is exemplary of a range of similar, more secular, devotions that revolve around thoughtfulness, caring, and doing good work (see, e.g., Bellah, Madsen, Sullivan, Swidler, & Tipton, 1985; Crawford, 2009; Robinson, 2010; Thompson, 2002).

Thus, these two examples—Thai and American—suggest a sense of social gravity that favors those working for the common good. And because it is care for shared commitments and enterprises, it means that those who take up such work also experience the benefits of the care they provide. This tradition lies dormant in America, but some have advised reclaiming it (Bellah et al., 1985). The alternative remains possible in rural America, even if the prevailing ideology has worked for a long time to eliminate it (Berry, 1970; Scott, 2012).

Thus what we are suggesting is the development of STEM talent with "higher purpose" that is relevant to students' rural home territory. Certainly one has to make a living, but one does not actually have to be very well paid to live well in rural places (as our own families know). Can people so widely believe that engineering, scientific inquiry, and mathematics are relevant to rural places only for generating personal wealth someplace else? One hopes not.

For one example of the possibility of STEM talent doing good in rural places, consider Wes Jackson. He is an ecologist, geneticist, and rural thinker who lives in rural Kansas. His "higher purpose" across an entire career is to support sustainable agriculture (see, e.g., Jackson, 1996, 2011). Jackson, though, is in very good company with a great many others who live happily in rural places. Some are writers and novelists (e.g., novelists Wendell Berry and Barbara Kingsolver); many, many others, perhaps equally thoughtful and purposive, are not, of course, famous (see Jacob, 1997, for one account). Much might be done rurally to weaken American individualism and greed. It seems like good work to us.

The Aesthetic Dimension

Overall, we want to highlight this dimension, in fact, as one that illustrates higher purpose. In an age that values (in dollars) science and mathematics above all else, the artistic spirit struggles more than ever, which we take to be a good thing. In our interpretation, art is by definition both difficult and intrinsically connected to higher purpose (see, e.g., Robinson, 2010). This section proceeds in three parts: a discussion of art as difficult practice, characterization of the familiar urban pathway, and exploration of alternative rural pathways.

Leaving or Staying Home

We borrow the phrase "aesthetic dimension" from Herbert Marcuse's 1978 book of the same title. Like him, we too believe that art is dangerous intellectual territory, and that anyone hearing the word should instantly appreciate the fact (see Descollonge & Eisner, 2003, for an ironic treatment of this fact). But how can this be? Aren't "the arts" supposed to be *entertaining*? Isn't music supposed to make us *feel better*?

In a word: No. Judging the difference between art and distracting entertainment is part of what makes art different from "the arts." Art, on this view, represents one of those "higher powers" available to human engagement, as noted in the previous section. Artistic talent, as compared to STEM talent, however, is not typically motivated by money; the "starving artist" is iconic. But the difficulty here is also cultural.

Art as Difficult Engagement

One novelist who understood the distinction was Graham Greene, author of *The Power and the Glory* (1940). Greene was happy to call some of his novels (not the one mentioned) "entertainments," and these he thought of as lesser works.[8] Proof of the salient distinction between "the (easy) arts" and actual *grit*? Twentieth Century Fox sued Greene for libel in Britain (Anderson, 2014) over his review of the very diverting *Wee Willie Winkie* (a Shirley Temple vehicle, directed by John Ford with a score by Alfred Newman). Greene found it manipulative. The studio found it profitable.[9] Greene lost.

Today, of course, the Disney conglomerate is a big supporter of "the arts." The purpose of serious art (as contrasted with the jejune catchall of "the arts," which pertains mostly to Disney-like kitsch) makes it inevitably a preoccupation of the few rather than the many. Its creation (in literature, music, and fine art among others) uses standards from the accumulated works of the past.[10]

---

8   Some of Greene's espionage novels have been rendered as films, for instance, *The Honorary Consul* (1973) and *The Human Factor* (1978), the former starring Richard Greer and Michael Caine in its adaptation, and the latter adapted via a screenplay by dramatist Tom Stoppard.

9   Temple's films were a major profit stream for 20th Century Fox during the Great Depression. Based on a Rudyard Kipling story, *Wee Willie Winkie*, like all the star's mid-career films, was hugely successful. By 1938 Temple's films had earned the studio *profit* of $496 million (2012 constant dollars) and saved it from bankruptcy (Cline, 2014).

10   Directly and appreciatively or in critical repudiation. For one canon relevant to literature, see Bloom (2014). Neither we nor Bloom would regard *Wee Willie Winkie* as harboring a useful standard, of course.

Urban-Centered Pathways to Engagement

Great cities have great museums, private galleries, symphony orchestras, dance and opera companies, art shows, jazz festivals; and renowned universities and music schools (e.g., Julliard in New York, the Conservatoire de Paris in France, and so forth). Many such establishments have become active in city schools in recent decades, in part because they recognize the need to recruit future audiences for the project of performing and creating difficult works in a world awash with easy entertainment.

Some city residents, and those in affluent suburbs, thus have access to a substantial array of art venues—school programs, sometimes, but especially private lessons of all sorts; and concerts, dance performances, gallery shows, and so forth. In general, metropolitan students gifted in an art form will likely come from families themselves engaged in literature, music, or art (Cskiszentmihalyi, Rathunde, & Whalen, 1997). And these families will—as they often have done—ensure the participation of their children. Gifted classical and jazz musicians need access to private lessons and special institutions (Julliard's precollege program comes to mind) to realize the full potential of extraordinary talent. We ourselves are comfortable enough with the uncomfortable truth of these circumstances, but as rural educators we understand something more. The urban-centric mode of thinking about art is understandably facilitated by the upper echelon's city understandings of the meaning of life: In order to be successful, one needs the best (and, by extension, to *be* "the best").

This "best," however, is by no means a universal best, but only one sort. It works as one gauge of excellence, to be sure. (In summer 2014, we watched a 15-year-old play a Prokofiev piano concerto brilliantly, and we were indeed astonished—these are supremely difficult works.) Nonetheless, the aesthetic domain covers other difficult performances because aesthetic sensibility is not limited to a metro-centric echelon's construction of the artful best.

Rural-Centered Pathways to Engagement

Raymond Williams (1921–1988) is best known as one of the originators of the field of cultural studies, a field that takes seriously the culture of ordinary life. He famously claimed that *culture is ordinary* (Williams, 1958/2001). His cultural standpoint on this issue was notably, and avowedly, rural. Notable, too, was his application of the claim of ordinariness to the realm of high culture (e.g., literature, philosophy, and mathematics). It was ordinary too, in the conditions of its production, and for most of human history (*written history*), those conditions have been rural.

And rural conditions still exist, of course. Williams's (1973) *Country and the City* (with "country" first) was a retelling, in part, of English literature from a rural vantage that remains nearly unique. Our rural colleague Paul Theobald, has, moreover, in recent years established the Rural Lit Rally (see http://rural-litrally.org/) in the U.S. to promote the great 20th-century rural novels that, although not much championed, constitute the now oddly neglected backbone of American literature.

So we have in mind rural pathways into art (serious cultural productions) of all sorts—the difficult artfulness of ordinary rural productions as well as the engagement of rural people in the "high" culture of literature, fine art, and jazz or classical music. That is, from a rural standpoint, one must include not only "high" (elite and metro-centric) art in this domain, but also "the (rural) arts;" traditional music making, folk and fine art productions, and fiction with rural themes. This legacy is submerged, by comparison, to metropolitan and national "popular" [11] productions, but rural "deficiency" is a cultural asset here, in fact. With just 20% of the U.S. population, less densely clustered ("isolated"), rural areas are less profitable; broadband Internet and cable networks don't reach very far into the countryside for the same reason. Rural is a small and difficult market share. It thus offers a bit more purchase on reality; and a bit more purchase on the human condition than the cosmopolitan elite can access. Raymond Williams (1989) advised just such marginalized places as most promising for serious cultural work.

Rural places offer potential for artfulness that the mass-culture version of "the (distracting) arts" cannot. Local rural communities almost everywhere exhibit some of this potential, even if it too rarely darkens schoolhouse doors. Indeed, accounts of these sorts of opportunities actually exist in the education literature, although they are hardly best sellers. The field of place-based education is the venue to consult (see, e.g., Donehower et al., 2012; Lewicki, 2010; Smith, 2007; Theobald, 1997). The idea of basing instruction on place (*place-based*) makes it problematic for placeless locales like suburbs (where residence—and therefore community—is transient) and city neighborhoods (where no land remains in sight). Our point in this chapter, however, is that

---

11 Williams's *Keywords* (1976) also usefully explains the word "popular." The present common meaning appeared in 1697 as "courting the favor of the people by undue practices" (p. 237). Most mass entertainments are rife with "undue practices," of course: gratuitous violence, sexual exploitation, bad physics—whatever it takes. In 2015 as compared with 1697, of course, the obvious manipulations are augmented by undue practices of creation, distribution, and marketing—arrangements that are trade secrets.

rural is a cultural margin in which much that is artfully impossible elsewhere remains possible.

Following the precepts of place-based education, then, rural schools might connect their students who show unusual capacity (e.g., 1/33—the standard gifted rarity) for art to *locally artful people*. Rural schools often behave as if they do not even know—in our experience—who these local people are; they are plagued with the state's bequest of a distracting mission and are too often, though understandably, blinded by it. The unseeing is understandable and regrettable, but it is also *avoidable*. Rural schools *can* make the discovery and exploit it. Some families with students disposed to rural artfulness will already be making the connections. Simple Internet searches using the keywords in this chapter (e.g., place-based education, the arts, and rural) will provide interested readers with tools for the proposed work of resistance and invention. Within place-based efforts, art projects are probably as common as science projects, and both are (unfortunately) much more common than math projects (Howley et al., 2011; Showalter, 2013).

The aesthetic dimension (meaningfulness, insight, critique, graceful production) inevitably carries beyond both "the (distracting) arts" and (elite metro-centric) art and into rather more ordinary rural productions. Much that exists in the rural world has always been approached artfully (e.g., wood cutting, care of the land, knitting and sewing, cooking, housekeeping). These ordinary tasks harbor meaningfulness and grace that few Americans any longer appreciate, but for exceptional accounts of such artfulness see Wendell Berry's entire output, and also Pat Thompson's 2002 *The Accidental Theorist: The Double Helix of Everyday Life*.

The neglect arises in large measure, we think, from the 20th-century valuation of career, individualism, and movement. In this nexus of cultural values, domesticity is the loser. Domesticity, however, remains (in our experience) important to rural men and women because devotion to the homeplace and extended family remains important to so many rural people, families, and communities. That attachment, that affection, motivates the choice to remain rural. This realm of reality is one that the "knowledge economy" cannot appreciate and has little patience for (see, e.g., Burnell, 2003; Howley et al., 2013; Theobald, 1997). So we turn next to rural pathways for practical knowledge—less abstract than STEM and aiming rather less at transcendence than art.

Staying (or Leaving) With Practical Knowledge

Some gifted students in the United States prefer practical and vocational pursuits to traditional academic pursuits, even though the large majority report an interest in acquiring the knowledge and credentials needed for careers supposed to require abstract cognitive skills: scientist, lawyer, or physician (Sparfeldt, 2007; for a thoughtful critique from one such student, who now repairs motorcycles, see Crawford, 2009). Schools, moreover, typically encourage all gifted students to enroll in a college preparatory curriculum in order to gain access to a professional or managerial occupation (Sytsma, 2000) even if their interests and aptitudes lie elsewhere (Bals, 1999; Milgram & Hong, 1999).

For many American educators, the prospect of a gifted student taking up a trade over managerial-professional work seems a waste of talent (e.g., Leung, Conoley, & Scheel, 1994; Plank & Jordan, 2001). These educators believe that the possession of talent *requires* individuals to pursue the careers for which they are ostensibly best suited (e.g., Jung, 2012; Milgram & Hong, 1999): the managerial and professional careers that will make them national leaders (Subotnik, Olszewski-Kubilius, & Worrell, 2012). Apparently, no longer can anyone repairing motorcycles or building houses become a national leader. (Why would anyone not want to be rich in America?) This short-sighted perspective also reflects the substantial differentials in prestige, power, and financial reward for those performing mental work on the one hand and manual work on the other (e.g., Penn, 1975). And, according to Tomlinson (2008), many in the field presume that gifted students *deserve* to reap the rewards associated with professional and managerial careers (see, e.g., Renzulli, 2012; Subtonik & Rickoff, 2010; Subotnik, Olszewski-Kubilius, & Worrell, 2011).[12]

From this standpoint, as well, we can turn to other countries for an alternative model. In some Western European countries, in contrast to the United States and Britain, the material and status differentials between vocational and academic paths are not so stark (Sanderson, 1993; but cf. Young, 1993). Education systems in these countries—Germany, Switzerland, and the Netherlands, in particular—have developed vocational paths that lead to skilled employment in practical occupations. Predictably, technical schools and apprentice programs in these countries encounter academically talented students whose vocational interests and aptitudes are particularly strong. In other words, these nations

---

12   In addition to Tomlinson, Grantham (2012, p. 216) also agreed with our assessment of the "just deserts" presumptions of those cited: "They articulate a new goal of gifted education: adult eminence." This goal, of course, is not much different from Terman's.

have some experience with capable students who demonstrate "giftedness" for practical endeavors (Bals, 1999; Stamm & Niederhauser, 2008).

Discussion of programs for bright students with unusual aptitudes for practical work also appeared in U.S. education literature from the 1970s through the 1990s (e.g., Brann, 1988; Milne, 1982; Taylor, 1995). But according to some commentators (e.g., Fletcher, 2006), the No Child Left Behind Act and now Common Core and College and Career readiness initiatives require that school districts treat the college preparatory curriculum as necessary for *all* students. This development has had predictable consequences for career and technical education (CTE) for students in general, and certainly for those students who exhibit high levels of academic talent. Furthermore, CTE in the United States has come under criticism for its limited ability to prepare students for actual employment opportunities (e.g., Fletcher, 2012).

Rural Assets

Irrespective of these cultural and economic dynamics, several circumstances suggest that the cultivation of practical giftedness makes sense for rural schools. First, practical problem solving represents an asset in many rural communities and therefore offers a resource to rural schools, many of which lack other resources for establishing and sustaining meaningful talent development programs.

Second, practical problem solving entails complex and sophisticated intellectual work that is productive of significant cognitive growth. Both Crawford (2009) and Rose (2004) have demonstrated the intellectual depth that excellent craft requires. One might also observe that fiction (see the novels of Wendell Berry, or those at the Rural Lit Rally) has also demonstrated this vastly neglected fact quite well to those who read it.

Third, rural and urban communities need technicians with well-honed skills who are capable of problem solving and innovation (Crawford, 2009). They also need local entrepreneurs who are willing to invest resources and whose locally centered efforts contribute to sustaining rural places (Theobald, 1997).

Finally, many rural places embrace life choices made on the basis of meaningfulness for family and community (Burnell, 2003), not solely on the basis of individual or career benefit.[13] This again is one version of the "higher purpose" considered in previous sections of this chapter.

An important insight from recent literature on rural resilience is that the challenges persistently confronting rural people and their communities contribute to the development of characteristics such as innovativeness, adaptability, and resourcefulness (Scott, 2013). Resilience enables rural residents, at least in some places, to reinvigorate their economies and community support structures (McManus et al., 2012). The existence in such communities of adults whose own experiences have helped them cultivate these assets is an accessible source of help in expanding the practical problem-solving capabilities of rural students, including those who demonstrate extraordinary aptitude for such work.

The Intellectual Merits of Manual Work

Conventional wisdom contrasts mental with manual work, favoring the former both in rhetorical and material ways (Hubbard, 1988). Nevertheless, as some recent writers have argued, the distinction is false: To perform manual work well requires intellectual engagement; to perform it extraordinarily well involves a considerable amount of intellectual talent (Crawford, 2009; Rose, 2004).

Despite the devaluing of manual work in national culture and ideology, rural communities still continue to treat it as virtuous (Sage & Sherman, 2014). Many rural children and youth, therefore, observe the adults around them participating in work that entails effort, persistence, and sacrifice (Nelson & Smith, 1999). For some students, observing family struggles of this sort suggests that rural life is inhospitable (Carr & Kefalas, 2009); for others, though, it offers a model of how life might be lived well through the application of local knowledge on the one hand (Shava, Krasny, Tidball, & Zazu, 2010) and enterprise on the other (e.g., Akgun, Baycan-Levent, Nijkamp, & Poot, 2011).

---

13   Emerging under the rubric of "sense of place," a small literature addresses the human need for attachment to land, family, and community. Note that the American model of a mobile suburbia is at issue as destructive of such a sensibility; a hypermobile metropolitan population necessarily abandons a sensibility of place in favor of professional and financial opportunity. See James Kunstler's wonderful *The Geography of Nowhere* (1993) for an account of the American suburban ethos (the contrary sensibility to sense of place). Kunstler is particularly concerned with the ugliness of the culture known as suburban.

The Need for Innovative Technicians and Entrepreneurs

For rural youth with all levels of academic ability, practical considerations regarding work frequently eclipse middle-class aspirations about college attendance followed by the pursuit of a professional or managerial career (e.g., Burnell, 2003; Howley, 2006). Despite what some educators may think, this circumstance hardly represents a disastrous waste of talent. Rather, many capable rural students simply prefer to enter the workplace early or to pursue jobs that allow them to work with their hands (e.g., Burnell, 2003). Based on recent research showing that high-achieving rural students are more attached to their communities than their less-talented counterparts (Hektner, 1995; Howley et al., 1996; Petrin et al., 2014), one might also assume that some choose practical careers in order to remain close to home. These possibilities cannot be discounted even if rural gifted students, in general, appear to share equally high aspirations for college attendance as their nonrural peers (Howley, 2006).

Moreover, finding ways to prepare rural students for technical jobs (what some call "middle-skill" jobs) may help ensure their future employment irrespective of where they choose to live (Kochan, Finegold, & Osterman, 2012). Jobs in the trades and technical jobs in health care, manufacturing, and communications, for instance, offer security and flexibility. Employment in such jobs, in fact, often offers opportunities for innovation and problem solving as well as for career advancement (e.g., Kochan et al, 2012).

So too does small-scale business ownership. In fact, rural areas across the world may increasingly become sites for new business ventures—both those started by rural residents who seek to improve their communities and those started by newcomers who hope to exploit opportunities in communities that need the goods and services they provide (Akgun et al., 2011). Entrepreneurship education has, moreover, played a significant role over the years in rural community development (Nachtigal & Haas, 2000; Pitzel et al., 2007).

Meaningful Life Choices

One other consideration has a bearing on the merits of rural school programs with this focus. Whereas so much of what has been written about talent development justifies special programming by citing its importance for supplying the political economy with the highly skilled professionals and other leaders it needs (e.g., Schwartz, 1994), this view of educational purpose may significantly distort the connection between education and the "good life" (for a similar argument from a British perspective, see Tomlinson, 2008). Not only does it construct the individual benefits of education in terms of narrow, arguably venal, "goods" such as greed and personal power, it removes the community—the place where education actually takes place—from the list of education's beneficiaries. Talent development in the practical domain, by contrast, places a more worthy set of purposes at the center of the educational effort.

Discussion and Recommendations

Our argument is a lot for gifted education scholarship and practice to absorb. The values and insights it proposes are orthogonal to mainstream purposes. State schooling in America has been designed across an entire century to serve national defense and national economic purposes (see, e.g., Blacker, 2013; Scott, 2012); rural was to be left behind, for good (Theobald, 1997). The redesign took local public schools that once served communities and families—in a national population that was mostly rural—and reformed them all along the lines of industrial production (see, e.g., Callahan, 1962; Molnar, 1996). In America, only the Amish have successfully resisted (see Dewalt, 2006).

The difficulty of reforming the factory schools that now confront us arguably stems from the continued dominance of the business and national defense purposes, but also the continued usefulness of factories. In this scheme of things a more domestic, ad hoc, and rural outlook on the meaning of life has little place—especially as a national school reform concern. It really is little wonder that the market-based "solution" to the perceived problems is simply to let corporations manage schooling altogether (see, e.g., Hill, 2006). The community dimension of rural life is also a poor fit with the very strong individualist dimension of American national culture (Hofstede, 2001). Gifted students are seen first as a national resource, enriched with rights of conventional success that trump community attachments (see, e.g., Carr & Kefalas, 2009; Corbett, 2007; National Science Board, 2010; cf. Schwartz, 1994). In the national imaginary, then, little room remains for a rural alternative—especially in state schooling, a national project, according to some observers, for socializing the young to corporate norms and aspirations (see, e.g., Blacker, 2013; Glass, 2007; Theobald, 2009). Changing the mindset of professionals *who are themselves socialized* to do this work is immensely difficult (Theobald & Campbell, 2014). Perhaps, as Blacker (2013) concluded, it is impossible.

We have often, in other work, characterized this contrasting—nonrural—mindset as "cosmopolitan" (e.g., Howley et al., 2005). The term embeds the prejudicial misunderstandings about *rural*: rude, parochial, homely, and ignorant as against the esteemed sophistication, urbaneness, glamorousness, and remarkable talent of the (global, cosmopolitan) metropolis. Why (on earth) would anyone of merit want to be rural?

We have, we are, and we do. Our lives in a sense are part of the argument, though largely between the lines in our academic work. Both as writers and as natives, then, we offer a few simple and practical recommendations. We refrain, however, from offering school reform recommendations relevant to pedagogy, curriculum, or policy because we understand the key issues as ideological and cultural. Education philosopher Thomas Popkewitz (2007) concluded that education reform is the corporate redefinition of public purpose. The education profession, therefore, should be doing something else for the moment.

On this basis, we therefore offer recommendations that anyone who is interested can apply to their own lives and their own thinking about what a decent, rurally relevant education might be for children and youth with academic, artistic, and practical talents—talents that should be accessible for use in the homeplace *more* than other places:

1. Turn off the noise. The meaning of life is not embedded in personal wealth. Develop talents, not greed. The simple advice can be very difficult to follow because the noise is pervasive and seems convincing.
2. Recognize talents as connecting to higher purposes, purposes that can be addressed anywhere. For gifted rural students, that anywhere is an actual known and often beloved somewhere. These students already have the necessary allegiances (except for the noise).
3. Foster rural gifted students so as to realize their talents as more a responsibility than a gift. Identification of talent in order to bestow privileges is in fact mistreatment of talent.

Greater talent means harder work and it leads those who develop it toward difficult and unsettling insights. We are offering that sort of effort, in fact, in this chapter, knowing well that the ideas and outlooks on offer are culturally discordant with state schooling in America, and with some or much of the prevailing wisdom both in rural education and in gifted education. Nonetheless, a strong motive for us to do this work is the affection we hold for the rural places and people we know. They once had schools that served them better (see Dewalt, 2006). And we think they deserve better from the state and the corporations that now dominate their schools. But rural educators and rural families can best access that improvement with their own children and their own thinking: They are not going to get much help elsewhere, in our view.

As researchers have warranted elsewhere with both relevant arguments and empirical studies (Burnell, 2003; Carr & Kefalas, 2009; Corbett, 2007; Hektner, 1995; Howley et al., 1996; Huang et al., 1997), gifted students are those nearly everyone believes *should* leave their rural homeplaces behind *for good*; national purpose requires it. Communities and wise educators can mitigate this risk better without the help of reform than with it.

References

Akgun, A. A., Baycan-Levent, T., Nijkamp, P., & Poot, J. (2011). Roles of local and newcomer entrepreneurs in rural development: A comparative meta-analytic study. *Regional Studies, 45*(9), 1207–1223.

Anderson, L. (2014, Feb. 12). What was the deal with Graham Greene calling Shirley Temple "A fancy little piece"? *Browbeat: Slate's culture blog*. Retrieved from http://www.slate.com/

Bals, T. (1999). Fostering talents in vocational training: Current strategies in Germany. *High Ability Studies, 10*(1), 97–105.

Bellah, R. N., Madsen, R., Sullivan, W. M., Swidler, A., & Tipton, S. M. (1985). *Habits of the heart: Individualism and commitment in American life*. Berkeley: University of California Press.

Berry, W. (1970). *The hidden wound*. San Francisco, CA: North Point Press.

Berry, W. (2010). *What matters most: Economics for a renewed commonwealth*. Berkeley, CA: Counterpoint.

Blacker, D. (2013). *The falling rate of learning and the neoliberal endgame*. United Kingdom: Zero Books.

Bloom, H. (2014). *The western canon*. New York, NY: Houghton Mifflin Harcourt.

Brann, R. E. (1988). *The PRO-TECH Program: A program for gifted and talented high school students in Connecticut's vocational-technical school system*. Hartford, CT: Connecticut Department of Education. Retrieved from ERIC database. (ED311218)

Bureau of the Census. (2007). *Population 1790 to 1990: United States urban and rural population* (Table 4). Washington, D.C.: Author. Retrieved from http://www.census.gov/population/censusdata/table-4.pdf

Burnell, B. A. (2003). The "real world" aspirations of work-bound rural students. *Journal of Research In Rural Education, 18*(2), 104–113.

Callahan, R. (1962). *Education and the cult of efficiency*. Chicago, IL: University of Chicago Press.

Carr, P., & Kefalas, M. (2009). *Hollowing out the middle: The rural brain drain and what it means for America*. Boston, MA: Beacon Press.

Cline, M. (2014, Feb. 11). Shirley Temple movies provided escape during Depression era. *Salisbury Post*. Retrieved from http://m.salisburypost.com/2014/ 02 /11/ mike-cline-column-shirley-temple-movies-provided-escape-during-depression-era/

Cogan, L., Schmidt, W., & Wiley, D. (2001). Who takes what math and in which track? Using TIMSS to characterize US students' eighth-grade mathematics learning opportunities. *Educational Evaluation and Policy Analysis, 23*(4), 323–341.

Colangelo, N., Assouline, S., & New, J. (1999). *Gifted education in rural schools: A national assessment*. Iowa City, IA: Blank International Center for Gifted Education and Talent Development. Retrieved from http://www.nagc.org

Conant, J. (1959). *The American high school today*. New York, NY: McGraw-Hill.

Conkin, P. (2009). *A revolution down on the farm: The transformation of American agriculture since 1929*. Lexington: The University Press of Kentucky.

Corbett, M. (2007). *Learning to leave: The irony of schooling in a coastal community*. Halifax, Nova Scotia: Fernwood.

Crawford, M. B. (2009). *Shop class as soulcraft: An inquiry into the value of work*. New York, NY: Penguin.

Csikszentmihalyi, M., Rathunde, K., & Whalen, S. (1997). *Talented teenagers: The roots of success and failure*. New York, NY: Cambridge University Press.

De Tocqueville, A. (1848). *De La démocratie en Amérique*. Paris, France: Pagnerre.

Deresiewicz, W. (2014). *Excellent sheep: The miseducation of the American elite*. New York, NY: Simon & Schuster.

Descollonges, H., & Eisner, E. (2003). Protecting our children from the arts: Ten not-so-serious recommendations for policy makers. *American School Board Journal, 190*(10), 28–31.

Dewalt, M. W. (2006). *Amish schools in the United States and Canada*. Lanham, MD: R & L Education.

DeYoung, A. (1995). *The life and death of a rural American high school: Farewell, Little Kanawha*. New York, NY: Garland.

Donehower, K., Hogg, C., & Schell, E. (Eds.). (2012). *Reclaiming the rural: Essays on literacy, rhetoric, and pedagogy.* Carbondale: Southern Illinois University Press.

Douglas, S., & Walker, A. (2013). *Coal mining and the resource curse in the eastern United States.* Morgantown, WV: Social Sciences Research Network. Retrieved from http://papers.ssrn.com/sol3/Delivery.cfm/SSRN_ID2385560_code59895.pdf?abstractid=2385560&mirid=1

Fletcher, E. C. (2006). No curriculum left behind: The effects of the No Child Left Behind legislation on career and technical education. *Career & Technical Education Research, 31*(3), 157–174.

Fletcher, E. C. (2012). Demographics, tracking, and expectations in adolescence as determinants of employment status in adulthood: A study of school-to-work transitions. *Career & Technical Education Research, 37*(2), 103–119.

Gagné, F. (1998). A proposal for subcategories within the gifted or talented populations. *Gifted Child Quarterly, 42,* 87–95.

Gardner, H. (1983). *Frames of mind: The theory of multiple intelligence.* New York, NY: Basic Books.

Gibbs, R. M., & Cromartie, J. B. (1994). Rural youth outmigration: How big is the problem and for whom? *Rural Development Perspectives, 10*(1), 9–16.

Glass, G. (2007). *Fertilizers, pills, and magnetic strips: The fate of public education in America.* Charlotte, NC: Information Age Publishing.

Grantham, T. C. (2012). Eminence-focused gifted education: Concerns about forward movement void of an equity vision. *Gifted Child Quarterly, 56*(4), 215–220.

Greene, G. (1978). *The human factor.* London, England: The Bodley Head.

Greene, G. (1973). *The honorary consul.* London, England: The Bodley Head.

Greene, G. (1940). *The power and the glory.* London, England: Heinemann.

Gross, P., & MacLaury, B. (2003). *Learning for the future: Changing the culture of math and science education to ensure a competitive workforce.* New York, NY: Committee for Economic Development. Retrieved from https://www.ced.org/pdf/Learning-for-the-Future.pdf

Haller, E. J., & Monk, D. H. (1992). Youth migration from rural areas. In *Who pays for diversity? Population yearbook of the American Education Finance Association* (pp. 48–70). Thousand Oaks, CA: Corwin Press.

Healy, J. (2015, January 4). Heavyweight response to local fracking bans. *The New York Times,* p. A11.

Hektner, J. M. (1995). When moving up implies moving out: Rural adolescent conflict in the transition to adulthood. *Journal of Research in Rural Education, 11*(1), 3–14.

Herzog, M. J., & Pittman, R. (1995). Home, family, and community: Ingredients in the rural education equation. *Phi Delta Kappan, 77*(2), 13–18.

Hill, P. (Ed.). (2006) *Charter schools against the odds: An assessment by the Hoover Institution's Koret Task Force on K12 education.* Stanford, CA: Hoover Institution.

Hobsbawm, E. (1962). *The age of revolution, 1789–1848* (Vol. 1st). Cleveland, OH: World Publishing Company.

Hofstede, G. (2001). *Culture's consequences: Comparing values, behaviors, institutions, and organizations across nations* (2nd ed.). Thousand Oaks, CA: Sage.

Howley, A., Howley, C., & Pendarvis, E. (2003). The possible good gifted programs in rural schools and communities might do. In J. Borland (Ed.), *Rethinking gifted education* (pp. 80–104). New York, NY: Teachers College Press.

Howley, A., Showalter, D., Howley, M., Howley, C., Klein, R., & Johnson, J. (2011). Challenges for place-based mathematics pedagogy in rural schools and communities in the United States. *Children, Youth, and Environments, 21*(1), 101–127.

Howley, C., Harmon, H., & Leopold, G. (1996). Rural scholars or bright rednecks? Aspirations for a sense of place among rural youth in Appalachia. *Journal of Research in Rural Education, 12*(3), 150–160.

Howley, C., Howley, A., & Huber, D. S. (2005). Prescriptions for Rural Mathematics Instruction: Analysis of the Rhetorical Literature. *Journal of Research in Rural Education (Online), 20*(7), 1. Retrieved from http://www.jrre.psu.edu/articles/20-7.pdf

Howley, C., Howley, A., & Johnson, J. (Eds.). (2014). *Dynamics of social class, race, and place in rural education.* Charlotte, NC: Information Age Press.

Howley, C., Howley, A., & Yahn, J. (2014). Motives for dissertation research at the intersection between rural education and curriculum and instruction. *Journal of Research in Rural Education, 29*(5), 1–12.

Howley, C., Showalter, D., Klein, R., Sturgill, D. J., & Smith, M. A. (2013). Rural math talent, now and then. *Roeper Review, 35*(2), 102–114.

Howley, C. W. (2006). Remote possibilities: Rural children's educational aspirations. *Peabody Journal of Education, 81*(2), 62-80. doi:10.1207/S15327930pje8102_4.

Howley, M., Howley, A., & Eppley, K. (2013). How agricultural science trumps rural community in the discourse of selected U.S. History textbooks. *Theory and Research in Social Studies Education, 41*(2), 187–218.

Hubbard, R. (1988). Science, facts, and feminism. *Hypatia, 3*(1), 5–17.

Huang, G. G., Weng, S., Zhang, F., & Cohen, M. P. (1997). Outmigration among rural high school graduates: The effect of academic and vocational programs. *Educational Evaluation & Policy Analysis, 19*(4), 360–372.

Jackson, W. (1996). *Becoming native to this place.* Washington, D.C.: Berkeley, CA: Counterpoint.

Jackson, W. (2011). *Consulting the genius of the place: An ecological approach to a new agriculture.* Berkeley, CA: Counterpoint.

Jacob, J. (1997). *New pioneers: The back-to-the-land movement and the search for a sustainable future.* University Park, PA: Pennsylvania State University Press.

Jacobs, J. (1986). *Cities and the wealth of nations.* New York, NY: Penguin.

Jamieson, L. (2000). Migration, place, and class: Youth in a rural area. *Sociological Review, 48*(2), 203–223.

Jung, J. Y. (2012). Giftedness as a developmental construct that leads to eminence as adults: Ideas and implications from an occupational/career decision-making perspective. *Gifted Child Quarterly, 56*(4), 189–193.

Kannapel, P., & DeYoung, A. (1999). The rural school problem in 1999: A review and critique of the literature. *Journal of Research in Rural Education., 15*(2), 67–79.

Kochan, T., Finegold, D., & Osterman, P. (2012). Who can fix the "middle-skills" gap? *Harvard Business Review, 90*(12), 81–90.

Kunstler, J. H. (2005). *The long emergency: Surviving the end of oil, climate change, and other converging catastrophes of the twenty-first century.* New York, NY: Grove Press.

Leung, S., Conoley, C. W., & Scheel, M. J. (1994). The career and educational aspirations of gifted high school students: A retrospective study. *Journal of Counseling & Development, 72*(3), 298–303.

Lewicki, J. (2010). *To know the joy of work well done: Place-based learning and sustaining school communities.* Westby, WI: coopecology.com.

Lewis, J. D., & Hafer, C. (2007). The challenges of being gifted in a rural community. *Digest of Gifted Research.* Retrieved from http://tip.duke.edu/node/842

Lévy, B. H. (2007). *American vertigo.* New York, NY: Random House.

Lichter, D. T, & Brown, D. L. (2011). Rural America in urban society: Changing spatial and social boundaries. *Annual Review of Sociology, 37,* 565–592.

Lowell, B. L., Salzman, H., Bernstein, H., & Henderson, E. (2009). *Steady as she goes? Three generations of students through the science and engineering pipeline.* New Brunswick, NJ: Blaustein School, Rutgers University.

Retrieved from http://www.heldrich.rutgers.edu/uploadedFiles/Publications/ STEM_Paper_Final.pdf

Marcuse, H. (1978). *The aesthetic dimension: Towards a critique of Marxist aesthetics*. Boston, MA: Beacon Press.

Mathez, E. (2009). *Climate change: The science of global warming and our energy future*. New York, NY: Columbia University Press.

McManus, P., Walmsley, J., Argent, N., Baum, S., Bourke, L., Martin, J., & . . . Sorensen, T. (2012). Rural community and rural resilience: What is important to farmers in keeping their country towns alive? *Journal of Rural Studies, 28*(1), 20–29.

Miéville, C. (2009). *The city & the city*. London: Macmillan.

Milgram, R. M., & Hong, E. (1999). Multipotential abilities and vocational interests in gifted adolescents: Fact or fiction. *International Journal of Psychology, 34*(2), 81–93.

Milne, B. G. (1982). *Vocational education for gifted and talented students*. (Information Series No. 236). Columbus: National Center for Research in Vocational Education, Ohio State University. Retrieved from ERIC database. (ED216206)

Molnar, A. (1996). *Giving kids the business: The commercialization of America's schools*. Boulder, CO: Westview Press.

Nachtigal, P., & Haas, T. (2000). *Annenberg Rural Challenge: School reform from a slightly different point of view*. (Keynote Address). Retrieved from ERIC database. (ED455047)

National Science Board. (2010). *Preparing the next generation of STEM innovators: Identifying and developing our nation's human capital*. Arlington, VA: National Science Foundation (NSB 10-33).

Nelson, M. K., & Smith, J. (1999). *Working hard and making do: Surviving in small town America*. Berkeley: University of California Press.

Olsen, B., & Sexton, D. (2009). Threat rigidity, school reform, and how teachers view their work inside current education policy contexts. *American Educational Research Journal, 46*(1), 9–44.

Pendarvis, E., Howley, A., & Howley, C. (1990). *The abilities of gifted children*. Englewood Cliffs, NJ: Prentice Hall.

Penn, R. (1975). Occupational prestige hierarchies A great empirical invariant? *Social Forces, 54*(2), 352–364.

Petrin, R. A., Schafft, K. A., & Meece, J. L. (2014). Educational sorting and residential aspirations among rural high school students: what are the contributions of schools and educators to rural brain drain? *American Educational Research Journal, 51*(2), 294–326.

Pitzel, G. R., Benavidez, A. C., Bianchi, B. C., Croom, L. L., de la Riva, B. R., Grein, D. L., & . . . Rendon, A. T. (2007). Rural revitalization in New Mexico: A grass roots initiative involving school and community. *Rural Educator, 28*(3), 4–11.

Plank, S. B., & Jordan, W. J. (2001). Effects of information, guidance, and actions on postsecondary destinations: A study of talent loss. *American Educational Research Journal, 38*(4), 947–979.

Popkewitz, T. (2007). *Cosmopolitanism and the age of school reform: Science, education, and making society by making the child.* New York, NY: Routledge.

Renzulli, J. S. (2012). Reexamining the role of gifted education and talent development for the 21st century: A four-part theoretical approach. *Gifted Child Quarterly, 56*(3), 150–159.

Robinson, M. (2010). *Absence of mind: The dispelling of inwardness from the modern myth of the self.* New Haven, CT: Yale University Press.

Rose, M. (2004). *The mind at work: Valuing the intelligence of the American worker.* New York, NY: Viking Penguin.

Sage, R., & Sherman, J. (2014). The fate of rural communities and schools in a corporation-dominated political economy: A historical interpretation. In Howley, C., Howley, A., & Johnson, J. (Eds). *Dynamics of social class race, and place in rural education* (pp. 67–94). Charlotte, NC: Information Age Publishing.

Sanderson, M. (1993). Vocational and liberal education: A historian's view. *European Journal of Education, 28*(2), 189–196.

Schwartz, L.L. (1994). *Why give "gifts" to the gifted?: Investing in a national resource.* Thousand Oaks, CA: Corwin Press.

Scott, J. (1998). *Seeing like a state: How certain schemes to improve the human condition have failed.* New Haven, CT: Yale University Press.

Scott, J. (2012). *Two cheers for anarchism: Six easy pieces on autonomy, dignity, and meaningful work and play.* Princeton, NJ: Princeton University Press.

Scott, M. (2013). Resilience: A conceptual lens for rural studies? *Geography Compass, 7*(9), 597–610.

Shava, S., Krasny, M. E., Tidball, K. G., & Zazu, C. (2010). Agricultural knowledge in urban and resettled communities: applications to social-ecological resilience and environmental education. *Environmental Education Research, 16*(5/6), 575–589.

Showalter, D. A. (2013). Place-based mathematics education: A conflated pedagogy? *Journal of Research in Rural Education, 28*(6), 1–13. Retrieved from http://jrre.psu.edu/articles/28-6.pdf

Solomon, S. (2010). *Water: The epic struggle for wealth, power, and civilization.* New York, NY: Harper Perennial.

Smith, G. A. (2007). Place-based education: Breaking through the constraining regularities of public school. *Environmental Education Research, 13*(2), 189–207.

Sparfeldt, J. R. (2007). Vocational interests of gifted adolescents. *Personality and Individual Differences, 42*(6), 1011–1021.

Stamm, M., & Niederhauser, M. (2008). Giftedness and gender in vocational training. *European Journal of Vocational Training, 45*(3), 109–120.

Sternberg, R. J. (1985). *Beyond IQ: A triarchic theory of intelligence.* Cambridge, MA: Cambridge University Press.

Subotnik, R. F., Olszewski-Kubilius, P., & Worrell, F. C. (2011). Rethinking giftedness and gifted education: A proposed direction forward based on psychological science. *Psychological Science in the Public Interest, 12,* 3–54.

Subotnik, R. F., Olszewski-Kubilius, P., & Worrell, F. C. (2012). Nurturing the young genius. *Scientific American Mind, 23*(5), 50–57.

Subotnik R. F., & Rickoff, R. (2010). Should eminence based on outstanding innovation be the goal of gifted education and talent development? Implications for policy and research. *Learning and Individual Differences 20*(4), 358–364.

Sytsma, R. (2000). *Gifted and talented programs in America's high schools: A preliminary survey report.* Storrs, CT: The National Research Center on the Gifted and Talented.

Taylor, L.A. (1995). *Undiscovered Edisons: Fostering the talents of vocational-technical students.* Storrs, CT: National Research Center on the Gifted and Talented. Retrieved from ERIC database. (ED402706)

Theobald, P. (1997). *Teaching the commons: Place, pride, and the renewal of community.* Boulder, CO: Westview.

Theobald, P., & Campbell, C. (2014). The fate of rural communities and schools in a corporate-dominated political economy: A historical interpretation. In C. Howley, A. Howley, & J. Johnson (Eds.), *The dynamics of social class, place, and race in rural education* (pp. 95–108). Charlotte, NC: Information Age Publishing.

Thompson, P. (2002). *The accidental theorist: The double helix of everyday life.* New York, NY: Peter Lang.

Tomlinson, S. (2008). Gifted, talented and high ability: Selection for education in a one-dimensional world. *Oxford Review of Education, 34*(1), 59–74.

Walzer, M. (1988). *The company of critics: Social criticism and political commitment in the twentieth century.* New York, NY: Basic Books.

White, S., & Corbett, M. (2014). *Doing educational research in rural settings*. New York, NY: Routledge.

Williams, R. (1973). *The country and the city*. London, England: Verso.

Williams, R. (1976). *Keywords: A vocabulary of culture and society*. New York, NY: Oxford University Press.

Williams, R. (1989). *The politics of modernism*. London, England: Verso.

Williams, R. (2001). Culture is ordinary. In J. Higgins (Ed.), *The Raymond Williams reader* (pp. 10–24). Oxford, UK: Blackwell Publishers. Original work published 1958.

Young, M. (1993). Bridging the academic/vocational divide: Two Nordic case studies. *European Journal of Education, 28*(2), 209–214.

CHAPTER 3

Education in Rural America
Challenges and Opportunities

Marybeth J. Mattingly, Ph.D., and Andrew Schaefer

Introduction

Ask people to evoke images of rural America and many different scenarios come to mind. Many will think of agrarian communities rife with livestock and agricultural production. Others will see the idyllic panorama of some rural settings amidst mountains, lakes, and trees. Still others may think about deep rural poverty, families living "at the end of the road" with limited resources or connections to the larger world. So which of these images typify rural America today? They all do. Indeed, rural America represents an array of community types, lifestyles, and opportunities. In a 2008 report, Hamilton, Hamilton, Duncan, and Colocousis described four types of rural communities: amenity rich, or communities that are attractive to outsiders, particularly for their beautiful scenery and recreational opportunities; declining resource-dependent, or places that once relied on agriculture, manufacturing, or extraction industries (like logging or mining) but now face depleted resources and population loss; amenity/decline, or places that once depended on now-depleted environmental resources but have amenities that might attract outsiders and potentially lead to growth; and chronically poor, rural places that have experienced decades of economic deprivation and are left with inadequate resources and infrastructure.

In addition to changes in the economic structure of rural America, changing racial-ethnic composition is also evident (Johnson, 2012; Johnson, 2014; Lichter, 2012), particularly among children (Johnson, Schaefer, Lichter, & Rogers, 2014). Historically, clear patterns of minority representation across rural America are evident. The South has historically been characterized by a high concentration of Black residents, the U.S.-Mexico border regions have a high level of Hispanic residents, and Native Americans are concentrated on reservations in the Southwest and Great Plains (Johnson, 2012). Despite this characterization, overall, the nation's rural places are and have been disproportionately White. Across nonmetropolitan counties, 79.7% of residents are non-Hispanic White, as compared to 60.9% of residents in metropolitan counties. Indeed, despite some rural places characterized by large minority concentrations, many other rural places have been disproportionately White including across Appalachia and the Ozarks. Recently, however, scholars have noted increasing racial-ethnic diversity in rural America, particularly as Hispanics reach new destinations in large numbers (Lichter & Johnson, 2009). Not only do Hispanic women have substantially higher fertility rates than their non-Hispanic counterparts, the Hispanic population is younger, on average, than the national population, with a larger share of women in or soon entering peak childbearing years. Taken together, these suggest the Hispanic population across nonmetropolitan America is growing not merely as a result of migration but also due to natural increase (Johnson, Schaefer, Lichter, & Rogers, 2014). Traditional communities are faced with accommodating new residents who look different and may have a different cultural heritage. Additionally, much of the increased diversity is among lesser skilled residents seeking opportunities in the service and agricultural sectors: jobs that are low paying and unstable but may be the only ones available. Children may be entering rural schools having newly moved or having challenges that have not historically been as common.

Variation and change across rural America are key to understanding the challenges and opportunities in rural America today. In this chapter, we outline how people living in rural places often have different challenges than their suburban or central city counterparts. We look specifically at how rural people, particularly school-aged children and young adults, experience barriers to success that are different from those facing their peers in other communities. We also highlight differences between rural communities where contrasts can be just as striking as those between rural and nonrural places. We conclude by documenting not just challenges for implementing education and economic policy in rural places, but opportunities unique to rural areas that can be leveraged to make problems in these places more manageable.

Rural Poverty

Although rural poverty today is not typically the same as that depicted in the Dust Bowl of the 1930s, as in the novel *Grapes of Wrath*, it remains prevalent, and rural children face only slightly lower poverty rates than their peers in central cities. Indeed, the most recent official poverty statistics suggest that 26% of rural children lived in poor families in 2013, as did 29% of children residing in central cities. By contrast, poverty rates were much lower in the suburbs, where 17% of children were growing up poor (Mattingly, Carson, & Schaefer, 2014).[1] In fact, data suggest that poverty rates for both Black and White children were higher in rural America than in central cities or the suburbs in 2013, but it is the high concentration of White children—whose poverty rates are far lower than Black children's—in rural places that bring overall rates below those in central cities. As rural America diversifies, its poverty may climb with larger populations of demographic minorities who tend to have higher poverty rates.

In Figure 3.1, we show the distribution of counties with high child poverty between the years 2008–2012. For these purposes, we categorize a county as having high child poverty if at least 20% of its children live in families with incomes below the poverty line. As is evident from the shading on the map, high child poverty is common in the United States. The majority of U.S. counties (58%) had high child poverty during this time period, particularly across the South and less so in parts of the Northeast and Midwest. The prevalence of the darkest shading on the map indicates that high child poverty is more likely across rural America. Of the high child poverty counties, 70% are nonmetropolitan, or rural—a disproportionately high share, given that rural counties only represent 63% of all counties across the nation. In other words, children growing up across rural America have a higher probability of growing up in a high poverty county than do their urban peers.

Not only is rural child poverty high, in many places it has persisted for generations. In Figure 3.2, we show the counties that have experienced high child poverty in the 1980, 1990, and 2000 U.S. Decennial Censuses and the 2008–2012 American Community Survey Five-Year estimates. Of those counties with high child poverty at each decennial mark for at least four decades—dubbed "persistent child poverty" counties—581 are rural, representing 77% of all persistently poor counties. Again, considering that only 63% of all counties are rural, we find a rural disadvantage in persistent child poverty. Chronic pov-

---

[1] Note, however, that Supplemental Poverty Rate estimates suggest somewhat lower poverty in nonmetropolitan areas. (see Short, 2014)

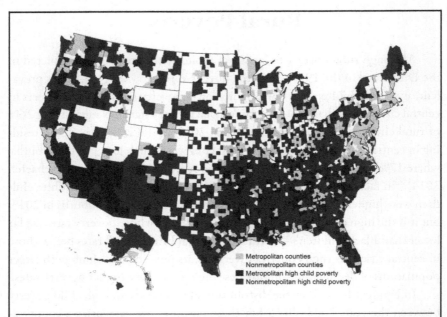

Figure 3.1. Authors' analysis of high child poverty counties by metropolitan status, 2008–2012.

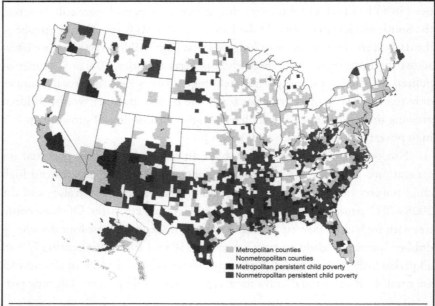

Figure 3.2. Authors' analysis of persistent child poverty counties by metropolitan status, 1980–2012.

erty in a county can have particularly pernicious effects. These places likely have fewer role models and examples of individuals who have carved out successful life paths that children and young adults can draw on or use for inspiration in their own lives. Like high child poverty counties, persistent child poverty counties are heavily concentrated in the South, with fewer present in the Northeast, Midwest, and Western regions of the nation.

Although official poverty rates are important for understanding these enduring patterns, measuring poverty in this way may mask the true underlying economic need families are facing. Indeed, basic needs budget estimates from the National Center on Child Poverty suggest families need between 2.5 and 3.5 times the official poverty threshold to meet their necessary expenditures on things like child care during work hours, food, shelter, utilities, and transportation to work, but excluding such luxuries as meals eaten out and child care during any nonwork time (Dinan, 2009). We calculated the share of rural residents living in low-income families (defined here as having incomes below twice the poverty threshold) to get a conservative estimate of those who may be struggling to make ends meet. Estimates suggest that in 2013, more than 1 in 2 children in rural America live in these types of families. These data have implications for educators living or working in rural America.

Barriers to Educational Success

"So the concept that an education is important is there, but that you can do it, it doesn't exist . . . The concept that you can have a good-paying job or that you don't need to be on disability to be able to meet your needs, it's just not there."—Service Provider in New England[2]

Poverty

Over the past couple of decades, rural poverty has been increasingly associated with both the lack of a middle class and little investment in infrastructure, including schools (see Duncan, 1999). Additionally, in many rural places, economic restructuring has resulted in the disappearance of jobs in manufacturing and the extractive industries (Duncan, 1999; Lichter & Graefe, 2011; Sherman,

---

2   Quotes used throughout this chapter are derived from a broader project being conducted by the Vulnerable Families Research Program at the Carsey School of Public Policy to better understand how families are getting by in rural America.

2009) alongside an increased reliance on jobs in the service sector, particularly in places with natural amenities (McGranahan, 1999). These low-skill manufacturing and extraction jobs tended to offer living wages and decent benefits without requiring much formal education (Kalleberg, 2011). In many places, completing high school was unnecessary because work in local extraction industries required on-the-job training that did not necessitate investment in academic pursuits (Corbett, 2007). In such places, where returns to education have been historically low, where high school dropouts may have had the same job successes as their parents, and where jobs for the better educated were scarce, there was little investment in the schools. The community culture did not value formal education as a practical necessity for a successful future, and for some, getting an education meant moving away. Such a history poses challenges to the establishment and provisioning of the most advanced educational opportunities across many rural communities.

Furthermore, as jobs became less and less available, rural communities have been transformed. What were once solid, hardworking communities are now home to economic disadvantage and little opportunity for children. In many places, such transformations began long before the Great Recession and the aftermath has implications for gender ideology (Sherman, 2011), family structure and formation (McLaughlin & Coleman-Jensen, 2011; Snyder, 2011), and general employment outcomes for both men and women (Jensen & Jensen, 2011; Smith, 2011), among others (Smith & Tickamyer, 2011). Not surprisingly, the lack of jobs is a major concern in many rural places. Many who can, do move away in search of better opportunities (Carr & Kefalas, 2009). Those left behind may not have the resources to invest in educational opportunities.

Teacher Quality and Preparation

Across rural America, student achievement often lags behind that of their urban peers. Graham and Teague (2011) documented that rural children less often achieve grade-level reading benchmarks by third grade, an achievement correlated with later academic and work success (Snow, Burns, & Griffin, 1998), than do their peers residing in cities and suburbs. The gap was particularly large for those entering kindergarten without adequate reading skills. Graham and Provost (2012) further documented that students from rural places and central cities start kindergarten behind their suburban peers in math, and this achievement gap grows over time. Rural adolescents are also more likely to drop out of high school and have lower academic achievement in terms of math and reading standardized assessments than their nonrural counterparts (Roscigno & Crowley, 2001; Roscigno, Tomaskovic-Devey, & Crowley, 2006). Research from the National Center for Education Statistics (2013) indicated that much of the difference between rural and nonrural students can be attributed to particularly high scores among some students in some suburban school districts, who are considered nonrural in analyses that don't break out suburban and urban places.

Opportunities for teachers and teacher quality also differ in rural America. Whereas 40% of teachers in cities and suburbs had access to professional development opportunities in their schools, only 27% of rural teachers did (Graham & Provost, 2012). Further, rural schools have a disproportionate number of new teachers (in their first or second year of teaching) as compared to those in the suburbs (although those in central cities have the highest concentration of new teachers). This distribution may indicate high turnover and signify a prevalence of teachers who lack experience managing a classroom and developing lesson plans compared with their more seasoned peers (Gagnon & Mattingly, 2012). Districts in poor, rural areas (and poor large cities) are also more likely to have a disproportionate number of new teachers compared to poor districts in suburban areas (Gagnon & Mattingly, 2012).

Access

Not surprisingly, opportunities for students also vary. Graham (2009) found that "suburban and urban schools, on average, offer three to four more courses in advanced mathematics than rural schools." And Gagnon and Mattingly (2015) found that not only are rural students less often enrolled in Advanced Placement courses, when they are enrolled, they are less often successful in obtaining final exams scores adequate for conferring college credits. Furthermore, while affluent school districts in rural areas have higher AP success rates than those in less affluent areas, suburban and urban affluent districts still fare better than their rural counterparts (Gagnon and Mattingly, 2015).

Taken together, the lack of opportunities coupled with lower student achievement means that many rural high school graduates are likely ill prepared for employment and have less access to "good" jobs (if they exist) that provide a stable schedule, paycheck, and adequate benefits. For many, college enrollment is also prohibitive, whether due to finances, skill levels, or the limited opportunities for higher education in many rural places. Further, many rural adolescents who are academically qualified leave rural places to seek jobs and educational opportunities that better match their skill sets when they reach adulthood (Carr & Kefalas, 2009).

Another way to explore the mismatch between career opportunities and educational attainment in rural places is to compare the "disconnected" youth there to those in urban places. Disconnected youth, often referred to as "idle" youth, are defined as those between 16 and 19 years old who are not enrolled in school and not in the labor force (either employed or unemployed). In the nation as a whole, a relatively small share of the youth population falls into this category: 5.4% (Figure 3.3). In contrast, 6.5% of rural youth are considered disconnected, a substantially larger percentage than their urban (5.2%) counterparts. We also see differences in the prevalence of disconnected youth *within* rural places. For instance, approximately 5.5% of rural youth living in counties not characterized by persistently high child poverty are disconnected compared to 9% of their counterparts in persistently high child poverty counties. In short, rural youth are more likely to be disconnected from the labor force and formal educational institutions than are their nonrural counterparts, and rural youth living in chronically poor places are especially at risk.

The Job Market

> "I've applied everywhere. I mean, local convenience stores, anything just so I have a job."—Rural New England Resident Living in a Poor County

Complicating matters for many rural residents, as previously noted, is a dearth of job opportunities. Concurrent with high poverty, many rural Americans face challenging job prospects. As the quote above illustrates, in many places, jobs are scarce. Opportunities are few and far between. Up until the early 1990s, jobs in manufacturing industries dominated rural America and provided living wages with benefits (Smith & Tickamyer, 2011). Service sector jobs that have replaced many of the steady jobs in manufacturing and extraction—and that dominate the tourism industry in amenity-rich places—are often less stable, offer lower pay and fewer benefits, and provide little opportunity for career advancement. Additionally, many rural places have seasonal variation in the jobs available. For example, harvesting core crops may provide several weeks of intense farm labor, while tourism or holiday industries may offer additional months of work. Although residents may experience increases in their incomes during these months, the income must last through many

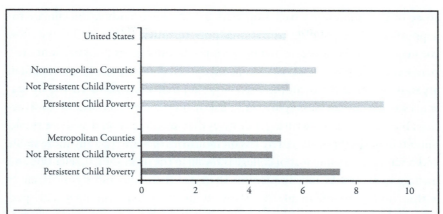

Figure 3.3. Percentage of youth age 16–19 disconnected by metropolitan and persistent child poverty county status, 2008–2012. *Note.* Differences between and within places are all statistically significant ($p<0.05$).

months when work is scarce. As a result, many families piece together what they can, working, bartering, or selling products for cash, as described by one resident, trained as a carpenter:

> I just can't rely on carpentry around here to keep the ball rolling. I've always grown a big garden ... I've sold organic vegetables privately and also to restaurants and whatnot ... I own a bunch of land ... And I've cut and sold firewood in the past when I'm not doing carpentry and not doing gardening and other things to keep the ball rolling in that regard. So I've developed a number of skills to, you know, make, you know, to bring it all together because carpentry in this area is seasonal to a degree ... That's the way it is ... For a number of years, I was a captain of an aquaculture boat in the salmon farms ... It gave me a fallback as well as [when] the carpentry slowed down or whatever, I could still use those carpentry skills ... So I'm maintaining that because it takes many different—for me, in my lifetime—different facets and aspects to keep the ball rolling, not just carpentry. I've worked out of the area on some different jobs ... Pieced together.—Widowed Dad of One Adult Daughter

One way to assess differences in the job structure between rural and urban places as well as within rural places is to look at industry breakdowns. Understanding the different industrial composition of America illuminates some of the community backdrop essential to understanding the climate for supporting and expanding educational opportunities. In Figure 3.4, we show the major industry categories in nonmetropolitan and metropolitan counties by persistent child poverty status. Compared to their counterparts in metropolitan areas, nonmetropolitan counties rely more on industries characterized by seasonal work or less-stable employment, like farming and extraction and construction, but also in manufacturing industries that are often touted as more stable. Simultaneously, these places rely less on industries that are typically more stable and often require some sort of college training in the professional, scientific and management, and finance industries. There are also some industry differences within nonmetropolitan places. Many nonmetropolitan counties with persistently high child poverty have smaller shares of jobs in manufacturing industries, finance or professional industries, and recreation and accommodation industries than other nonmetropolitan places. This indicates some difference in the kinds of job opportunities available to young adults finishing high school in persistently poor rural places. Offering expanded educational opportunities to students may better prepare them to move away and pursue higher education, or efforts for less skilled students could better prepare them for the available mix of jobs and life skills they will need to navigate less stable employment.

Population Decline

The United States has been growing older since the turn of the 20th century, and rural places in particular have continued this trend into recent years (Krout & Hash, 2015). This is due to a complex mix of low fertility, particularly in farming counties (Johnson, 2013), and outmigration of young adults to metropolitan areas (Johnson, Winkler, & Rogers, 2013). As a result, some rural communities are experiencing population decline. In many places, those seeking and holding educational credentials leave, often remaining away from the community in favor of places affording more career opportunities (Carr & Kefalas, 2009). In some places, families may even discourage their children from going to college, knowing that those who can leave often do and that has implications for family solidarity. As one rural service provider put it:

> I think there's a strong pull to not change. We've had a number of students who, from this area, who've actually gotten into college . . . and were all ready to go, and then when they graduated from school and were back home, they chose not to. And, even though the parents were

	United States	Nonmetropolitan			Metropolitan		
	Total	Total	Persistent Child Poverty	Not Persistent Child Poverty	Total	Persistent Child Poverty	Not Persistent Child Poverty
Agriculture, forestry, fishing and hunting, and mining	1.9	5.7[1]	6.6	5.5[2]	1.3	2.0	1.2[2]
Construction	6.5	7.4[1]	7.4	7.4	6.3	5.7	6.4[2]
Manufacturing	10.6	13.9[1]	12.4	14.4[2]	10.1	7.3	10.5[2]
Wholesale trade	2.8	2.3[1]	2.2	2.4[2]	2.9	2.6	2.9[2]
Retail trade	11.6	11.9[1]	11.8	11.9	11.5	11.0	11.6[2]
Transportation and warehousing and utilities	5.0	5.2[1]	5.4	5.2[2]	5.0	5.5	4.9[2]
Information	2.2	1.4[1]	1.2	1.4[2]	2.3	2.5	2.3[2]
Finance and insurance, and real estate and rental and leasing	6.7	4.3[1]	3.9	4.4[2]	7.1	7.1	7.1
Professional, scientific, and management services	10.7	6.0[1]	5.3	6.1[2]	11.4	11.0	11.5[2]
Educational services, and healthcare and social assistance	22.9	23.3[1]	24.8	22.9[2]	22.8	24.8	22.6[2]
Arts, entertainment, and recreation, and accommodation services	9.2	8.4[1]	7.8	8.6[2]	9.3	9.8	9.2[2]
Other services, except public administration	4.9	4.7[1]	4.8	4.7	5.0	5.1	5.0[2]
Public administration	4.9	5.4[1]	6.6	5.0[2]	4.9	5.6	4.8[2]

Figure 3.4. Percentage of youth age 16–19 disconnected by metropolitan and persistent child poverty county status, 2008–2012. *Note.* [1]Differences between nonmetropolitan and metropolitan totals are statistically significant (p<0.05). [2]Differences between persistent child poverty and not persistent child poverty are statistically significant (p<0.05).

very proud of them and . . . were so great, there is that fear of—for the kids too—'I don't want to leave my family,' you know? Think about it. That's their strongest connection, their strongest support. So I think there is that fear and, you know, I think maybe down the road—I think their eyes have been opened to something, and I think down the road maybe they'll pursue that."—Rural New England Service Provider

Among rural communities experiencing growth, much is driven by in-migration from other counties, largely Hispanic migration to new immigrant destinations (Johnson & Lichter, 2008), which in turn, contributes to the observed growing racial-ethnic diversity in rural America (Lichter, 2012).

Transportation

If I didn't have transportation, I don't know what I would do. You need transportation around here, 100%."—Rural New England Resident

Underlying many of the challenges facing rural America is the relative isolation of the population. Nonmetropolitan counties have much lower population density (45 people per square mile, on average) than their counterparts on the fringes (393 people per square mile) and cores (1,140 people per square mile) of metropolitan areas. Distances between schools and homes, homes and jobs, and amenities and residential areas can be vast. Further, public transportation is typically very limited, if available at all.

Thus, it can be particularly challenging to provide enriched opportunities for students outside of the school day. Wauchope and Stracuzzi (2010), for example, cited weak transportation services and lower population density as major barriers to rural families with children who are trying to access the USDA Summer Food Service Program. Even when services are delivered to people's doors, with "home visitors" traveling to meet clients in their homes, transportation can still complicate the service delivery processes. One rural New England provider described the way that transportation challenges affect both providers and clients, noting:

> Say you're a mom who doesn't have a car. Her neighbor drops in and says, 'I'm going to the store.' And, you know, she doesn't have a phone that can go across the county, 'cause she doesn't have that phone service. So she goes, 'Oh my god, okay, I'll go,' and she gets her kid together, and she goes out the door. And she may know that her home visitor is coming, but if given the choice of getting to the grocery store because she's out of Pampers . . . She goes thinking maybe she'll be back in time . . . [but her ride] wants to stop and get their pharmacy stuff, so she's back an hour and a half after the worker got there. So 5 hours, easily, out of her worker's day has ended up with no billable [client contact time].—Rural New England Service Provider

Implications for Education and Policy

Despite the challenges outlined in this chapter, there is reason for optimism. The small scale of rural America offers an ideal laboratory for testing new approaches, and relatively small investments can reach all students in given places (Jimerson, 2006). Thus, in many ways, the challenges facing rural America are on a relatively manageable scale.

The changing faces of rural America might also provide new opportunities for doing things differently. As communities transform, new residents may bring new ideas, new energy, and a desire to do better for their children.

Along these lines, some argue that schools in rural areas arguably play a larger role in fostering community cohesion and solidarity than schools in urban areas because of their smaller size, greater parental involvement, and their tendency to employ a large part of the community (Schafft & Biddle, 2014). Researchers in this field note that the key to creating education policy that works for rural schools is to capitalize on the expanded role that rural schools play in their towns. Because of the greater interconnectedness of rural schools and the communities they serve, policies that strengthen rural schools, like those that encourage new teachers to return to rural communities to work in their schools by providing them with increased training and certifications (Collins, 1999), can also impact labor markets in those places, as well as other structures that influence community solidarity (Schafft & Biddle, 2014).

Others similarly argue that a good place to start in rural communities is by identifying industries that are lacking employees and infrastructure, like health services and education (Peaslee & Hahn, 2011). This research cites the effectiveness of educational programs that prepare rural students to enter these underserved field, and then reward them for returning to rural places once they have received their training (Peaslee & Hahn, 2011). Policies like these could have multiple benefits, such as encouraging higher educational attainment among rural students, giving recent graduates incentives for returning home to their communities, and increasing the quality of institutions in the education and health sectors that have been degraded over the years due to a lack of funding and interest. Sections two and three of this book highlight specific programs, strategies, and policies that will promote these ideas through the lens of gifted education.

The changing faces of rural America might also provide new opportunities for doing things differently, although implications of increased diversity and migration to some rural areas are not necessarily all positive. On the one hand, as communities transform, new residents may bring new ideas, new energy and a desire to do better for their children. Furthermore, as diversity increases in many parts of rural America, interactions between people of different racial/ethnic groups provide the opportunity for increased understanding. On the other hand, migration to rural places can have adverse consequences, particularly if migrants less interested in funding education move in, like retirees or people purchasing second homes to take advantage of seasonal recreation opportunities. Also, increased diversity can have negative effects, especially if diversity is not evenly spread across rural places and economic and educational access and success are not available to all. Nonetheless, in-migration and diversity will continue to change and shape the landscape of rural America. In order to be effective, policy will have to take into account the changing landscape.

Conclusion

With a focus on barriers to education in rural places, we set out to describe several pernicious aspects of rural communities that can lead to (or result from) economic stagnation and decline, including impoverished families and educational structures, a lack of opportunities for jobs that provide living wages and benefits, transportation difficulties, and what is often referred to as the rural "brain drain" (Carr & Kefalas, 2009) that pushes the best students out of rural communities due to a lack of opportunity at home. On top of these challenges, "one size fits all" education policies based on national principles tend to be a poor fit for rural schools and have been accused by some researchers, with good supporting evidence, of favoring schools in densely populated school districts with more resources than schools in rural areas (Schafft & Biddle, 2014). However, we highlight how policies specifically geared for rural places can have positive impacts across the economic, social, and educational infrastructures in rural places. We further highlight the changing faces or rural communities caused by increased migration of some groups to rural places as well as increased diversity and note that new policies aimed at rural education will have to take these new realities into account.

References

Carr, P. J., & Kefalas, M. J. (2009). *Hollowing out the middle: The rural brain drain and what it means for America.* Boston, MA: Beacon Press.

Collins, T. (1999). *Attracting and retaining teachers in rural areas.* Charlestown, WV: ERIC Clearinghouse on Rural and Small Schools.

Corbett, M. (2007). *Learning to leave: The irony of schooling in a coastal community. Halifax, Nova Scotia*: Fernwood Publishing.

Dinan, K. A. (2009, March). *Budgeting for basic needs: A struggle for working families.* National Center for Children in Poverty, Mailman School of Public Health: Columbia University. Retrieved from http://academiccommons.columbia.edu/item/ac:126290

Duncan, C. M. (1999). *Worlds apart: Why poverty persists in rural America.* New Haven, CT: Yale University Press.

Gagnon, D., & Mattingly, M. J. (2012). *Beginning teachers are more common in rural, high-poverty, and racially diverse schools.* Carsey Issue Brief No. 53. Retrieved from http://scholars.unh.edu/cgi/viewcontent.cgi?article=1172&context=carsey

Gagnon, D., & Mattingly, M. J. (2015). *Limited access to AP courses for students in smaller and more isolated rural districts.* Carsey Issue Brief No. 80. Retrieved from http://scholars.uuh.edu/cgi/viewcontent.cgi?article=1234&context=carsey

Graham, S. (2009). *Students in rural schools have limited access to advanced mathematics courses.* Carsey Issue Brief No. 7. Retrieved from http://scholars.unh.edu/cgi/viewcontent.cgi?article=1088&context=carsey

Graham, S., & Provost, L. (2012). *Mathematics achievement gaps between suburban students and their rural and urban peers increase over time.* Carsey Issue Brief No. 52. Retrieved from http://scholars.unh.edu/cgi/viewcontent.cgi?article=1171&context=carsey

Graham, S., & Teague, C. (2011). *Reading levels of rural and urban third graders lag behind their suburban peers.* Carsey Issue Brief No. 28. Retrieved from http://scholars.unh.edu/cgi/viewcontent.cgi?article=1135&context=carsey

Hamilton, L. C., Hamilton, L. R., Duncan, C. M., & Colocousis, C. R. (2008). Place matters: Challenges and opportunities in four rural Americas. *Carsey Institute Reports on Rural America, 1*(4). Retrieved from http://scholars.unh.edu/cgi/viewcontent.cgi?article=1040&context=carsey

Jensen, L., & Jensen, E. B. (2011). Employment hardship among rural men. In K. E. Smith & A. R. Tickamyer (Eds.), *Economic Restructuring and Family Well-Being in Rural America* (pp. 40–59). University Park: Pennsylvania State University Press.

Jimerson, L. (2006). *The hobbit effect: Why small works in public schools.* Washington, DC: The Rural and Community Trust.

Johnson, K. M. (2012). Rural demographic change in the new century: Slower growth, increased diversity. Carsey Issue Brief No. 44. Retrieved from http://scholars.unh.edu/cgi/viewcontent.cgi?article=1158&context=carsey

Johnson, K. M. (2013). Deaths exceed births in record number of U.S. counties. Carsey Institute Fact Sheet No. 25. Retrieved from http://scholars.unh.edu/cgi/viewcontent.cgi?article=1190&context=carsey

Johnson, K. M. (2014). Demographic trends in nonmetropolitan America: 2000 to 2010. In C. Bailey, L. Jensen, & E. Ransom (Eds.), *Rural American*

In a Globalizing World: Problems and Prospects for the 2010s (pp. 311–329). Morgantown: West Virginia University Press.

Johnson, K. M., and Lichter, D. T. (2008). Population growth in new Hispanic destinations. Carsey Issue Brief No. 8. Retrieved from http://scholars.unh.edu/cgi/viewcontent.cgi?article=1041&context=carsey

Johnson, K. M., Schaefer, A., Lichter, D. T., & Rogers, L. T. (2014). The increasing diversity of America's youth. Carsey Institute National Issue Brief No. 71. Retrieved from http://scholars.unh.edu/cgi/viewcontent.cgi?article=1211&context=carsey

Johnson, K. M., Winkler, R., & Rogers, L. T. (2013). Age and lifecycle patterns driving U.S. migration shifts. Carsey Issue Brief No. 62. Retrieved from http://scholars.unh.edu/cgi/viewcontent.cgi?article=1191&context=carsey

Kalleberg, A. L. (2011). *Good jobs, bad jobs: The rise of polarized and precarious employment systems in the United States, 1970–2000*. New York, NY: Russell Sage Foundation.

Krout, J. A., & Hash, K. M. (2015). What is rural? Introduction to aging in rural places. In K. M. Hash, E. T. Jurkowski, & J. A. Krout (Eds.), *Aging in Rural Places: Policies, Programs, and Professional Practice* (pp. 3–22). New York, NY: Springer Publishing Company.

Lichter, D. T. (2012). Immigration and the new racial diversity in rural America. *Rural Sociology, 77*(1), 3–35.

Lichter, D. T., & Graefe, D. R. (2011). Rural economic restructuring: Implications for children, youth, and families. In K. E. Smith & A. R. Tickamyer (Eds.), *Economic Restructuring and Family Well-Being in Rural America* (pp. 25–39). University Park: Pennsylvania State University Press.

Lichter, D. T., & Johnson, K. M. (2009). Immigrant gateways and Hispanic migration to new destinations. *International Migration Review, 43*(3), 496–518.

Mattingly, M. J., Carson, J. A., & Schaefer, A. (2014). Cause for optimism? Child poverty declines for the first time since before the great recession. Carsey School of Public Policy National Issue Brief No. 76. Retrieved from http://scholars.unh.edu/cgi/viewcontent.cgi?article=1220&context=carsey

McGranahan, D. (1999, Sept.). Natural amenities drive population change. Agricultural Economic Report No. (AER-781). USDA Economic Research Service, Washington, D.C. Retrieved from http://www.ers.usda.gov/media/252390/aer781.pdf

McLaughlin, D. K., & Coleman-Jensen, A. (2011). Economic restructuring and family structure change, 1980 to 2000: A focus on female-headed families with children. In K. E. Smith & A. R. Tickamyer (Eds.), *Economic*

Restructuring and Family Well-Being in Rural America (pp. 105–123). University Park: Pennsylvania State University Press.

National Center for Education Statistics. (2013, May). The condition of education: The status of rural education. Washington, D.C.: Institute of Education Sciences. Retrieved from https://nces.ed.gov/programs/coe/indicator_tla.asp

Peaslee, L., & Hahn, A. (2011). Strengthening rural communities through investment in youth education, employment, and training. In K. E. Smith & A. R. Tickamyer (Eds.), *Economic Restructuring and Family Well-Being in Rural America* (pp. 233–255). University Park: Pennsylvania State University Press.

Roscigno, V. J., & Crowley, M. L. (2001). Rurality, institutional disadvantage, and achievement/attainment. *Rural Sociology, 66*(2), 268–292.

Roscigno, V. J., Tomaskovic-Devey, D., & Crowley, M. (2006). Education and the inequalities of place. *Social Forces, 84*(4), 2121–2145.

Schafft, K. A., & Biddle, C. (2014). Education and schooling in rural America. In C. Bailey, L, Jensen, & E. Ransom (Eds.), *Rural America in a Globalizing World: Problems and Prospects for the 2010s* (pp. 556–572). Morgantown: West Virginia University Press.

Sherman, J. (2009). *Those who work, those who don't: Poverty, morality, and family in rural America*. Minneapolis: University of Minnesota Press.

Sherman, J. (2011). Men without sawmills: Job loss and gender identity in rural America. In K. E. Smith & A. R. Tickamyer (Eds.), *Economic Restructuring and Family Well-Being in Rural America* (pp. 82–104). University Park: Pennsylvania State University Press.

Smith, K. E. (2011). Changing roles: Women and work in rural America. In K. E. Smith & A. R. Tickamyer (Eds.), *Economic Restructuring and Family Well-Being in Rural America* (pp. 60–81). University Park: Pennsylvania State University Press.

Smith, K. E., & Tickamyer, A. R. (2011). *Economic restructuring and family well-being in rural America*. University Park: Pennsylvania State University Press.

Snow, C. E., Burns, S. M., & Griffin, P. (Eds.). (1998). Preventing reading difficulties in young children. Washington, D.C.: National Academy Press.

Snyder, A. (2011). Patterns of family formation and dissolution in rural America and implications for well-being. In K. E. Smith & A. R. Tickamyer (Eds.), *Economic Restructuring and Family Well-Being in Rural America* (pp. 124–135). University Park: Pennsylvania State University Press.

Wauchope, B., & Stracuzzi, N. (2010). Challenges in serving rural American children through the summer food service program. *Carsey Issue Brief No. 13*. Retrieved from http://scholars.unh.edu/cgi/viewcontent.cgi?article=1107&context=carsey

Author Note

This chapter draws, in part, on Carsey School research and analyses funded by the Annie E. Carsey Foundation, the W. K. Kellogg Foundation, the U.S. Department of Health and Human Services, and anonymous donors. We gratefully thank colleagues at the Carsey School of Public Policy, including Jessica A. Carson for her role in collecting qualitative interview data on rural New Englanders, Barb Cook for her assistance with mapping, and Jennifer Clayton for formatting.

CHAPTER 4

Like Finding a Needle in a Haystack
Gifted Black and Hispanic Students in Rural Settings

Donna Y. Ford, Ph.D.

Introduction

The search for scholarship on gifted students in rural settings is an arduous one. Little exists on this student population, especially compared to the volume of work in urban settings. Even more difficult to locate are articles, chapters, and studies on gifted Black and Hispanic students who attend rural schools, despite the reality that gifted students exist in rural schools and that there is an increasingly high percentage of Black and Hispanic students in rural settings. Hence, the title of this chapter. Finding scholarship on rural gifted Black and Hispanic students was time consuming, like searching for and finding a needle in a haystack. This chapter presents an overview of these limited findings and juxtaposes them, where befitting, with such students in urban settings. The intent is to compare and contrast the issues and needs of students in both settings, but more importantly to shed light on the overlooked gifted Black and Hispanic students in rural schools. The focus on *rural* and *urban* is intentional given that, unlike suburban schools and communities, these two share the economic challenges of poverty. Recommendations for supporting gifted Black and Hispanic students in rural areas are similar to those in urban areas—culturally responsive education in terms of philosophy, learning environment, assessment, instruction, and curriculum. A model of culture is shared for Black and Hispanic students, along with the Bloom-Banks Matrix (Ford, 2011).

Rural Context: An Overview

In the 2010–2011 school year, about one-third of all public schools were in rural areas, while about one-fourth of all public school students were enrolled in rural schools. (Kena, Aud, Johnson, Wang, Zhang, Rathbun, Wilkinson-Flicker, & Kristapovich, 2014; Provasnik, KewalRamani, Coleman, Gilbertson, Herring, & Xie, 2007). In only three states, more than half of all students were enrolled in rural districts: Vermont (57.5%); Maine (57.2%); and Mississippi (56.5%). In 13 other states, more than one-third of all students were enrolled in rural school districts—in descending order: North Carolina, Alabama, South Dakota, Kentucky, South Carolina, Tennessee, Arkansas, West Virginia, North Dakota, Iowa, Georgia, Montana, and New Hampshire (Johnson, Showaler, Klein, & Lester, 2014, p. 7).

As in urban areas, poverty is prevalent in rural areas. According to the U.S. Department of Agriculture (USDA), in 2012, 15% of the nation's population lived in poverty, and poverty rates were higher in rural than in urban areas. In 2012, 17.7% of the population living in rural areas was poor. The higher incidence of rural poverty relative to urban poverty has existed since the 1960s, when poverty rates were first officially recorded (USDA, 2014b).

In 2012, the South had a rural poverty rate of 22%—about 7 percentage points higher than in the region's urban areas (USDA, 2014a). Race and poverty in both locales are different as well. Areas with a high incidence of poverty often reflect the low income of their racial and ethnic minorities. Rural Blacks had the highest incidence of poverty in 2012 at 40.6%. That rate is three times the rate for rural Whites in 2012 (13.5%). The 2012 poverty rate for rural Hispanics was 29.2%.

Who Are Rural Students of Color? Geographic and School Profiles

Geography

Nationally, almost 30% of rural students are children of color. The range among states is very large, from 4.6% in Rhode Island and New Hampshire to 82.5% in New Mexico. It is worth noting that about 70% of all rural minority students in the U.S. are concentrated in the 13 states where they make up one-third or more of the state's rural student population. In four states—New Mexico, California, Alaska, and Arizona—rural minority students make up more than half of the rural student population. In nine other states, more than one-third of rural students are students of color (in descending order, Texas, Louisiana, Florida, Mississippi, North Carolina, South Carolina, Oklahoma, Georgia, and Delaware; Johnson, Showaler, Klein, & Lester, 2014).

States vary considerably with regard to the racial and ethnic composition of their rural minority student populations. One of the states with the largest percentages of rural minority students (Alaska) has a rural population predominantly comprised of Alaska Natives. Others (e.g., New Mexico, Arizona, and Oklahoma) rank high because of combinations of Hispanic and American Indian populations. It may come as no surprise that in the South, states rank high primarily on the basis of their sizable African American populations (e.g., Louisiana, South Carolina, Mississippi, North Carolina, and Florida). California's rural minority student population is predominantly Hispanic (Johnson, Showaler, Klein, & Lester, 2014), and the rural Appalachian area is predominately White. Because of this, rural districts cannot be treated the same, as they differ in many ways based on their specific populations, cultures, and subcultures.

Schools

From 1995 to 2004, rural schools in the United States reported a 55% increase in minority students (Howley, Rhodes, & Beall, 2009). As of 2010–2011, in rural areas, 71% of public school students were White, 13% were Hispanic, and 10% were Black; Asian/Pacific Islanders and American Indian/Alaska Natives accounted for another 2% each.

Most, meaning 60%, of all rural minority students in the U.S. attend school in just eight states (in descending order of enrollment size, Texas, North Carolina, Georgia, California, South Carolina, Mississippi, Florida, and Arizona). The three states with the largest rural minority enrollments (Texas, North Carolina, and Georgia) serve one-third of all rural minority students in the U.S. Texas alone has more rural minority students than the 29 lowest ranking states on this indicator combined (Johnson, Showaler, Klein, & Lester, 2014).

Different Locale; Similar Outcomes

"Urban" has become the code word for Black and sometimes Hispanic, while "rural" is equated with White; and both are viewed as low income. As noted above and later, such interpretations are inaccurate, failing to capture the large and increasing student population who are culturally different. Stated another way, although the literature on Black and Hispanic students in urban settings is burgeoning, little attention has centered on those in rural schools and communities, which presents an incomplete and even distorted picture of life for these students. And one is hard pressed to find works that compare students from both settings. However, there is a great deal of speculation and conjecture, as reflected in Figure 4.1. A rudimentary search of the literature using "urban versus rural" resulted in a few documents that compared the locales' relative size, income, demographics, educational levels, occupation types, population density, and achievement data.

Communities are unique, and local or contextual values, traditions, and opportunities exert influences on the attitudes of students and their families about education and careers, for better or worse. Rural districts certainly face different challenges than urban districts, but the ultimate issues (e.g., providing children with high-quality teachers and rigorous, college-preparatory curricula) are the same as those faced by urban districts (Biddle, 2011).

Despite very different contexts—demographics, issues, and needs—the outcomes end up being quite similar for Black and Hispanic students in both settings. Noticeably, an unsettling finding is that these students are experiencing poor school outcomes in both settings, and they are underrepresented in gifted programs in both settings (Howley et al., 2009).

Although urban districts are home to half of the nation's dropout factories, defined as high schools with graduation rates of 60% or lower, 20% of persistently failing high schools are located in rural communities. Only 54% of Black

Gifted Black and Hispanic Students in Rural Settings

	Rural	Urban
Income	Low income; high poverty	Low income; high poverty
Demographics	Mostly White	Mostly non-White
Education Levels	Lower graduation and college rates	Higher graduation and college rates; more advanced degrees
School And Class Size	Smaller	Larger
Family Size	Larger	Smaller
Population Density	Sparsely populated per square mile; isolated; green spaces and land	Densely populated per square mile; concentrated; cement
Occupation Types	Blue collar	White collar
Economy	More agricultural	More industrial
Age	Older	Younger
Access To Resources	Less access to medical care, grocery stories, technology, etc.	More access to medical care, grocery stories, technology, etc.

Figure 4.1. Some perceptions regarding rural versus urban communities. *Note.* For more information, see http://www.ers.usda.gov/topics/rural-economy-population/rural-poverty-well-being/poverty-demographics.aspx and http://www.ers.usda.gov/topics/rural-economy-population/rural-poverty-well-being/geography-of-poverty.aspx.

ninth graders attending rural high schools graduated during the 2005–2006 school year, just 8 points higher than the graduation rates for their counterparts in urban schools. Also similar are low reading and math scores for urban and rural Black students on the 2009 National Assessment of Educational Progress (Biddle, 2011). Hines (2012) studied school experiences of rural Black students and found that in both rural and urban locales, Black students faced low teacher expectations and high rates of school disconnect and failure. Strayhorn (2009) studied the educational aspirations of Black males in urban, suburban, and rural high schools. He examined a nationally representative sample of respondents to the National Educational Longitudinal Study and found similarly low aspiration for Black males in urban and rural settings.

While by no means a comprehensive treatment or comparison of both locales, due to space limitations, I conclude this section with commentary by Biddle (2011):

> We have to stop looking at children through the location of the schools they attend and just look at them for who they are: Young men and women who deserve a high-quality education no matter where they live. And the schools and people who serve them, no matter where they are, must do better by all of them (para. 11).

Needle in a Haystack: Rural Gifted Black and Hispanic Students

Spicker, Southern, and Davis (1994) noted the lack of research on rural students, indicating that "when researchers—or at least the principal sponsors of poverty research—think poverty, they think city, not town or country" (p. 4). Little research exists on gifted students in rural environments, and even less research has examined gifted Black and Hispanic students who live in rural settings or locales.

Given that both locales share their respective and context-based burden of poverty, a look at poverty alone is important and telling. The National Education Longitudinal Study from 1988 reported that only 9% of students in gifted programs were in the bottom quartile of family income, while 47% of program participants were from the top quartile in family income (see U.S. Department of Education, 1993). These percentages by no means reflect the economic makeup of our schools and nation. Renzulli (1973) admonished policymakers decades ago that gifted, culturally different children in impoverished environments were being neglected and their gifts wasted:

> There can be little doubt that our nation's largest untapped source of human intelligence and creativity is found among the vast numbers of individuals in the lower socioeconomic levels . . . an invaluable natural resource is being wasted daily by a system of education that has shut its eyes and turned its back on [these children]. (p. 437)

Spicker, Southern, and Davis (1987) noted major obstacles in meeting the needs of rural gifted students. They indicated that, within rural school districts, acceptance of the status quo and resistance to change made it difficult to initiate new programs for gifted students. Along with limited financial resources for programs perceived as benefitting only a few students, rural schools were unable to provide adequate specialized teachers, counselors, school psychologists, and curriculum specialists to assist in providing appropriate services for high-ability youngsters (See Hébert & Beardsley, 2001).

Herzog and Pittman (1995) reported that students in rural settings suffered from negative stereotypes because of their rural background and internalized antirural prejudices, and they "exhibited an inferiority complex about their origins" (p. 114). They found that students educated in rural communities attended poorly funded schools and experienced both a lack of quality facilities and limited educational programs, while their teachers struggled with limited access to cultural information and resources. Further university teacher training programs and professional development did not adequately prepare them with specialized training to work in rural schools (Herzog & Pittman, 1995; Spicker, Southern, & Davis, 1987).

Howley et al. (2009) explained that as rural areas experience increased diversity, teachers who once served primarily homogenous populations are now faced with the challenge of identifying and nurturing giftedness in students from many different cultural backgrounds. Doing so is not likely to be any easier in rural schools than in schools in other locales. That is to say, given the high rates of poverty in rural and urban America, these culturally different students are doubly disadvantaged—often denied access to gifted education based on race and income (Ford, 2010, 2013).

Decades of data from studies and reports reveal a consistently stubborn and pervasive problem—Black and Hispanic students nationally and in most school districts seldom have access to gifted education classes. Nationally, their underrepresentation ranges from 40%–55%, depending on the year, with Black students being the most underrepresented of all groups every year. The Office for Civil Rights' Civil Rights Data Collection (U.S. Department of Education, 2009, 2011) does not disaggregate gifted education representation by locale or income. This is clearly needed to understand such differences and to advocate for rural and urban gifted students, their families and educators, and policymakers.

Recommendations for Change: Multicultural Gifted Education

In both rural and urban locales, where schools are increasing rapidly in the number of non-White students, a culturally responsive educational system is necessary for students, from all racial backgrounds, including those in gifted education.

Howley et al. (2009) and Hébert and Beardsley (2001) challenged rural schools to create culturally responsive experiences and learning opportunities for gifted students in rural settings. The same has been urged for decades by Baldwin (1987), Barkan and Bernal (1991), Bernal (2007), Castellano and Frazier (2010), Ford (2010), Frasier (1987), and Grantham et al. (2011) for students in urban settings.

Ford (2011) conceptualized six components of multicultural education (also referred to as culturally responsive education), based on the works of Banks (2010, 2015), Gay (2010), and Ladson-Billings (2009): (1) philosophy, (2) learning environment, (3) curriculum, (4) instruction, and (5) assessment. When an education is culturally responsive, it permeates all aspects of education and all students. Culturally responsive education is not colorblind; rather, it affirms the dignity and worth of students by attending to their lives, interests, and needs as cultural beings.

Multicultural education is a philosophy, goal, and process. It is a philosophy based on the fundamental belief that all people must be accorded respect, regardless of age, race, ethnicity, gender, income, religion, physical ability, and mental ability. It is predicated on the belief that all people have intrinsic worth. Thus, multicultural education seeks to affirm individual differences and human diversity through the elimination of prejudices, biases, and stereotypes based on sociocultural demographic variables. The goal of multicultural education is to improve the academic achievement of culturally different students while developing and nurturing their racial and cultural identities.

The education that teachers deliver can only be culturally responsive when educators value the culture of their students. This requires that educators explore their philosophy about working with culturally different students and seek substantive training to be responsive to their students as cultural beings and how context (e.g., locale) influences their work.

When teaching from a culturally responsive philosophy and perspective, educators and students challenge and interrogate assumptions, biases, prejudices, and stereotypes; they examine curriculum from a broader and more comprehensive point of view and in an inclusive, assertive, and proactive manner. They educate and prepare all students for life during and after school by increasing students' understanding of cultural diversity and differences.

A culturally responsive philosophy supports classroom and learning environments that are welcoming and supportive. Gifted Black and Hispanic students who tend to feel alienated and isolated now feel a part of the classroom community. They feel a sense of belonging and have positive relationships with school personnel and classmates. This sense of belonging is essential when there are few culturally different gifted students in their classes and schools and related activities (e.g., competitions).

Further, a culturally responsive philosophy and perspective helps to promote culturally congruent teaching strategies because teachers collect, interpret, and make instructional and management decisions based on students' sociocultural information. Thus, teachers are empowered intellectually, socially, culturally, emotionally, and politically by using cultural referents to impart knowledge and to guide their skills, attitudes, or dispositions with gifted Black and Hispanic students in both urban and rural settings.

Instruction must also match students' culturally influenced learning styles. When teaching styles and learning styles are congruent, Black and Hispanic students are more engaged, their achievement increases, and relationships with their teachers are more positive (Ford, 2010, 2011). Figure 4.2 highlights some characteristics of Hispanic culture(s), particularly Mexicans, who comprise slightly more than 60% of Hispanics living in the U.S. (Kena et al., 2014). Hispanic children are taught the importance of (1) a deep sense of family responsibility, commitment, and obligation; (2) respectful and reverent treatment of elders and authority figures; (3) cooperation and collectivism with family, friends, and authority figures; and (4) rigid gender roles (e.g., head of house, childrearing, machismo).

Educators should consider these characteristics as they design instructional strategies and as they complete referral forms and checklists. For instance, if many Hispanic children are raised to not question adults, such students may not participate, ask questions, or challenge ideas in class. This may be misinterpreted as disengagement and lacking curiosity. If such students are more cooperative than competitive, their humility may be misinterpreted as lacking motivation. These misinterpretations contribute to underreferrals and thus underrepresentation.

Relative to culturally responsive instruction for African Americans, Cartledge, Gardner, and Ford (2008); Ford (2010, 2011); and Ford and Kea (2009) illustrated how this works using the framework of Boykin et al. (2006), whose Afro-centric model delineates several core characteristics of Black culture, including spirituality, harmony, movement, verve, oral tradition, expressive individualism, communalism, and social time perspective. These features, along with sample teaching strategies, appear in Figure 4.3. Blacks and Hispanics share many cultural values and characteristics. Blacks tend to be Christians (Baptists) rather than Catholics, but both share a strong sense of spirituality and faith. Both are collective and family oriented, with reverence for elders, children, and large and extended families; both have a relaxed sense of time. Differences are more evident

Characteristics	Descriptions and Examples
Spiritual and Religious	» Very religious, spiritual, and faithful (majority are Roman Catholic) » Religion is central to family life and marriage » External locus of control guided by faith in a higher being
Family	» Generational hierarchy; respect for elders, love for the family, and affection for children » Children and adolescents learn to show respect for authority, the patriarchal family structure, and extended family members » Strong bonds and frequent interaction among a wide range of kin » Places the needs of the family before personal needs » Large families; motherhood is highly valued and dependence on parents is promoted » Permissive parenting style is common
Communalism/ Collectivism	» Cooperative and collaborative; interdependence is valued » Collective, group identity; interdependence; emphasis on interpersonal relations; standing out among one's peers (lacking humility) must be avoided » Relationship and people oriented » Feel much more comfortable responding in groups, doing exercises together, and helping each other
Affect	» Warm, sensitive, and demonstrative » Restraint of feelings, particularly anger and frustration » Less assertive in expressing themselves to peers and adults and rely on authority figures to resolve interpersonal problems » Machismo is common—male's manhood, courage to fight, honor and dignity, keeping one's word, and protecting one's name
Orality/Verbal	» Formal with elders and authority figures » Limited verbal expressions toward authority figures and elders, which shows a reverence for them
Nonverbal	» Preference for closer personal space; avoidance of eye contact with authority figures
Social Time Perspective (Polychronic)	» Present-time perspective; relaxed about time and punctuality; and immediate short-term goals

Figure 4.2. Sample characteristics of Hispanic culture(s). Data from from "Cultural Values of Latino Patients and Families," by M. Carteret, 2011. Retrieved from http://www.dimensionsofculture.com/2011/03/cultural-values-of-latino-patients-and-families/. Copyright 2011 by M. Carteret. Adapted with permission.

Characteristics	Sample Instructional Strategies
Communalism Harmony Affect	» Build a sense of family and/or community; social activities » Cooperative learning; group work/activities and projects/assignments » Service and community involvement » Opportunity to help others (e.g., tutoring, mentoring) » Make learning relevant; connections between lesson and personal life/lives » Constructive feedback based on skill » Concrete rules, procedures, directions, expectations, and examples
Social Time Perspective Affect	» Deadlines with reminders; posting deadlines » Time management skills » Organizational skills; graphic organizers » Connect lessons to students' interests, passion, backgrounds
Harmony Movement Verve Expressive Individualism	» Active learning; physical activity; tactile and kinesthetic activities » Creative movement; mime; dance, drama » Role-plays, simulations, tableau technique » Experiments » Manipulatives » Field trips » Poetry; creative writing; journals » Music; background music; playing instrument; singing, humming, whistling, chanting » Creating melodies, songs, etc.
Oral Tradition Expressive Individualism	» Student choice in assignments, rules, etc. » Lectures » Seminars, discussions, and dialogues » Oral presentations and speeches » Debates » Word games (e.g., metaphors, idioms, jokes, riddles, homonyms, anagrams) » Poetry » Storytelling, creative writing » Reading (choral, peer, individual) » Journal writing

Figure 4.3. Black cultural styles and sample instructional strategies. Data adapted from "Creating Culturally Responsive Instruction: For Students' Sake and Teachers' Sake" by D. Y. Ford and C. D. Kea, 2009, *Focus on Exceptional Children, 41*(9), 1–18. Copyright 2009 by The Council for Exceptional Children. Adapted with permission.

in orality and verbal communication, with Blacks being more direct and blunt. Although family elders are esteemed and placed on higher level, teachers and other authority figures must earn the respect of African American students and families. There is no hierarchy.

Curriculum can also be culturally responsive as Banks (2009, 2015) described in terms of infusing multicultural content into education for all students. The focus levels or approaches range from most common to least common and from lack to depth to substance. The lowest level, the Contributions Approach, is also referred to as the "four Fs"—food, fun, fashion, and folklore. This is the most common approach adopted in schools, the most basic, and the least substantive due to lack of depth and breadth. Students learn about cultural artifacts and events, but not the people (e.g., beliefs and values). Students acquire stereotypes or stereotypes are reinforced at this level.

Albeit higher, the second lowest level, the Additive Approach, is also very common in schools. Students learn about culturally different groups and events in a fragmented manner, often during special events and times, such as Black History Month (February) and Hispanic Heritage Month (September). Although students are introduced to multicultural ideas and topics, this is done in a safe way and via one perspective or point of view (often Eurocentric). This is a safe, non-controversial approach that lacks substance, and what is read or taught is not integral to the district's overall curriculum and goals.

The third level, the Transformation Approach, is not very common in schools. Here, the curriculum is transformed in deep and powerful ways; significant cultural ideas, concepts, events, and people are immersed in the curriculum throughout the year and in all subject areas. Further, students are presented with multiple and even opposing perspectives in order to be critical thinkers and empathetic learners. Depth and breath are evident.

The highest level, the Social Action Approach, is the least common in schools but the most substantive. Based on previous levels, especially transformation, students become social activists and change agents. Students develop and/or improve their problem-solving skills, as well as their skills in self-advocacy and advocating for culturally and racially different groups. Students are provided with pertinent information needed to take action that approves the lives of others with equity and justice in mind.

In 2011, Ford updated the Bloom-Banks Matrix (also known as the Ford-Harris Matrix), which was designed to provide educators with a tool to ensure rigor and relevance in their lesson plans and is explained next. Students in rural areas, in particular those gifted classes where they are racially isolated, benefit from seeing themselves reflected and affirmed in lesson plans and materials. This

Gifted Black and Hispanic Students in Rural Settings

increases engagement and achievement. White students also benefit from lesson plans that are multicultural; they learn about other groups and increase in their regard for these groups. And, as just stated, culturally responsive education improves relationships (harmony and understanding) among students from different backgrounds (Banks, 2010, 2015; Gay, 2010).

As stated earlier, a curriculum is incomplete if students are not taught think and learn beyond the scope of themselves and if the cannot see world from the viewpoints of others. The Bloom-Banks Matrix (Ford, 2011) merges the components of Bloom's (1985) taxonomy and Banks' Multicultural Curriculum model to provide teachers with a framework that allows them to create lesson plans at different critical thinking levels (rigor) and different multicultural levels (relevance). The resultant 4 x 6 matrix is comprised of 24 cells that are divided into four quadrants (Figure 4.4). Trotman Scott (2014) added colors to the four quadrants for a clearer visual model.

» Red/Stop = Quadrant 1 (in normal print in Figure 4.4): Low on both levels of Bloom's taxonomy and Banks' Multicultural model. When low on Bloom's taxonomy (e.g., knowing, understanding, applying) and low on Banks' multicultural levels (e.g., contributions and additives), students will superficially know, understand, and apply information about cultural elements, groups, and concepts. Gifted students are not being challenged with rigor or relevance. This is a place to start but not to stop.

» Yellow/Caution = Quadrant 2 (in italics in Figure 4.4): High on Bloom's taxonomy and low Banks' Multicultural Levels—high rigor but low relevance. This quadrant requires students to use higher level critical thinking (i.e., analyzing, studying, creating) skills, but teachers should proceed with caution. Minimal cultural substance is learned, which may lead to students not grasping multicultural content in substantive ways. Ford (2011) argued that this quadrant is common in gifted education where critical thinking is espoused but in a colorblind way (additive and contributions).

» Blue/Guarded = Quadrant 3 (in bold in Figure 4.4): Low on Bloom's taxonomy but high on Banks' Multicultural levels. Ford (2011) noted that multicultural experts not familiar with how to promote critical thinking might operate in this quadrant. This quadrant provides students with opportunities to view cultural events, concepts, and themes through the lens of others and from multiple perspectives; however, there is little critical thinking involved; rigor is low (knowing, under-

	Knowing	Understanding	Applying	Analyzing	Studying	Creating
Contributions	Students are taught and know facts about cultural artifacts, events, groups, and other cultural elements.	Students show an understanding of information about cultural artifacts, groups, and so forth.	Students are asked to and can apply information learned on cultural artifacts, events, and so forth.	Students are taught to and can analyze (e.g., compare and contrast) information about cultural artifacts, groups, and so forth.	Students are taught to evaluate facts and information based on cultural artifacts, groups, and so forth.	Students are required to and can create a new product from the information on cultural artifacts, groups, and so forth.
Additive	Students are taught and know concepts and themes about cultural groups.	Students are taught and can understand cultural concepts and themes.	Students are required to and can apply information learned about cultural concepts and themes.	Students are taught to and can analyze important cultural concepts and themes.	Students are taught to and can critique cultural concepts and themes.	Students are asked to and can synthesize important information on cultural concepts and themes.
Transformation	Students are given information on important cultural elements, groups, and so forth, and can understand this information from different perspectives.	Students are taught to understand and can demonstrate an understanding of important cultural concepts and themes from different perspectives.	Students are asked to and can apply their understanding of important concepts and themes from different perspectives.	Students are taught to and can examine important cultural concepts and themes from more than one perspective.	Students are taught to and can evaluate or judge important cultural concepts and themes from different viewpoints (e.g., racially and culturally different groups).	Students are required to and can create a product based on their new perspective or the perspective of another group.
Social Action	Based on information on cultural artifacts, students make recommendations for social action.	Based on their understanding of important concepts and themes, students make recommendations for social action.	Students are asked to and can apply their understanding of important social and cultural issues; they make recommendations for and take action on these issues.	Students are required to and can analyze social and cultural issues from different perspectives; they take action on these issues.	Students critique important social and cultural issues and seek to make national and/or international change.	Students create a plan of action to address a social and cultural issue(s); they seek important social change.

Figure 4.4. Revised Bloom-Banks Color Matrix. Data adapted from *Multicultural gifted education: Rationale, models, strategies, and resources* (2nd ed.), by D. Y. Ford, 2011, New York, NY: Taylor & Francis. Copyright 2011 by Taylor & Francis; and "Using the Blooms-Banks Matrix to Develop Multicultural Differentiated Lessons for Gifted Students," by M. Trotman Scott, 2014, *Gifted Child Today, 37*, 163–168. Copyright 2014 by Sage. Adapted with permission.

standing, applying) regarding such culturally diverse content (transformation, social action).
- » Green/Go = Quadrant 4 (in bold italics in Figure 4.4): High on both Bloom's taxonomy and Banks' Multicultural levels. Instruction and assignments allow students to think critically and solve problems and, importantly, they seek to make social change(s) related to justice. This, as Ford (2011) indicated, is the ultimate destiny—curriculum is rigorous *and* relevant. This is the win-win quadrant for all students due to rigor (analyzing, studying, and creating) and relevance (transformation, social action).

Conclusion

Although cognizant of serious problems facing rural schools, fewer researchers undertake studies in rural settings in this country than in urban or suburban settings. In addition, there is limited research on special populations of students in rural settings. Unfortunately, one population of students missing from much of the research literature on rural schools is gifted students. (Hébert, 2001, p. 86)

Hébert's assertion, like many others shared herein, remains as relevant today as it was years ago. This is a sad commentary. Not much has changed in recent years regarding scholarship on gifted students who live in rural locales, and even less is known about Black and Hispanic students who are gifted and live in rural locales. From what has been reviewed, I find more similarities than differences in the lives of gifted Black and Hispanic students in rural and urban areas. Poverty is a reality, neither group is reaching its potential, underrepresentation in gifted education is a problem, and schools are not meeting their needs as cultural beings. This represents a clarion call for more research on these students and for more training for educators to be culturally competent.

More Research

Compared to scholarship in urban settings, relatively little systematic research has been conducted in rural schools (Gándara, Gutièrrez & O'Hara, 2001). More than 30% of U.S. schools are in rural communities, yet less than

6% of research conducted in schools has included rural schools (Hardré, 2007, 2008). Rural schools serve large numbers of minority students, families in socio-economic distress, and many single-parent families with little education. Rural students are at risk for low motivation and lack of school success (Hardré, Sullivan, & Crowson, 2009; Lichter, Roscigno & Condron, 2003); this is particularly the case for Black and Hispanic students living in rural settings as they grapple with both classism and racism.

More Training

Teachers must decrease and, better yet, eliminate their prejudice or stereotypes in order to accept the child as a person who is potentially capable of high achievement (Baldwin, 1987). Effective teachers of culturally different students understand and respect cultural differences and have a high degree of tolerance and respect for behavioral characteristics, which do not fit usual conceptions of giftedness, as reflected in Boykin et al.'s (2006) model (Ford, 2011, 2013). They also understand the similarities and differences between rural and urban locales from cultural, racial, economic, and geographic perspectives.

Hébert's (2001) case study of Jermaine, a third-grade Black male and a rural gifted student reminded us that intelligence tests do not also reflect performance and achievement, that there is merit to social and practical intelligence, and many rural students display creative positives per the vast work of E. Paul Torrance (1969, 1977; e.g., an ability to express feelings and emotions, articulateness in role-playing and storytelling, enjoyment and ability in visual art, expressive speech, responsiveness to the kinesthetic, a sense of humor, richness of imagery in informal language, and originality of ideas in problem solving). Associated with being a gifted rural Black male, Jermaine had some challenges with fitting in, with identity, and with being understood via cultural lens. Too few teachers recognized Jermaine as gifted. This is true for many gifted Black students in both rural and urban settings (Ford, 2010, 2011, 2013).

As has been discussed, in both locales, poverty adds another layer of complexity to problems facing students. African American children in the South have borne a disproportionate share of the burden of poverty in America for decades. Although the overall rate of rural poverty is higher than urban poverty, the difference in rural and urban poverty rates varies significantly across regions. Yet, as Frasier (1987) cautioned, we must not oversimplify the problem because "there are too many examples of gifted adults who come from less advantaged backgrounds to make a tenable argument that culture, class, or environment are permanent obstacles to achievement" (p. 174). Neither genes nor zip code is cause for inequitable treatment and ignoring needs.

References

Baldwin, A. Y. (1987). Undiscovered diamonds: The minority gifted child. *Journal for the Education of the Gifted, 10,* 271–285.

Banks, J. A. (2010). Approaches to multicultural curriculum reform. In J. A. Banks & C. A. M. Banks (Eds.), *Multicultural education: Issues and perspectives* (7th ed., pp. 233–258). Hoboken, NJ: John Wiley & Sons.

Banks, J. A. (2015). *Cultural diversity and education: Foundations, curriculum and teaching* (6th ed.). Boston, MA: Pearson, Allyn & Bacon.

Barkan, J. H., & Bernal, E. M. (1991). Gifted education for bilingual and limited English proficient students. *Gifted Child Quarterly, 35*(3), 144–147.

Bernal, E. M. (2007). The plight of the culturally diverse student from poverty. In J. VanTassel-Baska & T. Stambaugh (Eds.). *Overlooked gems: A national perspective on low-income promising learners* (pp. 27–30). Washington, D.C., and Williamsburg, VA: National Association for Gifted Children and College of William and Mary.

Biddle, R. (2011). The myth of differences between urban and rural schools. Retrieved from http://dropoutnation.net/2011/08/02/the-myth-of-differences-between-urban-and-rural-schools/

Bloom, B. S. (1985). *Developing talent in young people.* New York, NY: Ballantine Books.

Boykin, A. W., Tyler, K. M., Watkins-Lewis, K. M., & Kizzie, K. (2006). Culture in the sanctioned classroom practices of elementary school teachers serving low-income African American students. *Journal of Education of Students Placed At-Risk, 11,* 161–173.

Carteret, M. (2011). Cultural values of Latino patients and families. Retrieved from http://www.dimensionsofculture.com/2011/03/cultural-values-of-latino-patients-and-families/

Cartledge, G., Gardner, R., & Ford, D. Y. (2008). *Diverse learners with exceptionalities: Culturally responsive teaching in the inclusive classroom.* Columbus, OH: Merrill Education.

Castellano, J. A. & Frazier, A. D. (2010). *Special populations in gifted education: understanding our most able students from diverse backgrounds.* Waco, TX: Prufrock Press.

Ford, D. Y. (2010). *Reversing underachievement among gifted Black students: Theory, Research and Practice* (2nd ed.). Waco, TX: Prufrock Press.

Ford, D. Y. (2011). *Multicultural gifted education: Rationale, models, strategies, and resources* (2nd ed.). Waco, TX: Prufrock Press.

Ford, D. Y. (2013). *Recruiting and retaining culturally different students in gifted education.* Waco, TX: Prufrock Press.

Ford, D. Y., & Kea, C. D. (2009). Creating culturally responsive instruction: For students' sake and teachers' sake. *Focus on Exceptional Children, 41*(9), 1–18.

Frasier, M. M. (1987). The identification of gifted Black students: Developing new perspectives. *Journal for the Education of the Gifted, 10,* 155–180.

Gándara, P., Gutiérrez, D., & O'Hara, S. (2001). Planning for the future in rural and urban high schools. *Journal of Education for Students Placed At-Risk, 6*(1), 73–93.

Gay, G. (2010). *Culturally responsive teaching: Theory, research, and practice* (2nd ed.). New York, NY: Teachers College Press.

Grantham, T. C., Ford, D. Y., Henfield, M., Trotman Scott, M., Harmon, D., Porchér, S., & Price, C. (2011). *Gifted and advanced Black students in school: An anthology of critical works.* Waco, TX: Prufrock Press.

Hardré, P. L. (2007). Preventing motivational dropout: A systemic analysis in four rural high schools. *Leadership and Policy in Schools, 6*(3), 231–265.

Hardré, P. L. (2008). Taking on the motivating challenge: Rural high school teachers' perceptions and practice. *Teacher Education and Practice, 21*(1), 72–88.

Hardré, P., Sullivan, D., & Crowson, H. (2009). Student characteristics and motivation in rural high schools. *Journal of Research in Rural Education, 24*(16). Retrieved from http://jrre.psu.edu/articles/24-16.pdf

Hébert, T. P., & Beardsley, T. M. (2001). Jermaine: A critical case study of a gifted Black child living in rural poverty. *Gifted Child Quarterly, 45,* 85–103.

Herzog, M. J., & Pittman, R. B., (1995). Home, family, and community: Ingredients in the rural education equation. *Phi Delta Kappan, 77*(2), 113–118.

Hines III, M.T. (2012). An in depth analysis of African American students' schooling experiences: A rural school district in review. *National Forum Of Applied Educational Research Journal, 35*(3), 1–20.

Howley, A., Rhodes, M, & Beall, J. (2009). Challenges facing rural schools: Implications for gifted students. *Journal for the Education of the Gifted, 32*(4), 515–536.

Johnson, J., Showaler, D., Klein, R., & Lester, C. (2014). *Why rural education matters: The condition of rural education in the 50 States.* Washington, D.C.: The Rural School and Community Trust.

Kena, G., Aud, S., Johnson, F., Wang, X., Zhang, J., Rathbun, A., Wilkinson-Flicker, S., & Kristapovich, P. (2014). *The Condition of Education 2014* (NCES 2014-083). Washington, D.C.: U.S. Department of Education, National Center for Education Statistics.

Ladson-Billings, G. (2009). *The dreamkeepers: Successful teachers for African-American children* (2nd ed.). San Francisco, CA: Jossey-Bass.

Lichter, D. T., Roscigno, V. J., & Condron, D. J. (2003). Rural children and youth at risk. In D. L. Brown & L. E. Swanson (Eds.), *Challenges for rural America in the twenty-first century* (pp. 97–108). University Park: Pennsylvania State University Press.

Provasnik, S., KewalRamani, A., Coleman, M. M., Gilbertson, L., Herring, W., & Xie, Q. (2007). *Status of Education n Rural America* (NCES 2007-040). Washington, DC: National Center for Education Statistics, Institute of Education Sciences, U.S. Department of Education.

Renzulli, J. S. (1973). Talent potential in minority group students. *Exceptional Children, 39,* 437–444.

Rivera, B. D., & Rogers-Adkinson. D. (1997) Culturally sensitive interventions: Social skills training with children and parents from culturally and linguistically diverse backgrounds. *Intervention in School and Clinic. 33*(2), 75–80.

Spicker, H., Southern, T., & Davis, B. (1987). The rural gifted child. *Gifted Child Quarterly, 31,* 155–157.

Strayhorn, T. L. (2009). Different folks, different hopes: The educational aspirations of Black males in urban, suburban, and rural high schools. *Urban Education, 44*(6), 710–731.

Torrance, E. P. (1969). Creative positives of disadvantaged children and youth. *Gifted Child Quarterly, 13,* 71–81.

Torrance, E. P. (1977). *Discovery and nurturance of giftedness in the culturally different.* Reston, VA: Council for Exceptional Children.

Trotman Scott, M. (2014). Using the Blooms-Banks Matrix to develop multicultural differentiated lessons for gifted students. *Gifted Child Today, 37,* 163–168.

U.S. Department of Agriculture. (2014a). Geography of poverty. Retrieved from http://www.ers.usda.gov/topics/rura-economy-population/rural-poverty-well-being/geography-of-poverty.aspx

U.S. Department of Agriculture. (2014b). Poverty overview. Retrieved from http://www.ers.usda.gov/topics/rural-economy-population/rural-poverty-well-being/geography-of-poverty.aspx

U.S. Department of Education. (1993). *A national case for excellence: Developing America's talent*. Washington, D.C.: Author.

U.S. Department of Education. (2009). The Office for Civil Rights' Civil Rights Data Collection. Washington, D.C.: Author.

U.S. Department of Education. (2011). The Office for Civil Rights' Civil Rights Data Collection. Washington, D.C.: Author.

Part I Summary

We as editors find ourselves in an interesting position of bringing light to the many different contexts in which rural gifted students reside while also acknowledging the unique challenges and opportunities these students have. Educators may be surprised by some of the concepts discussed in Part I of this book, especially the most important one: What "ruralness" is, what it looks like, and what is meant when it is brought up in conversation or addressed in a text.

First, rural is its own culture, one that is changing. When thinking about rural, perhaps the first image is bucolic rolling fields of wheat, with a small red barn in the background. Although that is indeed one image of rural life, rural communities are also fishing villages, timber industries, mountain regions, cattle ranges, as well as agrarian farms. Every state has rural areas. Rural is the Pacific Northwest, the Midwest, the Northeast, the South, and the West. It is Washington, Maine, Arizona, South Carolina, and Hawaii. Rural America is also not White America. Every rural community has a different demographic constitution, and many are changing to include more students of color. Not every rural community is challenged by poverty, declining populations, or shrinking job markets but many are. So what does that mean for gifted students from these communities?

Giftedness is its own culture. As Nick Colangelo's foreword suggests, these students have unique needs; yet as budgets shrink and resources become scarcer, these students are the least mentioned when it comes to service in the schools. As Ford points out in her chapter, culturally diverse gifted students may demonstrate their giftedness through behavioral characteristics that do not fit the stereotypical conceptions of giftedness. Teachers working in rural schools will have a range of training; they may or may not have the expertise to identify gifted students, especially gifted students of color, and to provide the enrichment or differentiation required to meet their intellectual needs. If stereotypical thinking drives service, then rural schools equate gifted programming as, to quote Howley, Howley, and Showalter in their chapter, bestowing "privileges," which is a "mistreatment of talent". If the student's school cannot provide for advanced achievement or enrichment, these students may not have the skills for future steady employment—which can facilitate their choice to leave the community to seek jobs, or seek additional educational opportunities for additional skill-sets. Within rural situations, gifted students may find fewer students like themselves, which may also drive the need to leave their community. These students may also struggle to make meaning of a variety of conflicting messages regarding education, behavior, college and careers, wealth, their place in the community, and how their rural culture views their nature of giftedness.

And rural is a culture. There is a sense of belonging and connectedness that many gifted students experience in their communities. As Richards and Stambaugh suggest, gifted students may want to stay and live in the place they are known and loved if that has been their experience. The rural "essence" can provide these students with a sense of place, traditions, and community pride. But if the community places more value on athletics, or has a practical or utilitarian stance towards education—as preparation for community work—then some gifted students may feel the distinct rub of not being valued for their talents and guilty for wanting to forge a new path. Parents and community members may question this path: "Does it mean the children leaving the community forever? For a time? Will they come back? Would leaving benefit the child? Will they come back and lend their expertise and skills to the community to help it thrive?" But "going away to college" may not be a panacea for community or student, and the career chosen postgraduation may not lead to the ephemeral "success" that students may believe is important. Gifted students must decide for themselves what success looks like and what they find meaningful, alongside honoring ties to their family, beauty, and patriotism, as examples of rural values suggested by Richards and Stambaugh.

If gifted students stay, what then? The community must answer, "Do we have what we need to enable our children to be successful and find meaning here?" Howley, Howley, and Showalter contest that yes, rural communities do

Part I Summary

have what is needed—the chance for these children to be loved and known and with the needed relationships to be successful and quite possibly, happy. What these gifted students need is a "noise-free" environment where they can think about the talents they have, and the degree to which what they do with those talents is a responsibility to themselves and to the community.

As Mattingly and Schaefer write, "Variation and change across rural America are key to understanding the challenges and opportunities in rural America today." With changing populations in their community, gifted students will have the chance to learn from diverse perspectives and experiences in their schools and rural communities. Those who do choose to leave for a time to pursue college or other educational opportunities may find that the diversity of people and of thought in their community is an asset in their adaptation to college culture. Gifted students will become gifted adults who must find a path that they can walk that embraces their gifts and talents, and their culture. That path can be supported by best practices in identification, service, and programming—all of which have roots in both research and in the practicalities of the "known and often beloved" of place-based education (Howley, Howley, & Showalter, this volume). We hope that Part II of this book provides educators with a "how" to match the issues of the "what" that Part I shed light on.

PART II

Identification, Curriculum, and Instruction for Rural Gifted Learners

CHAPTER 5

Celebrating Talent
Identification of Rural Gifted Students

Tamra Stambaugh, Ph.D.

Introduction

Gifted students are as different as they are alike. They come from all backgrounds and ethnicities. They can be wealthy or poor; live in a rural, urban, or suburban area; have a learning disability in conjunction with their giftedness; or be culturally different (e.g., Black, Hispanic, ELL). Combinations of locale, income level, race/ethnicity, and family will impact who a gifted child is and what he or she values. Gifted students have different strengths, varying levels of ability, and they come to school with different experiences, different interests, and even different priorities. Some of these combinations of locale, ethnicity, and income level are more easily recognized through traditional identification methods, yet many gifted students—especially in rural areas—are missed and their talents unrecognized by schools, especially if they are also poor or minority. It is only when one recognizes the unique characteristics of gifted students within the context of place that identification methods can be tailored to highlight gifted students' strengths and talent development opportunities to nurture their gifts. Through this lens, the following questions are explored:

» Are rural students really that different from non-rural gifted students?
» What does the research say about the identification of rural gifted students from varying backgrounds?

> How can rural gifted students best be identified and provided appropriate services matched to their individual and community strengths?

Are Rural Students Really That Different From Other Students?

Rural gifted students, their educators and families view the world through a unique lens. The rural life, while varied by region, embraces different sets of values, beliefs, and cultural norms. Slama (2004) argued that rural is its own culture and that there are "degrees of rurality" (p. 10) that determine to what extent the individuals living there adhere to the beliefs and values of rural life more than they embrace the American mainstream values. For example, those who live in touristy parts of rural America (e.g., lakefront properties or high-end mountain areas) tend to embrace the values, traditions, and beliefs of suburbanites more readily than those who live farther away from these areas. Individuals who live in more remote rural areas adhere to a completely different set of values and beliefs than those on the fringes of larger cities. The beliefs, values, and experiences in the deep rural South, for example, differ significantly from those who live in the Appalachian mountain areas or the rural northeast (Dillon & Savage, 2006; Duncan, 1999), yet there are some similarities as well.

Educators must first understand the values, belief systems, and characteristics of their locale before they can understand how these apply to giftedness. That said, each student is an individual, and we must also be careful not to stereotype when outlining common patterns or making generalizations as we focus on the rural gifted learner and how to best identify him or her.

Belief Systems and Common Characteristics of Different Rural Regions

Rural Appalachia appears to be researched more than other rural regions. Jones (1994) outlined common attributes found in rural Appalachian families. In essaying his life experiences he explained that most rural Appalachian families posses 10 common values, which he explained in detail:
1. *Individualism and pride*: Given their history on the frontier and as pioneers, Appalachian families have had to rely on their own ingenuity and survival skills to endure. As such, they value this characteristic

in themselves and others. This spirit of individualism is what led many to settle in America as a way to sustain their freedoms and those of others.
2. *Religious beliefs*: Jones explained that although not all rural Appalachians go to church, they rely on their faith—especially in the midst of hard times. He explained that many social reformers criticize this aspect of Appalachian values, but it is integral to who they are such that one cannot understand those in rural Appalachia without understanding their religion.
3. *Neighborliness and hospitality*: Rural Appalachians are more willing to help out others and invite them in for a meal or to spend the night, even when there may not be enough food or places for everyone to sleep.
4. *Familism*: The emphasis on and loyalty to family is another factor common among rural Appalachians. Jones explained that this extends beyond the normal nuclear family to first, second, and third cousins as well as aunts and uncles.
5. *Personalism*: Rural families are generally not confrontational. They will avoid conflict as much as possible and stand up and confront only when absolutely necessary. They value relationships above all else, are easy to talk to, and are very open and personable.
6. *Love of place*: Rural families who move away from Appalachia go "home" as much as possible. The draw to the rural area is strong, and this is one reason many do not leave or if they do, they return often, even when the economy is not as strong.
7. *Modesty*: Rural Appalachian families are modest. They care more about the person than what the person does. Fame, education, and status do not impress as much as being a good person who is personable, trustworthy, and caring.
8. *Strong sense of beauty*: This sense of beauty, according to Jones, is manifest through the folk arts and crafts as well as everyday language. Colloquialisms, metaphors, similes, and vivid descriptors are part of everyday vernacular and are quite creative. Working with one's hands to create something is also highly valued, as is songwriting and art forms that play into the ideas of self-reliance and require intense commitment and dedication to the craft (e.g., wood carvings).
9. *Sense of humor*: Jones explained that it is this sense of humor that has helped rural Appalachians get through hard times. Those who survived were able to see the humor in life and themselves. This humor is

generally more self-depreciating and humble, although generally not deserved.
10. *Patriotism*: This is the characteristic that brought those who have settled in rural Appalachia to America in the beginning. There is a strong sense of pride for America and the flag. Many who fought in the Revolutionary War were given land near the Appalachian Mountains in exchange for their service; thus, the history for this patriotism has been strong for generations.

Several of the characteristics of Appalachians described by Jones (1994) have been touted as characteristics of rural individuals living in regions other than Appalachia, too. In particular, religion (also described in the literature as traditionalism, morality, and spirituality), love of place (or sense of place), individuality and independence, and a strong commitment to family are repeated themes in the rural literature. Most of the research about belief systems and values is conducted through political science and policy fields, with little research found on potentially defining characteristics of rural gifted students and how these impact their education. We will examine the available research next.

School-Based Characteristics of Rural Gifted Students

Educators need to know and understand their students if they are to positively impact learning. Students who live in a high-poverty, predominately White rural area will likely have different experiences and values than those who live in a high-poverty, predominately Black or Hispanic rural area. (See the Ford and Griffith and Wood chapters in this book for more information.) The cultural context matters, and even more so when adding the layer of giftedness. Although limited and dated, a few studies have examined the characteristics of gifted rural students, especially those who are low income.

Spicker, Fletcher, Montgomery, and Breard (1993) identified specific characteristics that are detrimental in finding rural gifted students of poverty and explained that many of these students "speak a non-standard English, are less verbal in oral communication skills, tend to be passive participants in classroom activities, are relatively unaffected by time pressures, are likely to be lax in completing assignments and homework, and are not likely to perform well on standardized tests" (p. 4). They also explain how gifted students who are disadvantaged have strengths that may go unnoticed if teachers do not know how to recognize their gifts and talents. For example, gifted students who are low income are more likely to show an uneven profile of performance and testing, meaning that they may exceed in only one subject area instead of many (Spicker et al., 1993). Moreover, they are likely to have strong content-based products but with poor grammar, form, and handwriting, and they are also more likely to show their strengths in the community instead of the classroom through projects related to 4-H, FFA, the performing arts, auto repair, or specific rural-related knowledge about their surroundings.

Capitalizing on their region's emphasis on relationships, cultural understanding, and hands-on applied problem solving, Spicker and Aamidor (1996) conducted a follow-up study to Project Spring. They created a checklist of gifted characteristics that was more culturally relevant. Items included: "thinks of unusual ways to solve problems; is clever about making things out of ordinary materials; understands the importance of culture and family; understands the importance of nature in relation to farming; helps others solve problems; knows how to interact and get along with a lot of different people" (p. 184). Community members and teachers completed this behavioral checklist as one part of a comprehensive identification system.

As indicated, educators, administrators, and school counselors who are unaware of the strengths and beliefs of their rural community or how their students live outside of the classroom are less likely to notice the talents of their gifted students. Many rural gifted students, especially those who are low income, are more likely to show their strengths within the applied context of their lived experience and their community than in school. Without a relevant schoolwide identification system that recognizes the unique characteristics of the rural child, and in the absence of professional development specific to one's particular rural population, it is unlikely that teachers are able to recognize, let alone develop, the talent of their rural students.

What Works Best When Identifying Rural Gifted Students?

So, what do these characteristics of rural have to do with how we best identify gifted students from rural areas? Research on gifted identification specific to rural is scant. A PsycInfo database search using the key terms of "rural, gifted, and identification" (and multiple variations of those terms) yielded only five articles written on the topic in the past 10 years. When extending the search to the past 20 years, an additional nine articles were found. Only two of the nine articles focused specifically on the identification of rural gifted students: one case study of a rural district's journey to reverse the underrepresentation of gifted poor and minority students in rural areas (Pendarvis & Wood, 2009) and one descriptive study on a project geared toward identifying artistically gifted rural students (Clark and Zimmerman, 2001). The remainder of the articles fit into one of two categories: The article mentioned rural as the geographic location for a study but focused on another concept with a brief mention of identification, or the article focused on identification and mentioned rural as one of the groups studied in the sample; however, the differences and similarities in locales were not disaggregated such that we knew how gifted rural students performed in relation to their urban and suburban counterparts.

Many authors point out the confounding issues in identifying rural gifted students (Bull & Fishkin, 1987; Fishkin & Kampsnider, 1996; Pendarvis & Wood, 2009), especially those who are poor and/or culturally diverse (Pendarvis & Wood, 2009; Montgomery, 2001; Hebert & Beardsley, 2001; Clark and Zimmerman, 2001; Abell & Lennex, 1999; Davalos & Griffin, 1999). Because many students of poverty live in rural areas, it is difficult to unravel the differences in characteristics of poverty, rural life, and differing ethnicities, as these are intertwined. It is even more difficult to parcel these factors in order to determine the extent to which the rural life impacts identification more or less than ethnicity or income levels.

Including characteristics of giftedness adds another layer of complexity. In a review of the literature on rural giftedness, Lawrence (2009) pointed out that "The anxieties of gifted children about fitting in and being accepted; finding challenging courses, and later, jobs; encountering unsympathetic teachers; and having to leave home to find suitable work all increase their level of stress" (p. 10). She further explained that gifted students in rural communities may be hesitant to stand out or excel when they are of the minority (simply by being gifted) or in a community where social norms and expectations hinder their progress. This is exacerbated for gifted rural students who may be low income or minority.

So, what do we know about how to best identify gifted students? Much of the research has focused on traditionally underrepresented gifted students in rural areas (e.g., those who are Black, Hispanic, or low income). Pendarvis and Wood (2009) studied a district's attempt to identify rural gifted students who are poor or minority. In order to increase the identification of underrepresented gifted students, the district added a nonverbal assessment (i.e., the Universal Nonverbal Intelligence Test, UNIT) and a widely known checklist of behaviors (i.e., Gifted and Talented Education Scales, GATES) to their traditionally accepted test scores on individual achievement and ability assessments.

Training was provided to teachers so that they recognized unique characteristics of students of poverty and differing ethnicities. As a result, the training had a strong and positive impact on the number of referrals for testing. However, the addition of a nonverbal assessment and checklist of behaviors was not helpful in identifying more underrepresented gifted students, and, in most instances, had the opposite effect.

The authors concluded that professional development on specific characteristics of gifted minority and low-income students led to increased referrals that, in turn, allowed more students to have access to individual testing. Yet the addition of a nonverbal assessment and checklist of gifted characteristics did not provide any beneficial information to support the talent identification of gifted students. In all but one instance, the addition of a checklist and nonverbal assessment actually prohibited identification, as most students performed lower on the nonverbal assessment and the nationally normed characteristics checklist. Instead, test scores from the individual ability and achievement measures were the most liberal in finding gifted students if subtests scores instead of full-scale battery scores were used. Specifically, the authors noted widely discrepant scores among various subtests of their low-income and minority students' testing profiles. By accepting a score approximately 2 standard deviations above the mean on any one index score (i.e., verbal, perceptual reasoning) of an IQ assessment and/or achievement content area, they identified significantly more rural underrepresented students (Pendarvis & Wood, 2009).

Spicker and colleagues (1993) also found an uneven profile to be a typical identification pattern among many rural gifted children, especially those who are low income. They explain that gifted students from rural Appalachia areas, in particular, are more likely to show strengths in one specific area with average or even below average abilities in others. They also found that rural students of poverty and minority status are more likely to show their strengths and abilities outside the classroom, such as in the mechanical and environmental science areas or the arts. Therefore, traditional measures that rely heavily on full-scale comprehensive scores and commonly held notions about what school-based (versus experience-based) intelligence looks like do not accurately measure the strengths of rural gifted learners, especially those of poverty.

As part of a federally funded project (Project Spring I) that sought to identify more underrepresented gifted students from rural areas, Spicker and colleagues (1993) created and delivered professional development modules for teachers (see Spicker & Poling, 1993) to help them better understand the unique characteristics of gifted students from rural schools. They encouraged the use of a variety of assessments matched to rural gifted learner's environment and strengths, including student observations, portfolio assessment with specific criteria, standardized assessments (as a secondary source), and creativity (i.e., Torrance Test of Creative Thinking). Then the researchers created curriculum that matched the identification processes so that each was congruent with the other. Through the use of alternative measures, significantly more underrepresented gifted students were identified. However, even after the curriculum intervention, those alternately identified students still underperformed on general achievement measures when compared to more traditionally identified students, with the exception of the nonverbal creativity measures, creative writing samples, and self-concept—these areas were equivalent among both groups of students (Spicker, 1993).

In 2007, Aamidor located the students from the Project Spring II study, who were now in high school, and examined the extent to which they were achieving. She found significant differences in student achievement favoring the traditionally identified gifted students over the Project Spring identified students. She also found that the self-concept of Project Spring students was higher than that of nongifted students, and than traditionally identified gifted students in one of the two high schools where the participants attended. Project Spring students were also administered a college and career inventory (i.e., Interest Determination, Exploration, and Assessment System [IDEAS]) to assess career interests. Although there were few differences on most of the items, the Project Spring students scored higher on the Realistic Theme for career identification than the traditionally identified students. The Realistic Theme includes preferences for occupations such as mechanical engineering, protective services (police, fire), and nature-related outdoor jobs. This again supports the need for recognizing experiential and community-based strengths of some rural gifted students.

In a different federally funded project, Montgomery (2001) created methods to identify rural Native American gifted students using student portfolios that included "writing samples, an interest survey, and portfolio examples in addition to the classic standardized test scores and grades" (p. 470). This information was entered into a matrix that logged grades, nomination scores, interest survey results, nomination rankings, and product analysis scores, as well as the review team recommendations. A case study approach, as opposed to a total matrix score, was used for identification. Through this method, an additional 87% of students were identified as compared to traditional methods. Although portfolios can be admittedly subjective, the researcher noted that it showcases the unique strengths of students and is more equitable than typical identification methods in finding students who show their talents in unique ways.

Once the project was underway, students were provided enriched curriculum units that honored the traditions of Indian tribes and developed in partnership with "Indian Education Specialists" within the school and community. Efforts to connect students with community leaders, develop relationships between schools and families, and to work within community norms were paramount. Upon conclusion of the project, students' ACT/SAT scores increased and more students decided to apply for college (Montgomery, 2001).

Similarly, Clark and Zimmerman (2001) used locally developed tools to find more students gifted in visual and performing arts. They encouraged study participants from three different states to develop their own identification methods based on their locale, after a professional development seminar on identification. The majority of sites selected nomination forms, portfolios, and achievement test scores. In addition, the Torrance Test of Creativity and Clark's Draw A Person Test (CDAT) were administered and included for research purposes. Regardless of the methods used, the authors found that state test achievement test scores were correlated to the Torrance and the CDAT. They hypothesized that the Torrance and CDAT may better identify rural gifted students for other domains, as the high-achieving students in the visual and performing arts were also the high-achieving students in math and reading.

What Are the Practical Applications for Identifying Gifted Students From Rural Areas?

Based on the varying characteristics of students in rural places, the differences in rural locales and those who live there, and differing levels of socio-economic status and ethnicities within and between rural areas, it is difficult to generalize who rural gifted students are and how to best identify them. The uniqueness of each locale cannot be ignored when crafting an identification system to best identify these students. However, there are noted patterns of successful strategies that educators and policy makers may find useful when crafting a comprehensive identification system for rural gifted learners:
1. Use place-based identification methods. The context of place cannot be underestimated when identifying rural gifted students. In each of

the studies previously explained, characteristics checklists and identification methods were specifically crafted for the given population. For example, Spicker and colleagues (1993, 1996) designed gifted behavior checklists typical of Appalachia students of poverty while Montgomery (2001) and Clark and Zimmerman (2001) used local product-based measures as indicators to identify more students. The use of place-based identification methods ensure that students have the necessary tools to showcase their talent in ways that are appreciated within their community and in ways that they have experienced or have access, which is more equitable. Place-based methods of identification may include *empirically validated* characteristics checklists unique to the rural population of a given area, portfolios that showcase a student's successes with family and community involvement outside of school, interviews of students and their families, model lessons and student observations when teaching a specific culturally appropriate thinking skills lesson, and interest and performance-based opportunities for students to showcase talents in a hands-on way.

2. Provide ongoing, context-based professional development to teachers. Each of the studies emphasized the need to educate teachers, families, and administrators in the nature and needs of gifted students in their particular rural area. Atypical characteristics were shared with educators and case study approaches were used to support discussion in how giftedness may be manifest. Through this approach, teachers felt more confident in identifying gifted students and also referred more students for gifted services and further assessment (see Pendarvis and Wood, 2009; Montgomery, 2001; and Spicker et al, 1993, 1996).

3. Involve the family and community in identifying gifted students. As family plays an important role in the lives of rural gifted students, they need to be part of the identification process from the beginning. Many innovative studies seeking to find more rural gifted students—especially of poverty or minority status—recognize the important influence of family on the lives of gifted students and the need to involve them in the identification process. Many times families can identify characteristics that some gifted students may not exhibit at school—especially if they show their talents through faith-based organizations, community organizations such as 4-H, dance, or work in a local business.

4. Use local norms or accept test profiles more indicative of the population, such as subtest instead of full-scale scores. Although uneven test

score profiles are typical for many gifted students, more discrepant and significant uneven profiles may be indicative of rural gifted students of poverty or minority status (Pendarvis & Wood, 2009). Using subtest scores instead of a full battery ability score is an accepted method of identification for students of poverty in general, as is identifying gifted students of poverty in one specific content area (e.g., math, science, reading) instead of by overall achievement (VanTassel-Baska & Stambaugh, 2007). Likewise, local norms, or accepting the top 5%–10% of scores in each school building or district instead of using a cut-off score that is more nationally accepted (e.g., 2 standard deviations above the mean), will also identify more gifted students.

5. Rural school administrators and policy makers need to practice flexibility when implementing or crafting policies related to identification so that these methods can be tailored to rural gifted students' specific needs. Many of the studies that focused on better ways to identify rural gifted students—especially those who are traditionally underrepresented—had to bend the rules or veer from state-based methods in order appropriately identify rural gifted students. This included using more flexible scoring systems and nontraditional methods of identification that matched the locale.

6. Match the program to the identification methods. If rural gifted students are identified by alternative, place-based identification methods, the services provided must follow suit. Students identified by performance-based methods need talent development opportunities and services that are performance-based and hands-on in nature if they are to thrive. Montgomery (2001) found that students identified by alternative means thrived when provided with locally created, culturally appropriate curriculum. Similarly, Spicker and colleagues (1996) found that rural gifted were more likely to show their giftedness in practical ways through environmental or application-based sciences and needed more opportunities in these areas.

7. Place-based education is a common theme in the rural education literature. Place-based education refers to the connection of educational curriculum to the local community (Shamah & MacTavish, 2009). The culture of the community is embedded within the curriculum outcomes and activities. Azano, Callahan, Missett, and Brunner (2014) piloted a language arts curriculum in rural schools and found that although rural educators did not implement the curriculum with fidelity, the students still showed gains as the teachers adapted the

units to fit the rural community culture and learning needs of their students. Similarly, Leonard, Russell, Hobbs, and Buchanan (2013) created a mathematics unit that highlighted the cultural capital of the community and introduced several ways in which mathematics can be taught through the community-based activities and authentic learning opportunities. This place-based approach capitalizes on the strengths of the community, involves students with community professionals and potential mentors, and provides unique opportunities for accelerated and individualized learning as well as hands-on and relevant experiences that rural students will find more meaningful to their every day lives.
8. Use multiple measures and a team approach for identification. Of all the innovative projects that successfully identified more rural gifted students—especially those who are minority or poor—more than one assessment was used. Place-based identification measures and subjective tools were combined with more traditional assessments. No one test or measure excluded or included a rural gifted student for access to services. Instead, teams of trained educators carefully considered the unique profiles of each student and made the best determination for appropriate services based on individual student needs and strengths.

Conclusion

Rural places are unique. There are defining characteristics of rural individuals and especially those who are gifted and live in rural areas. However, these characteristics, beliefs, and values differ based on the rural region in which a student resides as well as his or her ethnicity, income status and experiences. Educators need to understand the context of their specific rural locale and match identification methods to their students' needs. The use of a variety of measures, flexibility of methods used, understanding the context and community in which a rural gifted student resides, and challenging preconceived notions of giftedness through professional development are essential in crafting appropriate identification systems for rural gifted students.

References

Aamidor, S. (2007). Identification and intervention for rural, low-income, gifted students: A follow-up study. *Gifted Children, 2,* 1–5.

Abell, D. J., & Lennex, L. (1999). *Gifted education: Don't overlook the disadvantaged.* Point Clear, AL: Mid-South Educational Research Association. (Eric Document Reproduction Service No. ED436918)

Azano, A. P., Callahan, C. M., Missett, T. C., & Brunner, M. (2014). Understanding the experiences of gifted education teachers and fidelity of implementation in rural schools. *Journal of Advanced Academics, 25,* 88–100.

Bull, K., & Fishkin, A. (1987). Should rural gifted education be different? A survey of teacher education. *Research in Rural Education, 4,* 73–75.

Clark, G., & Zimmerman, E. (2001). Identifying artistically talented students in four rural communities in the United States. *Gifted Child Quarterly, 45,* 104–114.

Davalos, R., & Griffin, G. (1999). The impact of teachers individualized practices on gifted students in rural, heterogeneous classrooms. *Roeper Review, 21,* 308–314.

Dillon, M., & Savage, S. (2006). Values and religion in rural America: Attitudes toward abortion and same-sex relations. *The Carsey School of Public Policy at the Scholars' Repository.* Paper 12. Retrieved from http://scholars.unh.edu/cgi/viewcontent.cgi?article=1011&context=carsey

Duncan, C. M. (1999). *Worlds apart: Why poverty persists in rural America.* Hartford, CT: Yale University Press.

Fishkin, A. S., & Kampsnider, J. J. (1996). WISC-III subtest scatter patterns for rural superior and high-ability children. (ERIC Document Reproduction Service No. 394783). Retrieved from http://scholars.unh.edu/carsey/12

Hebert, T. P., & Beardsley, T. M. (2001). Jermaine: A critical case study of a gifted Black child living in rural poverty. *Gifted Child Quarterly, 45,* 85–103.

Jones, L. (1994). *Appalachia values.* Ashland, KY: The Jesse Stuart Foundation.

Lawrence. B. K. (2009). Rural gifted education: A comprehensive literature review. *Journal for the Education of the Gifted, 32,* 464–491.

Leonard, J., Russell, N. M., Hobbs, R. M., & Buchanan, H. (2013). Using GIS to teach place-based mathematics in rural classrooms. *Rural Educator, 34,* 10–17.

Montgomery, D. (2001). Increasing Native American Indian involvement in gifted programs in rural schools. *Psychology in the Schools, 38,* 467–475.

Pendarvis, E., & Wood, E. W. (2009). Eligibility of historically underrepresented students referred for gifted education in a rural school district: A case study. *Journal for the Education of the Gifted, 32,* 495–514.

Shamah, D., & MacTavish, K. A. (2009). Rural research brief: Making room for place-based knowledge in rural classrooms. *Rural Educator, 30,* 1–4.

Slama, K. (2004). Rural culture is a diversity issue. *Minnesota Psychologist, 53,* 9–13.

Spicker, H. (1993). Final report Project SPRING special populations rural information network for the gifted (USDOE No. R206A00169). Washington, D.C.: U.S. Department of Education.

Spicker, H., & Aamidor, S. E. (1996). Project Spring II: Identifying rural disadvantaged and ethnically diverse gifted students. (ERIC Document Reproduction Service No. ED 404791)

Spicker, H., Fletcher, R., Montgomery, D., & Breard, N. (1993). Rural gifted education in a multicultural society. Proceedings from *Rural America: Where All Innovations Begin.* Savannah, GA: EDRS.

Spicker, H., & Poling, S. N. (1993). *Identifying rural disadvantaged gifted students. Project Spring: Special Populations Resource Information Network for the Gifted.* Bloomington: Indiana University. (ERIC Document Reproduction Service No. ED365065)

VanTassel-Baska, J., & Stambaugh, T. (Eds.). (2007). *Overlooked gems: A national perspective on low-income promising learners.* Washington, D.C.: National Association for Gifted Children.

CHAPTER 6

Grouping and Instructional Management Strategies

Kristen Seward and Marcia Gentry, Ph.D.

Developing the strengths, potentials, and talents among gifted, rural youth is an important task rife with challenges specific to rural areas. Because rural students comprise greater than 20% of public school students in the United States, it follows that one-fifth of all gifted students hail from rural areas as defined by the National Center for Education Statistics' (NCES) "locale code system . . . specifically, locale codes 41(rural fringe), 42 (rural distant), or 43 (rural remote)" (Johnson, Showalter, Klein, & Lester, 2014, p.27). Rural gifted students are fascinating, as they bring their practical yet creative intelligences to their learning experiences, and teaching them can be an inspiring, fulfilling endeavor. However, teachers in rural contexts are called to serve many roles within their school districts, which often involve teaching multiple subjects (or sections) to classrooms of students ranging widely in achievement and readiness levels, in addition to coaching, serving on committees, and being involved in clubs and activities within the school community. These teachers, and the administrators who guide them, need to organize educational experiences wisely in order to achieve maximum effects with the least amount of burnout. Just as teachers encourage students to study smarter, not harder, by explicitly teaching mnemonics, note-taking, and time management skills, teachers and administrators in rural schools need to work smarter, not harder, to effectively meet the needs of rural students of all achievement levels. Following, we pro-

111   DOI: 10.4324/9781003237938-8

vide a structure and specific programming strategies appropriate for use in rural schools which effectively group students within classrooms as well as among grade levels and in entire schools.

Special Issues in Educating Gifted Students in Rural Schools

District Perspective

Challenges facing rural schools have dramatic effects on gifted students' educational experiences. Among these challenges are disparity in school funding with rural schools frequently underfunded; an overburden of federal and state mandates; persistent poverty; a lack of economic advancement accompanied by depopulation; and fewer educational resources, including highly qualified teachers (Bryant, 2007; Howley, Rhodes, & Beall, 2009). These issues have had devastating consequences for rural school district budgets and on the quantity and quality of gifted education services offered in their schools (Haney, 2013). Across the country, gifted education is inadequately funded and is frequently one of the first areas eliminated when districts consider budget cuts (National Association for Gifted Children [NAGC] & Council of State Directors of Programs for the Gifted, 2013; Purcell, 1994; Renzulli, 2005). Many rural schools function without a gifted education coordinator, trained teachers, or specific services for their gifted students. According to the NAGC (2014) *2012-2013 State of the Nation* report, only "three states require general education teachers to have some type of training in gifted education" (p. 2), and only half of the states provide any funding at all for gifted programs. In addition, only one (Kentucky) of the 42 states reporting requires gifted education coursework for all preservice teachers (NAGC & Council of State Directors of Programs for the Gifted, 2013). Thus, in the majority of states, the education of gifted students falls to general education teachers who may or may not have backgrounds in working with gifted students or be willing to provide appropriately challenging learning experiences.

For those school districts that reside in states that provide some level of funding for gifted education, these limited funds are stretched among instructional resources and professional development in gifted education (VanTassel-

Baska, 2006). For most rural districts, professional development funding has become directly tied to school improvement plans and to Common Core State Standards achievement, which generally do not include special attention to gifted students' needs (Marrongelle, Sztajn, & Smith, 2013). District administrators' and principals' regard for educating gifted students in their districts often suffer under the pressure of meeting demands for overall student achievement and growth and other school accountability measures. In addition, changing student demographics in many rural areas and teacher accountability concerns dictate administrators' decision making with regard to culturally, linguistically, and ethnically diverse (CLED); special needs; and gifted student placement across classrooms to minimize the negative impact of new teacher evaluation methods (Howley et al., 2009). However, district-level gifted education practices do exist that can strengthen achievement for gifted students and their same age peers.

School Perspective

Teachers and school-level administrators in rural contexts are the face of education for the community, for it is at the school and in classrooms that education becomes personalized and meaningful to rural students and their families. Because these professionals are confronted daily with the challenges mentioned above, they may often feel the weight of these pressures more strongly than teachers in larger suburban or urban schools. Bryant (2007) observed that many state and federal mandates, which were likely written with larger urban schools in mind, have forced rural schools to channel already limited funds to programs that support these mandates. In addition, teachers in rural schools frequently have lower wages than those in suburban and urban areas (Provasnik et al., 2007), and with new regulations involving competition for merit pay and fewer teachers among which to spread the pay, demoralization may occur. In many rural elementary schools, fewer teachers at each grade level means larger class sizes, and in many rural middle and high school contexts, one teacher may be responsible for teaching more than one subject area, making the attainment of "highly qualified" status in each of those subjects difficult to achieve (Rosenburg, 2011). Often the number of teachers available is based on the number of students per grade level rather than any other measure, such as the number of students performing at certain achievement levels (Lavigne, 2014). A plausible solution that may alleviate these concerns is for school-level administrators to think differently regarding teacher assignments and traditional student grouping procedures.

In rural high schools, these concerns are further complicated by the small number of teachers who hold certification and/or qualification to teach certain subjects or more advanced coursework in core subject areas. According to federal government statistics, only 43% of rural teaching staff has attained at least a master's degree compared with 49% of urban and 52% of suburban teachers (Provasnik et al., 2007). In addition, newly graduated teachers often choose positions in higher paying, suburban or urban schools, or they move on to these positions after a few years' experience at a rural school (Simmons, 2005). To address these concerns, school-level administrators could develop the teaching talents of their faculty by implementing professional development plans that address the needs of gifted learners and their teachers and at the same time improve learning for all students. Rewarding the implementation of effective gifted education practices such as curriculum compacting (Reis, Westberg, Kulikowich, & Purcell, 1998; Starko, 1986), acceleration (Colangelo, Assouline, & Gross, 2004), cluster grouping (Gentry, 2014), and differentiation (Kanevsky, 2011; Tomlinson et al., 2003; Wormeli, 2011) in teacher evaluations can help reinforce the use of the strategies learned in professional development.

Classroom Perspective

Teachers in rural schools are challenged to meet the needs of a wide spectrum of learners, and no matter how well-meaning, rural teachers will struggle to meet these needs as effectively as they would like to. Rural teachers need to advocate for themselves so that they can more effectively impact all students' learning. Existing gifted education practices can assist the teacher in managing their workloads more effectively, including grouping strategies that can address the learning needs of all students. For rural gifted students, this means that they, too, may have to advocate for educational experiences that challenge them every day. The consequences for lack of challenging curriculum and instruction for the most capable rural students are high school dropout and lack of preparation for college success (Aamidor, 2007; Zabloski & Milacci, 2012) These consequences are too severe to be overlooked simply because funding is lacking or school personnel's attitudes regarding gifted education are languid. An atmosphere of support for gifted students and their education is important for their success. Determining ways in which teachers can work smarter, not harder, is essential. How can this be accomplished, especially in rural schools that often lack human and financial resources? One answer can be found in specific gifted education practices, that when implemented with integrity and with school personnel support, can turn a struggling teacher, a struggling school, and a struggling rural district around.

Generalizations

Effective Grouping Strategies in Meeting the Needs of Rural Gifted Students

Several different kinds of grouping practices are effective with gifted students. Most of these practices group students according to similar readiness levels, achievement levels, and/or ability, and when used in conjunction with appropriate gifted education strategies, these grouping practices can promote learning with all students (Gentry, 2014; Kulik & Kulik, 1992; Rogers, 1991). Mixed-ability grouping, however, is not advised for gifted students when learning course content is the primary goal (as opposed to social skills development). When gifted students are placed in heterogeneous groups, they may fall victim to the other group members' expectation that the smartest kid will do all the work or to their own "façade of effort and ability" (Gentry 2014, p. 22) as they underperform while still maintaining an acceptable degree of academic reputation in the classroom (Kulik, 2003; Rogers, 2002). Like all students, gifted students deserve to be challenged academically and to learn something new every day.

Too often in education today, the term "ability grouping" receives a suspicious glance, as if some covert, devious treatment were about to be inflicted on innocent school children, but ability or achievement grouping is simply a tool that when used appropriately can help teachers better target their instruction. Researchers have shown that all students, regardless of ability or achievement level, can benefit from flexible ability grouping strategies when accompanied by differentiated curriculum and instruction (Gentry, 2014; Gentry & Owen, 1999; Kulik, 2003; Loveless, 2013; Rogers, 1993; Tieso, 2003). Flexible skills groups in which teachers group students with similar readiness levels can help the teacher target content and instructional levels in specific subject areas and provide these groups with appropriate differentiated curriculum and instruction. This may be especially true for gifted students in rural contexts where resources are limited. Unlike tracking, the goal of flexible ability grouping is to provide appropriately paced, individualized instruction as determined by each student's academic readiness (Olszewski-Kubilius, 2013). When students are grouped according to ability, provided with appropriately challenging material and instruction, and re-evaluated for group placement at regular intervals, achievement gains result for students at all levels (Brulles, Peters, & Saunders, 2012; Gentry & Owen, 1999; Matthews, Ritchotte, & McBee, 2013; Pierce et al., 2011). The practice of flexible grouping is enhanced by the expectation that students will regularly move among groups as readiness and achievement levels improve (Gentry, 2014; Gentry & Owen, 1999).

Cross-graded or cross-age groups are populated based on achievement levels in various subject areas, not on students' ages or traditional cohort groups (Lloyd, 1999). Often referred to as multi-age classrooms, these groups allow for targeted skill development and appropriate challenge, especially for gifted students in rural schools (Pratt, 1986). Cross-age grouping may seem unnatural to many education stakeholders, but consider that this practice is already in place in every school in the United States. It's called retention, a more negative, reactionary cross-age grouping practice. Cross-age grouping as a proactive practice that groups students according to achievement levels has the potential to maximize classroom time on appropriate learning tasks that will result in marked achievement gains.

Cluster grouping, a popular programming strategy in elementary schools, places several gifted students together in one classroom with other students of varying abilities in order to help teachers focus on the affective and academic needs of these students. Teachers with training, experience, and/or background in gifted education work with these clusters of gifted students (Gentry, 2014). But in this general application of cluster grouping, no thought is given to the composition of the other classrooms or the training of the other teachers in the building. One specific form of cluster grouping, Total School Cluster Grouping (TSCG; Gentry, 2014), has been shown to be effective as a program model that integrates differentiated instructional strategies with grouping practices across all classrooms. This model will be discussed in detail in the following section as a way for rural schools to work smarter as they address the learning needs of all students, including gifted students.

Collaborative learning is another grouping practice that can be used with gifted youth. Collaborative learning groups are most effective when: a) students of similar achievement levels are grouped together; b) students have specific individual contributions to make to the group; c) students who share interests are grouped together; and/or d) teachers want to promote skill development in group work (Kulik, 2003; Kulik & Kulik, 1987; Lou et al., 1996). Gifted students, like all students, need to develop skills to work with others effectively; collaborative learning groups provide skills training in teamwork, communication, and conflict resolution (Patrick, Bangel, Jeon, & Townsend, 2005) important to their social-emotional growth.

Meeting the Needs of Gifted Students Using Total School Cluster Grouping

Cluster grouping is an organizational model that must be considered within the broader context of ability grouping in general. Many thousands of studies over the years have been done, with some revealing the positive effects and others revealing the negative effects of ability grouping. Several different researchers have conducted a number of meta-analyses trying to make some sense of these individual studies and with variable findings (e.g., Goldring, 1990; Henderson, 1989; Kulik, 1985; Kulik & Kulik, 1982, 1984, 1987, 1992; Lou et al., 1996; Mosteller, Light, & Sachs, 1996; Noland & Taylor, 1986; Slavin, 1987, 1990, 1993). According to Gentry (2014),

> Conflicting results, conclusions, and opinions exist regarding ability grouping. The practice has been both touted as an effective means for promoting student achievement (Kulik, 2003) and decried as an evil force contributing to the downfall of America's schools (Oakes, 1985). However, the "real" answer lies somewhere in the middle and depends largely upon the context and application of the ability grouping. (pp. 16–17)

For years, calls to completely eliminate ability grouping and implement full inclusion have occurred, while at the same time resources have decreased and class sizes have increased. Classroom teachers across the country work every day to address individual students' needs while under increased pressure to improve student performance on state tests. Thus, it is becoming more and more difficult for teachers to meet the disparate individual needs of their students. Additionally, despite those who believe ability grouping is "bad," Loveless (2013) reported that analyses of National Assessment of Educational Progress (NAEP) data revealed that the use of ability grouping has continued to increase since the year 2000. Most researchers agree that students of all achievement levels benefit when teachers adjust their curriculum and instruction to the skill level of the child. This sensible approach to achievement grouping is how Total School Cluster Grouping works.

TSCG has a growing body of research that suggests all students can benefit from its implementation. The original quasi-experimental research conducted in two rural schools on TSCG showed that, over time, more students were identified as high achieving (+50% to +100%), fewer students were identified as low achieving (-66% to -100%), student achievement increased compared to control-school students ($F=16.98, p<.001, R^2=.18; F=10.14, p<.001. R^2=.11$), and teachers' practices improved as they implemented strategies in general classrooms often reserved for students in gifted programs (Gentry & Owen, 1999).

More recent quasi-experimental research has revealed similar findings and has shown that TSCG resulted in larger numbers of students from traditionally underrepresented groups being identified as gifted and that these students experience achievement growth (Brulles, Saunders, & Cohn, 2010; Brulles, Peters, & Saunders, 2012; Collins & Gan, 2013; Gates, 2011; Gentry & McDougall, 2009; Matthews, Ritchotte, & McBee, 2013; Pierce et al., 2011). Additionally, these researchers found no negative effects of cluster grouping on any children—so lower performing children were not harmed, and in some cases were helped, by grouping high-achieving students in a clustered model. In fact, Matthews et al. (2013) found that TSCG positively influenced math achievement for gifted and for typical learners. Brulles et al. (2012) found that typical learners experienced similar growth in mathematics regardless of whether they were groups with high-achieving students. Pierce et al. (2011) examined math achievement for gifted and typical students in total school applications of cluster grouping and found performance gains for both groups of students in mathematics. Gentry and MacDougall (2009) found increased representation rates for students with free or reduced lunch assistance (+33%), English language learners (+10%), and students from underrepresented racial/ethnic groups (African American, +12%; Latino/a, +10%) after just one year of TSCG programming. A controlled evaluation study of a 3-year implementation of TSCG in an urban area revealed average NCE achievement gains across five treatment schools in reading (+3.28) and math (+7.07) for all students; gains among students identified as high achieving in reading (+7.31) and in math (+8.32); and treatment schools outperforming their matched comparison schools in achievement. This evaluation study also revealed an increase in the number of students from low-income (+24%) and African American (+21%) families identified as high achieving and an increase in the number of students from underserved populations who qualified as gifted under state guidelines (+100% on average at each school; Gentry, 2012). TSCG capitalizes on the common belief that gifted education practices can be effective when used with students of varying abilities (Gentry, 2014). In short, TSCG "uses the achievement performance levels of all students in the school to create classes of students characterized by a reduced range of student achievement levels, but including students who achieve at above average levels in every classroom" (Gentry, 2013, p. 110). Annual evaluation of student achievement cluster group placement and ongoing professional development for all teachers (with the expectation that all teachers will use gifted education practices such as differentiation, flexible grouping, and curriculum compacting) enhance learning for all students in the school, not just gifted students (Gentry, 2014). Gentry (2014) defined TSCG as having the following features:

> Total School Cluster Grouping takes general cluster grouping several steps further to consider the placement and performance of *every* student in the school together with the students who might traditionally be identified as gifted and placed in the cluster classroom under the general model . . . . cluster grouping . . . differs from general clustering in the following important ways:
> 1. Identification occurs yearly on the basis of student performance, with the expectation that student achievement will increase as students grow, develop, and respond to appropriately differentiated curricula.
> 2. Identification encompasses the range of low-achieving to high-achieving students, with all student achievement levels identified.
> 3. The classroom(s) that contain clusters of high-achieving students contain no above-average-achieving students, as these students are clustered into the other classrooms.
> 4. Some classrooms may contain clusters of special needs students with assistance provided to the classroom teacher.
> 5. Teachers may flexibly group between classes or among grade levels as well as use a variety of flexible grouping strategies within their classrooms.
> 6. All teachers receive professional development in gifted education strategies and have the opportunity for more advanced education in gifted education and talent development through advanced workshops, conferences, and coursework.

7. The teacher whose class has the high-achieving cluster is selected by an enrichment team or his or her colleagues and provides differentiated instruction and curriculum to these students as needed to meet their educational needs. (pp. 19–20)

TSCG offers schools a smarter way to effectively meet the learning needs of all students; it makes sense that teachers and students will benefit from more targeted/focused instructional experiences. In rural schools, to some degree, cluster grouping may already be practiced, as students are frequently grouped according to achievement levels in English/language arts and math in particular. For example, many schools, including rural schools, group students in accelerated or honors courses for these subjects from grade 5 or 6 through graduation, often culminating in Advanced Placement or dual credit/dual enrollment courses in the upper levels of high school. TSCG can strengthen these existing practices by also considering the learning needs of students in elementary schools and by helping them learn to achieve at higher levels.

What Is the Same or Different for Rural Gifted Learners?

Quite possibly, TSCG in rural settings may be more manageable and effective than in larger urban schools that experience intra- and interdistrict mobility at high rates. Due to smaller populations in rural schools, teachers often know students well, which assists in the clustered classroom placements, even in multi-age classrooms. Teachers in rural schools also know one another well and may be able to work together effectively and support one another throughout the TSCG process. Indeed, with regard to informal professional development, TSCG teachers who worked with gifted cluster groups often served as day-to-day resources for fellow teachers, and gifted education strategies were used with students of all achievement levels (Gentry & Keilty, 2004).

Gifted and general learners in rural settings will benefit from TSCG, as they are challenged with like-minded peers and somewhat shielded from the pressure of "acting dumb" in order to fit in. Additionally, able students who are not initially recognized as gifted benefit, over time, from being stereotyped as "second best," when the top achievers are clustered together in one classroom while these students become the top achievers in other classroom. Their confidence and skills grow, and so does their achievement—when the highest achievers are placed elsewhere. TSCG will allow gifted students to receive full-time services in their areas of exceptionality within the classroom, and this model also works in conjunction with any pull-out programs that may exist. By ensuring rigor and challenge beginning in elementary school, rural gifted students will be better prepared for whatever they choose to do after high school.

Specific Strategies

District-Level Considerations: Gifted Program Services, Identification, and Staff

District administrators, including gifted education coordinators, should consider their gifted education program mission statement and program goals as they consider implementing TSCG. Will TSCG be implemented as a service option or as a program model? How will teachers be trained and how will TSCG be supported by each school's staff? Will TSCG be welcomed as a refreshing approach to meeting the needs of all students, or will it be received as another time-consuming add-on? Administrator attitudes and support are vital in the implementation and development process.

One strength of TSCG is that it integrates well with the general education program, especially when utilized as a program model that can enhance gifted behaviors in all students (Gentry, 2014). An overall emphasis on the talent development of all students, especially when promoted as a reframing of the often-negative teacher perception of diagnosing and remediating student weaknesses, may breathe fresh air back into an overworked teaching staff. And talent development should not be focused solely on students but on teachers as well; professional development in gifted education that nurtures the talents of teachers, that enriches their professional experiences through supportive encouragement that assists them in working smarter, not harder, will also receive a warm welcome from staff.

The gifted program's continuum of services will be strengthened by the adoption of TSCG. Another key feature of TSCG is that teachers are collaborative developers of the program as they identify the kinds of professional development experiences that they need in order to develop their teaching talents in the classroom (Gentry & Keilty, 2004). As all teachers in a school are instructed in effective gifted education practices and positively implement them in their classes, more and more students are exposed to these practices and student achievement increases. The gifted education continuum of services expands, and all students benefit from differentiated instructional practices. Figure 6.1 (Gentry, 2009) depicts a comprehensive continuum of services for gifted students, including several services suitable for all students (see shaded area). Teachers working together within grade levels and schools should strive to include as many of these services as possible during in- and out-of-school hours to enhance learning for all students. Rural schools might also consider collaborating with other rural schools or utilizing distance learning options to provide these services and enhance talent development among their students.

Identification procedures in gifted programs will also be enhanced with TSCG. As all teachers are trained in and use various gifted education strategies in their classrooms, more students will be identified as high achieving (Gentry & Owen, 1999), and the achievement of all students will improve (Brulles et. al., 2012; Gentry & Owen, 1999; Pierce et. al., 2011). In this way, identification procedures will be strengthened as teachers begin to recognize emerging talents in their students. Because student achievement data is reviewed every year for grouping purposes, the identification process is ongoing. In addition, TSCG does not impose a cap or limit on the number of students identified, thereby opening wide the doors of inclusion in the high-achieving group(s) (Gentry, 2014).

Staffing gifted programs has often been a challenge for rural schools with limited resources. TSCG can address these challenges by incorporating the talent and motivation of existing staff. First, teachers who are willing and committed to work with high-ability clusters of students are specially trained (or have been specially trained) in gifted education, likely resulting in a certification or endorsement in gifted education (Gentry & Keilty, 2004). Ideally, these teachers can be identified by their colleagues with support of administration by virtue of their ability (manifest or emerging) and desire to work with gifted students. These teachers will then serve as school-based resources for gifted education practices and other effective TSCG strategies. Second, as all staff are trained in gifted education practices that can be effective with all students—such as differentiation, curriculum compacting, and higher order thinking skills—district-level administrators will recognize the benefits as student achievement rises without additional funds being expended.

A Comprehensive Continuum of Gifted Education and Talent Development Services[1,2]

Elementary School	Middle School	High School
General Classroom Enrichment, Talents Unlimited, Junior Great Books	General Classroom Enrichment	General Classroom Enrichment
Discovery, Inquiry, Problem Based Learning	Discovery, Inquiry, Problem Based Learning	Discovery, Inquiry, Problem Based Learning
Enrichment Clusters	Academies of Inquiry	Academies of Inquiry
Differentiation	Differentiation	Differentiation
Curriculum Compacting	Curriculum Compacting	Curriculum Compacting
Individual and Small-Group Counseling	Individual and Small-Group Counseling	Individual and Small-Group Counseling
Social, Emotional, Physical Health	Social, Emotional, Physical Health	Social, Emotional, Physical Health
Independent Study in Interest Area	Independent Study in Interest Area	Independent Study in Interest Area and Self-Designed Courses
Product/Service in Interest Area	Product/Service in Interest Area	Product/Service in Interest Area
Career Awareness	Career Counseling	Career and Educational Counseling
Within-Class Cluster Grouping	Small-Group Flexible Grouping and Differentiation, Achievement Grouping	Advanced Placement Courses
Total School Cluster Grouping		
Between Class Grouping by Skill Level	Advanced Options in Leadership, Music, Visual and Performing Arts	Advanced Options in Leadership, Music, Visual and Performing Arts

Figure 6.1. A comprehensive continuum of gifted education and talent development services. Adapted from *Schools for Talent Development: A Practical Plan for Total School Improvement* (p. 78), by J. S. Renzulli, 1994, Mansfield Center, CT: Creative Learning Press. Adapted with permission. *Note.* Services for all young people are highlighted in grey, and these options do not constitute gifted services but do set the stage for discovery and development of talent in more youth and children.

A Comprehensive Continuum of Gifted Education and Talent Development Services[1,2]		
Elementary School	Middle School	High School
Nongraded Cluster Grouping	Within and Across Grade Level Advanced/Honors Classes	Honors Courses
Within and Across Grade Pull-Out by Targeted Ability, Subject, and Interest Areas	Resource Room Send-Out to Facilitate Advanced, Student-Based Study	International Baccalaureate
Self-Contained Classes (Single or Multigrade)	Self-Contained Classes (Single or Multigrade)	Advanced Academies
Magnet Schools	Magnet Schools	Magnet Schools, Special Schools
Integrated Technology	Integrated Technology	Integrated Technology, Career and Technical Education Courses
Multicultural/Foreign Language Study	Multicultural/Foreign Language	Multicultural/Foreign Language
Individual Options: Internships, Apprenticeships, Mentorships, IEP, Dual Exceptionalities	*Individual Options:* Internships, Apprenticeships, Mentorships, IEP, Dual Exceptionalities	*Individual Options:* Internships, Apprenticeships, Mentorships, IEP, Dual Exceptionalities
Acceleration Options: Early Admission, Grade Skipping, Subject Acceleration, Dual Enrollment in Middle School Classes	*Acceleration Options:* Grade Skipping, Subject Acceleration, Telescoping, Dual Enrollment in High School Classes	*Acceleration Options:* Subject Acceleration, Telescoping, Dual Enrollment in High School Classes, Dual Enrollment in College Classes, Early Admission to College
Special Talent Programs: Young Writers, Saturday and Summer Programs, Future Problem Solving, Math Olympiad, Science Olympiad, Math Leagues, Science Fairs, Talent Searches, Odyssey of the Mind, Destination Imagination, Invention Convention, Youth in Government, Close up, Governors' Schools and Academies, etc.		

Figure 6.1. *continued*

School-Level Considerations

TSCG has been shown effective at the elementary level in rural schools as a program model. However, teacher buy-in and principal support are vital in the program's effectiveness (Gentry & Keilty, 2004). Underlying negative attitudes regarding professional development or gifted education in general will undermine positive results. For this reason, Gentry and Keilty (2004) recommended a six-step process for successful implementation of TSCG at the school level:

1. Conversations are held regarding what staff members believe and hope with regard to education in general, and to gifted programming in particular, in order to solidify the school's mission and goals.
2. Research is conducted in order to alleviate doubts, correct misconceptions, and facilitate staff members' compliance with proven gifted education practices.
3. A long-term gifted program plan, which is based on previous conversations and research and aligns with the mission and goals of the school, is determined. The foundation of this plan is continuous, responsive staff development.
4. Implementation of the plan involves all members of the staff and secures teacher, administrator, and community buy-in as much as possible. Flexibility and defensibility based on the school's mission, goals, and the staff members' conversations and research in previous steps are vital aspects for the plan's success. Continually connecting the TSCG program to the general education program will remind everyone that the school is concerned with all of its students, not just its gifted students. In addition, implementation problems that arise should be addressed with problem solving rather than administrative dictates.
5. Support for the plan is strengthened through ongoing formal and informal staff development that is responsive to staff input and needs.
6. Maintenance and growth of the plan is enhanced by orienting new staff members to the plan, by ongoing research in effective gifted education practices, by encouraging ownership of the plan by staff members' action research and other supportive efforts, and by continually evaluating the program's effectiveness in relation to the school's ever-changing mission and goals.

Classroom-Level Considerations

Meeting the needs of all rural learners requires flexibility, expertise, and persistence in creating educational experiences that help diverse students learn something new every day. TSCG as a program model that addresses the learning needs of all students at the school level provides the structure for student success, but classroom teachers must complement this model with enthusiasm for understanding the unique academic, social, and emotional needs of their students and for appropriate differentiation of curriculum, instruction, and assessment to meet those needs. Successful teachers address the social/emotional elements embedded in curriculum, utilize flexible grouping strategies within their classrooms, and incorporate fun and challenge in every unit of study. Teachers in rural schools also appreciate and promote rural ways of knowing by matching their students' interests and abilities to place-based educational experiences as described above (Avery, 2013).

Differentiation that "demolishes ceilings" often experienced by gifted students is an essential component of the TSCG classroom (McIntosh, 2014, p. 99). Effective differentiation begins with preassessment of students' abilities, interest levels, process skills, familiarity with products, and affective needs related to the content. Preassessment results are thoroughly analyzed to determine each student's strengths and weaknesses in order to develop individualized learning experiences for all students. Table 6.1 includes several easy-to-use preassessment techniques for teachers' consideration, including Four Corners, Quick Writes, KWL Charts, and RAN Charts (McIntosh, 2014).

Providing appropriate academic challenge for gifted rural learners requires teachers who not only understand the unique learning characteristics of gifted students, but who also pursue alternative instructional opportunities which ignite these students' passions. Allowing gifted students to choose certain aspects of their learning experiences empowers them to become self-motivated, autonomous learners. This kind of deferential differentiation (Kanevsky, 2011) allows teachers to maintain their professional judgment regarding overall learning objectives, content, process, product, and assessment. Academic challenge for gifted students also incorporates expert-like processing skills related to the specific content being studied. Gifted students are often unchallenged, and their teachers sometimes struggle to provide appropriately challenging learning experiences. Both concerns can be addressed with providing learning experiences that would require the gifted student to demonstrate achievement levels that mirror expert performance in the field (McIntosh, 2014). When used appropri-

TABLE 6.1
Preassessment Techniques

Preassessment Techniques	
Pretest/Posttest Design	Give the test you plan to give at the end of the unit (or one similar) at the beginning of the unit.
Curriculum Maps and Markers	At the beginning of the year, ask the students to highlight on the curriculum map document what they already know in green, what they have been exposed to in yellow, and what they have never heard of in red.
Quick Write	Ask students to write everything they know about a topic in five minutes or less.
Concept Map	Ask students to create a concept map that includes the "big ideas" related to a topic.
Four Corners	Post one of the following signs in each of the four corners in the classroom: Novice, Apprentice, Practitioner, and Expert. After naming the topic or skill, ask the students to walk to the corner that represents their current level of understanding.
Informal Survey or One-on-One Interview	Ask students what they know about a topic through a survey or an individual discussion.
KWL Chart	Ask students to complete a modified KWL chart (K: what they already know; W: what they want to know; and L: where they learned it).
RAN Chart (Reading and Analyzing Nonfiction)	Create a chart with the following headings: 1) What I Think I know; 2) Confirmed; 3) Misconceptions; 4) New Learning; and 5) Wonderings. Students brainstorm what they think they know about a topic and write each fact on a Post-it note. As they read through a text and find confirmation for a fact, they then move its corresponding Post-it to the second column. The process continues as misconceptions are identified and new learning takes place. Finally, students are asked to list what they would still like to learn.

Adapted from "Curriculum Compacting: Organized Common Sense," by J. McIntosh, 2014. In M. Gentry (with K. A. Paul, J. McIntosh, C. M. Fugate, & E. Jen), *Total School Cluster Grouping and Differentiation: A Comprehensive, Research-Based Plan for Raising Student Achievement and Improving Teacher Practices* (2nd ed., pp. 121–143), New York, NY: Taylor & Francis. Copyright 2014 by Taylor & Francis. Adapted with permission.

ately, challenge and choice will increase gifted students' confidence, self-worth, and overall school satisfaction (McIntosh, 2014).

Recognizing and accepting that they can't provide every instructional experience for gifted students, teachers of gifted students in rural schools utilize local expertise and community resources, university partnerships, mentoring, and distance learning whenever available (Avery, 2013; Reis, Gentry, & Park, 1995). When paired with effective differentiation strategies such as problem-based learning, passion projects, and independent studies, rural gifted students can extend learning beyond the classroom, making it more relevant and meaningful (McIntosh, 2014). In addition, these experiences, when closely monitored by the classroom teacher, will foster students' investment in designing their own educational experiences.

Conclusions and Take-Away Points

In summary, despite the unique challenges they face, rural schools have many strengths from which to develop outstanding programs and services for their students. For example, rural educators know one another, they know the students and their families, and the students find their rural schools enjoyable places to be, likely due to this familiarity. However students report lower levels of challenge than their suburban peers, underscoring the need for direct, developed services for students (Gentry, Rizza, & Gable, 2001). By selecting options from the continuum of services (see Figure 6.1) that involve all students and teachers, a talent development culture can be cultivated (to use a rural metaphor). When a school is a place where it is "cool to be smart," all students win, and rural educators can build smart environments by using all the tools available to them and leveraging their connections to the students, their families, and the community. Grouping, when done thoughtfully as in the TSCG model, can help teachers work smarter, not harder, by targeting effective instruction to promote growth for all students, thereby enriching the challenge and learning experience for all.

References

Aamidor, S. (2007). Identification and intervention for rural, low-income, gifted students: A follow-up study. *Gifted Children, 2*(1), 1–5.

Avery, L. (2013). Rural science education: Valuing local knowledge. *Theory into Practice, 52*(1), 28–35.

Brulles, D., Peters, S. J., & Saunders, R. (2012). Schoolwide mathematics achievement within the gifted cluster grouping model. *Journal of Advanced Academics, 23*, 200–216.

Brulles, D., Saunders, R., & Cohn, S. (2010). Improving performance for gifted students in a cluster grouping model. *Journal for the Education of the Gifted, 34,* 327–352.

Bryant, J.A. (2007). Killing Mayberry: The crisis in rural American education. *The Rural Educator, 29,* 7–11.

Colangelo, N., Assouline, S., & Gross, M. U. M. (Eds.). (2004). *A nation deceived: How schools hold back America's brightest students.* Iowa City: University of Iowa, Connie Belin & Jacqueline N. Blank International Center for Gifted Education and Talent Development.

Collins, C. & Gan, L. (2013). *Does sorting students improve scores? An analysis of class composition.* Retrieved from http://www.nber.org/papers/w18848

Gates, J. (2011). *Total school cluster grouping model: An investigation of student achievement and identification and teachers classroom practices* (Doctoral dissertation, Purdue University). Available from ProQuest Dissertations and Theses database. (UMI No. 3479482)

Gentry, M. (2009). Myth 11: A comprehensive continuum of gifted education and talent development services: Discovering, developing, and enhancing young people's gifts and talents. *Gifted Child Quarterly, 53*(4), 262–265.

Gentry, M. (2012). *Total School Cluster Grouping, Urban Pilot Project, 2 years of Controlled Study Final Report on Academic Achievement, Identification, and Teacher Practices. Technical Report.* West Lafayette, IN: Purdue University.

Gentry, M. (2013). Cluster grouping. In C. M. Callahan & J. Plucker (Eds.), *Critical issues and practices in gifted education* (2nd ed., pp. 109–117). Waco, TX: Prufrock Press.

Gentry, M. (with Paul, K. A., McIntosh, J., Fugate, C. M., & Jen, E.). (2014). *Total school cluster grouping and differentiation: A comprehensive, research-based plan for raising student achievement and improving teacher practices.* (2nd ed.) Waco, TX: Prufrock Press, Inc.

Gentry, M. & Keilty, B. (2004). Rural and suburban cluster grouping: Reflections on staff development as a component of program success. *Roeper Review, 26*(3), 147–155.

Gentry, M. & McDougall, J. (2009). Total school cluster grouping: Model, research, and practice. In J. S. Renzulli, E. J. Gubbins, K. S. McMillen, R. D. Eckert, & C. A. Little (Eds.), *Systems and models for developing programs for the gifted and talented* (2nd ed., pp. 211–234). Waco, TX: Prufrock Press.

Gentry, M. & Owen, S. V. (1999). An investigation of total school flexible cluster grouping on identification, achievement, and classroom practices. *Gifted Child Quarterly, 43,* 224–243.

Gentry, M., Rizza, M. G., & Gable, R. K. (2001). Gifted students' perceptions of their class activities: Differences among rural, urban, and suburban student attitudes. *Gifted Child Quarterly, 45,* 115–129.

Goldring, E. B. (1990). Assessing the status of information on classroom organizational frameworks of gifted students. *Journal of Educational Research, 83*(6), 313–326.

Haney, P. (2013). The gifted commitment: Gifted education's unrecognized relevance in "thorough and efficient" public schools. *Case Western Reserve Law Review, 64*(1), 279–301.

Henderson, N. D. (1989). A meta-analysis of ability grouping achievement and attitude in the elementary grades. Unpublished doctoral dissertation, Mississippi State University at Mississippi.

Howley, A., Rhodes, M., Beall, J. (2009). Challenges facing rural schools: Implications for the gifted. *Journal for the Education of the Gifted, 32*(4), 515–536.

Johnson, J. Showalter, D., Klein, R., & Lester, C. (2014). *Why rural matters 2013–2014: The condition of rural education in the 50 states.* Retrieved from http://www.ruraledu.org/user_uploads/file/2013-14-Why-Rural-Matters.pdf

Kanevsky, L. (2011). Deferential differentiation: What types of differentiation do students want? *Gifted Child Quarterly, 55*(4), 279–299.

Kulik, C.-L. C. (August, 1985). Effects of inter-class ability grouping on achievement and self-esteem. Paper presented at the 93rd Annual Convention of the American Psychological Association, Los Angeles, CA.

Kulik, J. A. (2003). Grouping and tracking. In N. Colangelo & G. Davis (Eds.), *Handbook of gifted education* (pp. 268–281). Boston, MA: Allyn and Bacon.

Kulik, C.-L. C., & Kulik, J. A. (1982). Effects of ability grouping on secondary school students: A meta-analysis of evaluation findings. *American Educational Research Journal, 19,* 415–428.

Kulik, C.-L. C., & Kulik, J. A. (1984). *Effects of ability grouping on elementary school pupils: A meta-analysis.* Paper presented at the annual meeting of the American Psychological Association, Toronto, Canada. (ERIC Document Reproduction Service No. ED 255 329)

Kulik, J. A., & Kulik, C.-L. C. (1987). Effects of ability grouping on student achievement. *Equity & Excellence in Education, 23,* 22–30.

Kulik, J. A., & Kulik, C.-L. C. (1992). Meta-analytic findings on grouping programs. *Gifted Child Quarterly, 36,* 73–77.

Lavigne, A. (2014). Exploring the intended and unintended consequences of high-stakes teacher evaluation on schools, teachers, and students. *Teacher College Record, 116,* 1–29.

Lloyd, L. (1999). Multi-age classes and high ability students. *Review of Educational Research, 69*(2), 187–212.

Lou, Y., Abrami, P. C., Spence, J. C., Poulsen, C., Chambers, B., & d'Apollonia, S. (1996). Within-class grouping: A meta analysis. *Review of Educational Research, 66,* 423–458.

Loveless, T. (2013). *The 2013 Brown Center Report on American Education: How well are American students learning?* (Volume 3; Number 2). Retrieved from http://www.brookings.edu/research/reports/2013/03/18-tracking-ability-grouping-loveless

Marrongelle, K., Sztajn, P., & Smith, M. (2013). Scaling up professional development in an era of common state standards. *Journal of Teacher Education 64*(3), 202–211.

Matthews M. S., Ritchotte, J. A. & McBee, M. T. (2013). Effects of schoolwide cluster grouping and within-class ability grouping on elementary school students' academic achievement growth. *High Ability Studies, 24,* 81–97.

McIntosh, J. (2014). Differentiation: Demolishing ceilings. In M. Gentry (with K. A. Paul, J. McIntosh, C. M. Fugate, & E. Jen), *Total school cluster grouping and differentiation: A comprehensive, research-based plan for raising student achievement and improving teacher practices* (2nd ed., pp. 99–119). Waco, TX: Prufrock Press.

Mosteller, F., Light, R.J., & Sachs, J.A. (1996). Sustained inquiry in education: Lessons from skill grouping and class size. *Harvard Educational Review, 66,* 797–842.

National Association of Gifted Children. (2014). *2012–2013 State of the nation in gifted ducation: Work yet to be done.* Retrieved from http://www.nagc.org.442elmp01.blackmesh.com/sites/default/files/Advocacy/State%20of%20the%20Nation.pdf.

National Association for Gifted Children, & Council of State Directors of Programs for the Gifted. (2013). *2012–2013 State of the states in gifted education: National policy and practice data.* Washington, D.C.: Authors.

Noland, T. K., & Taylor, B. L. (1986). The effects of ability grouping: a meta-analysis of research findings. Paper presented at the 70th Annual meeting of the American Educational Research Association, San Francisco, CA. (ERIC Document Reproduction Service No. ED 269 541)

Oakes, J. (1985). *Keeping track: How schools structure inequality.* New Haven, CT: Yale University Press.

Olszewski-Kubilius, P. (2013). Setting the record straight on ability grouping. *Education Week Teacher.* Retrieved from http://www.edweek.org/tm/articles/2013/05/20/fp_olszewski.html

Patrick, H., Bangel, N., Jeon, K., & Townsend, M. (2005). Reconsidering the issue of cooperative learning with gifted students. *Journal for the Education of the Gifted, 29*(1), 90–108.

Pierce, R., Cassady, J., Adams, C., Neumeister, K., Dixon, F., & Cross, T. (2011). The effects of clustering and curriculum on the development of gifted learners' math achievement. *Journal for the Education of the Gifted, 34,* 569–596.

Pratt, D. (1986). On the merits of multiage classrooms. Research in Rural Education, 3(3), 111–115. Retrieved from http://jrre.vmhost.psu.edu/wp-content/uploads/2014/02/3-3_3.pdf

Provasnik, S., KewalRamani, A., Coleman, M.M., Gilbertson, L., Herring, W., and Xie, Q., National Center for Education Statistics, Institute of Education Sciences, & U.S. Department of Education. (2007). *Status of education in rural America* (NCES 2007-040). Retrieved from http://nces.ed.gov/pubs2007/2007040.pdf

Purcell, J. (1994). The status of programs for high ability students (CRS94306). Storrs, CT: The National Research Center on the Gifted and Talented.

Reis, S. M., Gentry, M., & Park, S. (1995). *Extending the pedagogy of gifted education to all students: The enrichment cluster study. Technical Report.* Storrs, CT: The National Research Center on the Gifted and Talented.

Reis, S., Westberg, K., Kulikowich, J., & Purcell, J. (1998). Curriculum compacting and achievement test scores: What does the research say? *Gifted Child Quarterly, 42*(2), 123–129.

Renzulli, J. S. (1994). *Schools for talent development: A practical plan for total school improvement.* Mansfield Center, CT: Creative Learning Press.

Renzulli, J. S. (2005). A quiet crisis is clouding the future of R & D. *Education Week, 24,* 32–33, 40.

Rogers, K. B. (1991). *The relationship of grouping practices to the education of the gifted and talented learner.* Storrs, CT: The National Research Center on the Gifted and Talented.

Rogers, K. B. (1993). Grouping the gifted and talented: Questions and answers. *Roeper Review, 16,* 8–12.

Rogers, K. B. (2002). Re-forming gifted education. Scottsdale, AZ: Great Potential Press.

Rosenberg, S. J. (2011). The challenges in implementing school improvement grant models in rural high schools (Alliance for Excellent Education report). Retrieved http://dukespace.lib.duke.edu/dspace/bitstream/handle/10161/3681/Rosenberg%2c%20Sarah%20MP.pdf?sequence=1

Simmons, B. J. (2005). Recruiting teachers for rural schools. *Principal Leadership: Middle Level Edition, 5*(5), 48–53.

Slavin, R. E. (1987). Ability grouping and student achievement in elementary schools: A best-evidence synthesis. *Review of Educational Research, 57,* 293–336.

Slavin, R. E. (1990). Achievement effects of ability grouping in secondary schools: A best-evidence synthesis. *Review of Educational Research, 60,* 471–499.

Slavin, R. E. (1993). Ability grouping in the middle grades: Achievement effects and alternatives. *The Elementary School Journal, 93,* 535–552.

Starko, A. (1986). Meeting the needs of the gifted throughout the school day: Techniques for curriculum compacting. *Roeper Review, 9*(1), 27–33.

Tieso, C. L. (2003). Ability grouping is not just tracking anymore. *Roeper Review, 26,* 29–36.

Tomlinson, C., Brighton, C., Hertberg, H., Callahan, C., Moon, T., Brimijoin, K., Conover, L., & Reynolds, T. (2003). Differentiating instruction in response to student readiness, interest, and learning profiles in academically diverse classrooms: A review of literature. *Journal for the Education of the Gifted, 27,* 119–145.

VanTassel-Baska, J. (2006). A content analysis of evaluation finding across 20 gifted programs: A clarion call for enhanced gifted program development. *The Gifted Child Quarterly, 50*(3), 199–215.

Wormeli, R. (2011). Differentiated instruction: Setting the pedagogy straight. *Middle Ground, 15,* 39–40.

Zabloski, J., & Milacci, F. (2012). Gifted dropouts: Phenomenological case studies of rural gifted students. *Journal of Ethnographic & Qualitative Research, 6*(3), 175–190.

Appendix 6.1: Practical Resource Recommendations

The authors recommend the following resources to those interested in learning more about Total School Cluster Grouping.

Books, Chapters, and Articles

Gentry, M. (2014). *Total school cluster grouping and differentiation: A comprehensive, research-based plan for raising student achievement and improving teacher practices* (2nd ed.). Waco, TX: Prufrock Press.

Gentry, M. (2009). Cluster grouping. In B. Kerr (Ed.) *Encyclopedia of giftedness, creativity, and talent* (pp. 140–144). Thousand Oaks, CA: Sage.

Gentry, M., & Owen, S. V. (2004). An investigation of the effects of total school cluster grouping on identification, achievement, and classroom practices. In S. M. Reis & L. E. Brody (Eds.), *Grouping and acceleration practices* (pp. 115–146). Thousand Oaks, CA: Corwin Press.

Gentry, M., Renzulli, J., & Reis, S. (2014). *Enrichment clusters: A practical plan for real-world, student-driven learning* (2nd ed.). Waco, TX: Prufrock Press.

Johnson, J. Showalter, D., Klein, R., & Lester, C. (2014). *Why rural matters 2013–2014: The condition of rural education in the 50 states.* Retrieved from http://www.ruraledu.org/user_uploads/file/2013-14-Why-Rural-Matters.pdf

National Association of Gifted Children. (2014). *2012–2013 State of the nation in gifted education: Work yet to be done.* Retrieved from http://www.nagc.org.442elmp01.blackmesh.com/sites/default/files/Advocacy/State%20of%20the%20Nation.pdf

Renzulli, J., Gentry, M., & Reis, S. (2014). *Enrichment clusters: A practical plan for real-world, student-driven learning.* Waco, TX: Prufrock Press.

Web Resources

- » Total School Cluster Grouping: http://www.purduegeri.org/
- » Authentic Enrichment Clusters: http://www.gifted.uconn.edu/sem/semart01.html
- » Schoolwide Enrichment Model: http://www.gifted.uconn.edu/SEMR/
- » Purdue University Gifted Education Resource Institute (GERI): http://www.purdue.edu/geri

CHAPTER 7

Challenges and Solutions for Serving Rural Gifted Students
Accelerative Strategies

Susan G. Assouline, Ph.D., Kristin Flanary, and Megan Foley-Nicpon, Ph.D.

Introduction

Gifted students living in rural America represent a distinct population, and their educational needs deserve special consideration among educators. The specialness of any population implies two common questions: How unique is the population and what is the prevalence? For rural, gifted students, each is answered through data from the National Center for Education Statistics (Keaton, 2014). Regarding the first question, rural students themselves are not unique. With the exception of our nation's capital, rural students are in every state in the United States. They attend nearly one-third (29%) of the schools, and they represent nearly one in five (18.7%) of the 48, 539, 901 students reported for the 2012–2013 year (Keaton, 2014). Although rural students are found in every state, they are an important population with special learning circumstances that merit the concern and attention of America's educators.

The prevalence of rural *gifted* students, the second question, requires consideration of the definitions of giftedness, which are many and varied. The National Association for Gifted Children's website (NAGC, 2014; http://nagc.org) offers the following:

Gifted individuals are those who demonstrate outstanding levels of aptitude (defined as an exceptional ability to reason and learn) or competence (documented performance or achievement in the top 10% or rarer) in one or more domains. Domains include any structured area of activity with its own symbol system (e.g., mathematics, music, language) and/or set of sensorimotor skills (e.g., painting, dance, sports). (para. 5)

If the top-performing (10%) rural students are considered gifted, that would mean approximately one million students across the United States who attend rural schools fit this description. One million is a substantial number, again, deserving of our attention.

The roots of both general and gifted education are grounded in the rural history of this country, which predates its founding. An understanding of the historical challenges and strengths facing gifted rural students over the years has the potential to crystalize our philosophy and direct our actions for generations to come. A timeline of gifted education can be seen in Table 7.1.

Colangelo, Assouline, Baldus, and New (2003) reviewed the state of gifted education in rural schools and determined that empirical validation of best practices for gifted education in rural settings was limited. Several barriers were recognized, including (a) identification, (b) program opportunities, and (c) resources. Gentry, Rizza, and Gable (2001) also identified psychosocial issues as barriers to providing services in rural settings. Specifically, they found that compared to suburban and urban peers, gifted students from rural areas perceived less challenge and interest in their coursework. This is particularly disconcerting because students who are not interested or challenged are likely to become disengaged from developing their academic talent (Csikszentmihalyi, Rathunde, & Whalen, 1993). Academic acceleration, which can be delivered in a variety of forms, is one proven educational strategy (Colangelo, Assouline, & Gross, 2004) that has the potential to address the barriers impeding the academic development of rural gifted students. Furthermore, a commonly held belief that academic acceleration has a negative social-emotional impact on students has been disproved. (See Assouline, Colangelo, Van Tassel-Baska, & Lupkowski-Shoplik, 2015; Colangelo, Assouline, & Gross, 2004; Cross, Andersen, & Mammadov, 2015; and Robinson, 2004 for an extensive discussion of the impact of academic acceleration on the social-emotional development of gifted students.)

The focus of this chapter is on two forms of acceleration (Southern & Jones, 2015), a school-based Advanced Placement (AP) online academy for high schools students, and an extracurricular science and math program for gifted

TABLE 7.1
A Timeline of Rural Gifted Education[1]

Time Period	General Education	Rural Gifted Education	Gifted Education	Observations
1600s	First statute in the colonies to establish a school system (1647)		Harvard University is established (1636).	General education *is* rural education.
1700s	The European Enlightenment posits that children are "blank slates," in direct contrast to Calvinist doctrine that children are inherently evil.			
1800s	"Monitorial Schools," which are modeled after a factory model, are established in urban areas.	Education in rural areas is predominately represented by the one-room school house.	Gifted students work at their own pace.	Rural is not only farming and agricultural; however during the 19th century, this is the prevalent approach; agricultural workers decrease steadily from 58% in 1820 to 15% in 1850.
1836	McGuffey's Readers are published.	They are significant to country schools, which had few resources available.		Availability of resources would become an important educational and legislative theme.
1839–1855	Horace Mann establishes the first Normal Schools, which he hopes will become linked to common schools.	As of 1840, 25% of the adult population is illiterate.		Normal schools are the precursors of today's Colleges of Education.
	In 1855, Brown University offers education classes for teachers.			

Table 7.1. continued

Time Period	General Education	Rural Gifted Education	Gifted Education	Observations
1860–1900	The concept of kindergarten is established by two sisters, Mary and Sophia Peabody. Mary was married to Horace Mann and Sophia was married to Nathaniel Hawthorne. By the end of the 19th century, the number of kindergartens will grow from the original 25 to 4,363. In 1889, Columbia Teacher's College is established.		1868, St. Louis implements the St. Louis plan, which includes flexible promotion. In 1869, Sir Francis Galton (cousin to Charles Darwin) publishes *Hereditary Genius*. In 1884, Massachusetts implements grade skipping.	Massive immigration to the U.S. from many European countries; many go to cities, and the rest go to the Midwest and West. 80% of Americans live in rural communities with fewer than 2,500 residents.
1905–1925	Simon and Binet publish their first intelligence test in Paris, France (1905).	Leta Hollingworth is born in rural Nebraska.	Leta Hollingworth establishes a school for gifted students in NYC (The Speyer School). Lewis Terman publishes the first of four volumes of Genetic Studies of Genius, the first longitudinal study of giftedness.	Although it would be many years later, Julian C. Stanley, founder of the Talent Search Model, used Terman's and Hollingworth's work as a foundation for the Talent Search Model.

Table 7.1. continued

Time Period	General Education	Rural Gifted Education	Gifted Education	Observations
1925–1975	In 1955, the Ford Foundation establishes the College Board; 1975 marks passage of PL 94-142, special education law, which is the precursor to current special education legislation, known as IDEA.		In 1954, National Association for Gifted Children is established. In 1972 U.S. Congress commissions the S.P. Marland Report on the State of Gifted Education. In 1975, Federal Office of Gifted and Talented is established (dissolved in 1982).	This 35-year period was momentous for gifted education, especially the establishment of AP and the launching of Sputnik, which launched the STEM movement, although it would lay dormant for some years.
1975–present	No Child Left Behind (NCLB) is enacted in 2001. NCLB focuses on increasing accountability and achievement in schools. However, because the goal is grade-level proficiency, it does not meet the needs of gifted students who, by definition, exceed the grade-level placement of their peers.	In 1984, there are still 430 one-room school houses in operation in the U.S.	In 1980, talent search organizations are established at Johns Hopkins University, Duke, and Northwestern. Other centers for gifted education established, including the Belin-Blank Center at the University of Iowa (1988). Several states establish residential STEM high schools; Javits Gifted and Talented Act (1988) is passed. *A Nation Deceived* is published in 2004; *A Nation Empowered*, published 2015.	

Note. Some information from this table is from Colangelo, Assouline, and New (1999), *Gifted Education in Rural Schools: A National Assessment*.

middle schools students. Both programs are housed in a university center for gifted education, and the two programs share a common goal to prepare students and their teachers for advanced high school science and math courses, specifically through AP coursework.

Academic Acceleration

Pressey (1949) defined academic acceleration as an educational intervention that moves high-ability students through an educational program at a rate faster or an age younger than typical. Southern and Jones (2015) documented 20 forms of academic acceleration that range from curriculum compacting to radical grade skips of 2 or more years. The various forms have also been characterized as two broad categories, content-based and grade-based (Institute for Research and Policy on Acceleration, National Association for Gifted Children, & Council of State Directors for Programs for Gifted 2009; Rogers, 2004; Southern & Jones, 2015). The distinction between content-based and grade-based categories is centered upon whether the accelerative strategy shortens the number of years in the K–12 system. Grade-based strategies, including grade skipping, early entrance to kindergarten or first grade, or early entrance to college, shorten the number of years that a student is in the K–12 system. Whereas grade-based strategies may be more extreme than content-based acceleration, they are the least salient to other students or teachers (Southern & Jones, 2015). Content-based strategies allow the student to remain with chronological peers, but instruction is at a higher level, and this form of intervention may be more noticeable to others (Southern & Jones, 2015). Content-based instruction refers to single-subject acceleration, credit-by-examination, extracurricular programs, and AP (Rogers, 2015; Southern & Jones, 2015).

Advanced Coursework for Academically Talented Students

A rigorous high school curriculum is one of the best predictors of college completion (Adelman, 1999), and The College Board's AP Program is considered a gold standard of such curriculum (Bleske-Rechek, Lubinski, & Benbow, 2004; Rogers, 2015). The AP Program allows students to pursue college-level studies and take college-level exams while in high school. In May 2014 (most recent data available), more than 2.3 million students across the country took 4.2 million AP Exams in 34 subjects (College Board, 2015). Students can earn college credit or advanced placement in college courses at thousands of colleges and universities with a qualifying AP Exam score. For all participants, AP exams provide a uniform standard of academic accomplishment across geography, economic status, ethnicity, and school size. An AP Exam score of 5 (the exam scores are on a scale of 1–5) is considered top-level work in a corresponding college course; an exam score of 3 is recognized as a qualifying score for college credit or advanced placement in college courses at many colleges and universities.

AP courses and exams help students experience college-level academics while still in high school. Students who participate in the AP program benefit academically from the experience during their college years (Rogers, 2015; Wai, 2015). Students who complete AP coursework perform as well or better in upper level college courses in the content area of their AP course(s) (Sadler & Tai, 2007), earn higher GPAs in college (Eimers & Mullen, 2003), have higher college graduation rates (Adelman, 1999; Dougherty, Mellor, & Shuling, 2006), and are more likely to graduate college in 4 years or fewer (Hargrove, Godin, & Dodd, 2008; Mattern, Marini, & Shaw, 2013) and to go on to obtain an advanced degree (Bleske-Rechek et al., 2004).

Because rural high schools are less likely to be prepared for advanced classes, let alone have access to AP courses or other advanced coursework, rural gifted students are unlikely to have the same postsecondary advantages as their urban and suburban counterparts (Azano, Callahan, Missett, & Brunner, 2014; Colangelo et al., 2003). Moreover, AP teachers and courses must be certified by the College Board, resulting in the observation that rural schools often do not have faculty who are qualified to teach specialized or advanced courses (Aronson & Timms, 2004) and cannot justify paying for certification when only a few students each year may be likely to take a particular AP course (Colangelo, Assouline, & New, 2001). These concerns represent systemic issues that are unique to the rural setting. Technology literally serves as a bridge to geographic barriers previously impeding access to high-level courses like AP. Extracurricular programming at the middle school level is a psychological bridge because such programming prepares students academically and socially-emotionally for accelerated coursework in high school.

Iowa: A Case Example of an Extracurricular Middle School Program That Prepares High-Ability Rural High School Students for Distance Education

When geographical barriers limit access to advanced coursework, online learning opportunities can sometimes help close these gaps (Hannum, Irvin, Banks, & Farmer, 2009). At the beginning of the 21st century, Iowa's students were limited in opportunities for AP courses and exams because of the large number of rural and small schools. According to the National Center of Education Statistics (2012), 74% of schools in Iowa are in rural communities. Approximately 44% of all public school districts in the state of Iowa have a K–12 enrollment of 599 or fewer (Iowa Department of Education, 2013a). It is not cost effective to offer AP courses in rural and small schools because class sizes would be too small. As a result, a culture of knowledge about and appreciation for AP remains underdeveloped in these schools.

In response to the inequitable access to AP coursework, the University of Iowa's Belin-Blank International Center for Gifted Education and Talent Development has made a concerted effort since 2001, through the Iowa Online AP Academy (IOAPA), to bring AP and advanced learning opportunities to all high schools in Iowa (see Colangelo et al., 2003). The IOAPA has a special focus on serving rural and small high schools so that Iowa's geography does not determine educational opportunity. The program accomplishes these goals through four primary areas of activity: (a) online AP coursework; (b) online, instructor-led AP exam reviews; (c) professional development about AP courses, provided by College Board consultants; and (d) above-level assessments to middle schools students, which provide specific data indicating readiness for accelerated, extracurricular programming. The case study addressed both the AP online coursework as well as the middle school extracurricular programming that prepares students for AP.

IOAPA, funded by a state legislative initiative, enrolls students in online AP coursework through a third-party course provider at no cost to the student. IOAPA also covers all associated course fees. Schools provide course materials and any necessary technological equipment (usually a computer with Internet access), along with time in the student's regular course schedule and space in the school building for the student to complete the coursework. During two enrollment periods—one in the late fall and one in the late spring—schools register with the IOAPA and enroll students for courses. The online nature of the course offers flexibility that traditional brick-and-mortar courses cannot provide; progress is self-paced and coursework can be completed virtually anywhere with Internet access. This is ideal for gifted students in rural schools, who may prefer a faster pace and/or have complicated schedules due to participation in several extracurricular activities (a hallmark of small, rural schools).

Several key personnel contribute to IOAPA operations. Each registered school assigns a site coordinator and a mentor from among its faculty and staff to supervise and support that school's IOAPA students. Site coordinators are typically the school counselor or talented and gifted coordinator, and they are responsible for most logistical and communication issues. Site coordinators oversee registration and enrollment, make any necessary arrangements at the school, and keep in contact with IOAPA staff. Mentors are typically state-licensed classroom teachers, often with a background in gifted education, and provide active student support throughout the year. They monitor student progress, proctor exams, facilitate communication between students and instructors, help troubleshoot problems, and offer encouragement and advice. The third-party course provider employs licensed, content-certified online instructors to deliver all course content, assign and grade course activities and exams, and answer questions about course material. Finally, the Belin-Blank Center for Gifted Education and Talent Development provides university-based assistance in the form of an IOAPA administrator, clerical staff, and a graduate assistant who provide support to the school personnel and help monitor student progress. The infrastructure provided by the gifted education center is critical to the success of the IOAPA.

The AP exam is the culminating event of an AP course, and students only receive college credit by earning a qualifying score on this optional exam. In order to promote exam taking, the IOAPA also covers the cost of registration for online AP exam reviews through the same third-party provider. Students in any Iowa accredited school registered with the IOAPA, not just those in IOAPA courses, may register for the exam reviews.

To address the shortage of qualified AP teachers in rural districts, the IOAPA offers grants to Iowa teachers that cover registration fees for an Advanced Placement Summer Institute sponsored by the Belin-Blank Center. The Advanced Placement Teacher Training Institute (APTTI) provides teachers interested in the AP Program comprehensive preparation for developing and teaching an AP course. In addition to discussing questions about AP subject-area content, teachers receive an overview of the AP program and can receive AP certification from the College Board. Certified teachers are then qualified to return to their home schools and introduce a new AP course into the curriculum and/or improve existing AP courses.

While providing access to college-level coursework for academically talented high school students is a worthwhile and critical endeavor, access alone is insufficient if students have not been adequately prepared in middle school and their first 2 years in high school to succeed in these courses. To assist in that goal, the IOAPA expanded in two ways. First, extracurricular programming is being offered to high-need, underresourced middle schools. Extracurricular programs provide opportunities for in-depth study and enriched learning environments where achievement is valued (Olszewski-Kubilius & Thomson, 2014). Furthermore, there are positive effects from out-of-school activities on the educational success of students who are at risk due to poverty (Olszewski-Kubilius, 2006). The purpose of extracurricular middle school programming is to equip students with the skills and background knowledge that will prepare them for the advanced content and difficulty level of future AP courses.

Determining readiness for an extracurricular middle school program is based upon above-level testing such as that provided through talent search programs to upper elementary and middle schools students (Assouline & Lupkowski-Shoplik, 2011). Because gifted students' grade-level assessment scores often reach a ceiling, above-level testing is needed to reveal the necessary level of challenge. Scores on these above-level assessments can then demonstrate what students are ready to learn and inform classroom instruction at the middle school level so they are prepared to take AP courses in high school.

Is the Iowa Online Programming Successful?

Rogers (2015) documented the very strong academic effects of both AP coursework and online coursework. The impact of this accelerative option is validation for the efforts to provide AP online programming to rural schools. The College Board has documented that Iowa student participation in the AP program has increased dramatically since 2001 (The College Board, 2014a), when the IOAPA was implemented. Additionally, the percentage of Iowa high school graduates earning a score of 3 (the qualifying score) or better on at least one AP exam has almost doubled during the 10-year period from 2003–2013 (5.9% of 2003 graduates versus 11.1% of 2013 graduates), although it is still lower than the national average of 20.1% (Iowa ranks 40th nationally).

IOAPA students also perform well in their AP coursework. In the 2013–2014 academic year (most recent data available), 87% of IOAPA students completed their course(s); 94% of completing students received a passing final grade. In comparison, national online learning retention rates hover around 30%–50% (Irvin, Hannum, Farmer, de la Varre, & Keane, 2009). As Irvin et al. (2009) noted, online courses involve a certain level of distance between students and instructors, who are usually located in different geographical areas. The instructors may or may not be able to see their students' faces and nonverbal cues, and vice versa. This stands in stark contrast to the level of familiarity and close student-teacher interactions characteristic of most small, rural schools. Therefore, the daily face-to-face support provided by the IOAPA mentors in the schools is crucial to this level of student success, and an in-person component should not be ignored when implementing online advanced learning opportunities (Irvin et al., 2009).

Dual Enrollment: Another College Experience

Other options for students to earn college credit while still in high school include concurrent enrollment in community college courses and postsecondary enrollment options (PSEO) through community colleges or other institutions of higher education. Both dual enrollment and PSEO provide opportunities for many high school students; however, Rogers (2015) documented that the academic impact of such coursework is moderate in comparison to AP coursework. Therefore, community college coursework may superficially appear to meet the needs of high school students who are gifted; however, because there is no national credentialing body such the College Board of Educational Examiners, they cannot be considered to offer a consistent experience across the country. A student in the most rural Iowa community who takes AP English Literature and Composition has a course that adheres to the exact same standards as the student who takes AP English Literature and Composition at a private preparatory school in a suburban or urban community.

Without question, AP is the gold standard for a national, advanced, college-level content. Many Iowans participate; as mentioned above, Iowa's participation in AP has doubled over the past decade (The College Board, 2014b). Still, the participation rate remains relatively low compared to other states (ranked 43rd nationally, in terms of the number of seniors taking an AP exam; ranked 40th nationally in terms of number of graduates scoring a 3 or better on an AP exam). This may be due to dual enrollment in community college courses.

Many more students who earn college credit during the high school years are currently pursuing dual enrollment through community colleges, rather than AP courses, despite the fact that the rigor of the AP program more closely matches the level of 4-year university courses (Colangelo et al., 2003). In 2013 (most recent data available), more than 40,000 Iowa high school students enrolled in community college courses (Iowa Department of Education, 2013b), while 11,084 students enrolled in AP courses (The College Board, 2014b). This trend demonstrates a need to prepare middle school students for advanced coursework in high school and to emphasize the benefits of AP to schools and high-ability students for whom more rigorous coursework is not only appropriate, but essential to their success in 4-year institutions.

Summary and Recommendations

The ideal of a bucolic, agricultural environment, which emphasizes cooperation and community values, veils issues that are salient in rural educational settings. The primary issue concerns resources (see Appendix 7.1 for accessible resources) and reflects the impact of geography and low-population density. Students who live in low-population density areas do not have the same access to educational opportunities as their urban and suburban peers; this means that the college and career playing fields are not level, which will have negative impact on gifted students who live in these communities. However, technology has great potential to change this situation and bridge the achievement gap between gifted students in rural settings and urban/suburban peers. In particular, technological access to AP courses goes a long way toward leveling the college, and hence the career, playing fields. There are two reasons for this: equal access and consistent standards. Online access to standardized curriculum makes it such that where one lives no longer has to dictate what advanced educational opportunities are available.

The IOAPA program, including the expanded middle school extracurricular offering in preparation for high school online AP courses, is presented as a best practice model of how rural communities nationwide can reduce educational access inequalities between rural and urban settings. This model becomes possible with funding and support from state constituencies who recognize the need to develop talent in their students from diverse locations across their state. With increased communication and collaboration, the acceleration opportunities for gifted learners from our rural communities will continue to grow far into the future.

References

Adelman, C. (1999). *Answers in the tool box: Academic intensity, attendance patterns, and bachelor's degree attainment.* Washington, D.C.: Office of Educational Research and Improvement, U.S. Department of Education.

Assouline, S. G., Colangelo, N., VanTassel-Baska, J., & Lupkowski-Shoplik, A. E. (Eds.). (2015). *A nation empowered: Evidence trumps excuses holding back America's brightest students.* Iowa City: The University of Iowa, Connie Belin & Jacqueline N. Blank International Center for Gifted Education and Talented Development.

Assouline, S. G., & Lupkowski-Shoplik, A. E. (2011). The talent search model of gifted education. *Journal of Psychoeducational Assessment,* 1–15.

Aronson, J. Z., & Timms, M. J. (2004). *Net choices, net gains: Supplementing high school curriculum with online courses* (Knowledge Brief). Retrieved from http://www.wested.org/online_pubs/KN-03-02.pdf

Azano, A. P., Callahan, C. M., Missett, T. C., & Brunner, M. (2014). Understanding the experiences of gifted education teachers and fidelity of implementation in rural schools. *Journal of Advanced Academics, 25,* 88–100.

Bleske-Rechek, A., Lubinski, D., & Benbow, C. P. (2004). Meeting the educational needs of special populations: Advanced Placement's role in developing exceptional human capital. *Psychological Science, 15,* 217–224.

Colangelo, N., Assouline, S. G., Baldus, C. M., & New, J. K. (2003). Gifted education in rural schools. In N. Colangelo & G. A. Davis (Eds.), *Handbook of Gifted Education* (pp. 572–581). Boston, MA: Allyn & Bacon.

Colangelo, N., Assouline, S. G., & Gross, M. U. M. (2004). *A nation deceived: How schools hold back America's students.* Iowa City: The University of

Iowa, Connie Belin & Jacqueline N. Blank International Center for Gifted Education and Talent Development.

Colangelo, N., Assouline, S. G., & New, J. K. (2001). *Gifted voices from rural America*. Iowa City: The University of Iowa, Connie Belin & Jacqueline N. Blank International Center for Gifted Education and Talent Development, the University of Iowa.

College Board. (2014a). *10th annual report to the nation: Iowa state supplement*. Retrieved from http://media.collegeboard.com/digitalServices/pdf/ap/rtn/10th-annual/10th-annual-ap-report-state-supplement-iowa.pdf

College Board. (2014b). *10th annual report to the nation*. Retrieved from http://media.collegeboard.com/digitalServices/pdf/ap/rtn/10th-annual/10th-annual-ap-report-to-the-nation-two-page-spread.pdf

College Board. (2015). *About the exams*. Retrieved from http://professionals.collegeboard.com/testing/ap/about

Cross, T. L., Andersen, L., & Mammadov, S. (2015). Effects of academic acceleration on the social and emotional lives of gifted students. In S. G. Assouline, N. Colangelo, J. VanTassel-Baska, & A.E. Lupkowski-Shoplik (Eds.), *A nation empowered: Evidence trumps excuses holding back America's brightest students* (pp. 31–42). Iowa City: The University of Iowa, The Connie Belin and Jacqueline N. Blank International Center for Gifted Education and Talented Development.

Csikszentmihalyi, M., Rathunde, K., & Whalen, S. (1993). *Talented teenagers: The roots of success and failure*. New York, NY: Cambridge Press.

Dougherty, C., Mellor, L., & Shuling, J. (2006). *The relationship between advanced placement and college graduation* (2005 AP Study Series, Report No. 1). Retrieved from http://broadprize.org/symposium/2006BroadSymposiumRelationshipBetweenAPandCollegeGrad.pdf

Eimers, M. T., & Mullen, R. (2003). *Dual credit and Advanced Placement: Do they help prepare students for success in college?* Paper presented at the 43rd Annual Association of Institutional Research Conference, Tampa, FL.

Gentry, M., Rizza, M. G., & Gable, R. K. (2001). Gifted students' perceptions of their class activities: Differences among rural, urban, and suburban student attitudes. *Gifted Child Quarterly, 45,* 115–129.

Hannum, W. H., Irvin, M. J., Banks, J. B., & Farmer, T. W. (2009). Distance education use in rural schools. *Journal of Research in Rural Education, 24,* 1–15.

Hargrove, L., Godin, D., & Dodd, B. G. (2008). *College outcomes comparisons by AP and non-AP high school experiences* (College Board Research Report No. 2008-3). New York, NY: The College Board.

Iowa Department of Education. (2013a). *The annual condition of education report*. Des Moines: Iowa Department of Education. Retrieved from https://www.educateiowa.gov/documents/annual-condition-education-report-pk-12/2014/01/annual-condition-education-report-2013

Iowa Department of Education. (2013b). *Joint Enrollment Report*. Des Moines: Iowa Department of Education. Retrieved from https://www.educateiowa.gov/documents/joint-enrollment/2014/03/2013-joint-enrollment-report

Institute for Research and Policy on Acceleration, National Association for Gifted Children, & Council of State Directors of Programs for the Gifted. (2009). *Guidelines for developing an academic acceleration policy*. Washington, D.C.: National Association for Gifted Children.

Irvin, M. J., Hannum, W. H., Farmer, T. W., de la Varre, C., & Keane, J. (2009). Supporting online learning for advanced placement students in small rural schools: Conceptual foundations and intervention components of the facilitator preparation program. *The Rural Educator, 31,* 29–37.

Keaton, P. (2014). *Selected statistics from the public elementary and secondary education universe: School year 2012–13* (NCES 2014-098). Washington, D.C.: National Center for Education Statistics. Retrieved from http://nces.ed.gov/pubsearch

Mattern, K., Marini, J. P., & Shaw, E. J. (2013). *Are AP students more likely to graduate on time?* (College Board Research Report 2013-5). New York, NY: The College Board.

National Association for Gifted Children. (2014). *Definitions of giftedness*. Retrieved from http://www.nagc.org/resources-publications/resources/definitions-giftedness

National Center for Education Statistics. (2012). *Number of public school districts, by district locale and state or jurisdiction: School year 2011–12*. Retrieved from http://nces.ed.gov/surveys/ruraled/districts.asp

Olszewski-Kubilius, P. (2006). Addressing the achievement gap between minority and nonminority children: Increasing access and achievement through Project EXCITE. *Gifted Child Today, 29*(2), 28–37.

Olszewski-Kubilius, P., & Thomson, D. (2014). Talent search. In J. A. Plucker & C. M. Callahan (Eds.), *Critical issues and practices in gifted education. What the research says* (pp. 633–644). Waco, TX: Prufrock Press.

Pressey, S. L. (1949). *Educational acceleration: Appraisals and basic problems* (Bureau of Educational Research Monographs, No. 31). Columbus: Ohio State University Press.

Robinson, N. (2004). Effects of academic acceleration on the social-emotional status of gifted students. In N. Colangelo, S. G. Assouline, & M. U. M Gross

(Eds.), *A nation deceived: How schools hold back America's students* (pp. 59–68). Iowa City: The Connie Belin & Jacqueline N. Blank International Center for Gifted Education and Talent Development.

Rogers, K. B. (2004). The academic effects of acceleration. In N. Colangelo, S. G. Assouline, & M. U. M. Gross (Eds.), *A nation deceived: How schools hold back America's brightest students* (pp. 47–57). Iowa City: The Connie Belin & Jacqueline N. Blank International Center for Gifted Education and Talent Development.

Rogers, K. B. (2015). The academic, socialization, and psychological effect of acceleration: Research synthesis. In S. G. Assouline, N. Colangelo, J. VanTassel-Baska, & A. E. Lupkowski-Shoplik (Eds.). *A nation empowered: Evidence trumps excuses holding back America's brightest students* (pp. 19–30). Iowa City: The University of Iowa, Connie Belin & Jacqueline N. Blank Center for Gifted and Talented Education.

Sadler, P. M., & Tai, R. H. (2007). Advanced placement exam scores as a predictor of performance in introductory college biology, chemistry, and physics courses. *Science Educator, 16,* 1–20.

Southern, W. T., & Jones, E. D. (2015). Types of acceleration: Dimensions and issues. In S. G. Assouline, N. Colangelo, J. VanTassel-Baska, & A. E. Lupkowski-Shoplik (Eds.), *A nation empowered: Evidence trumps excuses holding back America's brightest students* (pp. 9–18). Iowa City: The University of Iowa, Connie Belin & Jacqueline N. Blank International Center for Gifted Education and Talent Development.

Wai, J. (2015). Long-term effects of educational acceleration. In S. G. Assouline, N. Colangelo, J. VanTassel-Baska, & A. E. Lupkowski-Shoplik (Eds.), *A nation empowered: Evidence trumps excuses holding back America's brightest students* (pp. 73–83). Iowa City: The University of Iowa, Connie Belin & Jacqueline N. Blank International Center for Gifted Education and Talent Development.

Appendix 7.1: Practical Resource Recommendations

Institutions

» The Connie Belin & Jacqueline N. Blank International Center for Gifted Education and Talent Development: http://belinblank.org

- > Acceleration Institute: http://www.accelerationinstitute.org/
- > The Belin Family Research Library: http://bbcdata.honors.uiowa.edu:8080/webopac/main
- > Iowa Online AP Academy: http://belinblank.org/ioapa
- > Student programming (including STEM opportunities): http://belinblank.org/students
- > Belin-Blank Center Assessment and Counseling Clinic: http://belinblank.org/clinic

» Davidson Institute for Talent Development: http://www.davidsongifted.org/
» Duke University Talent Identification Program: http://tip.duke.edu/
» Johns Hopkins Center for Talented Youth: http://cty.jhu.edu/
» National Association for Gifted Children: http://www.nagc.org/
» Northwestern University Center for Talent Development: http://www.ctd.northwestern.edu
» Stanford University Education Program for Gifted Youth: http://giftedandtalented.com
» Vanderbilt Programs for Talented Youth: http://pty.vanderbilt.edu/

Recommended Reading

Among the most requested Belin-Blank Center publications are:
» *A Nation Deceived: How Schools Hold Back America's Brightest Students* (2004): http://www2.education.uiowa.edu/belinblank/pdfs/ND_v1.pdf
» The Iowa Acceleration Scale—3rd Edition (2009): http://www.greatpotentialpress.com/iowa-acceleration-scale-3rd-edition-manual
» A three-report series on the status of gifted education in rural America: *Gifted Education in Rural Schools: A National Assessment* (1999): http://www2.education.uiowa.edu/belinblank/Researchers/1999_rr_schools.pdf
» *Gifted Voices from Rural America* (2001): http://www2.education.uiowa.edu/belinblank/Researchers/2001_rr_voices.pdf
» *Gifted in Rural America: Faces of Diversity* (2006): http://www2.education.uiowa.edu/belinblank/Researchers/2006_rr_diversity.pdf
» *The Nature and Needs of Rural Gifted Programs*: http://www.ncagt.org/sites/default/files/files/RuralGifted.pdf

- » *Attending to the Gifted in Rural Schools*: http://www.aasa.org/SchoolAdministratorArticle.aspx?id=20066
- » *Meeting the Needs of the Gifted in Rural Areas through Acceleration*: http://www.davidsongifted.org/db/Articles_id_10249.aspx
- » *The Education of Promising Students in Rural Areas: What Do We Know and What Can We Do?*: http://pty.vanderbilt.edu/cms/wp-content/uploads/StambaughGiftedRural.pdf
- » *The Challenge of Being Gifted in a Rural Community*: http://tip.duke.edu/node/842

Other Resources for High-Ability Students

- » Distance Learning Resources, compiled by Johns Hopkins Center for Talented Youth: http://cty.jhu.edu/imagine/resources/distance_learning.html
- » NAGC's Gifted and Talented Resource Directory: http://giftedandtalentedresourcesdirectory.com/
- » NAGC's list of gifted and talented organizations by state: http://www.nagc.org/resources-publications/gifted-state
- » http://EdX.org: Offers a variety of courses from prestigious universities; most are offered free of charge
- » http://www.HippoCampus.org: Offers multimedia based courses for free (but no credit); can be an additional way to prepare for AP coursework and exams
- » http://www.HoagiesGifted.org: Database of resources for high-ability students, and their parents and educators
- » Gifted teachers listserv: To subscribe to the Gifted Teachers e-mail list, send an email to listserv@list.uiowa.edu and, in the text of your message (not the subject line), write: SUBSCRIBE GIFTED-TEACHERS First-Name Last-Name
- » The Virtual High School: http://thevhscollaborative.org/

Journals

- » *Advanced Development*: http://www.gifteddevelopment.com/products/adj
- » *Gifted Child Quarterly*: http://gcq.sagepub.com/
- » *Gifted Child Today*: http://gct.sagepub.com/

- *Gifted Education Communicator*: http://giftededucationcommunicator.com/
- *High Ability Studies*: http://www.tandfonline.com/toc/chas20/current#.VKMbKyvF98E
- *Journal of Advanced Academics*: http://joa.sagepub.com/
- *Journal for the Education of the Gifted*: http://jeg.sagepub.com/
- *The Rural Educator*: http://ruraleducator.net/

CHAPTER 8

Serving the Rural Gifted Child Through Advanced Curriculum

Joyce VanTassel-Baska, Ph.D., and Gail Fischer Hubbard

When we consider the vast needs of gifted students nationally, gifted students from rural areas are not frequently considered as a special group in need of differentiated services. Because of their isolation, their underfunded schools, and their lack of trained teachers, especially in specialty areas like STEM or gifted education, these students' needs are often not considered. Rural schools have enough difficulty staying afloat and providing basic and mandated services. Yet these gifted and potentially gifted students represent an important group that is in need of specialized programs and services that may advance the learning of our most able learners. The purpose of this chapter then is to focus on appropriate curriculum and program interventions for rural gifted students, based upon available research and effective practices. The interventions will be discussed at two levels: (1) at the school and community level where educators and others may offer effective services, and (2) at the classroom level where teachers may employ differentiated strategies.

Who Are the Gifted in Rural America?

Nearly 10 million students—or 20% of all students—in the United States attend school in the 49.9% of school districts that are designated as rural by federal definition based on the federal National Center for Education Statistics (NCES) urban-centric code system (Johnson, Showalter, Klein, & Lester, 2014; NCES, 2012). Although 1,972 of these districts are within a 5-mile radius of an urban-suburban area and considered fringe rural districts, 3,262 districts within 5 to 25 miles of an urban-suburban area are considered distant rural districts, and the 2,576 districts beyond a 25-mile radius are considered remote rural districts (Provasnik et al., 2007; NCES, 2012).

Using a conservative estimate, at least the top 5% of students in rural districts, approximately 500,000 students, need gifted services. Because these students reside in over 7,000 school districts, the number of students needing services in any given district, spread over the number of grades the district includes, would differ from district to district, but still would be a small number of students. This means that gifted students are frequently isolated within their classrooms and schools as well as geographically isolated from educational resources and opportunities outside of school.

Persistent, multigenerational poverty defines the lives of nearly half of all rural students (Johnson et al., 2014). The poverty rate among rural students has increased by more than 10% since 2000, with 46.6% of rural students eligible for subsidized meals (Johnson et al., 2014). In certain regions of the country, social stratification results from students in middle- and upper-class families enrolling in private schools, leaving students of poverty in the public schools (Duncan, 1999). Fundamental needs for food, clothing, and shelter also have to be considered in addition to educational opportunities in order to find and serve promising rural learners of poverty (Stambaugh, 2010).

The rural student population composition continues to change. Minority students make up 26.7% of all rural students (Johnson et al., 2014). Depending upon the region, using NCES codes, minority students may be American Indian/Alaskan Native, Asian/Pacific Islander, African American, Hispanic, and Two or More Races (Johnson et al., 2014). In four states—New Mexico, California, Alaska, and Arizona—rural minority students make up more than half of the rural student population. In the past decade, the number of rural Hispanic students has more than doubled. The publication *Gifted in Rural America: Faces of Diversity* (Colangelo, Assouline, & New, 2006) responded to the complex question of who the gifted in rural America are through a series of reflective case studies. By focusing on students of promise in two Alabama communities, on Hispanic students of promise in a bilingual program in rural Iowa, on learners of promise from families of migrant workers enrolled in advanced programs in a high school in Washington, and on students participating in a gifted program integrating educational opportunity with Hawaiian culture, this study helped to define the diverse needs of rural learners of promise.

Poverty issues are also often accompanied by minority status, an increasing issue in rural areas where minority status constitutes more than 26% of the population. Finding and serving gifted rural students from minority backgrounds requires an understanding of the culture of these students. With regard to those rural students who are English language learners (ELLs), this service also needs to include support for language learning.

Very few empirical studies have been done that lend themselves to understanding the educational outcomes for these learners. One such study has suggested that underachievement in math, in comparison to peers from suburban school districts, is often the result. In a study tracking math achievement across the K–8 spectrum, Graham and Provost (2012) found that significant differences existed at kindergarten level and continued to grow as students advanced in school. The authors suggested that parental expectations linked to their educational level might have accounted for some of the differences found. Yet rural schooling was also indicated; the authors noted that no preschool opportunities were available to rural children in the study and limited opportunities were provided afterward due to lack of teacher preparation in mathematics. In another report in Ohio, data indicate that fewer Advanced Placement (AP) courses were offered to students in rural counties than in ones that were more populous, documenting the lack of educational opportunity linked to college-level work (Candisky & Siegel, 2014). Although these studies provide some insight into the context of rural learning environments, there is also a modest amount of literature pertaining to gifted students in these contexts.

Review of the Literature

Much of the literature on rural students is contained within government or agency reports that present the overall general picture of the educational shortcomings faced by students who reside in rural areas. One report had an important quotation regarding the following issue: "When you've seen one rural area, you've seen one rural area" (Rural Poverty Research Center, 2004, p. 3). This quote exemplifies the diversity of rural areas and therefore the difficulty in setting research and policy agendas to study the phenomenon effectively.

Studies in gifted education that focus on the rural gifted attempt to document incidence rates and describe general conditions in rural schools that would impact the gifted student. Case studies that describe specific rural areas also feature a gifted student growing up in that area, providing a more specific vision of the diversity among rural areas and the myriad different problems that gifted students encounter (Colangelo, Assouline, & New, 2006). Only a few actually focus on the specific kinds of interventions that have worked and would work with this population (Stambaugh, 2010). Curriculum work in gifted education, for the most part, has not been refined to the point of studying either the contextual aspects of rural settings that would affect interventions, nor has curriculum work examined the modification necessary to adapt sufficiently for rural students.

A recent review of findings from Project Spring (Aamidor, 2007), a federally funded project that focused on the rural gifted student identification approaches, has found that:

> To effect a positive change in the academic achievement and aspiration outcomes of rural, economically disadvantaged, gifted children, the findings of this study would suggest that when alternative identification is employed, the curriculum intervention must be sufficiently challenging and consistently implemented to mediate between the expectations of school and the child's early experiences. (p. 4)

In other words, identification without faithful implementation of appropriate interventions over time will produce no effects on learning.

Yet some attempts have been made to provide appropriate intervention to the gifted rural student at secondary levels. The provision of distance learning opportunities (Colangelo, Assouline, & New, 1999) in the form of foreign language courses and advanced courses, sometimes including Advanced Placement courses, have been offered to many rural students (e.g., Barbour & Mulcahy, 2006; Murphy & Coffin, 2003). Dual enrollment arrangements (e.g., between high schools and local 4-year and community colleges) provide another way for small rural schools to expand their curricular offerings (Johnson & Brophy, 2006).

Many studies also note the importance of providing early childhood experiences for the rural child. The argument is often the same as is made for the urban child except for the issue of geographic isolation. These children cannot access so readily resources seen as common to urban children—libraries, museums, and other community agencies that offer additional educational opportunities. However, recommendations for early childhood opportunities are emerging as policy recommendations from the last two national reports on the state of gifted students and poverty (VanTassel-Baska & Stambaugh, 2006; Olszewski-Kubilius & Clarenbach, 2012).

Another area of recommendations for helping the rural gifted student has been to focus on the parents and their understanding of their child's abilities and needs (Aamidor, 2007; Cross & Burney, 2005). With regard to education in particular, various conditions in rural schools serving low-income communities can hamper opportunities for gifted students including the following: (a) distance to programs and services, (b) accessibility to resources, (c) transportation to extracurricular activities, and (d) limited interaction with other high-achieving students (Cross & Burney, 2005). In addition, participants from the Cross and Burney (2005) study cited concerns that parents of rural gifted students are unlikely to support what they do not understand or value (e.g., student involvement in gifted programs that take place in the evenings or on the weekends and that therefore interfere with family responsibilities). Care of siblings, household chores, and work to help support the family all may limit the time available for parental participation in school-related activities organized to aid the talent development of gifted students (Cross & Burney, 2005). Thus, parent education programs, held at times and in community venues more accessible and convenient to parents and community members, may help provide the needed understandings.

Working With Promising Students in Rural America: Programmatic Issues and Interventions

Because rural areas in America are so diverse, curriculum design and instructional strategies that are successful with gifted students in one community may not be effective in a different community (Johnson et al., 2014). Certain common curricular and instructional themes do emerge from the research literature and may be considered across the range of rural communities.

» **Supportive Learning Environments With Peers:** Because rural gifted students tend to have few intellectual peers in their school communities, forming communities of learners is especially important to establish supportive learning environments for these students. Such learning environments might be established through using virtual learning opportunities or through using flexible and multi-age grouping to allow gifted students to create peer groups for themselves within and across school contexts (Rogers, 2006).

» **Access to Multicultural Materials and Resources:** Because rural gifted students tend to be in geographically isolated communities, providing materials and resources with information on different cultures, different regions of the world, and, if possible, different languages, offers these students opportunities to explore worlds beyond their communities. Moreover, for minority students, such access validates their cultural identity (Colangelo, Assouline, & New, 2006).

» **Curriculum That Emphasizes Critical Thinking and Problem-Solving Skills:** Because rural gifted students tend to be in small school systems with few resources for local curriculum development, having access to nationally researched curriculum materials that provide complex and in-depth content, require critical thinking and problem solving, and provide research-based assessment of student learning is especially critical. Such curriculum provides models for thinking that they can apply to real life settings (VanTassel-Baska, 2013a).

» **Project- and Problem-Based Learning:** Because rural gifted students have very different experiences depending upon the community in which they live, these students need a range of options for project work. They also can benefit from the application of real-world higher level thinking to their work. Because rural students frequently are working independently, it is important that rubric-based assessments provide structure for the implementation of the project as well as for assessment of the final product (VanTassel-Baska, 2013a).

» **Access to a Range of Educational Opportunities:** Because gifted students in rural settings lack access to curriculum and instruction that is focused on their particular learning needs, it will be necessary for these students to access learning opportunities beyond their schools and communities. This is especially important for students who need advanced curriculum and instruction targeted in specific subject areas. It also applies to students of poverty who need access to opportunities for cultural enrichment (Lewis & Hafer, 2007).

» **Assessment of Learning in a Wider Context:** Because a rural student may be the most outstanding student in a given school or school system, it is difficult for these students to measure their learning against advanced academic standards. Nationally normed achievement tests, SAT or ACT assessments, and Advanced Placement or International Baccalaureate examinations help these students assess their learning in a wider context. Participation in talent searches at an early age also provides an excellent basis for calibrating their level of talent in a given academic area and encouraging further development in that area (Subotnik, Tai, Almarode, & Crowe, 2013).

Addressing the needs of rural gifted learners thus requires a systematic approach to program development that includes multiple avenues of access. The following programmatic approaches may be useful in working with the rural gifted.

Technology

In 2013, the Federal government established an initiative, ConnectED, to address the issue that less than 40% of public schools have high-speed Internet in their classrooms. Over 5 years, the plan is to connect 99% of America's students to the digital age through next-generation broadband and high-speed wireless in their schools and libraries. ConnectED will also provide better broadband access for students in rural areas by expanding successful efforts to connect parts of the country that typically have trouble attracting investment in broadband infrastructure (Slack, 2013). In the 1% of rural communities that are so remote that access to the Internet will remain difficult, printed resources that can be obtained through interlibrary loan programs are a crucial resource for advanced learners (Lewis & Hafer, 2007).

Establishing opportunities for students to access Internet resources is a vital curricular support. Collaboration among schools through using Internet resources supports additional interaction among advanced and gifted learners. National projects, such as JASON Learning (http://www.jason.org), managed by Sea Research Foundation, Inc., in partnership with the National Geographic Society, provide advanced learning experiences. Such learning experiences in the science, technology, engineering, and mathematics (STEM) fields are especially important for rural students who may not have access to such specialized curriculum and instruction.

These learning experiences may include competitions selected to enhance the curriculum. Equitable access for rural learners, especially for learners in school districts with persistent poverty, is a necessary component for competitions to serve as effective learning extensions (Riley & Karnes, 2007). Often competitions require a team model to be employed with a school coach, such as the Future Problem-Solving competition or the Odyssey of the Mind. These competitions provide important opportunities for the rural gifted in respect to peer interaction as well as the use of higher level thinking and problem solving. Even individual competitions like Math Counts or Young Authors can provide important understanding of competency in a given area of learning and motivate a rural student to improve even more.

The use of technology to offer advanced classes and Advanced Placement courses online provides the opportunity for academically advanced students in rural schools to take courses not offered in their high schools. Virtual Virginia (http://www.VirtualVirginia.org), an Internet academy for advanced and Advanced Placement coursework supported by the Virginia Department of Education, is just one illustration of online course offerings provided by states and school districts. The talent search universities (i.e., Northwestern, Duke, and Johns Hopkins) all offer online coursework both nationally and internationally to students who meet the relevant score criteria. Dual enrollment courses where high schools and 4-year and 2-year colleges cooperate to offer coursework may also be offered online.

Opportunities for online learning are also available beyond the collaborative offerings of states, school districts, and schools. Private for-profit groups, such as Renzulli Learning, have organized online resources that link students to project-based opportunities.

Summer, Weekend, and Afterschool Programs

Summer residential programs with academic challenge are especially critical for gifted learners from rural America. Examples of such programs include Talent Search Programs, including the Johns Hopkins Center for Talented Youth, the Northwestern Center for Talent Development, and the Duke Talent Identification Program. These programs offer a network of services beginning in third grade.

A number of states offer state-funded summer residential programs, usually housed on college campuses, to provide summer educational opportunities for advanced high school students from all regions of the state (National Association for Gifted Children [NAGC], 2013). In some instances—the Hawaiian Na Pua

No'eau Program is an example—students are served through summer residential and weekend programs (Colangelo, Assouline, & New, 2006).

Academic-Year Specialized Programs

Twelve states report that they provide state-funded academic-year residential high school programs for gifted students within the state. In addition, there are four states with legislative authorizations for early college entrance residential programs. These early entrance programs provide an accelerated set of opportunities for students in those states to bridge high school and college work at earlier ages (NAGC, 2013; Cross & Miller, 2007). In some of the states, tuition and boarding costs are covered fully by state funding. In other states, tuition and/or boarding costs may be charged. Scholarship opportunities may be available where public funding does not cover the total cost.

Both types of residential programs offer exceptional educational opportunities for gifted learners, often in state-of-the-art facilities. Although some rural gifted students may choose to remain in their communities, others choose residential programs because of the opportunity to engage in more intensive curriculum work with a more extensive intellectual peer group. Table 8.1 delineates both the high school and early college entrance residential programs for use by district level program administrators who may want to explore these opportunities as models for program offerings for rural students in their states (NAGC, 2013; Cross & Miller, 2007).

In addition, nonresident specialized high school programs serve students in multiple school districts. Whether residential or nonresidential, in 1988 the programs focused on mathematics, science, and technology established the National Consortium for Specialized Secondary Schools of Mathematics, Science, and Technology, now named the National Consortium of Secondary STEM Schools (http://www.ncsss.org), to support continuing improvement of curriculum, instruction, and services for advanced learners.

Collaborative Services

Collaborative services may be provided by regional service centers, funded by the state or organized by nonprofit efforts. Such centers can offer specialized opportunities such as advanced math programs or foreign language academies or other needed classes. Such programs provide an intellectual peer group for gifted students to provide challenge and critical feedback. They also allow for

TABLE 8.1
State-Funded Academic-Year Residential High School Programs and Early College Entrance Residential Programs With Their Websites

State	State-Funded Academic-Year Residential High School Programs	Website
Alabama	Alabama School of Mathematics and Science	http://www.asms.net
Alabama	Alabama School of Fine Arts	http://www.asfa.k12.al.us
Arkansas	Arkansas School for Mathematics, Sciences, and the Arts	http://www.asmsa.org
Illinois	Illinois Mathematics and Science Academy	http://www.imsa.edu
Indiana	The Indiana Academy for Science, Mathematics, and Humanities	http://www.bsu.edu/academy
Kansas	Kansas Academy of Mathematics and Science	http://www.fhsu.edu/kams
Louisiana	Louisiana School for Math, Science, and the Arts	http://www.lsmsa.edu
Maine	Maine School of Science and Mathematics	http://www.mssm.org
Minnesota	Perpich Arts High School	http://www.mncae.k12.mn.us
Mississippi	The Mississippi School for Mathematics and Science	http://www.themsms.org
Mississippi	Mississippi School of the Arts	http://www.msa.k12.ms.us
North Carolina	North Carolina School of Science and Mathematics	http://www.ncssm.edu
North Carolina	University of North Carolina School of the Arts	http://www.uncsa.edu
Oklahoma	Oklahoma School of Science and Mathematics	http://www.ossm.edu
South Carolina	South Carolina Governor's School for Science and Mathematics	http://www.scgssm.org
South Carolina	South Carolina Governor's School for the Arts and Humanities	http://www.scgsah.org

State	Legislatively Authorized Early College Entrance Residential Programs	Website
Georgia	Advanced Academy of Georgia	http://www.advancedacademy.org
Georgia	Georgia Academy of Aviation, Mathematics, Engineering and Science (G.A.M.E.S.)	http://www.mga.edu/games
Kentucky	The Gatton Academy of Mathematics and Science in Kentucky	http://www.wku.edu/academy
Missouri	Missouri Academy of Science, Mathematics and Computing	http://www.nwmissouri.edu/MASMC
Texas	Texas Academy of Mathematics and Science	http://www.tams.unt.edu
Texas	Texas Academy of Leadership in the Humanities	http://www.lamar.edu/texas-academy-of-leadership-in-the-humanities

students to meet and learn across district lines in their areas of strength and interest. Often these classes are also across grade levels, allowing able students to have the experience of working with older and younger peers who have similar abilities and interests. Examples of such services have been provided in the Midwest through universities such as Kalamazoo College in Michigan, where students in the region meet to do advanced math once a week, returning to their schools with the appropriate homework to last the remaining 4 days. These courses are credit bearing for students from the participating school districts.

Mentorships, Internships, and Tutorials

Of special value to the rural gifted are individualized services, provided by adult mentors who can offer expertise and role modeling. These mentors may be retired community members, current educators or professionals in the community, or university personnel who can be accessed online. Several existing models for providing these individualized mentorship opportunities can be adapted for use in rural settings (Feng, 2007; Brody, 2007).

Summer programs may include opportunities for gifted students from rural areas to serve internships in settings of business or industry, hospitals, or university research laboratories. Internships may also take place in the student's own rural community if businesses, industry, or community service organizations support such internships. Structuring internships and monitoring and assessing the learning occurring through the internship process require ongoing, consistent professional support from school-based educators.

Tutorials can provide continuing support for individual advanced learners. Tutorials are interactive, seek to teach by example, and provide information to complete a given task. Although tutorials can be online or with teachers or other professional educators, members of the community who have specific skills can offer opportunities for individual students to acquire those skills.

Because rural communities often accept and accommodate differences among learners, individual opportunities for learning can be effective enhancements beyond the school curriculum (Lewis & Hafer, 2007). Individualized opportunities, including mentorships, internships, and tutorials, may provide avenues for connection of the gifted learner with the rural community.

Strategies That Matter for Classrooms

Despite all of the recommendations that have been made around the issues facing rural gifted students, little will change for these students in the educational arena without school and classroom interventions that address their educational needs for challenge directly (Gentry, Rizza, & Gable, 2001). The Common Core State Standards (CCSS) in language arts and mathematics represent a new effort to standardize curriculum across states and to elevate the levels of thinking within these subjects to conform to 21st-century skillsets needed for college and the workplace. As we discuss the appropriate curriculum for rural gifted students, it is necessary to suggest that curriculum will be implemented in a standards-based environment where teachers will need to differentiate for these students in order for their learning level to be met.

Fortunately, there are several common points of intersection of CCSS and differentiation of curriculum for the gifted. The areas of greatest alignment occur in using higher level skills to enhance learning in literacy, with major emphases on analysis and development of argument. In mathematics, the alignment is best accomplished in the use of higher level nonalgorithmic problem-solving approaches. Strategies for accelerating the standards for use with the gifted have also been developed. These strategies are described in some detail in a set of guides developed for use by practitioners (see Hughes, Kettler, Shaughnessy-Dedrick, & VanTassel-Baska, 2014; Johnsen, Ryser, & Assouline, 2014). Thus differentiation of curriculum must begin with the new standards and proceed from that point.

There are five areas of curriculum intervention that can make a real difference in the lives of these students if they are applied faithfully and consistently over time. Acceleration, structure and scaffolding, independent learning, use of higher level questions, and the inclusion of role models are discussed in more detail below.

Acceleration

This is still the best-researched strategy for any gifted child, but for the rural gifted, it is a lifeline to advanced work at the appropriate level (Howley, Rhodes, & Beall, 2009). In the classroom, content acceleration in areas of strength is essential, especially in world languages and mathematics. The use of diagnostic testing to find appropriate skill levels in the subject is central to beginning an advanced course of study for the rural gifted child. In reading, the Lexile level on which a child is reading should be the starting point for selecting appropriate level literature and nonfiction. Educators may wish to consult Standard 10 of the Common Core State Standards (CCSS) in English Language Arts (Hughes, Kettler, Shaughnessy-Dedrick, & VanTassel-Baska, 2014) to determine the need for finding the appropriate reading level as a basis for selecting text.

Structure and Scaffolding

Because many rural students live in lower income areas as previously discussed, many may benefit from strategies designed to work with students from poverty and/or diverse students of color. Curriculum developed under Javits Grant funding is particularly useful in supporting the learning of children of poverty with high potential. Examples of such research-based curriculum include Project M^3, Mentoring Mathematical Minds, which is focused on curriculum for mathematically promising students; Project Athena, focused on support for reading comprehension, literary analysis, and persuasive writing; and Project Clarion, focused on support for the development of scientific talent (Adams & Chandler, 2014).

The use of graphic organizers coupled with templates and rubrics for product development are essential tools to ensure student success in the classroom and beyond (Stambaugh & Chandler, 2012). Providing graphic organizers and then asking students to create them for newly read material is one way to ensure they have internalized the importance of finding the significant aspects of what they have read. Moreover, graphic organizers provide a way for these students to internalize their learning for use in other learning contexts. Thus learning how to analyze difficult text through examining theme, character motivation, and author's purpose prepares a student to tackle any text, cognizant of these elements and their importance in understanding text at higher levels. Jacob's Ladder is another material that informs the progressive development of higher level skills through questions and activities. The program has been found successful, especially with rural students (VanTassel-Baska & Stambaugh, 2006).

Independent Learning

Because of the issue of isolation, it is difficult for rural students to work in collaborative groups with equally gifted members. Therefore, independent work must be used to ensure rigor and challenge for the student. However, this work must be carefully organized and tailored to ensure that it is an optimal match for the student, whether it is a full tutorial in a subject or special projects lasting for more limited time frames. Independent study opportunities also need to be monitored carefully to ensure that students acquire deeper learning and higher level skills as a result of the work.

Use of Higher Level Questions

Working with the rural gifted student requires an emphasis on inquiry, on asking questions and encouraging the same in the student. Therefore, finding opportunities to form *multiage discussion groups* for purposes of addressing the ideas found in books and the pleasure in conversation with others who are interested in the same things is a critical component for development. These may be groups formed at the local library that include adults as well as gifted students of varying ages. Film discussion groups also serve a similar function for high-level discussion of ideas.

Role Models

Strong and supportive adult role models help rural gifted students understand and respond to their communities and culture. Curriculum and instruction embedded within the community and its culture with the support of appropriate role models can increase academic success for rural learners of promise (Colangelo, Assouline, & New 2006; Stambaugh, 2010). However, students with specific academic needs will need to look beyond the community for role models. Biographies and autobiographies can become a real tool for enhancing the lives of these students by providing the real-life examples of those who have contributed to our civilization in their areas of interest. They can read about the amazing discoveries of Benjamin Franklin in science and his contributions to foreign policy as well, the solitary life of Emily Dickinson and how it influenced her work, and the contributions of the Roosevelt family to our life today.

These strategies then are the bedrock of delivering an effective curriculum to gifted learners in rural areas. Delivery will require several of the approaches discussed earlier in this chapter, especially the use of distance learning tools. Delivering effective curriculum will require targeted training of teachers who can provide the structure and scaffolding necessary for effective classroom instruction. Finally, the facilitation of services with the agencies in the local community who can provide a common space for human interaction, such as churches or libraries, will be necessary.

The following section of this chapter will provide more specific applications of these strategies for use with teachers and other educators. The examples provided are all aligned with the relevant CCSS in language arts and mathematics (VanTassel-Baska, 2013b; Johnsen & Sheffield, 2013). In science, they align with the Next Generation Science Standards (Adams, Catobish, & Ricci, 2014).

Specific Application Examples

The Use of an Independent Learning Template for Conducting Research

The following example uses the Paul model of reasoning (Paul, 2012) to construct a series of questions around which students may proceed to conduct independent research on any topic of choice or one that has been pre-assigned. The questions are nonhierarchical but use a real world approach to higher level thinking about the world. As students become proficient in using this template, the model can be extended to include more questions at higher levels, more specifications about the number of resources used, the forms of note taking to be employed, and the use of bibliographic resources and their credibility. Educators may wish to use this once in the classroom in order to clarify questions about it and then assign it for outside research work. The model and its questions should be used repeatedly for all research projects in order to build the automaticity needed by the student in doing higher level work. Assessment of the products emanating from students should be based on the elements of thinking employed as demonstrated in the questions asked:

» What do you want to know about an issue or topic? Create a list of researchable questions. (concept/content knowledge)
» What questions have priority? (purpose/goals)
» What types of data will help you best answer those questions? Where will you find them? What data sources have you examined? What is your rationale for each? What contribution do they make to your overall understanding of the topic or issue studied? (data/evidence)
» What are your results, findings, conclusions? (inferences)

» What do they imply for application in the real world and future research? (consequences/implications)

Research is reasoning. Students can develop a five- to ten-page research paper that uses these questions as the outline of the paper and provide a reference list at the end of all data sources that were used to create the paper. Then students can assess the paper on the following criteria, using a 1–5 scale: (a) the quality of research questions asked; (b) the ability to discriminate questions of importance; (c) the explanation of data source material used and the inferences drawn from the data sources; and (d) the ability to articulate logical implications of the findings.

Using a Graphic Organizer for Reading Challenging Material in All Subject Areas

Using a graphic organizer to aid rural gifted students in doing independent work often requires providing the structure and scaffolding for them to carry it out successfully. The new CCSS standards in both math and language arts encourage students to read, interpret data, and articulate their understanding of it. Thus this graphic organizer emphasizes textual analysis and is useful to promote higher level thinking about challenging texts students are asked to read. An organizer can be used in part or wholly, asking some or all of the questions or adding questions as the teacher desires. In science, organizers are an especially useful tool to read short articles about new discoveries made, often in the form of newspaper articles. In social studies, an organizer is useful as a tool to study readings about current events, whether in newspapers or magazine material online. In language arts, organizers work well for short stories and novels, selecting the questions that best fit the text. In math, organizers provide a thinking tool that employs the use of data interpretation and representation. These applications then can vary by subject as well as grade level used. The text material employed determines how challenging the assignment will be. For rural gifted students, the reading level should be at least one to two grade levels above their tested Lexile level in order to ensure sufficient challenge. The graphic may be employed in the classroom or as outside work. Figure 8.1 illustrates a graphic that can be used with a group where assignments are made for each student for part of the organizer before students share outcomes from their part with their group. Further directions to students could include the following: "Read the text provided and work on answering the questions from the graphic organizer

Advanced Curriculum

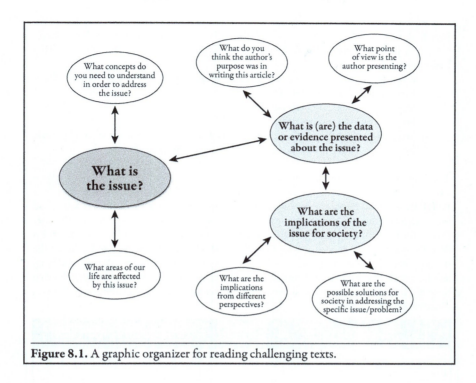

Figure 8.1. A graphic organizer for reading challenging texts.

that have been assigned to you. Represent your answers graphically or in the written form of your choice."

Use of Biography to Stimulate Interest in Careers and Life Choices

The need to expose students to direct experiences in their communities is an important part of their development. Students can learn a great deal about careers and life choices from members of their communities. However, opportunities to come to know great leaders in a number of fields are also important. In a series of readings and inquiry-based activities on leadership, students can get to know Clara Barton, Nelson Mandela, and Marie Curie, along with other great leaders, as exemplars of the fields of social work, politics, and science. They can also study their talent development process over their lifetimes and how their contributions to society were forged from the crucible of their lives. Through such study they can become close to understanding how they themselves may begin a journey of self-discovery and clarification of interests and abilities. The example of Picasso in Figure 8.2 is particularly apt for considering

Part I. Read online biographical material about Picasso, his life, and work (see websites below). Focus on his contributions to the art world that have qualified him to be called a leader in his field.
- http://www.pablo-picasso.paintings.name/biography (Advise students to read all sections of the biography at this site.)
- http://www.biography.com/people/pablo-picasso
- http://www.pablopicasso.org
- http://www.youtube.com/watch?v=_fNvBJAJw4s (for a 5-minute video clip made by a young student for show and tell and posted on April 23, 2009)

Then complete the activities in the next sections.

PART II. How was Picasso an art visionary with respect to form, theme, subject matter, and use of elements such as perspective, color, and mood? Ask students to select (or you may choose for them) three paintings representing three distinct periods in Picasso's career: his Blue Period, his Rose Period, and his Cubist Period. Have them compare and contrast the styles of these paintings, demonstrate how each period was evolutionary in Picasso's thinking, and how each of these periods contributed to the field of art as a whole. Use the following template to record responses, and then create a concept map that demonstrates Picasso's contributions to painting.

Periods	Picture selected	Style characteristics	Nature of evolution	Contribution to art
Blue				
Rose				
Cubist				

PART III. Create a journal entry, using the following questions as prompts:
- What did you learn from the biographical study of Pablo Picasso that is useful or interesting in your understanding of leadership?
- In what ways is Pablo Picasso a role model for you and other aspiring artists? Are there facets of Picasso's personality or behavior that you dislike or disdain?
- In what ways is leadership in the arts like leadership in the sciences? In what ways is it different?
- What were the original contributions that Picasso made to the art world?

Figure 8.2. Picasso: Leadership in art. Adapted from *Change for tomorrow: A leadership unit for middle school students* (Book 2; pp. 64–67), by J. VanTassel-Baska and L. Avery, 2012, New York, NY: Taylor & Francis. Copyright 2012 by Taylor & Francis. Adapted with permission.

the role of the arts in society and how one man had the capacity to change that world dramatically through innovative forms and the use of social criticism. The activities cited may be done independently or in dyads. They are designed for grades 6–8 but may be used through high school and can be done online as the material is readily available there (VanTassel-Baska & Avery, 2012).

These three examples provide a picture of the basis for classroom work with the rural gifted as well as a roadmap for outside project work that would be completed independently. They provide the most important aspects of a strong curriculum including the following: (a) advanced work; (b) structure for the student; (c) scaffolding of products to be created; (d) opportunities for creativity and interest-based activities; and (e) role models through the use of biographical material found online.

Teacher Preparation for Working With the Rural Gifted

Programs that support gifted learners beyond the classroom setting require personnel with an understanding of the subject matter and of the needs of gifted learners, a high-quality advanced curriculum based on best gifted education practices and student interests, and evaluation of student growth and program effectiveness (VanTassel-Baska, 2007). In order for students to receive appropriate programs and services in rural areas, their teachers need to have preparation in content, content pedagogy, and strategies, such as those delineated in this chapter. Evidence of effective professional development models have been discussed elsewhere (see Chapter 15 in this volume).

These models may need to be tailored for delivery to teachers in rural areas in much the same way that services are tailored for the students—through online modules and regional collaborative professional development sessions and through being provided differentiated materials and resources for use in classrooms. Professional development opportunities should be ongoing throughout the school year and provide real time conversations about practice among teachers in the same school and across schools in the same district. Moreover, developing a university partnership would enhance the possibilities for sustained connections, especially with one of the 25 centers for gifted education in the United States. In addition, over 150 universities offer some form of coursework in gifted education that may provide greater depth of training than is available through professional development workshops. Given the critical need for trained personnel in gifted education in rural areas, reaching out to universities for assistance is an important step in the right direction.

Conclusion

This chapter on the curriculum needs of the rural gifted has provided a portrait of what these children are like demographically, what they are like in respect to the geographic areas in which they reside, and therefore what their resultant needs are for programs and services, provided both in and outside of school. The themes of isolation and lack of movement toward opportunity complicate the suggestions made. However, the authors have also provided several concrete ideas for educators working in rural areas to offer advanced work to these rural students of promise. With such assistance, these students may come to realize their considerable potential in relevant domains of learning.

References

Aamidor, S. (2007). Identification and intervention for rural, low-income, gifted students: A follow-up study. *Gifted Children, 2,* 2–5.

Adams, C. & Chandler, K. (2014). *Effective program models for gifted students from underserved populations.* Waco, TX: Prufrock Press.

Adams, C., Cotabish, A., & Ricci, M. (Eds.). (2014). *Using the Next Generation Science Standards with gifted and advanced learners.* Waco, TX: Prufrock Press.

Barbour, M., & Mulcahy, D. (2006). An inquiry into retention and achievement differences in campus based and web based AP courses. *Rural Educator, 27*(3), 8–12.

Brody, L. (2007). Counseling highly gifted students to utilize supplemental educational opportunities: Using the SET Program as a model. In J. VanTassel-Baska, (Ed.), *Serving Gifted Learners Beyond the Traditional Classroom* (pp. 123–145). Waco, TX: Prufrock Press.

Candisky, C., & Siegel, J. (2014). Rural kids get fewer AP classes. *The Columbus Dispatch.* November 30.

Colangelo, N., Assouline, S. G., & New, J. K. (1999). *Gifted education in rural schools: A national assessment.* Iowa City: University of Iowa, Belin-Blank Center for Gifted Education and Talent Development.

Colangelo, N., Assouline, S. G., & New, J. K. (2006). *Gifted in rural America: Faces of diversity.* Iowa City: University of Iowa, Belin-Blank Center for Gifted Education and Talent Development.

Cross, T., & Burney, V. (2005). High ability, rural, and poor: Lessons from Project Aspire and implications for school counselors. *Journal of Secondary Gifted Education, 16,* 148–156.

Cross, T. & Miller, K. (2007). An overview of three models of publically funded residential academies for gifted adolescents. In J. VanTassel-Baska (Ed.). *Serving Gifted Learners Beyond the Traditional Classroom* (pp. 81–103). Waco, TX: Prufrock Press.

Duncan, C. M, (1999). *Worlds apart: Why poverty persists in rural America.* New Haven, CT: Yale University Press.

Feng, A. (2007). Developing personalized learning experiences: Mentoring for talent development In J. VanTassel-Baska (Ed.), *Serving Gifted Learners Beyond the Traditional Classroom* (pp. 189–212). Waco, TX: Prufrock Press.

Gentry, M., Rizza, M. G., & Gable, R. K. (2001). Gifted students' perceptions of their class activities: Differences among rural, urban, and suburban students. *Gifted Child Quarterly, 45,* 115–129.

Graham, S., & Provost, L. (2012). Mathematics achievement gaps between suburban students and their rural and urban peers increase over time. *Carsey Institute Issues Brief.* Montpelier: University of New Hampshire.

Howley, A., Rhodes, M., & Beall, J. (2009). Challenges facing rural schools: Implications for gifted students. *Journal for the Education of the Gifted, 32*(4), 515–536.

Hughes, C., Kettler, T., Shaughnessy-Dedrick, E. & VanTassel-Baska, J. (2014). *A teacher's guide to using the Common Core State Standards in English language arts.* Waco, TX: Prufrock Press.

Johnsen, S. K., Ryser, G. R., & Assouline, S. G. (2014). *A teacher's guide to using the Common Core State Standards in mathematics.* Waco, TX: Prufrock Press.

Johnsen, S. K., & Sheffield, L. (Eds.). (2013). *Using the Common Core State Standards in mathematics with gifted and advanced learners.* Waco, TX: Prufrock Press.

Johnson, J., Showalter, D., Klein, R., & Lester, C. (2014). *The condition of rural education in the 50 states.* Washington, D.C.: Rural School and Community Trust.

Johnson, T. E., & Brophy, M. (2006). Dual enrollment: Measuring factors for rural high school student participation. *Rural Educator, 28*(1), 25–32.

Lewis, J., & Hafer, C. (2007). The challenges of being gifted in a rural community. *Digest of Gifted Research*, Duke Talent Identification Program. Retrieved from http://tip.duke.edu/node/842

Murphy, E., & Coffin, G. (2003). Synchronous communication in a web-based senior high school course: Maximizing affordances and minimizing constraints of the tool. *American Journal of Distance Education, 17,* 235–246.

National Association for Gifted Children. (2013). State of the states in gifted education. Washington, D.C.: Author.

National Center for Education Statistics. (2012). *Number of public schools districts, by district, local and state or jurisdiction: School year 2011–12.* Washington, D.C.: U.S. Department of Education.

Olszewski-Kubilius, P., & Clarenbach, J. (2012). *Unlocking emergent talent: Supporting high achievement of low-income, high-ability students.* Washington, D.C.: National Association for Gifted Children.

Paul, R. (2012). *Critical thinking.* Sonoma, CA: Foundation for Critical Thinking

Provasnik, S., Kweal Ramani, A., Coleman, M. M., Gilbertson, L., Herring, W., & Xie, Q. (2007). *Status of education in rural America* (NCES 2007-040). Washington, D.C.: National Center for Education Statistics, Institute of Education Sciences, U.S. Department of Education.

Rogers, K. (2006). *A menu of options for grouping gifted students.* Waco, TX: Prufrock Press.

Riley, T., & Karnes, F. (2007). Competitions for gifted and talented students: Issues of excellence and equity. In J. VanTassel-Baska, (Ed.), *Serving gifted learners beyond the traditional classroom* (pp. 145–167). Waco, TX: Prufrock Press.

Rural Poverty Research Center. (2004). *Place matters: Addressing rural poverty.* Columbia, MO: Author.

Slack, M. (2013). ConnectED. Washington, D.C.: The White House Blog. Retrieved from www.whitehouse.gov/blog/2013/06/06

Stambaugh, T. (2010). The education of students in rural areas: What do we know and what can we do? In J. VanTassel-Baska, (Ed.), *Patterns and profiles from promising learners in poverty* (pp. 59–83). Waco, TX: Prufrock Press.

Stambaugh, T., & Chandler, K. (2012) *Curriculum for underrepresented gifted populations.* Waco, TX: Prufrock Press.

VanTassel-Baska, J., & Avery, L. (2012). *Change for tomorrow: A leadership unit for middle school students.* Waco, TX: Prufrock Press.

VanTassel-Baska, J. (2013a). Curriculum issues: Curriculum, instruction, and assessment for the gifted: A problem-based learning scenario, *Gifted Child Today, 36*(1), 71–75.

VanTassel-Baska, J. (Ed.). (2013b). *Using the Common Core State Standards for English language arts with gifted and advanced learners.* Waco, TX: Prufrock Press

VanTassel-Baska, J., & Stambaugh, T (2006). *Overlooked gems: A national perspective on low-income promising learners.* Washington, D.C.: National Association for Gifted Children.

VanTassel-Baska, J. L. (Ed.). (2007). *Serving gifted learners beyond the traditional classroom: A guide to alternative programs and services.* Waco, TX: Prufrock Press.

CHAPTER 9

Programming and Rural Gifted Learners
A Review of Models and Applications

Joan D. Lewis, Ph.D.

Introduction

In its review of the *State of the Nation in Gifted Education* (2012–2013) report conducted by the National Association for Gifted Children (NAGC) and the Council of State Directors of Programs for the Gifted (CSDPG), NAGC asserted that "to thrive in the 21st century we need a renewed commitment to excellence" (NAGC, n.d., p. 3). It is not enough to strive to close the achievement gap with slower students, as important as it is; *all* students, each individual student, need to be taught so they strive to reach the highest level of which they are capable, regardless of their entry points.

A recent analysis of data from the National Assessment of Educational Progress (NAEP) evaluated achievement gaps between high-achieving students. Very little gain was noted in reading and math for students from low socioeconomic families compared to those with higher socioeconomic status (Plucker, Burroughs, & Song, 2010). Although these data were not disaggregated by rurality, many of these students were likely from sparsely populated and isolated areas. Indeed, the Rural Family Economic Success Action Network's (n.d.) analysis of the 2014 Kids Count Data Book found that approximately 24% of children living in poverty are from the least densely populated rural counties and are more apt to experience long-term and extreme poverty (O'Hare, 2014).

Plucker et al. (2010) pointed out that focusing only on minimum competency or only on excellence is not apt to close the various achievement gaps, but rather the focus should be on both simultaneously. For rural communities, this is a major issue. They often need assistance developing the resources to fund quality education for all their students, including their most able (Lewis, 2009). The variability between individuals accounts for just what that level of excellence is independent of environmental differences. Closing the achievement gap caused by those environmental differences is critical; at the same time, policy makers and educators need to remember to include high-performing students in their plans. Providing quality gifted education services is essential for our nation's youth regardless of where they live in order to successfully compete in the global society (NAGC & CSDPG, 2013).

Educational leaders in rural areas struggle with meeting mandated reform initiatives due to competing priorities, high poverty, and the need to wear multiple hats in order not only to fulfill the mandated policy requirements but also to meet the expectations of the community. This is even more difficult when working with gifted students. Many times there is not a critical mass of gifted learners yet these students live in rural areas just as they do in urban and suburban areas. As such, they need appropriate services as part of an equitable education. The goals of this chapter are to investigate current gifted programming models and each model's suitability for implementation in rural schools and then provide examples of current reform initiatives and other models/strategies educators and leaders may consider when planning schoolwide programs for gifted learners.

Programming Models for the Gifted

Program Models for Rural Gifted: Do We Need to Make a Distinction?

Gentry (2009) described a gifted education program model as "a comprehensive set of responsive services spanning grade levels and subject areas, providing a variety of well-conceived opportunities to different students who have potential talent in many different domains" (p. 262). Program models are used to help educators structure curriculum and services for their students. Rural schools face many challenges that require flexible thinking in the program models they adopt including: (a) a smaller percentage of gifted students in the building that may not allow for critical mass in order for any one advanced class to be delivered; (b) diversity of communities and families even within the same district; (c) lack of material and financial resources coupled with remote geographical locales that may mean restricted professional development and/or gifted educators being shared across buildings and fewer qualified teachers due to lower pay. Selecting a model that will provide an effective guide for rural schools' gifted education programs is particularly challenging. The major and widely popularized models were not developed with rural students in mind. Coleman and Cross (2001) questioned if there is any benefit from the use of one *specific* model over another. Further, they asked if there is evidence that some content is particularly beneficial for advanced development. They concluded that a "right" answer doesn't appear possible. Instead, the most useful approach is to select the model that best suits a particular school and community. This approach is useful in all settings and especially in rural schools.

Many curriculum and program models have been reviewed to some extent. In one of the most comprehensive reviews conducted by VanTassel-Baska and Brown (2007), authors identified 20 program and curricular models. The following 11 models were evaluated in depth: (a) Julian Stanley's Talent Search; (b) Joseph Renzulli's Enrichment Triad, later infused into the Schoolwide Enrichment Model (SEM); (c) Howard Gardner's Multiple Intelligences (MI); (d) John Feldhusen's Purdue Three-Stage Enrichment Model and Purdue Secondary Model; (e) C. June Maker's The Matrix; (f) Carol Ann Tomlinson and colleagues' Parallel Curriculum Model (PCM); (g) Carol Schlichter's Talents Unlimited; (h) Robert Sternberg's Triarchic Componential Model; and (i) Joyce VanTassel-Baska's Integrated Curriculum Model (ICM). Betts' Autonomous Learner Model, Kaplan's Grid, and Meeker's Structure of Intellect were not included because they were "lacking clear research evidence of effectiveness," as were some other early models (VanTassel-Baska & Brown, 2007, p. 344). In their review, the models of Feldhusen, Renzulli, Schlichter, Stanley, Sternberg, and VanTassel-Baska met most or all of the specific criteria and demonstrated at least some support for gifted students' improved learning compared to nontreatment group students. Much of the evidence for Schlichter's Talents Unlimited model, however, was based on nongifted students (VanTassel-Baska & Brown, 2007, p. 351). From their analysis, they assembled several suggested "best practices" for instruction within any gifted program model (VanTassel-Baska & Brown, 2007, pp. 351–352):

» group[ing] gifted students instructionally by subject area for advanced curriculum work that would be flexibly organized and implemented

based on students' documented level of learning within the subject area;
» embedding multiple higher level thinking models and skills within core subject area teaching to enhance learning;
» the use of inquiry as a central strategy to promote gifted student learning in multiple modalities; and
» the use of student-centered learning opportunities that are issue- or problem-based and relevant to the students' world.

But what is the potential use of each model highlighted by VanTassel-Baska and Brown (2007) for gifted learners in rural settings? What should we consider? Based on the unique features of rural schools and potential barriers to implementation, as explained earlier in this chapter, criteria were crafted to examine popular programming models with rural schools in mind (see Table 9.1). Four curriculum/program models reviewed by VanTassel-Baska and Brown (2007) have documented evidence of success for gifted learners and meet at least half of the established criteria in the second column of Table 9.1: the Integrated Curriculum Model (ICM), the Purdue Three-Stage Model, the School-wide Enrichment Model (SEM), and the Talent Search model. Each of these models is discussed in more detail with applicability for rural schools. Because rural schools are not alike and other models beyond the limitations of this chapter may be appropriate for certain districts, Appendix 9.1 documents other known programming models as well as strengths and considerations for use in rural schools. The ones listed in the chapter are bolded in the appendix charts. For a more detailed description of each model, see Renzulli, Gubbins, McMillen, Eckert, and Little (2009).

Review of Selected Models

Integrated Curriculum Model (ICM, Joyce VanTassel-Baska). The ICM is comprised of three dimensions: (a) advanced content, (b) high-level process/product work, and (c) intra- and interdisciplinary concept development and understanding through studying issues and themes (Davis, Rimm, & Siegle, 2011). Gifted learners' need for advanced content delivered at a faster pace than typical is the focus of the content dimension. Content specialists need to be able to consult and collaborate with one another to develop the level of content and delivery required for highly able learners to progress at an appropriate level for them while ensuring all relevant standards are met. Professionals'

TABLE 9.1
Rural School Characteristics and Subsequent Criterion for Gifted Programming Models

Rural School Characteristics	Criteria for Programming Models
May not have a critical mass of gifted students	Can be implemented regardless of the number of gifted learners within a grade or district
Diversity of different rural communities—even within the same district	Flexibility of the model for different settings
Lack of material and financial resources	Doesn't require expensive materials or several individuals to implement with fidelity
Competing priorities of leaders and teachers in rural schools	Time commitment for teachers is not extensive
Fewer qualified teachers	Doesn't require a specialized gifted specialist to be onsite (versus online)
Professional development costs	Isn't dependent upon specialized professional development beyond basic knowledge of gifted learners
Remote geographic area locales	Isn't dependent upon the availability of high-speed Internet for resources
Need for research-based materials and models	Has a strong research base, preferably piloted with rural learners—even if not disaggregated

habits of mind are an important component of the advanced content dimension along with pertinent topics and concepts. Students develop advanced processes (e.g., critical and creative thinking, independent thinking, components of metacognition). Product requirements are integrated with activities focused on accelerated advanced content. The processes and products students create can be discipline specific or applicable to any subject. Interdisciplinary themes structure gifted learners' acquisition of content that exceeds discipline specific instruction. A focus on building understanding of concepts and generalizations across and within disciplines addresses gifted learners' need for greater complexity in their studies (Davis et al., 2011). Likewise, approaching key issues from various perspectives aids students' ability to think more broadly about the world around them. Specialized professional development is needed to effectively instruct students using the William and Mary units (VanTassel-Baska & Brown, 2007; VanTassel-Baska, 2013). The ICM can adapt as needed to fit with a district's current standards as well as the Common Core State Standards (VanTassel-Baska, 2013).

Researchers have documented educational gains for G/T learners in various school settings—including rural—compared to control groups using the core subject curriculum units that are an integral part of the ICM (VanTassel-Baska & Brown, 2007). Longitudinal studies also show efficacy for use with a variety of gifted learners (see VanTassel-Baska & Stambaugh, 2008 for a compilation of studies). VanTassel-Baska (2013) reported recent research showing benefits for low-income students and those of color with academic promise. She also cites evidence of educational benefits of the ICM from several quasi-experimental studies over the past two and half decades. Teacher training is an important component for the units to be implemented with fidelity. The ICM was developed specifically for intellectually and/or academically gifted learners. A great deal of research has gone into the development of the College of William and Mary interdisciplinary curriculum units. Each one is structured to build strong metacognitive skills while students are acquiring high level content (Davis et al., 2011; VanTassel-Baska & Brown, 2007; VanTassel-Baska, 2013). ICM units are available in language arts grades 1–12, science grades 1–8, social studies grades 2–12, and mathematics grades K–8. (See tinyurl.com/k6d7bnm for more information on the available units.)

The ICM provides one of the most rigorous educational opportunities of any model. Considerable training on the use of the curriculum units is essential. Meeting that requirement may be difficult in a rural school unless some accommodation is made without jeopardizing the quality of each curriculum unit. One of the many teleconferencing tools might be used for a trained gifted specialist to deliver the necessary professional development to those who need it. Rural teachers across several sites, even from different states, could receive training simultaneously. Another option is for local, regional, state, or national professionals to commit to delivering some of the instruction with cross-site transmission of academic content. Some distance learning systems allow interaction and grouping between sites so gifted learners would gain not only academically but also from social interaction with their intellectual peers. States or NAGC might be prevailed upon to support the development of training or delivery of instruction for rural communities that want to employ the ICM for their gifted learners. Six of the eight evaluation criteria can be clearly met in rural schools if approached creatively. A gifted specialist with the necessary professional development using the William and Mary units or the required training could be provided online, although this would require high-speed Internet. The various trade books could be borrowed from libraries across the region rather than purchasing them; however, the units themselves are expensive, especially when teachers' editions are included. Table 9.2 lists some selected models and their suitability for rural gifted students.

TABLE 9.2
Selected Models and Their Suitability for Rural Gifted Students Based on Set Criteria

Criteria	ICM	Purdue	SEM	Talent Search
Can be implemented regardless of the number of gifted learners within a grade or district	Yes	Yes	Yes	Yes
Model is flexible or adaptable to different settings	Yes	Yes	Yes	Yes
Can be implemented without expensive materials or additional purchases	No	Yes	Yes	Yes
Time commitment for teachers is extensive	No	Yes	No	No
Can be implemented without a specialized gifted specialist onsite (versus online)	Yes	Yes	Yes	Yes
Requires specialized professional development beyond basic knowledge of gifted learners to implement with fidelity	Yes	No	No	No
Can be implemented without the availability of high-speed Internet for resources	Yes	Yes	Partially	Yes
Has a strong research base, preferably piloted with rural learners—even if not disaggregated	Yes	Moderate	Yes	Yes

Purdue Three-Stage Model (John Feldhusen & Penny Kolloff). VanTassel-Baska and Brown (2007) reported that some research has been conducted supporting the effectiveness of this model to deliver academic and creative benefits for gifted learners. The Three-Stage Model's goals for identification and programming are clear, yet adaptable, and easily evaluated. The model is an uncomplicated framework for instruction that adapts to any content area because it doesn't prescribe a set curriculum. Rather, it depicts a set of learning processes such as creative and critical thinking skills, creative problem solving, and independent learning. Focus is on high-level differentiation of content, process, and product applied to any grade level to move students from novice to practitioner. To accomplish this, teachers need to be highly qualified with training in gifted education and have in-depth content knowledge, especially at the secondary levels. Implementation is sufficiently flexible that schools can select one of several delivery modes: pull-out, cluster grouping, self-contained content classrooms, whole-school enrichment, or afterschool or Saturday programs. All learners in the regular classroom can benefit provided the material is differentiated for the varying ability levels and entry points throughout grades K–12 (Moon, Kolloff, Robinson, Dixon, & Feldhusen, 2009).

Mastering the core curriculum is critical to any application of this model, elementary or secondary. The role of the teacher changes as students take on more responsibility for their learning with the teacher becoming a facilitator by the time students have progressed to Stage 3. In the first stage, students learn skills for higher level thinking and both divergent and convergent creativity using core content. The motivational activities can be completed during a typical class period. As students' skills develop, the teacher moves them into Stage 2, during which they continue to develop their thinking and creative problem solving skills with more challenging materials and practical situations, such as solving atypical math problems and those found in problem-based learning units. Students focus more on building their knowledge and skills in talent areas, preparing them to take on independent study of self-selected topics (Moon et al., 2009).

Throughout the stages, students are honing their self-monitoring, self-evaluation, and self-awareness abilities, enabling them to assume more ownership of their learning. These important life skills are extended in Stage 3 with students using what they have been learning to function more as professionals in their areas of interest. Products need to be developed for real audiences in preparation for their adult lives. Students develop proficient metacognitive skills through evaluating their own work and that of their peers. By this time, students should be directing their own activities with the teacher serving as a facilitator (Moon et al., 2009).

Secondary students continue to expand their proficiency with the core curriculum in talent areas and refine their application of essential process skills. At this level, the Three-Stage Model contains 11 components offering a comprehensive program of choices for gifted adolescents as they develop their own learning plans:

- counseling services,
- seminars,
- advanced placement courses,
- honors classes,
- math/science acceleration,
- foreign languages,
- arts,
- cultural experiences,
- career education,
- vocational programs, and
- extraschool instruction.

Three options for applying the Three-Stage Model at the secondary level include: differentiating advanced classes, offering independent study opportunities, and arranging disciplinary and interdisciplinary seminars (Moon et al., 2009). These examples are suited to rural high schools and middle schools by making use of materials on the Internet and face-to-face cross-site groupings that could reach far beyond the school and state.

Teachers trained in gifted education need to be able to locate, develop, and use a range of materials even though this model is not as resource-intensive as some and is also fairly low cost. As with any model used to structure gifted education services, a well-trained gifted teacher on site or within easy access would be best at all grade levels. Professional development for teachers to learn how to differentiate for gifted learners is essential, although it could be provided via distance technologies with teachers practicing the skills in their own classroom with peer support. High-speed Internet service opens up a wide range of resources for all levels of learning although the model isn't dependent on it. While access is still being extended to rural and other isolated areas, it is an essential support for modern education. The Three-Stage Model meets six and a half of the important rural needs for gifted programs; the demonstrated research support is not as strong as for the ICM, SEM, and Talent Search (VanTassel-Baska & Brown, 2007). The other three models have been used in many more contexts than has the Three-Stage Model. Easy access to a gifted specialist could be provided via high speed Internet or with an itinerant teacher. Either way, the specialist would need to visit frequently for enough time to satisfy student learning needs and to assist teacher development of high-quality, motivational activities that are a basis for this model.

Schoolwide Enrichment Triad Model (SEM, Joseph Renzulli). This widely used enrichment program applies gifted education methodologies to general education classrooms, having been used in schools across the country as well as internationally. Decades of research support it and several of its components and numerous books and articles have been published on this model. The methods (e.g., enrichment triad, curriculum compacting, independent study focused on student interest areas, real products for real audiences) are applicable to all grade levels and content areas in grades K–12. Research has demonstrated its effectiveness with high-ability learners in a variety of school sizes and locations, and students from a range of socioeconomic levels and ethnically diverse populations (Reis, n.d.). Compacting, a key instructional strategy, has research documenting that students' achievement is not harmed from its use (Renzulli et al., 2009). Much of the research lacks a comparison or control group, which would show the SEM approach provided more achievement than another program (VanTassel-Baska & Brown, 2007).

The SEM calls for 10%–20% of the student body being identified for the talent pool (Renzulli et al., 2009). In a small rural K–5 school with perhaps 10 children in each grade at most, that would be 6–12 members across all grades. In a K–8 school with the same general number of students per grade, approximately 9–18 students could be eligible for the talent pool. It would be possible to cross-age group students by educational need or learning level. The model consists of Type I, II, and III enrichment with varying levels of complexity. Type I enrichment is for everyone. The challenge for rural schools becomes what the rest of the students do while specialized enrichment activities are being provided to selected students if there are no extra staff. One teacher could teach the "talent" group with the other teachers doubling up to teach the remaining students. This arrangement might be an option for Type II activities. Type III activities might be handled on an individual basis matching the student with an appropriate teacher or a community mentor (Renzulli et al., 2009).

The SEM's requirement for a talent pool in each major subject at the secondary level would need to be modified for many if not all attendance centers serving rural populations. At this point a gifted specialist that can consult with content area teachers and possibly supervise Type 3 independent projects becomes important to the quality of learning for G/T students in academic and affective realms. Using distance learning technology, one gifted specialist might work with groups of gifted learners in their talent areas achieving talent pools across grade levels and schools for each subject. Mentors from professions or universities might be identified to consult with students as needed, if accessible to rural areas, although sometimes a difficulty due to distance and access. These individuals and their colleagues might be the audience for student projects with some presented to professional organizations or submitted for publication when appropriate (Renzulli et al., 2009).

The recently developed Renzulli Learning, an online application of the basic enrichment triad model (see http://www.renzullilearning.com), might be used in any school for all three enrichment types and varying levels of student readiness and interest regardless of class size reducing the need for an onsite gifted specialist and training on differentiation for the elementary grades. Field (2009) evaluated quantitative data from Renzulli Learning, finding achievement gains in some content areas for at-risk urban students after an intervention of 16 weeks. Reis (n.d.) described a 2006 honors project by Eleck that assessed students' success using Renzulli Learning, in which students were able to use the program with little instruction both in the regular and "enrichment" classroom. Eleck's and Field's studies suggest promise for rural students using Renzulli Learning as a way to differentiate their learning without employing additional personnel. Reliable access to high-speed Internet connections is necessary for effective instruction using this or any online instructional and content approach. The SEM rates a seven and a half on the rural evaluation criteria scale. The school would need enrichment materials, which entail an added cost. An onsite gifted specialist would not be necessary if one was available on a shared basis. High-speed Internet access would be needed for online materials whether for Renzulli Learning or other online sources, or for locating more traditional materials and possibly for obtaining gifted specialist's services. Renzulli et al. (2009) and Reis, Gelbar, and Renzulli (2013) explained the components of SEM and its research base and described the use of Renzulli Learning for readers who want more detail. VanTassel-Baska and Brown (2007) also described the background and research support for this model.

Talent Search Model (Julian Stanley). Unlike any other model, this is essentially an above-level testing program designed to identify students ready for advanced coursework and offer them instructional opportunities that match their strength areas. The title of Stanley's (2000) publication explains the purpose of his talent search model: "Helping students learn only what they don't already know." Csikszentmihalyi, Rathunde, and Whalen (1993) stressed that *"challenging opportunities* in academic settings" are critical for highly able students to remain engaged in their talent area(s) (as cited in Assouline, Blando, Croft, Baldus, & Colangelo, 2009, p. 3; italics are original). Students in any size school could benefit from this model with little additional cost.

The effectiveness of the talent search model has been demonstrated by extensive research spanning more than 40 years (Assouline & Lupkowski-Shoplik, 2012). A previous 20-year longitudinal study is currently being replicated. When completed in 2022, the researchers will have 50 years of data. It all began in 1971 with Julian Stanley's Study of Mathematically Precocious Youth (SMPY, now CTY) at Johns Hopkins University (VanTassel-Baska & Brown, 2007). There are four specific talent search locations across the country (see Chapter 5 for more information on talent searches across the United States). Initially, the program was strictly a diagnostic-prescriptive acceleration model for highly gifted seventh-grade (and occasionally a few eighth-grade) math students. They were given the Scholastic Aptitude Test (SAT, now called the Scholastic Assessment Test), an assessment normally used to evaluate college readiness of high school juniors and seniors. Scoring at the 51st percentile, as compared to college-bound high school young men, identified these students as needing accelerated mathematics instruction. Students were encouraged to take a variety of accelerative options (see Stanley, 1979, as cited in Davis et al., 2011). Fast-paced, 3-week summer classes, usually taught by college professors that required students to study 5–6 hours a day, delivered impressive results. Students were able to master 1–2 years of high school math, typically algebra and geometry, during those 3 weeks (Davis et al., 2011).

By 1979, Stanley added the SAT-V to identify gifted students with high verbal abilities, scores from the American College Test (ACT), and academic counseling. The summer programs have expanded to include many Advanced Placement (AP) courses. Additional courses are offered on Saturdays and weekends during the year and still more are offered online. Highly gifted elementary students in grades 2–6 (grade level depends on the university sponsor of the program) are assessed using above-level tests, such as EXPLORE and PLUS. Identified students from all these programs are offered enrichment course opportunities. Several studies show the long-term benefits of the Talent Search (as cited in Davis et al., 2011).

More rural students could have the opportunity to participate in one of the formal talent searches if someone in the district, regional service unit, state gifted association, or state department of education would take the responsibility of e-mailing a staff member the basic information (e.g., benefits of participation, eligibility criteria, testing schedule, application link) for the closest talent search program. A teacher, principal, or secretary could then forward the e-mail to parents and students. Every year the same e-mails could be sent with only minor date modifications and e-mail updates. Whether a student takes part in a formal search program or not, each program has many online resources listed on its website. A community member or group might be willing to arrange for funding assistance for registration and other supports as needed. Another arrangement could be for a district employee or state gifted organization committee or member to undertake some or all of these duties.

Furthermore, the Talent Search model could be modified slightly and used as a regular program in rural schools. The diagnostic-prescriptive model could be implemented at any grade level with or without standardized testing as the diagnostic piece. End of text assessments or those from higher grade levels could be used in most content areas for students of any age who consistently demonstrate they have mastered the state standards in one or more domains of knowledge. Teachers knowledgeable with both the student and the content area(s) could develop a scope and sequence to meet each student's strengths and relative weaknesses. This is a comparatively inexpensive program for increasing academic rigor for highly able students. Although the testing and program development would take a little time from one or more teachers, additional instructional materials would not necessarily be needed. The student(s) could walk to the appropriate grade-level class (e.g., reading, math, spelling, science, social studies), making this an attractive model for rural schools. For a more complete program, content differentiation to add enriching depth and breadth should also be part of learners' educational experiences. Access to advanced content beyond available high school courses and teacher experience would eventually be necessary for a few students entailing Internet access, although not necessarily high speed. Gifted students would also benefit from online communication with academic peers, especially in the upper grades. This is the only model that meets all eight evaluation criteria for ease of application in rural schools.

Alternative Programming

Besides structured programming models, different states have developed interesting options that may benefit rural gifted students and could be replicated elsewhere.

Governor's Schools. "The Governor School model is a highly effective way of delivering an accelerated and enriched curriculum that is not available to students in a regular high school setting" (McHugh, 2006, p 185). McHugh's review of research on governor's school participation showed students built friendships, gained confidence, and expanded their understanding of other perspectives, although the limited study designs failed to provide evidence of social and emotional benefits from participation as she had hoped.

Magnet schools. State or regional magnet schools may be an education option for rural gifted students. Several states (e.g., Maine, Mississippi, North Carolina) have built them over the last few decades, particularly targeting high-ability youth. Many large city districts have created them as well. Plucker et al.'s (1996, as cited in Lawrence, 2009) study found that 6th–12th-grade students attending Maine's magnet school expressed higher aspirations and perceived greater support for achievement than regular education students in typical high schools. Although there were limitations to the study that could affect the results, the finding is worth considering (Lawrence, 2009). The Magnet Schools of America's 2013 annual report stated that there are approximately 4,000 magnet schools in the United States. They range from elementary through high school and from district only to statewide. The National Consortium for Specialized Secondary Schools of Mathematics, Science and Technology (NCSSS, 2014) listed schools in 32 states that meet their guidelines. At least some of these schools are statewide, offering alternative educational opportunities for gifted students who choose to apply.

Iowa Excellence Program. Iowa Excellence begins with above-level testing similar to Stanley's Talent Search, then provides challenging learning opportunities through the Mitchell Excellence Curriculum delivered through the Israel Arts and Science Academy (IASA), located in Jerusalem. The math and science units these educators created were directed toward rural students in particular (Assouline et al., 2009, pp. 6–7). The IASA curriculum is also being used in a few locations in the U.S. (see http://tinyurl.com/ka8jmda). Advanced Placement courses are made available to Iowa students by the Iowa Online AP Academy run through the Belin-Blank Center at the University of Iowa. Research for Talent Search and ICM models provide support for the Iowa Excellence Program (Assouline et al., 2009). Although the complete model can be employed only in Iowa, the concept is well worth replication by other states in conjunction with one or more colleges or universities. The Iowa Excellence Program applies to limited grade levels and content; however, it is an interesting approach for serving rural students.

Other Local or State Programs Worth Replicating

Many states, especially those with larger rural populations have found innovative ways to provide opportunities for their students in rural areas. Although there are many and this is not a comprehensive list, a few a programs are described here. Table 9.3 includes a web address and grade levels served for the following programs as well as others that are worth investigating.

Aspirnaut™ Summer Research Internships for High School Students. This intense internship housed on the campus of Vanderbilt University is for high school students with career interests in science and engineering. Participants spend 6 weeks conducting biomedical research in STEM areas mentored by personnel from the university's Medical Center (Aspirnaut™, 2014, see http://www.aspirnaut.org). This remarkable experience is free for the students. Their BEAMING program (see http://www.aspirnaut.org/what-we-do/beaming-stem-labs) connects students in rural schools with Vanderbilt faculty and graduate and undergraduate students through videoconferencing. Students in rural schools, with the help of a teacher's aide or teacher help students, conduct science experiments and theme-based modules specifically designed by Vanderbilt faculty and students. Preliminary data show that this model has a positive impact on students' science achievement and understand-

TABLE 9.3
Alternative Materials and Programs

Online Materials and Programs	Grade	Website
Aspirnaut™ programs: STEM learning, summer internships at Vanderbilt University	Rural high school	http://www.aspirnaut.org/
Assessment and LEarning in Knowledge Spaces (ALEKS): commercial online math program	K–12	http://www.aleks.com, http://www.aleks.com/about_aleks/overview
Advancement Via Individual Determination (AVID): teacher training; focuses on students underrepresented in college; funding supports	K–12, summer STEM for middle school, higher education, career readiness	http://www.avid.org
Boys' State & Nation Girls' State	Summer after junior year	http://www.legion.org/boysnation/stateabout, http://www.alaforveterans.org/ala-girls-state/
Connections Academy: accredited by one or more of six regional accrediting organizations	Free K–12, gifted, honors, AP	http://www.connectionsacademy.com/
Governor's Schools	High school, usually summer of junior year	http://www.ncogs.org/index.php/programs-by-state
Hugh O'Brian Youth Leadership Program (HOBY)	High school sophomores	http://www.hoby.org/
Iowa Online AP Academy for students in IA	Belin-Blank Center, University of Iowa	http://www2.education.uiowa.edu/belinblank/students/ioapa/
The Jack Kent Cooke Foundation College Scholarship Program (other scholarships listed)	College	http://www.jkcf.org/scholarship-programs/college-scholarship
The Jack Kent Cooke Foundation Young Scholars Program	Eighth grade through high school	http://www.jkcf.org/scholarship-programs/young-scholars/
Jason Learning	STEM K–12	http://www.jason.org/

Table 9.3. continued

Online Materials and Programs	Grade	Website
Khan Academy	K–12+	http://www.khanacademy.org/
National Argonaut Program	Freshman or sophomore year of high school	http://www.jason.org/national-argonaut-program
North Carolina Investing in Rural Innovative Schools	High school	http://ncnewschools.org/educators-administrators/how-we-do-it/rural-schools-nc-iris
Project Lead The Way (PLTW): web-based, nonprofit organization	K–12 STEM curriculum	http://www.pltw.org
Renaissance Learning	K–12, Math, reading	http://www.renaissance.com
Renzulli Learning: web-based; based on research for Enrichment Triad Model; CompassLearning; RtI grant money	K–12	http://renzullilearning.com
Rural Connections at CTY	Seventh through ninth graders nationally	http://cty.jhu.edu/scholarships/jack_kent_cooke/index.html
Stanford University Online High School, fully accredited	Grades 7–12	http://ohs.stanford.edu
Summer Honors Program Educational Service Unit, Holdrege, NE	Grades 8–12, based on teacher nomination	http://esu11.org/departments/gifted-education/summer-honors-program
Talent Search Programs	Grades 6–12	http://www2.ed.gov/programs/triotalent/index.html
University of Nebraska online high school, fully accredited	Core, elective, and AP online courses	http://highschool.nebraska.edu/

ing of STEM (see http://www.aspirnaut.org/what-we-do/beaming-stem-labs). Funding comes from the National Institutes of Health (NIH) and the National Institute of Diabetes and Digestive and Kidney Diseases' (NIDDK) Short-Term Education Program for Underrepresented Persons (STEP-UP) grants. Other grants from the NIH, National Science Foundation (NSF), or other such funding agencies might be available for universities in other states. Search for suitable research funding proposals (RFPs) from these organizations; a quick Google search using "research funding announcements" delivered numerous possibilities.

Iowa Online AP Academy. The Belin-Blank Center at the University of Iowa provides an opportunity to take Advanced Placement classes for in-state students, an outreach that is essential for rural gifted learners. Universities in other states could emulate this model. High-ability youth across the state would benefit. Two or more states might coordinate the development and delivery of AP courses to reduce duplication of expenses and trained personnel. Results would mean far more bright rural students would have access to educational opportunities similar to peers in more populous localities.

North Carolina Investing in Rural Innovative Schools. This program "is aimed at exposing all high school students to a college-ready culture and creating new opportunities for all students to graduate from high school with some college credit" free of tuition costs (North Carolina Investing in Rural Innovative Schools, 2014, para. 1). Funding comes from a $15-million-dollar U.S. Department of Education grant and some matching private monies spread over 5 years. This model for providing advanced and supportive learning to rural schools in North Carolina is worth notice by other state departments of education and their community college and university systems.

The Summer Honors Program (SHP). Summer Honors is a competitive 2-week advanced program for students in grades 6–12 in rural Holdrege, NE. Begun in 1971, its strong and supportive alumni group is tribute to the quality of the experiences. Teachers come from many states and at least one other country. Some of the teachers are former students; most are so committed they return each year, as do many of the students. Both teachers and students are housed with community volunteers. Colangelo, Assouline, and New (1999, p. 35) described the program in *Gifted Education in Rural Schools: A National Assessment* as helping students make lifelong friends and giving them the opportunity to see a larger world. Other small communities could develop a similar program.

Young Scholars Program. Funded by The Jack Kent Cooke Foundation (2013) for "exceptionally promising students across the nation who have financial need," this program includes "comprehensive advising and financial support from the eighth grade through high school" (para. 1). Other educational foundations in conjunction with educational institutions could set up a similar scholarship and support system targeting rural students in particular.

Talent search programs. Talent searches continue to follow the basic model originally developed by Julian Stanley more than four decades ago. Program websites frequently provide learning materials and classes for academically talented students and resources for parents. Participants in their searches who meet specific criteria receive recognition, online resources, and become eligible for appropriately challenging educational opportunities to stretch their minds and maintain their interest in learning.

Linking Gifted Programming Models to Educational Reform Initiatives: RtI as a Model

Given the competing priorities of mandated reform initiatives, gifted services are likely to be overlooked or given a backseat on the priority list. In addition, leaders may see gifted programming and specific reform models as incompatible or separate. However, the alternative programs, programming models, and special opportunities can become part of mandated reform. One popular reform initiative, Response for Intervention (RtI; currently implemented in many states) can easily coincide with gifted programming. Merging reform initiatives such as RtI with solid gifted programming options can be a win-win for rural districts that need to save money, deal with limited special populations, and work with limited numbers of faculty and staff.

RtI is an easy fit for this type of merger. RtI begins with research-based curriculum, then matches the level of instruction with students' readiness, unlike reactive approaches to students with learning struggles that wait until students fail before beginning to teach them at the level they need. So, too, can potentially gifted learners receive the appropriate level of instruction without waiting for formal identification, provided that the assessments used for screening and progress monitoring have a high enough ceiling. Because many educators are already rethinking how students need to be taught so every child benefits, RtI appears to be a promising model for reaching gifted learners wherever they live and attend school.

Despite the expectations of the Individuals With Disabilities Education Act (IDEA; 2004), not all school districts or states have adopted RtI. Nevertheless, a logical first step in reviewing its implications for the field of gifted education is to begin with students who are twice exceptional (2e), meaning both gifted and learning disabled. Yssel, Adams, Clarke, and Jones (2014) discussed RtI for learners who are 2e and named numerous gifted and talented specialists who expressed concern for locating and serving 2e students (e.g., Adams, Yssel, & Anwiler, 2013; Crepeau-Hobson & Bianco, 2011; Volker, Lopata, & Cook-Cottone, 2006). Finding a model for identifying students' strengths in addition to their weaknesses would relieve a lot of suffering that these students and their families frequently experience. Harnessing their talents could have wide-ranging benefits, too. There are at least two models for working with 2e students: Baum's Talent Centered Model for Twice Exceptional Students (Baum, 2009; Baum et al., 2014) and the new Challenge Leading to Engagement, Achievement, and Results (CLEAR, McCallum et al., 2013).

Yssel et al. (2014) described universal screening of all students with quality assessments to determine who may need differentiated curriculum and instruction in order to demonstrate their interests and strengths, even when core curriculum is excellent. This screening should start in preschool and kindergarten so the benefits of instructional modifications begin early in a child's life before underachievement can set in. RtI is one method for accomplishing this goal (Horne & Shaughnessy, 2013). Yssel et al. (2014) concluded that components of Tier 1 would benefit other at-risk students too, including advanced learners. These students would also be identified if a strength-based model is institutionalized. Otherwise, these students risk wasting a lot of time practicing what they already know. Yssel et al.'s (2014) Table 2 on Dually Differentiated Interventions at RtI Tier 1 (pp. 47–48) displayed excellent guidelines for developing appropriate interventions for a 2e student. Their instructional examples could serve as a beginning guide for differentiating for other gifted learners.

Hughes and Rollins (2009) asserted a basic tenet of RtI is that Tier 1 curriculum needs to be high level and stimulating for all students, including those who are gifted. Tier 2 interventions might include enrichment and/or acceleration in domains of strength for individual students. Teachers could manage these modifications with contracts and develop compacting plans with the assistance of a gifted specialist. Finally, Tier 3 would consist of one or more forms of rapid acceleration (e.g., skipping one or more grades, early enrollment in AP courses, college courses in high school, entering college early).

Universal screening and progress monitoring are advantageous components of RtI for identifying and serving GT learners. Several experts have expressed concern that grade-level assessments are typically used for these assessments. Typical measures may not have a high enough ceiling to identify gifted learners (e.g., Bianco, 2010; Brown, 2011; Coleman & Johnsen, 2011; Hughes & Rollins, 2009; Johnsen & Sulak, 2013); may not recognize gifted students' academic growth, even when some students may be twice exceptional (e.g., Baum, Cooper, & Neu, 2001; Crepeau-Hobson & Bianco, 2011; Yssel et al., 2014); or may miss many gifted students who are English language learners (e.g., Bianco & Harris, 2014; Ford & Trotman Scott, 2013). Employing above-grade-level assessments when appropriate for universal screening and progress monitoring could provide the accountability.

Coleman and Shah-Coltrane (2011) envisioned Response to Intervention as a way to nurture potential. They compare progress monitoring to the Schoolwide Enrichment Model's (SEM) pre-assessment. Instruction is determined by what children already know and still need to learn. It has the potential to provide a more individualized education for every student, regardless of strengths and weaknesses or even if he or she is still learning English.

Four small qualitative studies evaluated RtI implementation in rural schools (see Greenwood et al., 2011; Robinson, Bursuck, & Sinclair, 2013; Shepherd & Salembier, 2011; Thompson & Fearrington, 2013). Findings showed that pre-K schools were just beginning to use RtI and found printed models a valuable resource (Greenwood et al., 2011). At the elementary level, evidence-based instruction, a central component of RtI, was difficult to implement and adequate professional development was essential, yet funds to pay for it were limited (Robinson et al., 2013). They emphasized that state-supported professional development was essential for rural districts. Implementation efforts in Shepherd and Salembier's (2011) study revealed an increase in data-based decision making, greater collaboration among SPED and classroom teachers, a better understanding of their RtI process, and changes in the role of principals to instructional leader. Adopting RtI requires major structural changes that challenge previously held beliefs and affect school culture. Thompson and Fearrington's (2013) study suggested that teachers need to become familiar with how the reform affects them so they aren't as easily intimidated. Support for teachers during the change process needs to reflect transitions in their concerns over time.

Research identifying and improving learning for gifted students with RtI could not be located. Nevertheless, the model may hold promise as a way to recognize talent in the general classroom and identify through assessment that a student has mastered the material. Thus, students' readiness for different learning opportunities is emphasized (Brown, 2011). Gifted and talented students are usually required to "learn" what they already know. The RtI concepts of universal screening and progress monitoring with end-of-unit or out-of-level assessments could put an end to this lack of awareness by teachers.

The models previously outlined in this chapter easily fit the RtI model. The ICM in conjunction with strengths of Response to Intervention (e.g., universal screening; progress monitoring; high-level, evidence-based general education curriculum) has the potential to increase advanced learning for rural gifted students. In Tier 1, the ICM can vary the reading level of a subject area and introduce specific process skills resulting in more sophisticated products. The use of scaffolds, such as literature webs, makes enhanced learning for many students possible in the general classroom. Similarly, scaffolds can enable problem-based learning opportunities for all learners. Tier 2 learning would only be available to more advanced readers (two or more grades above their placement and identified gifted learners). The ICM curriculum units would be used in Tier 3 to encourage individual development similar to other models' in-depth learning dimensions (VanTassel-Baska, 2013).

Similarly, SEM combined with RtI would be one option for a rural school searching for a model to provide more advanced learning for their GT students in addition to enriching the whole student body. Meshing Renzulli Learning (or other online resources) with SEM and RtI could ameliorate limited access to gifted specialists in rural communities. Renzulli et al. (2009) and Reis, Gelbar, and Renzulli (2013) described using SEM with RtI for reaching talented learners. They reported that one of the many benefits of RtI is that it targets the intensity of instructional supports to the level of student need. Reis et al. (2009) described Tier 1 and Type I enrichment as being general enhancements of the regular curriculum suitable for all students, such as strategies to build thinking and feeling skills. Tier 2 is still in the regular classroom. Type II enrichment for talent pool students would include more specific differentiation, such as curriculum compacting and some basic research methods to learn more about a topic of interest when students have mastered the core material. Type III enrichment would coincide with RtI's third tier. Gifted learners would receive educational guidance and support, including greater depth of individual research.

The Three-Stage Model also easily meshes with the concepts and strategies of the three tiers of a strength-based Response to Intervention. Tier 1 would consist of differentiated content and strategies from the Stage 1 delivered in the regular classroom. Depending on the number of students identified through universal screening and progress monitoring as needing more advanced differentiation from Stage 2, students could be clustered in one classroom or cross-age clustered. Cross-age clustering is a useful strategy for students in Stage 3.

Grouping students across grade levels so the teacher could facilitate a variety of students simultaneously allows for more flexibility to accommodate student needs.

The Talent Search Model also fits nicely into a strength-based RtI framework. High-quality curriculum is basic to any RtI model as a necessity for all students. Universal assessment and progress monitoring, both requirements of RtI, would only need to be modified by including above-level assessments to raise the ceiling so gifted learners' achievement could be identified. These students would be served through RtI's Tiers 2 or 3 in one or more content areas, progressing through required standards at a suitable pace for them. Differentiated instruction to add depth and breadth should be part of the curriculum at any level.

Synthesis of Ideas

After reviewing the large majority of program and curriculum models developed specifically for gifted learners as well as a few models originally created for other purposes, the feasibility of building a separate GT program within most rural schools does not appear practical for the delivery of quality enrichment. An exception would be those districts that bus their students from across a wide area to a central location so there are multiple sections of each grade. Then a separate gifted program could use cluster grouping within or across grade levels, pull-out or push-in programs, or occasionally even a separate class. For those districts, program model options are considerably broader (see Appendix 9.1). Still, the models discussed at length in this chapter are possibly the strongest choices because most of them have research evidence of their effectiveness, and many specifically for gifted learners.

Regardless of model, the level and quality of the curriculum are crucial for gifted and talented learners. Azano, Callahan, Missett, and Brunner (2013) studied the fidelity of curriculum for gifted learners in pull-out and self-contained classes in rural schools as part of a larger study. They found the most common rural school challenges (e.g., limited funding, staff, professional support, resources for students' learning, and time) frequently reported by other researchers along with a few specific to rural GT teachers. Some teachers of gifted serviced very large case loads in several schools. Their classes might range from one student to a large number of students drawn from most, or all, of the elementary grade levels. Driving over long distances to reach these students was exhausting for the teachers. Fidelity of curriculum delivery in this study was negated in some instances when GT teachers decided parts of the prescribed language arts content were too difficult for their third-grade gifted students and selected easier material (Azano et al., 2013). These educators might have pre-assessed the students and provided scaffolds if necessary to allow students to successfully tackle the intended materials. Gaining experience with challenging content and processes is a basic tenant of gifted and talented education. How often do GT teachers disregard what they learned during training for a particular curriculum or during classes or professional development?

It is essential that curriculum planning and instruction for GT learners is based on high-quality core curriculum, is supported by all relevant standards, and is differentiated through enrichment and acceleration appropriate to the readiness of each individual. Research-based models such as those provided in this chapter help guide the selection of strategies and materials (see Gifted Education Programming Standard 3 for guidance, NAGC, 2010). Outside sources are often needed to accomplish this goal. Sometimes developing the community's or state's capacity to serve rural gifted and talented learners is appropriate.

Regardless of the number of students at any one attendance center, availability of highly qualified staff for all content domains and especially gifted education may remain a major challenge, especially for very small schools. These latter schools are the ones that need to approach the education of their gifted learners in creative and perhaps less common ways.

Every program for gifted learners, despite size and location, should be developed and delivered with the 2010 NAGC Pre-K Grade 12 Gifted Standards in mind (see http://tinyurl.com/nj64ltx for an overview and links to the individual standards). These standards describe six fundamental "learner outcomes," each with one or more "evidence-based practices" for each standard. Standard 5 applies to programming for gifted and talented learners. Its seven outcomes for students are critical components for any program.

Concluding Thoughts

Increasingly depth, breadth, and complexity of enrichment and acceleration will require considerable knowledge and experience teaching gifted and talented learners and familiarization with specific content, regardless of educational model selected. For gifted and talented learners to truly gain academically, specialized personnel are needed. Although that has been a challenge for rural areas, regional consortia and educational service units could provide support. Additional training and support could be institutionalized through state-level gifted associations, NAGC, and university faculty specializing in gifted education. The cost of professional development and relevant instructional materials quickly adds up and could easily become burdensome for many rural schools and districts. This is a large area of need that local and state businesses could work to support, as could service organizations from more affluent parts of the state. Additionally, some state gifted organizations offer scholarships for students to attend a special program and for teachers to take a class on gifted education. They might also be willing to help provide the needed funding for talent search programs, specialized resources, or other expenses within their districts or states, regardless of program model choice. NAGC and CEC-TAG might offer similar supports. NAGC already offers professional webinars. Perhaps these organizations could help with the funding for teachers who cannot afford the registration fee.

Working together educators across the country and even internationally can improve the learning of their students. Good ideas know no borders. Technology is increasingly making wide-ranging collaboration possible. Tapping into service groups, professional organizations, businesses, industry, and the higher education system could help develop the necessary supports and funding to assist financially limited rural schools improve education for their gifted learners. Local, state, and national elected and appointed officials need to take responsibility for the increasing numbers of students who attend rural schools and help provide the infrastructure that will improve education for all, not focus solely on urban and suburban localities.

Ultimately, whichever gifted program model or combination of program models a district adopts isn't as important as building educator and community support for high-quality education for *every* student, including gifted learners. Their teachers need not be responsible for implementation on their own. A world of resources, including experts in many fields of study and materials for advanced learning, await their discovery. Technological advances have shrunk our world and made many forms of communication possible and will doubtless continue unabated. Educators, community members, and their students only need to reach out and make use of these tools.

References

Adams, C. M., Yssel, N., & Anwiler, H. (2013). Twice-exceptional learners and RtI: Targeting both sides of the same coin. In M. R. Coleman & S. K. Johnsen (Eds.), *Implementing RTI with gifted students: Service models, trends, and issue* (pp. 229–252). Waco, TX: Prufrock Press.

Aspirnaut™. (2014). Summer research internships for high school students. Retrieved from http://www.aspirnaut.org/what-we-do/summer-research-internship-for-rural-high-school-students/

Assouline, S. G., Blando, C. A., Croft, L. J., Baldus, C. M., & Colangelo, N. (2009). Promoting excellence through enrichment. In J. S. Renzulli, E. J. Gubbins, K. S. McMillen, R. D. Eckert, & C. A. Little (Eds.), *Systems & models for developing programs for the gifted and talented* (pp. 1–16). Waco, TX: Prufrock Press.

Assouline, S. G., & Lupkowski-Shoplik, A. (2012). The talent search model of gifted identification. *Journal of Psychoeducational Assessment, 30*(1), 45–59.

Azano, A. P., Callahan, C. M., Missett, T. C., & Brunner, M. (2014). Understanding the experiences of gifted education teachers and fidelity of implementation in rural schools. *Journal of Advanced Academics, 25*(2), 88–100.

Baum, S. M. (2009). Talent centered model for twice exceptional students. In J. S. Renzulli, E. J. Gubbins, K. S. McMillen, R. D. Eckert, & C. A. Little (Eds.). *Systems and models for developing programs for the gifted & talented* (pp. 17–48). Waco, TX: Prufrock Press.

Baum, S. M., Cooper, C. R., & Neu, T. W. (2001). Dual differentiation: An approach for meeting the curricular needs of gifted students with learning disabilities. *Psychology in the Schools, 38*(5), 477–490.

Baum, S. M., Schader, R. M., & Hébert, T. P. (2014). Through a different lens: Reflecting on a strengths-based, talent-focused approach for twice-exceptional learners. *Gifted Child Quarterly, 58*(4), 311–327.

Bianco, M. (2010). Strength-based RtI: Conceptualizing a multi-tiered system for developing gifted potential. *Theory Into Practice, 49*(4), 323–330.

Bianco, M., & Harris, B. (2014). Strength-based RTI: Developing gifted potential in Spanish-speaking English language learners. *Gifted Child Today, 37*(3), 169–176.

Brown, E. F. (2011). Is Response to Intervention and gifted assessment compatible? *Journal of Psychoeducational Assessment, 30*(1), 103–116.

Colangelo, N., Assouline, S. G., & New, J. K. (1999). *Gifted education in rural schools: A national assessment.* Iowa City: The Iowa University, Connie Belin & Jacqueline N. Blank International Center for Gifted Education and Talent Development.

Coleman, L. J., & Cross, T. L. (2001). *Being gifted in school: An introduction to development, guidance, and teaching.* Waco, TX: Prufrock Press.

Coleman, M. R., & Johnsen, S. K. (Eds.). (2011). *RtI for gifted students: A CEC-TAG educational resource.* Waco, TX: Prufrock Press.

Coleman, M. R., & Shah-Coltrane, S. (2011). Remembering the importance of potential: Tiers 1 and 2. In M. R. Coleman & S. K. Johnsen (Eds.), *RtI for gifted students: A CEC-TAG educational resource* (pp. 43–62). Waco, TX: Prufrock Press.

Crepeau-Hobson, F., & Bianco, M. (2011). Identification of gifted students with learning disabilities in a Response-to-Intervention era. *Psychology in the Schools, 48,* 102–109.

Csikszentmihalyi, M., Rathunde, K., & Whalen, S. (1993). *Talented teenagers: The roots of success and failure.* New York, NY: Cambridge University Press.

Davis, G. A., Rimm, S. B., & Siegle, D. (2011). *Education of the gifted and talented* (6th ed.). Boston, MA: Pearson.

Eleck, S. (2006). *Students' perceptions of Renzulli Learning Systems.* Unpublished honors project, Neag School of Education, University of Connecticut.

Field, G. B. (2009). The effects of the use of Renzulli Learning on student achievement in reading comprehension, reading fluency, social studies, and science: An investigation of technology and learning in grades 3–8. *iJET, 4(1),* 29–39.

Ford, D. Y., & Trotman Scott, M. (2013). Culturally responsive Response to Intervention: Meeting the needs of student who are gifted and culturally different. In M. R. Coleman & S. K. Johnsen (Eds.), *Implementing RTI with gifted students: Service models, trends, and issues* (pp. 209–228). Waco, TX: Prufrock Press.

Gentry, M. (2009). Myth 11: A comprehensive continuum of gifted education and talent development services: Discovering, developing, and enhancing young people's gifts and talents. *Gifted Child Quarterly, 53*(4), 262–265.

Greenwood, C. R., Bradfield, T., Kaminski, R., Linas, M., Carta, J. J., & Nylander, D. (2011). The Response to Intervention (RTI) approach in early childhood. *Focus on Exceptional Children, 43*(9), 1–22.

Horne, J., & Shaughnessy, M. F. (2013). The Response to Intervention program and gifted students: How can it facilitate and expedite educational excellence for gifted students in the regular education setting? *International Journal of Academic Research Part B, 5*(3), 319–324.

Hughes, C. E., & Rollins, K. (2009). RtI for nurturing giftedness: Implications for the RtI school-based team. *Gifted Child Today, 32*(3), 31–39. Retrieved from http://eric.ed.gov.proxy.lib.siu.edu/PDFS/EJ849373.pdf

Johnsen, S. K., & Sulak, T. N. (2013). Screening, assessment, and progress monitoring. In M. R. Coleman & S. K. Johnsen (Eds.), *Implementing RTI with gifted students: Service models, trends, and issue* (pp. 26–46). Waco, TX: Prufrock Press.

Individuals With Disabilities Education Act, 20 U.S.C. § 1401 et seq. (2004).

Jack Kent Cooke Foundation. (2013). Young scholars program. Retrieved from http://www.jkcf.org/scholarship-programs/young-scholars/

Lawrence, B. K. (2009). Rural gifted education: A comprehensive literature review. *Journal for the Education of the Gifted, 32*(4), 461–494.

Lewis, J. D. (2009). The challenges of educating the gifted in rural areas. In F. A. Karnes & K. R. Stephens (Eds.). *Practical strategies series in gifted education.* Waco, TX: Prufrock Press.

Magnet Schools of America. (2013). *2013 annual report: Taking bold steps toward a brighter future.* Washington, D.C.: Author.

McCallum, R. S., Bell, S. M., Coles, J. T., Miller, J. C., Hopkins, M. B., & Hilton-Prillhart, A. (2013). A model for screening twice-exceptional students (gifted with learning disabilities) within a Response to Intervention paradigm. *Gifted Child Quarterly, 57*(4), 209–222.

McHugh, M. W. (2006). Governor's Schools: Fostering the social and emotional well-being of gifted and talented students. *Journal of Secondary Gifted Education, 17*(3), 50–58.

Moon, S. M., Kolloff, P., Robinson, A., Dixon, F., & Feldhusen, J.F. (2009). The Purdue Three Stage Model. In J. S. Renzulli, E. J. Gubbins, K. S. McMillen, R. D. Eckert, & C. A. Little (Eds.), *Systems and models for developing programs for the gifted and talented* (pp. 289–322). Waco, TX: Prufrock Press.

National Association for Gifted Children. (2010). *2010 Pre-K–Grade 12 Gifted Programming Standards.* Retrieved from http://www.nagc.org/resources-publications/resources/national-standards-gifted-and-talented-education/pre-k-grade-12

National Association for Gifted Children. (n.d.). *State of the nation in gifted education: Work yet to be done.* Washington, D.C.: Author. Retrieved from http://tinyurl.com/Kllcf2j

National Association for Gifted Children, & the Council of State Directors of Programs for the Gifted. (2013). *State of the states in gifted education: National policy and practice data 2012–2013*. Washington, D.C.: Authors. Retrieved from http://tinyurl.com/lhtfpzh

National Consortium for Specialized Schools of Mathematics, Science and Technology. (2014). Profile and member directory. Chevy Chase, MD: Author.

North Carolina Investing in Rural Innovative Schools. (2014). Retrieved from http://ncnewschools.org/educators-administrators/how-we-do-it/rural-schools-nc-iris

O'Hare, W. (2014). *Poverty is a persistent reality for many rural children in U.S.* Retrieved from http://www.prb.org/Publications/Articles/2009/ruralchildpoverty.aspx

Plucker, J. A., Burroughs, N., & Song, R. (2010). *Mind the (other) gap! The growing excellence gap in K–12 education*. Bloomington: School of Education, University of Indiana.

Reis, S. M. (n.d.). *Research that supports using the Schoolwide Enrichment Model and extensions of gifted education pedagogy to meet the needs of all students*. Retrieved from http://www.gifted.uconn.edu/sem/semresearch.html

Reis, S. M., Gelbar, N. W., & Renzulli, J. S. (2013). *The Schoolwide Enrichment Model: Responding to talent within an RtI Framework*. In M. R. Coleman & S. K. Johnsen (Eds.), *Implementing RTI with gifted students: Service models, trends, and issues* (pp. 123–148). Waco, TX: Prufrock Press.

Renzulli, J. S., Gubbins, E. J., McMillen, K. S., Eckert, R. D., & Little, C. A. (Eds.). (2009). *Systems and models for developing programs for the gifted and talented*. Waco, TX: Prufrock Press.

Robinson, G. G., Bursuck, W. D., & Sinclair, K. D. (2013). Implementing RTI in two rural elementary schools: Encouraging beginnings and challenges for the future. *The Rural Educator, 34*(3), 1–9.

Rural Family Economic Success Action Network. (n.d). *Rural counts: 6.1 million kids in poverty*. Retrieved from http://rufes.org/2014/10/06/rural-child-poverty/

Shepherd, K., & Salembier, G. (2011). Improving schools through a Response to Intervention approach: A cross-case analysis of three rural schools. *Rural Special Education Quarterly, 30*(3), 3–15.

Stanley, J. C. (2000). Helping students learn what they don't already know. *Psychology, Public Policy, and Law, 6*(1), 216–222.

Thompson, L. J., & Fearrington, J. Y. (2013). Teacher concerns pertaining to Response to Intervention. *School Psychology Forum: Research in Practice, 7*(3), 65–75.

VanTassel-Baska, J. (2013). The Integrated Curriculum Model: A basis for RtI curriculum development. In M. R. Coleman & S. K. Johnsen (Eds.), *Implementing RTI with gifted students: Service models, trends, and issues* (pp. 169–186). Waco, TX: Prufrock Press.

VanTassel-Baska, J, & Brown, E. F. (2007). Toward best practice: An analysis of the efficacy of curriculum models in gifted education. *Gifted Child Quarterly, 51*(4), 342–358.

VanTassel-Baska, J., & Stambaugh, T. (2008). *What Works: 20 years of research and curriculum development for gifted learners, 1988-2008*. Retrieved from http://eric.ed.gov/?id=ED506369

Volker, M. A., Lopata, C., & Cook-Cottone, C. (2006). Assessment of children with intellectual giftedness and reading disabilities. *Psychology in the Schools, 43,* 855–869.

Yssel, N., Adams, C., Clarke, L. S., & Jones, R. (2014). Applying an RTI model for student with learning disabilities who are gifted. *Teaching Exceptional Children, 46*(3), 42–52.

Appendix 9.1: Models for Structuring Programs, Curriculum, Evaluation, Collaboration, and Conceptions of Gifted Students and Services

Models	Research evidence of effectiveness with gifted	Focus	Strengths for rural schools	Weaknesses for rural schools
Curriculum Models				
An Antimodel[1]	No direct evidence	Curriculum-based differentiation and acceleration	Works in gifted or regular classroom, large or small number of students	Needs teacher expertise with gifted; difficult to implement; elementary only
Autonomous Learner Model (ALM; Betts & Carey, 2013)[1]	No direct evidence	Enrichment	Works in gifted or regular classroom, large or small number of students, all grades and content areas; can be scheduled period at secondary levels	Needs local gifted specialist, professional development on model and materials; needs money for materials; time to implement
Catalyst Model: Resource Consultation and Collaboration[1]	No direct evidence	Collaboration and consultation, not direct instruction	Works in gifted or regular classroom, large or small number of students, all grades and content areas; gifted specialist is shared between schools	Needs gifted specialist, professional development on differentiation for gifted, common planning time; may require long driving time from school to school
Challenge Leading to Engagement, Achievement, and Results (CLEAR; McCallum et al., 2013)	Little evidence	Enrichment	Rural schools with pull-out and special-class delivery; could be adapted to small number of students	Needs teacher expertise with gifted; needs source of enriched curriculum

Appendix 9.1. *continued*

Models	Research evidence of effectiveness with gifted	Focus	Strengths for rural schools	Weaknesses for rural schools
Cognitive-Affective Interaction Model (Friedman & Lee, 1996)	Little evidence	Enrichment	Works in gifted or regular classroom, large or small number of students, all grades and content areas	Need teacher expertise with gifted, professional development on gifted and model
Differentiation[1]	No direct evidence, related research lends support	Enrichment	Works in gifted or regular classroom, large or small number of students, all grades and content areas	Needs ongoing professional development on differentiation, especially for gifted; difficult to do well; time intensive to develop and implement
DISCOVER Assessment and Curriculum Model[2]	Moderate (VanTassel-Baska & Brown, 2007)	Identification and Enrichment	Parts can be implemented separately, can be used with all ages & contents; identifies & serves students with ethnic differences too	Difficult for small districts; requires professional development on identification & curriculum; time intensive to develop & implement
Enrichment Matrix[1]	No direct evidence	Enrichment	Individualized program, works with large or small number of students, all grades & content areas	Needs teacher expertise with gifted; time intensive to develop & implement
Enrichment Triad[2]	Some research (VanTassel-Baska & Brown, 2007)	Enrichment	Works in gifted or regular classroom, large or small number of students, all content areas, adapts to student interests	Limited talent pool; needs teacher expertise with gifted, especially for Type III activities, professional development on gifted; primarily for elementary
The Grid[1]	No direct evidence	Differentiated enrichment curriculum	Works in gifted or regular classroom, large or small number of students, all grades and content areas	Needs ongoing professional develop on differentiation for gifted; time intensive to develop and implement

Appendix 9.1. continued

Models	Research evidence of effectiveness with gifted	Focus	Strengths for rural schools	Weaknesses for rural schools
Integrated Curriculum Model[1,2]	Evidence from research on each type of unit, range of student characteristics (Hockett, 2009; VanTassel-Baska & Brown, 2007; Renzulli et al., 2009)	Advanced enrichment	Curriculum units for most grades in main content areas; could be taught by off-site teacher using Internet	Needs specialized professional development to teach units with fidelity; expensive materials
Integrative Education Model[1]	Applies brain research to improve teaching and learning; no evidence for model itself	Enrichment	Works in gifted or regular classroom, large or small number of students, all grades and content areas	Needs ongoing professional development for gifted and on model; time intensive; difficult to use in most schools
Iowa Excellence Program[1]	Limited research, no comparison groups on this model specifically; extensive evidence for talent search and enrichment triad portions (Assouline et al., 2009)	Enrichment for 6–8, acceleration for 9–12	Developed for rural schools; early enrichment preparation for AP; other states could adopt model	Professional development for early enrichment; needs local gifted specialist; limited to math and science; limited grades; needs university partnership; time intensive to develop and implement
Multiple Intelligences (Regular education)[2]	Moderate (VanTassel-Baska & Brown, 2007)	Enrichment	Works in gifted or regular classroom, large or small number of students, K–8, all content areas	Needs teacher expertise differentiating for gifted; professional development on model and differentiating for gifted; needs money for materials, time to select and differentiate them; not practical in high school

Appendix 9.1. *continued*

Models	Research evidence of effectiveness with gifted	Focus	Strengths for rural schools	Weaknesses for rural schools
Multiple Menu Model[1]	None (Hockett, 2009)	Enrichment	Works in gifted or regular classroom, large or small number of students, all grades and content areas	Needs teacher expertise with gifted and curriculum development for them; ongoing professional development for gifted and on model; time intensive to develop and implement
Parallel Curriculum Model[2]	No direct evidence at present (Hockett, 2009; VanTassel-Baska & Brown, 2007)	Enrichment	Works in gifted or regular classroom or schoolwide, large or small number of students, K–8, and all content areas; one or all strands can be implemented	Needs teacher expertise with gifted; needs professional development on gifted and model; time intensive to develop and implement; not suitable for high school
Problem-Based Learning[1], originated in medical schools	Strong evidence with medical students, growing evidence with K–12 (Renzulli et al., 2009)	Enrichment, builds content knowledge, increases thinking skill development	Can be used in regular or gifted classes with all ages and contents; commercially prepared units available, e.g., William & Mary units	Needs professional development on model, teacher who understands problem well; time intensive to prepare; cost of materials; not connected to state standards
Purdue Three-Stage Model[1,2]	Moderate (VanTassel-Baska & Brown, 2007)	Enrichment	Flexible implementation; large or small number of students, all contents and grades; can use materials from other sources	Needs teacher expertise with gifted

Appendix 9.1. *continued*

Models	Research evidence of effectiveness with gifted	Focus	Strengths for rural schools	Weaknesses for rural schools
Purdue Secondary Model[2]	Some research (VanTassel-Baska & Brown, 2007)	Enrichment	Flexible implementation; suitable for all class size, content, and secondary grades; could be adapted with online classes, materials, teachers, and other supports	Limited specialty courses and teachers; needs professional development on advanced differentiation for gifted; needs high-speed Internet; cost of online courses
Talent Search Model[1,2], based on Study of Mathematically Precocious Youth (SMPY)	Some research (VanTassel-Baska & Brown, 2007); extensive assessment of math and verbal benefits (Lubinski & Benbow, 1994, as cited in Renzulli et al., 2009)	Test and accelerate	Could be adapted to any grade and content; unaffected by class or school size; cost effective; could use above grade level, curriculum-based assessments and textbook tests	Availability and cost of published tests; time for teacher(s) to select and use alternate assessments; needs teachers with advance content knowledge, especially in upper grades
Talent Centered Model for Twice-Exceptional Students[1]	Qualitative and quantitative (compared to a standard) and longitudinal case studies (Baum, 2009; Baum et al., 2014)	Enrichment	Could be implemented with one or two students at any grade or content area	Needs gifted specialist or counselor with expertise with twice-exceptional students; needs enrichment resources for individual interests that don't require reading; time-intensive application

Appendix 9.1. *continued*

Models	Research evidence of effectiveness with gifted	Focus	Strengths for rural schools	Weaknesses for rural schools
Talents Unlimited[1,2] based on Calvin Taylor's Talents Model	Some, primarily on nongifted (Renzulli et al., 2009; VanTassel-Baska & Brown, 2007); evidence of benefits for GT lacking	Enrichment	Nurtures talent in all students at any grade level or content	Requires specialized training; not differentiated for gifted; cost of training
Trifocal Model for Preventing and Reversing Underachievement[1]	Controlled and informal research on some parts	Informational about underachievement	Can be informally applied by teachers and counselors; not affected by class size or content area	Needs trained counselor; teachers working with students need training; difficult to implement; expensive testing and materials; time intensive to develop and conduct testing
Trigram Model (Coon, 2004)	Limited observational evidence from WV only	Enrichment	Works in gifted or regular classroom, large or small number of students, all content areas; suitable for rural schools	Needs teacher expertise with gifted, professional development with model; primarily elementary
U-STARS~PLUS (Coleman & Shah-Coltrane, 2013; Regular education)	None yet	Enrichment and student support	Nurtures potential of at-risk K–3 students in regular class; works with RtI	Needs professional development on model, gifted, and RtI
Triarchic Componential	Moderate (VanTassel-Baska & Brown, 2007)	Describes types of giftedness	Flexible, low cost, works in gifted or regular classroom, large or small number of students, all content areas	Needs teacher expertise with gifted, professional development on model; time intensive to develop and implement

Appendix 9.1. *continued*

Models	Research evidence of effectiveness with gifted	Focus	Strengths for rural schools	Weaknesses for rural schools
WICS as a Model of Giftedness[1]	No direct evidence	Enrichment built on Triarchic concepts	Flexible, low cost; works in gifted or regular classroom, large or small number of students, all content areas	Needs teacher expertise with gifted, professional development on model; time intensive to develop and implement
Schoolwide Structure				
Continuous Progress (Mack, 2008; regular education)	No direct evidence	Acceleration, can include enrichment	Works in all classrooms schoolwide, large or small number of students, all grades and content areas; low to moderate cost	Needs teacher expertise differentiating for gifted; restructures school; needs management system for monitor student progress
International Baccalaureate (IB; Regular education)	Unknown	Inquiry-based advanced, thematic instruction	Not available in rural areas	Requires highly trained teachers; professional development on model and specialized curriculum; restructures school
Levels of Service (LoS)[1], originally Individual Programming Planning Model (IPPM)	Indirect evidence of benefits	Enrichment	Works in gifted or regular classroom, large or small number of students, all grades and content areas	Needs teacher expertise differentiating for gifted, especially for Levels III & IV; complex and difficult to implement
Multiage Classrooms (Lloyd, 1999; Miller, 1990; Regular education)	Consistent evidence of cognitive and affective benefits (Lloyd, 1999)		Works in regular classroom, large or small number of students, all grades and content areas; structural changes may be easiest for small schools; cost effective	Need ongoing professional development on differentiating for gifted; needs professional development on model; restructures school

Appendix 9.1. *continued*

Models	Research evidence of effectiveness with gifted	Focus	Strengths for rural schools	Weaknesses for rural schools
Multiage Learning (Stone, 1997; Regular education)	No direct evidence		Works in gifted or regular classroom, large or small number of students, K–8 and content areas; structural changes may be easiest for small schools	Need ongoing professional development on differentiating for gifted; professional development on model; restructures school; not for high school
Response to Intervention (RtI) (Coleman & Johnsen, 2011; Regular education)	Very limited in SPED, none in GT at present	Continuous progress based on formative assessment	Works in gifted or regular classroom with large or small number of students, all grades and content areas; required by IDEA (2004) for SPED; could use process for GT and ELL	Needs ongoing professional development on differentiation, especially for gifted; needs professional development on model and use of assessments; restructures school; requires more preparation time
Schoolwide-Enrichment Model[1,2]	Strong, some research evidence of affective benefits (VanTassel-Baska & Brown, 2007), some on gifted learning disabled, low SES (Renzulli et al., 2009)	Enrichment and acceleration	Schoolwide; works in any classroom with large or small number of students, all grades and content areas; flexible scope and sequence; adapts to student interests	Limited talent pool; needs teacher expertise with gifted, especially for Type III; many components; professional development on gifted and model; restructures school
Total School Cluster Grouping[1]	Indirect evidence, research supports ability grouping using challenging instruction, no direct evidence on model (Renzulli et al., 2009)	Enrichment	Low-cost schoolwide, full-time elementary gifted program	Needs ongoing professional development on differentiation, especially for gifted; time intensive to implement; restructures school; needs multiple sections at each grade level; elementary only

Note. Bold face type indicates possible adaptability for rural delivery. [1]See Renzulli, Gubbins, McMillen, Eckert, and Little (2009). [2]See VanTassel-Baska and Brown (2007).

Appendix 9.1 References

Assouline, S. G., Blando, C. A., Croft, L. J., Baldus, C. M., & Colangelo, N. (2009). Promoting excellence through enrichment. In J. S. Renzulli, E. J. Gubbins, K. S. McMillen, R. D. Eckert, & C. A. Little (Eds.), *Systems & models for developing programs for the gifted and talented* (pp. 1–16). Waco, TX: Prufrock Press.

Baum, S. M. (2009). Talent centered model for twice exceptional students. In J. S. Renzulli, E. J. Gubbins, K. S. McMillen, R. D. Eckert, & C. A. Little (Eds.). *Systems and models for developing programs for the gifted & talented* (pp. 17–48). Waco, TX: Prufrock Press.

Baum, S. M., Schader, R. M., & Hébert, T. P. (2014). Through a different lens: Reflecting on a strengths-based, talent-focused approach for twice-exceptional learners. *Gifted Child Quarterly, 58*(4), 311–327.

Betts, G. T., & Carey, R. (2013). Response to Intervention and the Autonomous Learner Model: Optimizing potential. In M. R. Coleman & S. K. Johnsen (Eds.), *Implementing RTI with gifted students: Service models, trends, and issue* (pp. 149–168). Waco, TX: Prufrock Press.

Coleman, M. R., & Johnsen, S. K. (Eds.). (2011). *RtI for gifted students: A CEC-TAG educational resource*. Waco, TX: Prufrock Press.

Coleman, M. R., & Shah-Coltrane, S. (2013). Recognizing and nurturing potential across the tiers: U-STARS~PLUS. In M. R. Coleman & S. K. Johnsen (Eds.), *Implementing RTI with gifted students: Service models, trends, and issues* (pp. 187–208). Waco, TX: Prufrock Press.

Coon, P. (2004). Trigram: A gifted program model all students can enjoy. *Rural Special Education Quarterly, 25*(1), 22–25.

Friedman, R. C., & Lee, S. W. (1996). Differentiating instruction for high-achieving/gifted children in regular classrooms: A field test of three gifted-education models. *Journal for the Education of the Gifted, 19*(4), 405-436. doi 10.1177/016235329601900403

Hockett, J. A. (2009). Curriculum for highly able learners that conforms to general education and gifted education quality indicators. *Journal for the Education of the Gifted, 32*(3), 384–440.

Individuals With Disabilities Education Act, 20 U.S.C. § 1401 et seq. (2004).

Lloyd, L. (1999). Multi-age classes and high ability students. *Review of Educational Research, 69*, 187–212.

Mack, J. (2008). Continuous progress schools see the "whole child." *Education, 129*(2), 324–326.

McCallum, R. S., Bell, S. M., Coles, J. T., Miller, J. C., Hopkins, M. B., & Hilton-Prillhart, A. (2013). A model for screening twice-exceptional students (gifted with learning disabilities) within a Response to Intervention paradigm. *Gifted Child Quarterly, 57*(4), 209–222.

Miller, B. A. (1990). A review of the quantitative research on multigrade instruction. *Research in Rural Education, 7(1)*, 1-8.

Renzulli, J. S., Gubbins, E. J., McMillen, K. S., Eckert, R. D., & Little, C. A. (Eds.). (2009). *Systems and models for developing programs for the gifted and talented.* Waco, TX: Prufrock Press.

Stone, S. J. (1997). The multi-age classroom: What research tells the practitioner. *ASCD Curriculum Handbook. 13.91-13.107.*

VanTassel-Baska, J, & Brown, E. F. (2007). Toward best practice: An analysis of the efficacy of curriculum models in gifted education. *Gifted Child Quarterly, 51*(4), 342–358.

CHAPTER 10

Best of Both Worlds
Technology as a Pathway for Meaningful Choice

Brian C. Housand, Ph.D., and Angela M. Housand, Ph.D.

About one-third of the public schools in the United States are located in rural areas and these schools serve roughly 12 million students representing 24% of the total enrollment in U.S. public schools (National Center for Education Statistics [NCES], 2013). These students and the communities in which they live face a number of challenges, including declining local populations, persistent poverty, geographic isolation, limited access to postsecondary educational institutions, restricted employment opportunities, and rural "brain drain" (Lichter & Johnson, 2007; Howley, Rhodes, & Beall, 2009; Carr & Kefalas, 2009; Corbett, 2009; Murray & Schaefer, 2006).

The rural brain drain is precipitated by the perception that in geographically isolated areas young adults, especially those who are gifted and talented, need to leave their family and community to seek advanced postsecondary education and employment opportunities commensurate with their abilities (Carr & Kefalas, 2009; Corbett, 2009). This loss of talent may exacerbate the rural community challenges such as declining population, restricted employment opportunities, and persistent poverty when the "best and brightest" leave to seek advanced educational opportunities and employment but do not return to the rural community with the skills, networks, and access to resources that might help mitigate the challenges faced by the rural community.

Technology and the affordances of technology (access to information, professional networks, and mobility) offer unique opportunities for surmounting the challenges that confront rural America. However, these technological advantages run the risk of being thwarted, as many elders may feel that technology use is contrary to rural values and may "fear that members of the next generation will become so dependent on information technology that they will lose their innate ability to function in their pragmatic sensible world" (Page & Hill, 2008, p. 61). In this chapter, we will examine what Cavanaugh et al. (2004) referred to as the fundamentally unique setting of rural education first through the lens of rural gifted students, and then through the lens of the role that technology can play in talent development. While one may be tempted to view the inclusion of computers and technology as a panacea for dwindling rural gifted programs, the authors would argue that rather than leaving gifted students to their own devices (pun intended), what is needed are adept teachers who possess an understanding of the promise and potential of gifted students and technology.

Rural Gifted Students

Rural Brain Drain and Outmigration

There is much debate about the sources of rural brain drain, or the outmigration of high-achieving students from rural areas (e.g., Petrin, Schafft, & Meece, 2014). Some perceive that there is an educational sorting where the "best and brightest," or those identified as gifted, receive the message that they will need to look beyond their communities to seek advanced learning opportunities or find meaningful career opportunities (Carr & Kefalas, 2009; Colangelo Assouline, & New, 1999; Corbett, 2009; Petrin et al., 2014). In fact, there is qualitative data that suggest educators and adult community members *do* encourage youth outmigration, but not without internal conflict and consideration of what is best for the affected youth (Petrin et al., 2014). Some parents and community members accept that their children may have to leave the community in order to fulfill their potential (Corbett, 2009; Petrin et al., 2014), but recent research suggests the pursuit of postsecondary education is not the only catalyst for outmigration. The rural challenges of persistent poverty and restricted employment opportunities may be the primary reason for outmigration. In a study of 8,754 diverse rural high school students, Petrin and colleagues (2014) found that economic opportunity was the strongest predictor of students' plans to leave their rural communities.

However, when students receive a college degree, they tend not to return to their rural communities (Corbett, 2009; Stricker, 2008), which creates a paradox for those communities. Rural communities are faced with the dilemma of needing to help students reach their potential, which seems to increase outmigration—the very thing rural communities need to avoid in order to retain the talent, innovation, and capacity for critical thinking and problem solving of these individuals for the good of the community. As Corbett put it, "rural communities may need the kinds of people who are most likely to leave" (2009, p. 8).

Aspirations and Rural Attachment

Despite the messages gifted students may receive that they will need to leave the community to pursue challenging academic opportunities and work commensurate with their abilities and skills, academically high-achieving students demonstrate the strongest attachment to their rural community and family life (Petrin et al., 2014).

This "rural attachment" can be characterized as an attachment to place, to the land and its natural resources, and to the local relationships with people (Howley, 2006). Rural youth may desire to maintain their attachment to family, community, and their rural lifestyle rather than seeking more self-serving goals, which in turn affects their aspirations. For example, using survey data from 2,907 children, Howley (2006) found that significant differences existed between rural youth and nonrural youth in their educational aspirations (i.e., the level of education they expected to attain). Rural youth tended to aspire to graduate from high school or community college. Nonrural youth were almost twice as likely to plan on attaining more than 4 years of postsecondary education. Research conducted by Petrin et al. (2014) suggested that there is a large proportion of rural students who aspire to leave their communities for advanced degrees with the intent of returning to similar rural areas if not their home communities. Often, however, postsecondary degrees are not needed for the kinds of job opportunities available in rural industries (e.g., agriculture, manufacturing, resource extraction, or service).

Attachment to place combined with limited diversity of available jobs and constrained educational opportunities may cause some rural students to become very strategic in their decision making and career pursuits as they settle for careers that can be pursued in the existing rural job market rather than aspiring to the highest levels of educational attainment (Howley, 2006; Petrin et al., 2014). How then do we resolve the conflict between gifted students heightened rural attachment and the ability to pursue advanced degrees, particularly when options for their educational and occupational aspirations may not be available in their community?

Corbett (2009) would suggest a two-fold solution: Either (a) continue to encourage students to pursue advanced educational opportunities and create the conditions in their rural communities that make returning feasible and appealing; or (b) as others suggest, rely on the "best and brightest" to create career opportunities in their community that are advantageous for all, thereby attracting talent from the outside (Howley et al., 2009; Lawrence, 2009; Woodrum, 2004).

Technology and Talent Development

Teachers

One of the most unyielding challenges for rural schools is attracting and retaining certified and highly qualified teachers (Barley & Brigham, 2008; Hobbs, 2004; Lowe, 2006; Monk, 2007). This challenge may be significantly magnified when looking for highly qualified teachers of the gifted to work in rural environments. As a consequence of these challenges, rural gifted students are often in danger of not having access to teachers trained in understanding or addressing their unique educational needs and "may not receive the critical academic stimulation and enrichment needed to support their full cognitive, social, and academic development" (Howley et al., 2009, p. 521).

In addition to the many challenges that gifted programs in nonrural environments face, rural gifted programs are often confronted with limited resources in the form of professional support and opportunities for students, as well as time constraints (Azano et al., 2014). Far too often, teachers of the gifted in rural settings are asked to do far more with far less than their nonrural colleagues. To further complicate matters, Azano et al. (2014) described "a lack of geographic connectivity, as well as a digital one" that impacted access to appropriate instructional resources and technology for gifted students and their teachers (p. 96). Meanwhile, today's students have grown up during a digital age where they may have greater access to technology outside of school than in the classroom. Howley, Wood, and Hough (2011) cautioned that when technology is not integrated into the learning environment or—even worse—when teachers choose to avoid the use of technology when available, "they may be distancing themselves from the world that their students now inhabit."

In a survey of 4,000 middle school students, Spires, Lee, Turner, and Johnson (2008) found that students generally perceived their teachers as being "out of touch" when it came to an understanding of the significant role that technology played in the lives of students. The students surveyed reported a disconnection between their technology use in school as compared to their digital lives outside of school. The students asserted if their teachers had a better understanding of this disconnect that they would actively seek ways in which to more extensively integrate technology into their classrooms (Spires, Lee, Turner, & Johnson, 2008).

Therefore, rural teachers for the gifted should not only have training in how to teach gifted students, but they should also have training in utilizing technology. Initiatives to increase technology use tend to focus on one of two objectives in isolation (Howley et al., 2011). Rural schools either focus on obtaining technology or using technology. Merely being provided with technology does not necessarily mean effective use (Park, Sinha, & Chong, 2007). Teachers should also be provided with training to effectively integrate technology into their curriculum.

To best meet the needs of rural gifted students in this digital age, we recommend that teachers continually seek professional development opportunities related to both gifted education and educational technology. Although this may come through local or state associations, many schools are reluctant to fund teachers to travel to conferences. Travelling to national conferences like the ones hosted by the National Association for Gifted Children (NAGC) or the International Society for Technology in Education (ISTE) may be a luxury that few rural gifted educators are ever able to afford. Thankfully, a growing number of organizations are offering free or low-cost professional development online to their members. By becoming a member of a professional organization at the state or national level, one is able to more readily connect to what is happening in the field of gifted education.

In addition to belonging to professional organizations, rural educators of the gifted should seek out additional ways to create a professional learning network through Internet resources. There is an increasing number of blogs dedicated to gifted education and to the use of technology in the classroom. A tech savvy teacher also looks for inspiration and connection via Twitter. Although one may learn a great deal by following others on Twitter, we would like to recommend looking into weekly Twitter chats dedicated to gifted education (#gtchat), rural education (#ruraledchat), or educational technology (#edtech chat). By participating in a variety of social media channels, we have the ability to connect with others and learn from their experiences while sharing our own experiences. Being a teacher of the gifted does not have to be an isolated experience. There is strength in numbers, and together we can empower ourselves to best serve our gifted students in this digital age.

Serving the Students

Although the problem of having access to technology tends to be dissipating, the issue of what to do with available technology is continuing to rise. Many schools have invested heavily in interactive whiteboards that primarily serve to strengthen the dependency on teacher-led instruction. Today's technology has the power to go far beyond a traditional lecture and the capacity to transcend the physical space of the classroom to bring the world to our students and to take our students to the world. However, none of this may be possible unless we allow technology to significantly redefine the learning task and the learning environment.

To help educators better understand the potential and power of technology and how educators can integrate technology with instruction in meaningful ways, Puentedura (2014) developed the SAMR Model. SAMR represents the **s**ubstitution, **a**ugmentation, **m**odification, and **r**edefinition of an instructional or student task by using technology. The following section will define each of the four components of the SAMR Model and apply the SAMR Model to the needs of gifted education in rural settings.

Using the SAMR Model in Rural Gifted Education

Substitution. Puentedura (2014) defined this as the lowest level in which computer technology is used to perform the same task as it was done before the use of computers. This level is characterized by technology acting as a direct tool substitute with no functional change. Substitution tends to be focused on the teacher rather than the student. Instead of merely focusing on substituting some type of device for paper and pencil, many rural gifted students may benefit from having virtual classes substituted for face-to-face ones.

A report from the National Center for Education Statistics (NCES) indicated that rural high school students have less access to advanced high school coursework (Planty, Provasnik, & Daniel, 2007). This stems from the multitude of challenges confronting rural schools, including attracting and retaining teachers to teach advanced courses (Monk, 2007). As a result, many rural schools have utilized distance education to expand the number of course offerings for gifted students in situations where they may not have qualified teachers, sufficient numbers of identified students, or be constrained by other funding considerations (Irvin et al., 2012).

The substitution of online courses potentially offers rural gifted students access to advanced courses and content and has been proposed as a viable solution in lieu of eliminating gifted programs or consolidating small rural schools (Burney & Cross, 2006; Hobbs, 2004). In a 2011 report from the NCES, 59% of rural school districts used distance education courses compared to 37% of urban and 47% of suburban school districts (Queen & Lewis, 2011).

Research on distance education has demonstrated the potential to effectively provide advanced coursework to gifted students through a variety means (Barbour & Mulcahy, 2006; Lewis & Hafer, 2007). Additionally, multiple studies have reported on gifted students' satisfaction and success with advanced courses offered via distance education (Adams & Cross, 1999/2000; Olszewski-Kubilius & Lee, 2004; Howley et al., 2009).

In a 2010 study of parents of children who participated in Gifted Learning Links (GLL) from the Center for Talent Development at Northwestern University, Blair identified three advantages of online gifted programs: flexibility, quality of instruction, and socialization. Online gifted programs offer the flexibility to take a course not offered at their school or to take a course not offered at their grade level or to accelerate in a subject area. Second, the quality of instruction was seen as a significant benefit to students who may not have access to academically excellent programs. Finally, the parents reported an increase in socialization of their children as a result of taking an online course. Blair (2010) reported on students developing self-confidence, independence, and deep relationships with their intellectual peers and online teachers.

Today, numerous online programs have been created specifically for gifted students. Many of these programs are sponsored by universities or by institutes for gifted students. Others are online consortiums that may or may not offer courses and programs specifically for gifted students. A listing of many of these can be found in the resource section at the end of this chapter (Appendix 10.1).

When considering any online option for gifted students, several important factors should be taken into consideration. First and foremost, one should ensure that the program is accredited and that the course taken will be accepted for credit by the student's school of residence (Housand & Housand, 2012).

Second, consider whether or not the student has the necessary skills to be successful. Online learning may not be optimal for every student and this type of learning requires a great deal of motivation and independence. In a study of rural administrators' satisfaction with distance education courses, the two most important factors leading to student success were students' preparation in study skills and computer skills (Irvin et al., 2012). When administrators felt that students were not prepared in their study skills, there was a strong correlation with low levels of satisfaction by rural administrators (Irvin et al., 2012).

Third, the distance in distance education can be an issue for almost any student, but it can be particularly problematic for rural students (Hobbs, 2004). Rural students are accustomed to being educated in learning environments with high levels of intimacy and teacher immediacy, and they typically feel a strong sense of belonging and connectedness both to school and community (de la Varre et al., 2010). De la Varre and coauthors (2010) recommended the use of facilitators in school to assist students as they take online courses in order to foster a better sense of connectedness. Facilitators can help students to overcome frustration and the feeling of being overwhelmed as well as isolation in online learning situations. In this way, students are able to access academically advanced courses that otherwise would have not been available.

Although many aspects of distance education and online learning have been researched, the bulk of the research has been conducted at the university level. Cavanaugh et al. (2004) advised us to resist the temptation to simply apply prior research to the "fundamentally unique" setting of K–12 distance education. De la Varre, Keane, and Irvin (2010) went on to add that rural K–12 distance education is fundamentally unique in a fundamentally unique setting. Although there exists the temptation to simply apply what works in other settings, one should proceed with caution and examine the unique characteristics of one's own rural community. The authors would also like to add that gifted education adds yet another fundamentally unique layer of complexity to this situation. Distance education is not a panacea and should not serve strictly as a substitute for rural gifted programs. Instead, rural educators should explore technology options to augment their current gifted programs and bolster their current best practices with online resources to personalize the learning for their gifted students.

Augmentation. Puentedura (2014) identified the level of augmentation as the point at which technology acts as a direct tool substitution with functional improvement. Like the level of substitution, Puentedura sees augmentation as an enhancement to the learning activity rather than a transformation of the task. For rural gifted programs, the Internet offers countless numbers of quality content resources that can significantly enhance curriculum. Rather than utilizing distance education courses as a substitution or a replacement, Irvin et al. (2012) felt that rural educators could more effectively and meaningfully construct or modify their own distance education courses by forming local, regional, or state consortiums to better meet the needs of rural youth.

To begin, educators might explore the multitude of course offerings presented via Massive Open Online Courses, or MOOCs. Consortiums such as edX (http://www.edx.org) and Coursera (http://www.coursera.org) have partnered with top universities and organizations worldwide to offer free courses for anyone to take online. Although the majority of the courses are at the college level, edX does offer dozens of courses at the high school level. Each course is taught by university faculty and varies in length. A wide range of subject areas is offered. For gifted students who are in need of acceleration or advanced content, MOOCs could provide an acceptable solution. As recommended by de la Varre et al. (2010) with regard to distance education courses, teachers should serve as facilitators to ensure student success. Also, keep in mind that although universities typically offer the MOOCs, there is no accompanying credit earned for completing the course.

Although MOOCs are a more recent development in online learning, iTunes U is an often-underutilized free online resource. Residing within the iTunes Store and available for either Mac or PC platforms, iTunes U is a continually expanding collection of over 800,000 free educational resources from universities, museums, and other institutions. Content may be streamed online or downloaded to any device, which may be especially useful if Internet connection speed is an issue. What began as a digital collection of recorded lectures from actual college courses taught at Stanford and Berkeley has expanded to include entire courses along with video lectures, readings, and assignments from hundreds of universities covering almost any topic imaginable. In addition to content from some of the worlds' leading institutions, there is a growing collection of materials targeted specifically for K–12 learners. iTunes U also has assembled Featured Collections of materials related to STEM education (http://bit.ly/itunesu-stem), virtual field trips (http://bit.ly/itunesu-vft), and resources for the classroom (http://bit.ly/itunesu-classroom).

Although iTunes U does provide a collection of primary sources (http://bit.ly/itunesu-primarysource) from institutions like the Library of Congress and the National Archives, teachers should also explore the teacher resources available from each. For example, the Library of Congress Teachers website (http://www.loc.gov/teachers/) contains digital versions of primary sources from the Library of Congress, as well as guides for integrating primary sources into the classroom. The National Archives has created an interactive collection of thousands of primary sources from its collection for educators at the site DocsTeach (http://www.docsteach.org). Teachers and students are able to not only explore and view digital versions of documents, but a collection of primary source-based activities designed to promote critical and historical thinking has been developed. Educators can also use the creation tool to design their own interactive activities.

The Google Cultural Institute (https://www.google.com/culturalinstitute) brings together millions of digital artifacts from numerous partners, including museums from around the world. The Google Cultural Institute is divided into three main sections: Art Project, Historic Moments, and World Wonders. Art Project features works from hundreds of art collections in ultra high-resolution images that allow one to zoom into the image to see intricate details. The Art Project section also features Street View images that allow one to virtually walk through many of the galleries to see the art as it is displayed in the actual museum. The Historic Moments section contains online exhibitions featuring documents, photos, and videos that detail the stories behind significant moments in human history. Finally, the World Wonders section combines Google Street View images with historic documents and images to allow for a deep exploration of some of the many wonders of the modern and ancient world. This powerful resource may help to serve to bring the world to classrooms of gifted students.

When augmenting lessons for gifted students, one should not overlook the wealth of free video content that is available online. Resources like TED (http://ted.com) present some of the greatest minds of our time, sharing brief yet powerful talks designed to inspire. TED has also created TED Ed (http://ed.ted.com), which contains "lessons worth sharing." Each of the hundreds of lessons contains a brief video typically about 5 minutes long, followed by a series of multiple choice and open-ended questions as well as a discussion forum, an extension activity, and additional readings. TED Ed also allows educators to customize any lesson to create their own questions and extensions to personalize the learning experience for their students. In addition, the Create a Lesson option (http://ed.ted.com/videos) allows a lesson to be created around any TED Ed video, TED Talk, or any video on YouTube.

With an estimated 300 hours of new video being uploaded to YouTube every minute, there is a lot to sort through to find the perfect companion to augment lessons and both inspire and inform students. Educators can find a video tutorial to teach them almost anything on the site. Indeed, Salman Kahn began Khan Academy (http://www.khanacademy.org) by recording more than 4,800 video tutorials. However, Khan Academy has continued to grow and develop beyond a collection of basic math tutorials recorded by one person. Teachers of the gifted should revisit the site and look for videos and lessons in the Partner Content section. Here, one will find video collections from museums like The Metropolitan Museum of Art (http://www.khanacademy.org/partner-content/metropolitan-museum) and the Exploratorium (http://www.khanacademy.org/partner-content/Exploratorium). In the Partners section, many students may be intrigued by content created by NASA, MIT+12, and Crash Course. John Green, author of *The Fault in Our Stars*, and his brother Hank Green have created CrashCourse, a collection of short video lessons designed to entertain and educate students on a variety of topics including world history, biology, and literature. Although a limited number of courses from this team are available on Khan Academy, their entire collection is available on their YouTube Channel (https://www.youtube.com/user/crashcourse).

By utilizing the vast array of rich and free content resources that are available on the Internet, teachers of the gifted in rural settings have the power to augment their available resources from the world to their students. However, augmenting is only part of the solution that technology offers.

Modification. Puentedura (2014) identified the level modification as the use of technology for significant redesign of the task. Unlike the previous two levels, which only allowed enhancement, the third and fourth levels provide for transformation of the learning task. One of the challenges that most gifted teachers face is the lack of time available to serve their gifted students. Although some are able to see their students on a regular basis several times a week, still many others are able to work with their gifted students only once per week for a limited time. In rural settings, this time may be even more constrained, as one teacher often is forced to serve multiple schools over the course of a week. However, the use of social learning platforms like Edmodo (http://www.edmodo.com) can easily modify the learning environment to allow for social interactions and learning to take place over the course of the week rather than just when the students are being pulled out for gifted services.

One of the potential pitfalls of technology integration is that it can detract from the learning, as many students are accustomed to utilizing technology to play games, access social networks, and consume video content (Spires et al., 2008; Howley et al., 2011). Rather than simply leaving our students to their own devices, teachers should provide a link between utilizing technology for personal reasons and help students to understand how it can be used meaningfully and with purpose.

Renzulli (1977) discussed the importance of creating learning experiences that helped students to transition from being merely consumers of information to being producers of new content, ideas, and information. One Internet resource that perfectly aligns with Renzulli's (1977) notion of creative productive giftedness is DIY (http://diy.org). According to the website, "DIY is a place for kids to share what they do, meet others who love the same skills, and be awesome." DIY is a community of creators designed for kids to develop skills through completing a series of challenges. Skills range from animator to zoologist in over 100 different areas. Each skill area is made up of a series of challenges, and interestingly, specific instructions are not provided as to how to complete the challenges. Instead, each individual is left to decide how to complete the challenge.

An increasing number of students are becoming obsessed with the idea of creating their own games and apps for their devices. Although learning to program a computer was once a rather daunting task filled with hours and hours of reading computer manuals, CODE.org has created an easy entry point into this virtual world with the free online materials designed to pique the interest of future computer programmers. Through the use of the introductory materials as part of the Hour of Code, any educator can easily modify their classroom environment into one that promotes creativity, critical thinking, and collaboration while students are introduced to coding.

One last recommendation for modifying the learning environment for gifted students is for both students and staff to recognize their technology talents and problem-solving skills by creating a "geek squad" within the school. A group of technologically gifted students could serve as trainers for teachers interested in exploring new applications. Together tech savvy teachers and students could help more reluctant users of technology in a school or community to modify traditional learning tasks and environments to allow for a significant redesign.

Redefinition. Technology allows for the creation of new tasks previously inconceivable; for redefining the way we think and behave. With this in mind, it might be prudent to consider how we might redefine the role of schools as a place for students to learn the necessary skills for global participation (meeting myriad educational standards along the way) by developing a "professional" digital identity that reflects students' interests, values, and capabilities.

The networks of affiliation in rural communities are already very strong with shared value for and attachment to the land and its resources, as well as the strong relational bonds that exist within educational settings and the larger community (Howley, 2006). Technology and access to the Internet affords individuals within rural communities the opportunity to attain skills and knowledge, develop networks of influence that extend beyond the rural community, gain access to assets outside the rural area, and all without ever leaving their community or family. For rural gifted students, access to a global community and nearly infinite sources of information can be very powerful as they reconcile attachment to their community with aspirations for an advantageous future for themselves and their rural community. Moreover, using technology to redefine the role of schools makes it possible to attain the ideal of relying on the "best and brightest" to create career opportunities in rural communities that are advantageous for all.

Technology does provide a unique opportunity for leveraging an egalitarian form of global affiliation through a complex web of social networks that make possible the exchange of information and the acquisition of skills (Burt, 1997; Nahapiet & Ghoshal, 1998). However, students must be taught the necessary skills to contribute to the Internet and have opportunities to take small steps toward global participation. In other words, they must build the skills of digital citizenship to gain access to a larger social network.

FutureCasting (http://futurecasting.org) is a pedagogical road map that enables students to connect their interests to desired academic outcomes as they develop their identity both within the school setting as well as on the global stage. Cultivating student interests to inform the talent development process is not new—Renzulli's (1977) Enrichment Triad Model has incorporated this approach for decades—but FutureCasting not only connects student interests to curricular rigor, it also helps students gain access to the networks and resources aligned with their "professional" interests, provides evidence of productivity in personal interest areas, and enables them to integrate their interests with academic rigor and curricular goals.

Leveraging the Internet, FutureCasting allows students to achieve integrated personal and professional success to attain life satisfaction and actualize potential. The process of forming a "professional" online identity requires students to:

- » examine their interests, values, and talents so that efforts toward goal attainment are achievable and fulfilling;
- » scrutinize their online identity to gain awareness about how what they produce in digital environments affects their reputation;
- » envision a future that aligns professional success with personal fulfillment;

» develop strategies and skills for self-determined success; and
» establish a network of support and garner influence by gaining access to affiliation networks in relevant domains (i.e., leveraging social capital in areas of interest).

Through the process, students pragmatically approach defining aspirations and planning future goals as they consider both the internal and external factors that might support or hinder success. Students decide *who* they want to be, rather than *what* they want to be. Focusing on *who* one wants to be allows for a concentration of efforts, time, and energy that minimizes distractions. FutureCasting provides the instructional framework that enables them to explore interests, engage mentors, gain access to resources, and yield creative products within domains of interest. In other words, FutureCasting allows rural students to begin transcending geographic isolation by leveraging networks of affiliation in domains of interest without ever leaving their rural community.

Considerations

In *The Road Ahead,* Bill Gates (1996) wrote, "We don't have the option of turning away from the future. No one gets to vote on whether technology is going to change our lives" (p. 11). Indeed, technology is not a passing phase that is going to go away. Instead, it is something that will only become more integral to our lives. We have reached a time of division where those who shy away from technology are in danger of being left behind. That being said, technology is constantly evolving at an increasingly rapid rate and in such a way that it is impossible for any one person to know everything that is possible. Instead of feeling that one has to understand all that technology is capable of, we would advise educators to critically look for opportunities for technology to significantly enhance and even redefine the learning environment.

We must also be cautious in falsely believing that simply because students were born in a digital age that they fully understand all of the power that technology possesses. As we learned from Stan Lee, creator of Spider Man, "With great power, must also come great responsibility." Part of our responsibility as educators of the gifted is to help teach our students to be proper citizens in digital and nondigital environments. They cannot do it alone, and technology cannot do it for them. Now more than ever, gifted students need high-quality teachers to help show them the way to a brighter future.

Conclusion

Although there may be conflict between a gifted student's aspirations, potential attainment, and cultural values, in the end, it is up to the gifted student to decide what is the right path for him or her. Whether students remain in their rural community and find fulfillment in a job that serves their family and friends, or they choose to leave their home to seek education and a job that continually challenges their ability, it is the job of education to prepare these students to be contributing members of society. Howley, Rhodes, and Beall, (2009) may have said it best:

> The paths to a fulfilling life, however, are many; and extraordinary accomplishment comes in many varieties. Arguably, in fact, the most gifted individuals in any group point the way to new paths rather than simply demonstrating high achievement in the already well-defined domains of accomplishment. (p. 528)

Technology provides opportunities that were not available to generations before including avenues for exploration, opportunities for creativity, and circumstances for engagement. As educators, we must give gifted rural students—and all students, really—the opportunity to define and participate on their terms using the tools to which they are accustomed. In so doing, we give them the freedom to enact change and with a love of place, likely change for the better.

References

Adams, C. M., & Cross, T. L. (1999/2000). Distance learning opportunities for academically gifted students. *The Journal of Secondary Gifted Education, 11,* 88–96.

Azano, A. P., Callahan, C. M., Missett, T. C., & Brunner, M. (2014). Understanding the experiences of gifted education teachers and fidelity of implementation in rural schools. *Journal of Advanced Academics 25*(2), 88–100.

Barbour, M., & Mulcahy, D. (2006). An inquiry into retention and achievement differences in campus based and web based AP Courses. *Rural Educator, 27,* 8–12.

Barley, Z. A., & Brigham, N. (2008). *Preparing teachers to teach in rural schools* (Issues & Answers Report, REL 2008–No. 045). Washington, D.C.: U.S. Department of Education, Institute of Education Sciences, National Center for Education Evaluation and Regional Assistance, Regional Educational Laboratory Central. Retrieved from http://ies.ed.gov/ncee/edlabs/regions/central/pdf/REL_2008045_sum.pdf

Blair, R. (2010). Online learning for gifted students from the parents' perspective. *Gifted Child Today, 34*(3), 28–30.

Burney, V. H., & Cross, T. L. (2006). Impoverished students with academic promise in rural settings: 10 lessons from Project Aspire. *Gifted Child Today, 29,* 14–21.

Burt, R. S. (1997). A note on social capital and network content. *Social Networks, 19,* 355–373.

Carr, P. J., & Kefalas, M. J. (2009). *Hollowing out the middle: The rural brain drain and what it means for America.* Boston, MA: Beacon Press.

Cavanaugh, C., Gillian, K., Kromney, J., Hess, M., & Blomeyer, R. (2004). *The effects of distance education on K–12 student outcomes: A meta-analysis,* Naperville, IL: Learning Point Associates.

Colangelo, N., Assouline, S. G., & New, J. K. (1999). *Gifted education in rural schools: A national assessment.* Iowa City: University of Iowa. (ERIC Document Reproduction No. ED430766)

Corbett, M. (2009). Rural schooling in mobile modernity: Returning to the places I've been. *Journal of Research in Rural Education.* Retrieved from http://jrre.psu.edu/articles/24-7.pdf

de la Varre, C., Keane, J., & Irvin, M. J. (2010). Enhancing online distance education in small rural US schools: A hybrid, learner-center model. *ALT-J: Research in Learning Technology, 18*(3), 193–205.

Gates, B. (1995). *The road ahead.* New York, NY: Viking Penguin.

Hobbs, V. (2004). *The promise and the power of online learning in rural education.* Arlington, VA: Rural School and Community Trust.

Housand, B. C., & Housand, A. M. (2012). The role of technology in gifted students' motivation. *Psychology in the Schools 49,* 706–715.

Howley, A., Rhodes, M., & Beall, J. (2009). Challenges facing rural schools: Implications for gifted students. *Journal for the Education of the Gifted, 32,* 515–536.

Howley, A., Wood, L., & Hough, B. (2011). Rural elementary school teachers' technology integration. *Journal of Research in Rural Education, 26*(9). 1–13.

Howley, C. W. (2006). Remote possibilities: Rural children's educational aspirations. *Peabody Journal of Education, 82,* 62–80.

Irvin, M. J., Byun, S., Meece, J. L., Farmer, T. W., & Hutchins, B. C. (2012). Educational barriers of rural youth: Relation of individual and contextual difference variables. *Journal of Career Assessment, 20*(1), 71–87.

Lawrence, B. K. (2009). Rural gifted education: A comprehensive literature review. *Journal for the Education of the Gifted, 32,* 461–494.

Lewis, J. D., & Hafer, C. (2007). The challenges of being in a rural community. *Duke Gifted Letter, 7*(2).

Lichter, D. T. & Johnson K. M. (2007). The changing spatial concentration of America's rural poor population. *Rural Sociology* 72(3), 331–358.

Lowe, J. M. (2006). Rural education: Attracting and retaining teachers in small schools. *Rural Educator, 27*(2), 28–32.

Monk, D. H. (2007). Recruiting and retaining high-quality teachers in rural areas. *The Future of Children, 17,* 155–174.

Murray, A., & Schaefer, V. (2006, Oct.). *Social and academic interventions for rural schools.* Presentation at the National Rural Education Association in Kansas City, MO. Retrieved from http://www.nrcres.org/presentations/NREA_2006_Murray.ppt

Nahapiet, J., & Ghoshal, S. (1998). Social capital, intellectual capital, and the organizational advantage. *Academy of Management Review, 23*(2), 242–266.

National Center for Education Statistics. (2013). *The status of rural education.* Retrieved from http://nces.ed.gov/programs/coe/indicator_tla.asp

Olszewski-Kubilius, P., & Lee, S. (2004). Gifted adolescents' talent development through distance learning. *Journal for the Education of the Gifted, 28,* 7–35.

Page, G. A., & Hill, M. (2008). Information, communication, and educational technologies in rural Alaska. *New Directions for Adult and Continuing Education, 117,* 59–70.

Park, E., Sinha, H., & Chong, J. (2007). Beyond access: An analysis of the influence of the E-Rate program in bridging the digital divide in American Schools. *Journal of Information Technology Education, 6,* 387–406.

Petrin, R. A., Schafft, K. A., & Meece, J. L. (2014). Educational sorting and residential aspirations among rural high school students: What are the contributions of schools and educators to rural brain drain? *American Education Research Journal, 51,* 294–326.

Planty, M., Provasnik, S., & Daniel, B. (2007). High school coursetaking: Findings from the condition of education 2007 (NCES 2007-065). Washington, D.C.: National Center for Education Statistics.

Puentedura, R. R. (2009). *As we may teach: Educational technology, from theory into practice*. Retrieved from http://tinyurl.com/aswemayteach

Queen, B., & Lewis, L. (2011). *Distance education courses for public elementary and secondary school students: 2009–10* (NCES 2012–008). Washington, D.C.: National Center for Education Statistics. Retrieved from http://nces.ed.gov/pubs2012/2012008.pdf

Renzulli, J. S. (1977). *The enrichment triad model: A guide for developing defensible programs for the gifted and talented*. Waco, TX: Prufrock Press.

Spires, H. A., Lee, J. K., Turner, K. A., & Johnson, J. (2008). Having our say: Middle grade student perspectives on school, technologies, and academic engagement. *Journal of Research on Technology in Education, 40,* 497–515.

Stricker, K. (2008, March). *Dakota diaspora: The out-migration of talented youth from one rural community*. Paper presented at the annual meeting of the American Educational Research Association, New York, NY.

Woodrum, A. (2004). State-mandated testing and cultural resistance in Appalachian schools: Competing values and expectations. *Journal of Research in Rural Education, 19,* 1–9.

Appendix 10.1: Resources

Virtual Courses for the Gifted

» Center for Talented Youth Online at Johns Hopkins University: http://cty.jhu.edu/ctyonline
» Education Program for Gifted Youth (EPGY) at Stanford University: http://epgy.stanford.edu
» Gifted Learning Links at Northwestern University Center for Talent Development: http://www.ctd.northwestern.edu/gll
» Florida Virtual School (FLVS): http://www.flvs.net
» Laurel Springs School: http://laurelsprings.com/our-families/gifted-talented/
» Connections Academy: http://www.connectionsacademy.com/curriculum/gifted-honors

Massive Open Online Courses (MOOCs)

- edX: https://www.edx.org
- Coursera: https://www.coursera.org
- iTunes U Resources
- STEM: http://bit.ly/itunesu-stem
- Virtual Field Trips: http://bit.ly/itunesu-vft
- Classroom Resources: http://bit.ly/itunesu-classroom
- Primary Sources: http://bit.ly/itunesu-primarysource

Content Resources

- Library of Congress: http://www.loc.gov/teachers/
- National Archives Docs Teach: http://docsteach.org
- Google Cultural Institute: https://www.google.com/culturalinstitute
- TED: Ideas Worth Spreading: http://www.ted.com
- TED Ed: Lessons Worth Sharing: http://ed.ted.com

Khan Academy Partner Content

- The Metropolitan Museum of Art: https://www.khanacademy.org/partner-content/metropolitan-museum
- Exploratorium: https://www.khanacademy.org/partner-content/Exploratorium
- NASA: https://www.khanacademy.org/partner-content/nasa
- MIT-K12: https://www.khanacademy.org/partner-content/mit-k12
- Crash Course: https://www.khanacademy.org/partner-content/crash-course1

Other Resources

- Crash Course YouTube Channel: https://www.youtube.com/user/crashcourse
- Edmodo: https://www.edmodo.com
- DIY: https://diy.org
- CODE: http://code.org

CHAPTER 11

Serving Rural Gifted Students Through Supplemental and Out-of-School Programming

Paula Olszewski-Kubilius, Ph.D., Susan Corwith, Ph.D., and Eric Calvert, Ph.D.

Introduction

The perspective underlying this chapter is that for all talent domains, including mathematics, sports, science, and the performing arts, the role of learning opportunities is critical, and these can be provided both within and outside of school. Some talent areas are developed primarily outside of school and others primarily within school, but no talent area is developed completely within school (Bloom, 1985; Olszewski-Kubilius, 2010). Hence the need for K–12 schools, community organizations, cultural institutions, and universities and colleges to offer supplemental, outside-of-school programming for gifted children and for society to support them. Talent development *requires* the provision of opportunities in the form of lessons, extracurricular activities, and summer programs, and is driven by expert teachers, mentors, and coaches. These must be made available more widely to all students with talent potential.

Empirical Support for the Effects of Out-of-School Programs on the Development of Talent

Research documents the importance of participation in out-of-school activities for talent development. Wai, Lubinski, Benbow, and Steiger (2010) examined this specifically in the STEM area. They found that students who had a "higher STEM dose" (p. 860) of precollege activities—defined as participation in a varied set of in-school and supplemental educational programs such as competitions, academic clubs, advanced courses, and summer programs—had a higher rate of exceptional and creative STEM accomplishments as adults, which included patents, papers published in prestigious journals, and acceptance to highly selective doctoral programs. Gifted students' participation in challenging, out-of-school activities in science, mathematics, the arts, and social leadership in adolescence has been found to predict their choice of adult occupations and their creative accomplishments (Milgram, 2003; Milgram & Hong, 1999).

There is strong research support for the efficacy of various types of out-of-school programs for gifted students and for their positive effects (see Olszewski-Kubilius & Lee, 2008, for a review). Importantly, these effects for participation in programs designed specifically for gifted students extend to their school achievement and include taking a more rigorous course of study, greater use of accelerative options in mathematics, and greater participation in math related extracurricular activities. They also include higher educational aspirations and matriculation at more academically selective institutions of higher education (Barnett & Durden, 1993; Olszewski-Kubilius, 2007, 2002; Olszewski-Kubilius & Grant, 1996; Swiatek & Benbow, 1991; Olszewski-Kubilius & Lee, 2008). Studies of gifted students' participation in distance education programs found evidence of enhanced independent study skills, a more realistic assessment of knowledge and skill level, increases in collaboration skills, and greater motivation and task commitment (Olszewski-Kuiblius, 2009; Olszewski-Kubilius & Lee, 2008, 2004a; McLoughlin, 1999; Ewing, Dowling, & Coutts, 1997; Wilson, Litle, Coleman, & Gallagher, 1998). The effects of participation in competitions include increased motivation and improved academic performance (Bronson & Merryman, 2013; Karnes & Riley, 2005; Subotnik, Miserandino, & Olszewski-Kubilius, 1997). Out-of-school programs can also affect children indirectly through their impact on parents' achievement expectations. For example, some parents of students participating in a weekend enrichment program raised their expectations regarding their child's achievement and proactively contacted their child's school to ask for more challenging classroom work (Olszewski-Kubilius & Lee, 2004a).

Effects of participation in outside-of-school service learning programs for students included enhanced problem solving, empathy and confidence, higher self-esteem, greater self-understanding, greater awareness of civic issues, and a stronger commitment to working in local communities (see Lee, Olszewski-Kubilius, Donahue, & Weimholt, 2007, for a review).

Benefits and Challenges of Educating Gifted Students in Rural Communities

It is possible to provide appropriate programming for gifted students in any community setting. Still, there are specific benefits and challenges unique to rural schools. Benefits of rural schools for gifted students include smaller class sizes, potentially resulting in more individualized instruction, closer teacher-student relationships, and opportunities for involvement in a range of school and community activities (Colangelo, Assouline, & New, 2001). However, there are several significant challenges that can co-exist with these benefits. The most common challenges reported in the literature include the following:

- fewer advanced courses offered in school;
- a smaller group of intellectual peers, which makes cluster grouping difficult and may lead to feelings of isolation;
- a more limited variety of professional role models, mentors, and career prospects in the immediate community;
- limitations in technology and consequently also in digital learning resources;
- significant physical distance to educational resources and programs, with accompanying transportation and logistical obstacles;
- fewer staff licensed or trained in gifted education and difficulty hiring teachers with significant content area expertise in a field;
- limited access to large-scale community resources such as museums and major libraries;
- significant numbers of students living in poverty and very high rates of identification of students with specific learning disabilities, with

accompanying school orientations toward remediation at the expense of talent development; and

» concerns about elitism when providing specialized programming for a small group of students or a general mistrust of programs that may be seen as disconnecting students from their rural communities (Goglin & Miller, 2014; Colangelo, Assouline & New, 2001).

Fortunately, through careful planning and forging partnerships with other educational institutions and community organizations, schools and families can maximize the benefits and minimize the impact of obstacles bright students frequently experience when growing up in rural environments.

Meeting the Needs of Rural Gifted Students Through Supplemental Programming

Supplemental programs are essential parts of high-quality service models for gifted students, a fact supported by the National Association for Gifted Children (NAGC, 2010) Pre-K–Grade 12 Gifted Programming Standards. In addition to the benefits outlined in the research, NAGC Programming Standard 5 reinforces the value of supplemental services:

Standard 5.1.2: Educators regularly use enrichment options to extend and deepen learning opportunities within and outside of the school setting.
Standard 5.1.5: Educators regularly use current technologies, including online learning options and assistive technologies to enhance access to high-level programming.

But how do rural schools overcome the very real challenges they face to give students access to the programs and resources they need? With creativity and commitment, it is possible to provide a range of supplemental learning opportunities for students that will develop their talents and allow them to pursue their passions. Goglin and Miller (2014) of the North Carolina Association for Gifted Children and Olszewski-Kubilius and Lee (2004b) identified a variety of strategies, utilizing online and face-to-face options, which have worked in rural

Supplemental and Out-of-School Programming

schools across the country. Following is an overview of these general strategies and ideas for incorporating various types of supplemental programming.

Build Connections With Nearby Schools to Share Resources and Create a Community

In many rural areas, neighboring districts are close enough in proximity to allow for regular communication and collaboration. Educators can establish—for themselves, parents, and even students—online groups and periodic in-person or virtual meetings with others in neighboring schools and communities to plan talent development opportunities and activities. Many districts already make use of this strategy to field athletic teams and cast theater productions, but the strategy can also be used to form multischool debate teams and interest-based clubs; plan programs such as mock trial, Model UN, and Science Olympiad; organize regional art and science fairs and competitions; or create opportunities for service learning.

Create Regional Networks for Extracurricular, Weekend Enrichment, and Hybrid Learning Programs

Many rural schools may not, on their own, have a sufficient critical mass of students to be able to support a wide range of programs for gifted students (Iatarola, Conger, & Long, 2011). However, groups of schools or districts can collaborate to sponsor specialized classes and competitions. With this approach, one district may supply the instructor or facilitator, and the other districts provide financial support, student participants, volunteers and support staff, and transportation. Districts can also cosponsor extracurricular programs that appeal to gifted students such as mock trial, Model UN, and Science Olympiad; regional art and science fairs and competitions; and opportunities for service learning.

Examples of networks created to provide specialized courses for advanced students include the Jackson River Governor's School for Science, Mathematics and Technology in Virginia, and the Wisconsin Center for Academically Talented Youth (WCATY) Academy Challenge courses in Wisconsin. In the Jackson River Governor's School collaboration, several school districts serving mostly rural communities partnered with a local community college to offer advanced courses to students in grades 11 and 12. In the WCATY Academy, schools in close proximity work with WCATY, a gifted education organization affiliated with the University of Wisconsin-Madison, to offer challenging hybrid courses for middle school students. WCATY Academy courses combine online learning with occasional regional face-to-face sessions. Some of these courses serve as a replacement for regular academic courses, while others are offered for enrichment and extension (Wisconsin Center for Academically Talented Youth, n.d.).

Leverage "Dual Enrollment" Programs to Provide Access to College and University Resources

For many students, dual enrollment is another option for advanced secondary students who need additional or replacement coursework. Dual enrollment allows high school students to enroll in college courses for credit prior to high school graduation. According to the Education Commission of the States (2013), at least 32 states have established policies for dual enrollment. Courses may be taken before, during, or after school hours on a college campus, online or at a high school, taught by a qualified educator. Although dual enrollment programs are not intended exclusively for gifted students, dual enrollment can provide many of the benefits of other forms of academic acceleration, including access to more advanced and appropriately challenging curricula and access to a more academically similar peer group. Unfortunately, some state policies include provisions that undercut gifted students seeking accelerated learning opportunities, such as capping the number of dual enrollment credits students may earn or restricting eligibility only to 11th-and 12-grade students. Therefore, gifted educators should advocate for the needs of rural students in policies governing dual enrollment and flexible credit.

Collaborate With Colleges and Universities to Create Dedicated Programs for Gifted K–12 Students

Many replicable models of school-university partnerships focused on the needs of gifted students exist. One such program is the Academically Talented Youth Program (ATYP), which operates throughout the state of Michigan. The program, founded by Carol McCarthy at Kalamazoo College and now based at Western Michigan University, operates at multiple sites in Michigan and is conducted by intermediate school districts (state-funded regional school service cooperatives) as well as universities and colleges. The basic model underlying this program is a telescoped curriculum and acceleration. Via off-level test scores, students are identified and begin an accelerated curriculum in the seventh or eighth grade in which 4 years of high school mathematics or 4 years of high school English are compressed into 3 years, thereby enabling students to start college classes as early as their junior year. Students take college-level classes at Michigan universities for their fourth or fifth years. ATYP students take these courses during the regular school day and are released from their schools to go to universities or central locations within their districts for a 2 1/2-hour weekly class. The instructional format is similar to college classes in that students are expected to do a great deal of work on their own at home with some additional supports provided by the program, such as study groups and tutoring. Other ways to deal with transportation barriers are to share transportation costs across districts and for colleges and universities to employ virtual class meetings and study sessions for students.

ATYP is a model of cooperation between multiple institutions and levels of schooling (Olszewski-Kubilius, 2012). A talent search organization provides testing to identify students. The middle and high school districts in Michigan agree to release their students to go to the classes and to honor the credits they earn in the program. The institutions of higher education provide the course instructors as well as advising for students regarding college classes. Because resources are pooled to control costs and program structures support shared trust in the quality and rigor of ATYP courses, the program has been sustained for more than 30 years.

Find Experts in the Community and Involve Them as Mentors, Resources, and Advocates

Mentorships are an excellent tool to help students explore their interests and develop their skills and abilities by working with adults with experience and expertise in a particular domain. Focused, individualized attention is afforded through a mentorship, allowing the student to develop important knowledge and skills at his or her own pace. In addition to developing skills, mentorships can help build confidence, self-esteem, and greater passion for study in the area of interest (Clasen & Clasen, 2003). Involving students in their communities and highlighting opportunities for cognitively and academically advanced students may help to moderate the "brain drain" that has negatively impacted the economies of many rural communities (Goglin & Miller, 2014, p. 3).

Mentorships can be created in a variety of ways. Mentorship can be provided online, for example, connecting a student with a professor or educator in a particular area of study for an independent study project. For a face-to-face experience, it is often possible to partner with local organizations and rural business enterprises, recognizing local sources of expertise. For example, modern farming is rich with opportunities to study STEM fields like chemistry, genetics, and mechanical engineering, as well as business. Therefore, a farmer may have shareable expertise and be able to provide authentic and (literally) "field-based" learning experiences for students interested in science. Program coordinators and educators should think creatively about how community members can be called upon to enrich the standard curriculum through job shadowing and internships.

There are also formal mentorship or internship programs for gifted students available through nonprofit organizations and colleges and universities throughout the country. In these programs, students are connected with experts to work on a predefined project, typically for several weeks over the summer. Examples include the UConn Mentor Connection Program, which provides opportunities for high school students to collaborate with a faculty member or graduate student on authentic research (Wray, 2002) and the Apprenticeship program from the Institute for Educational Advancement, which allows gifted students to work as members of research teams drawn from higher education and industry and to participate in supplemental cultural activities (Berger, 2013). The Davidson Institute for Talent Development has also created an online Mentoring Guidebook (available on the Davidson Institute website), which includes step-by-step guidance for developing a productive mentorship, as well as links to research on mentorship and profiles of model mentorship programs (Davidson Institute for Talent Development, 2014).

Make Use of Technology to Access Advanced Coursework, Connect With Experts, and Find Communities for Social Interaction

Technology, and the Internet specifically, can play a key role in overcoming barriers rural schools have traditionally faced when trying to address the needs of gifted students. As gifted students are, by definition, members of an exceptional population, small schools may lack a sufficient critical mass of gifted students to allow advanced classes and other services to be provided economically. However, as Chris Anderson has noted (2006), the Internet has a unique capacity to aggregate people with atypical needs and interests and provide affordable services for them by neutralizing the geographical limitations that prevent place-based institutions from reaching sustainable scales. Research has demonstrated that online programming can be an effective way to provide access to advanced learning opportunities (Ni, 2013), including gifted students (Thomson, 2010).

Several initiatives have demonstrated the potential for online programs to increase rural access to advanced learning options. For example, the Iowa Online AP Academy, overseen by the Belin-Blank Center at the University of Iowa with state support (Baldus, Assouline, Croft, & Colangelo, 2009), provides free access to online AP courses developed and delivered by for-profit online learning program, Apex Learning. This program has helped Iowa, an overwhelmingly rural state with a large number of small enrollment school districts, to nearly double participation in AP courses over the last decade (College Board, 2014). A similar state-funded program to provide online access to AP courses in Ohio allowed hundreds of gifted, many from rural schools, to participate in advanced online courses provided by the Center for Talent Development's Gifted LearningLinks program and other providers through a statewide portal. Before funding was eliminated, this program helped mitigate an "access gap" in a state where students enrolled in rural schools have access, on average, to only one-fourth the number of advanced courses available to suburban students within their regular schools (Candisky & Siegel, 2013).

In addition to addressing the need gifted students have for cognitively challenging and academically advanced coursework, online programs for gifted students can provide access to a community of peers with similar abilities and interests. For students attending small schools in isolated areas, this may help address some of the social and emotional aspects of giftedness, particularly the need to affiliate with a group of peers who have similar needs, interests, and experiences. Recognizing this need and the potential of the Internet as a platform for community building successfully demonstrated by social media enterprises, some online programs are beginning to complement online course offerings with online community spaces. For example, the Center for Talented Youth at Johns Hopkins University sponsors Cogito, an online community for high-ability students interested in STEM fields (Birch, Blackburn, Brody, & Wallace, 2011). Gifted LearningLinks (GLL) has adopted a new online learning platform modeled after social media sites that allows students, teachers, and mentors to interact not only within their own courses, but with others in interest-based groups using text, rich media, and video. GLL also works with students' schools to allow a local school-based advisor to monitor and support local students participating in online courses (Nelson, 2014).

However, rural students may face special barriers to successful participation in online programs. For example, although less than 20% of Americans live in rural areas (U.S. Census Bureau, 2010), 76% of Americans without access to broadband Internet service live in rural areas (U.S. Federal Communications Commission, 2012). Because students in rural schools are less likely than nonrural peers to have broadband Internet access at home, rural schools can help gifted students take advantage of online programs by providing time during the regular school day and computer access after school for students to engage in online activities. If time to participate during the school day cannot be arranged, rural schools may need to make special efforts to ensure that students have access to adequate technology and bandwidth at home. For households not served by wired broadband connections, schools may wish to investigate low-cost wireless data plans often offered at significant discounts for schools and libraries by mobile phone service providers.

In addition to addressing hardware and network access barriers to rural students' participation in online programs, it is also recommended that schools assess students' technology skills and provide support to help them participate successfully. Even very bright students who have had limited prior opportunities to use digital learning tools may have skill deficits in comparison to other students who have had more extensive experience using computers and online tools and resources. Schools can assist rural students by talking with online learning providers about the skills and technologies needed to successfully participate well in advance of the start of an online course to develop a plan to assess the students' needs and skills and provide targeted options for skill building.

Summer, School Break, and Weekend Programs

Many of the approaches described above focus on providing learning opportunities for rural gifted students within their home communities. However, it is valuable for all students, including rural students, to participate in programs outside their own communities, especially programs specifically designed to meet the needs of high-ability students. By doing so, students gain greater cultural awareness as well as greater awareness of options for future education and career pathways. In the following section we briefly examine supplemental summer, school break, and weekend programs and the unique challenges students in rural settings may experience and ways of overcoming them.

Many colleges, universities and educational organizations offer academic enrichment and accelerative programs for gifted students during the summer, over long weekends, or during winter or spring breaks during the school year. In addition to providing rigorous academics and access to intellectual peers, these programs often include a residential component, which gives students a preview of college life. Although these programs provide many benefits to gifted students, there are some considerations to address to assure access and help students get the most out of the program.

Tuition, Fees, and Transportation

The majority of supplemental programs charge tuition, and residential programs can average over a thousand dollars per week due to the costs involved in providing housing, meals, and 24-hour supervision. There may be additional fees for activities, lab supplies, or books, depending on the program. However, most programs offer need-based financial aid or scholarship opportunities, and it is possible that aid will cover the full cost of participation. Inquire early about financial aid and covered costs. Transportation may be another challenge, both because of distance to be traveled and the cost involved in doing so. In most cases, students will have to arrange their own transportation to the program site. Advance planning is critical so that the funds may be raised or set aside as early as possible.

Time Away From Home and Work

Summer and school break programs range from one week to 8 weeks long, with the average being 3 weeks. This is a significant time for students to be away from home, particularly if they are not used to living apart from family or their community. In addition, many high school students have summer jobs or other responsibilities, which may make it difficult to schedule time away for a program. Again, preplanning is critical for students to find the best program fit, arrange schedules with employers, and offload family responsibilities.

Community Norms

Rural students traveling to an urban program may find the transition exciting, but also challenging in a variety of ways. Students may not have had significant experience living independently or engaged with a wide range of individuals from different religious, cultural, racial, and socio-economic groups. Students need to be comfortable living away from home and in an environment that may have different rules and values.

Social and Academic Readiness

In smaller, rural schools, high-achieving students may have few opportunities to engage with intellectual peers or to take advanced courses, resulting in limited opportunities to experience competition and measure themselves against peers taking challenging curriculum. This can create a big fish, small pond situation where students have unrealistic views of their skills or abilities. When faced with new challenges, students may find themselves struggling for the first time and not knowing how to manage. It is important to prepare students and parents for what might be experienced and to cultivate coping strategies, from psychosocial skill development to study skills. If other students from the school have participated in supplemental programs previously, it is a good idea to arrange conversations about the experience and what to expect. Scaffolding opportunities, such as tutoring sessions, orientation programs, or shorter introductory experiences may be beneficial. And, if it is possible to send a small group of students to the same program, doing so can provide the support and confidence needed.

Professional Development

Educators, particularly those raised and trained in suburban and urban areas, may hold harmful stereotypes of rural students, including expectations of small-mindedness and a perception that students are culturally deprived due to a lack of exposure to diversity (McCracken & Miller, 1988). Therefore, explorations of rural students and cultures should be included in staff development related to diversity, particularly for educators in nonrural settings. While acknowledging the unique challenges rural students often face, teacher educators and professional development designers should also actively challenge negative stereotypes of rural students and strike a balance between valuing global and local perspectives. Incorporating "place-based education" (Gruenewald & Smith, 2008), in which participants are immersed in communities and are guided to recognize the inventiveness and adaptability of local culture to the geographical context through largely hands-on experiences, is one promising strategy for challenging negative stereotypes held by preservice teachers and helping rural teachers with urban and suburban upbringing to connect with the families and communities they serve.

Conclusion

Although the approaches to providing access to supplemental and out-of-school learning opportunities for gifted rural students described above are diverse, common threads can be found across approaches that are consistent with the values and strengths of rural America. First, resource sharing and collaboration are key. Connecting and collaborating with neighboring and regional schools and institutions can reduce the limitations of attending a small school while maintaining the benefits of membership in a close-knit community. Second, a culture of resourcefulness is essential in utilizing supplemental and out-of-school options effectively. Schools, organizations, and families serving rural students must be especially entrepreneurial with respect to recognizing and capitalizing on the affordances of their regions for learning while overcoming geographic and economic barriers. Third, leaders and participants in supplemental and out-of-school educational programs must actively foster environments that value and respect individual students and the cultures and communities from which they come. Particularly through programs that allow students from urban, suburban, and rural communities to collaborate and interact, students can learn to appreciate and balance global, connected, and local ways of knowing. When these principles are embraced, supplemental programs can reduce the rural opportunity gap and help rural students (and others) benefit from the unique cultural and knowledge resources of rural communities in an ever more diverse and interconnected nation of learners.

References

Anderson, C. (2006). *The long tail: Why the future of business is selling less of more.* New York, NY: Hyperion.

Baldus, C. M., Assouline, S. G., Croft, L. J., & Colangelo, N. (2009). The Iowa Online Advanced Placement Academy: Creating access to excellence for gifted and talented rural students. In L. Shavinina (Ed.), *International handbook on giftedness* (pp. 1225–1234). Netherlands: Springer.

Barnett, L. B., & Durden, W. G. (1993). Education patterns of academically talented youth. *Gifted Child Quarterly, 37,* 161–168.

Berger, S. (2013). *The best summer programs for teens.* Waco, TX: Prufrock Press

Birch, K., Blackburn, C., Brody, L., & Wallace, P. (2011). An online community for students who love STEM. *Science, 334*(6055), 467–468.

Bloom, B. (1985). *Developing talent in young people.* New York, NY: Ballantine.

Bronson, P., & Merryman, A. (2013). *Top dog: The science of winning and losing.* New York, NY: Twelve Books.

Candisky, C., & Siegel, J. (2013, Nov.) Rural kids get fewer AP classes. *Columbus Dispatch.* Retrieved from: http://www.dispatch.com/content/stories/local/2014/11/30/rural-kids-get-fewer-ap-classes.html

Clasen, D. R., & Clasen, R. E. (2003). Mentoring the gifted and talented. In N. Colangelo & G. A. Davis (Eds.), Handbook of gifted education (3rd ed., pp. 254–267). Boston, MA: Allyn & Bacon.

Colangelo, N., Assouline, S. G., & New, J. K. (2001). Gifted voices from rural America. Iowa city: The University of Iowa, The Connie Belin & Jacqueline N. Blank International Center for Gifted Education and Talent Development.

College Board. (2014). *The 10th annual report to the nation.* Retrieved from http://www.apreport.collegeboard.org

Davidson Institute for Talent Development. (2014). Davidson Institute for Talent Development mentorship handbook. Reno, NV: Davidson Institute for Talent Development.

Education Commission of the States. (2013). Dual enrollment: 50-state analysis. Retrieved from http://ecs.force.com/mbdata/mbprofallRT?Rep=DE13A

Ewing, J., Dowling, J., & Coutts, N. (1997). *STARS: Report on superhighway teams across rural projects* (ERIC Document Reproduction Service No. ED421319). Dunhee, Scotland: Northern College.

Supplemental and Out-of-School Programming

Goglin, E., & Miller, L. (2014). The nature and needs of rural gifted programs. North Carolina Association for the Gifted and Talented. Retrieved from http://www.ncagt.org/sites/default/files/files/RuralGifted.pdf

Gruenwald, D. A., & Smith, G. A. (2008). *Place-based education in the global age*. New York, NY: Lawrence Erlbaum Associates.

Iatarola, P., Conger, D., & Long, M. C. (2011). Determinants of high schools' advanced course offerings. *Educational Evaluation and Policy Analysis, (33)*3, 340–359.

Karnes, F. A. & Riley, T. L. (2005). *Competitions for talented kids*. Waco, TX: Prufrock Press.

Lee, S. Y., Olszewski-Kubilius, P., Donahue, R., & Weimbolt, K. (2007). The effects of a service-learning program on the development of civic attitudes and behaviors among academically talented adolescents. *Journal for the Education of the Gifted, 31*(2), 165–197.

McCracken, J. D., & Miller, C. (1988). Rural teachers' perceptions of their schools and communities. *Research in Rural Education, 5*(2), 23–26.

McLoughlin, C. (1999). Providing enrichment and acceleration in the electronic classroom: A case study of audiographic conferencing. *Journal of Special Education Technology, 14*(2), 54–69.

Milgram, R. M. (2003). Challenging out of school activities as a predictor of creative accomplishments in art, drama, dance, and social leadership. *Scandinavian Journal of Educational Research, 47*(3), 305–315.

Milgram, R. M., & Hong, E. (1999). Creative out-of-school activities in intellectually gifted adolescents as predictors of their life accomplishments in young adults: A longitudinal study. *Creativity Research Journal, 12*, 77–87.

National Association for Gifted Children. (2010). *Pre-K-grade 12 gifted programming standards: A blueprint for quality gifted programs*. Washington, DC: Author.

Nelson, A. (2014, Fall). Introducing schoology. *CTD Talent*. Retrieved from https://ctdnewsletter.wordpress.com/schoology/

Ni, A. Y. (2013). Comparing the effectiveness of classroom and online learning: Teaching research methods. *Journal of Public Affairs Education, 19*(2), 199–215.

Olszewski-Kubilius, P. (2002). Special summer and Saturday programs for gifted students. In N. Colangelo & G. Davis (Eds.), *Handbook of gifted education* (pp. 219–228). Boston, MA: Allyn and Bacon.

Olszewski-Kubilius, P. (2007). The role of summer enrichment programs in developing the talents of gifted students. In J. VanTassel-Baska (Ed.),

Serving Gifted Learners Beyond the Traditional Classroom (pp. 13–32). Waco, TX: Prufrock Press.

Olszewski-Kubilius, P. (2009). Working with academically gifted students in urban settings: Issues and lessons learned. In J. VanTassel-Baska (Ed.), *Patterns and Profiles of Low-Income Gifted Learners* (pp. 85–106). Waco, TX: Prufrock Press.

Olszewski-Kubilius, P. (2010). Special schools and other options for gifted STEM students. *Roeper Review, 32*(1), 61–70.

Olszewski-Kubilius, P. (2012). *What gifted education can teach general education: Sharing our stories of success.* Presidential address at the annual meeting of the National Association for Gifted Children, Denver, CO.

Olszewski-Kubilius, P. & Grant, B. (1996). Academically talented females and mathematics: The role of special programs and support from others in acceleration, achievement and aspirations. In K. Arnold, K. Noble, & R. F. Subotnik (Eds.), *Remarkable women: Perspectives on female talent development* (pp. 281–294). Cresskill, NJ: Hampton Press.

Olszewski-Kubilius, P., & Lee, S. Y. (2004a). Gifted adolescents' talent development through distance learning. *Journal for the Education of the Gifted, 28*(1), 7–35.

Olszewski-Kubilius, P., & Lee, S. Y. (2004b). The role of participation in in-school and outside-of-school activities in the talent development of gifted students. *Prufrock Journal, 15*(3), 107–123.

Olszewski-Kubilius, P., & Lee, S. Y. (2008). Specialized programs serving the gifted. In F. A. Karnes & K. P. Stephens (Eds.), *Achieving excellence: Educating the gifted and talented* (pp. 192–208). Columbus, OH: Pearson.

Subotnik, R. F., Miserandino, A. D., & Olszewski-Kubilius, P. (1997). The role of participation in in-school and outside-of-school activities in the talent development of gifted students. *Journal of Advanced Academics, 15*(3), 107–123.

Swiatek, M. A., & Benbow, C. P. (1991). Ten-year longitudinal follow-up of ability matched accelerated and unaccelerated gifted students. *Journal of Educational Psychology, 3*(4), 528–538.

Thomson, D. L. (2010). Beyond the classroom walls: Teachers' and students' perspectives on how online learning can meet the needs of gifted students. *Journal of Advanced Academics, 21*(4), 662–712.

U.S. Census Bureau. (2010). Frequently asked questions: What percentage of the U.S. population is urban or rural? Retrieved from https://ask.census.gov/faq.php?id=5000&faqId=5971

U.S. Federal Communications Commission. (2012). Eighth broadband progress report. Washington, D.C.: Federal Communications Commission.

Wai, J., Lubinski, D., Benbow, C. P., & Steiger, J. H. (2010). Accomplishment in science, technology, engineering, and mathematics (STEM) and its relation to STEM educational dose: A 25-year longitudinal study. *Journal of Educational Psychology, 102,* 860–871.

Wilson, V., Litle, J., Coleman, M. R., & Gallagher, J. (1998). Distance learning: One school's experience on the information highway. *The Journal of Secondary Gifted Education, 9*(2), 89–100.

Wisconsin Center for Academically Talented Youth. (n.d.). WCATY Academy. Retrieved from http://prgms.wcatyweb.com/index.php/school-year-programs/2014-09-02-19-05-04

Wray, J. (2002). Where are they now? Success stories from UConn Mentor Connection students. *UConn Advance, 5.*

Appendix 11.1: Program Options for Rural Gifted Students

Online Programs

- » Center for Talent Development: Gifted LearningLinks Program: http://www.ctd.northwestern.edu
- » Center for Talented Youth at John Hopkins University: CTY Online: http://www.jhu.edu/ctyonline/
- » Wisconsin Center for Academically Talented Youth: WCATY Academy: http://academy1.wcatyweb.org/

Talent Search Programs for Gifted Students

- » Northwestern University Midwest Academic Talent Search (NUMATS), Center for Talent Development, Northwestern University: http://www.ctd.northwestern.edu
- » Duke Talent Identification Program (Duke TIP), Duke University: http://www.tip.duke.edu

- Center for Talented Youth, Johns Hopkins University: http://www.cty.jhu.edu
- Western Academic Talent Search (WATS), Center for Bright Kids: http://centerforbrightkids.org
- Belin-Blank Exceptional Students Talent Search (BESTS), Belin-Blank International Center for Gifted Education and Talent Development, University of Iowa: http://www.education.uiowa.edu/belinblank

Part II Summary

Part II was designed with the educator in mind. Each chapter presents different issues pertaining to services for gifted students in rural contexts including identification, programming, curriculum, and accelerative and out-of-school options. A few themes stand out specifically and they are:
- » context is important to how we serve gifted students;
- » when working with any student, especially gifted students, educators must heed "goodness of fit" between the service and the student;
- » the services provided will vary depending on the school and what it can provide and the student and what he or she needs;
- » there is an unfortunate paucity of research that exists that can establish best practices in service provision for rural students in gifted contexts.

Each chapter underscores the reminder to educators that we must make sure the curriculum matches the cultural makeup of our students within our community.

Considerations of locale, a critical mass, access to a variety of talent development opportunities, availability of resources, student body makeup, and cultural differences all play an integral role and how gifted education is provided and to whom. Lewis' chapter highlights the need to evaluate models and programs to ensure the goodness of fit for the school district while accounting for the specific needs of gifted students. She writes that there is no one right answer in determining a choice of one model over another, rather that "the most useful approach is to select the model that best suits a particular school and community. This approach is useful in all settings and especially in rural schools." Lewis points out that regardless of model or program chosen, gifted students thrive by being supported in their striving for the "highest level of which they are capable." A strong curriculum match for gifted rural students is vital to their engagement and academic success. Curriculum must also be a match to the identification practices employed as described by Stambaugh. "Identification without faithful implementation of appropriate interventions over time will produce no effects on learning," write VanTassel-Baska and Hubbard in their chapter.

Appropriate curriculum must include advanced work, structure, scaffold, modeling, and opportunities for exploration and creativity. Without challenge, gifted students may not perceive the relevance of education nor become engaged in school. But no two gifted students are alike. Thus some students will require, as Assouline, Flanary, and Foley-Nicpon and authors suggest in their chapter, "academic acceleration, which can be delivered in a variety of forms" and which "has the potential to address the barriers impeding the academic development of rural gifted students." Assouline and authors provide examples of successful accelerative options for rural students, including online Advanced Placement classes, and conclude that "technological access to Advanced Placement courses goes a long way toward leveling the college, and hence the career, playing fields" for rural gifted students. "Online access to standardized curriculum makes it such that where one lives no longer has to dictate what advanced educational opportunities are available."

Housand and Housand outline Puentedura's SAMR Model, which provides educators with ideas for Substitution, Augmentation, Modification, and Redefinition of an instructional or student task by using technology. They write that although "technology provides opportunities that were not available to generations before including avenues for exploration, opportunities for creativity, and circumstances for engagement," rural gifted students "need high-quality teachers to help show them the way to a brighter future." Educators are the supportive and challenging models that help gifted rural students take the opportunities for participation and engagement "on their terms" and allow them the freedom to enact change and with a love of place.

Educators are those who "not only understand the unique learning characteristics of gifted students, but who also pursue alternative instructional opportunities, which ignite these students' passions." Kirsten Seward and Marcia Gentry offer in their chapter concrete suggestions of how educators of the gifted can use their understanding of their learners and their needs to create optimal environments for grouping in their classrooms and in schools. They write that "rural schools have many strengths from which to develop outstanding programs and services for their students. For example, rural educators know one another, they know the students and their families, and the students find their rural schools enjoyable places to be, likely due to this familiarity." These community strengths are also venues for out-of-school enrichment. Olszewski-Kubilius, Corwith, and Calver explain in their chapter how the community and state can play a role in supporting the talent of rural gifted students outside of the school day. These authors identify sharing and collaboration, creating a culture of resourcefulness, and the facilitation of environments that value and respect diversity of "place" as integral aspects of supplemental and out-of-school learning. "When these principles are embraced, supplemental programs can reduce the rural 'opportunity gap,' and help rural students (and others) benefit from the unique cultural and knowledge resources of rural communities in an ever more diverse and interconnected nation of learners." Taken together, providing challenge and support for gifted rural students is a complex matching process between what the school and community can provide and what the specific student needs.

It is also very clear that rural gifted is underrepresented in the literature and not much is known on this population in terms of how to identify it and to provide interventions and talent development opportunities that highlight its uniqueness and context. More research and attention to rural gifted students is needed in order for best practices to be established and empirically validated; then, educators of the gifted will have the repertoire of knowledge they need to create and defend their classroom and school practices.

PART III

Affecting Change for Gifted Learners in Rural Communities

CHAPTER 12

Counseling and the Rural Gifted

Susannah M. Wood, Ph.D., and Erin Lane, M.A.

In 2011 Hann-Morrison wrote the following in the Georgia School Counselor's Association journal:

> Some children require attention of a counselor if they are to resolve interpersonal and psychological issues that hinder their educational process.... Additionally the parents of these children often need clinical attention... Still others will require assistance to empower their children to aspire academic heights... (p. 26)

This quote referred to students in general; however, the assessment of the school counselor's role holds true specifically for gifted students and their parents as well. Although gifted students are no more or less likely to encounter mental health concerns than their nongifted peers (Colangelo, 2003), they require help and support just like any other student (Peterson, 2009). Unfortunately a common myth that pervades education is that gifted students are smart enough to handle concerns or issues on their own and should not need the assistance of a school counselor. Yet having a gift or a talent does not inoculate a student from experiencing stress, grief, conflict, or underachievement.

Being a gifted student in a rural setting may add both a secondary set of challenges as well as a distinctive and valuable perspective on the world. School counselors in rural settings are in a unique position to facilitate the positive growth and development of their gifted students. Unfortunately, few studies have focused on the interaction between gifted education or gifted students and school counselors, and research regarding gifted rural populations or rural school counseling is negligible. Thus, the purpose of this chapter is to delineate what is known about school counseling and rural gifted students and then to outline strategies school counselors can utilize to work with these youth in the academic, career, and personal-social domains. These strategies will be situated within the context of school counselors' facilitation of a comprehensive, developmental guidance program and will include ideas for data collection, accountability, advocacy, and leadership. The chapter will conclude with ideas for collaboration with mental health agencies and other entities and school counselors' professional development.

School Counseling and the Rural Gifted Student: What Do We Know?

Since the days of Leta Hollingworth, the field of gifted education has been a proponent of providing counseling as a vital element of educating gifted students. Unfortunately, there have been few studies focusing on how school counselors specifically work with their gifted students. Adding to this complexity is the paucity of research regarding the experiences of rural school counselors in general. However, there are some studies from which general themes can be drawn. Authors recommend that school counselors and gifted educators may wish to review these articles and book chapters together as a form of professional development in order to give both parties new ideas about how to effectively work with their gifted students.

Rural School Counselors

School counselors working in rural settings may have a qualitatively different experience than their urban or suburban counterparts. In 1997 Patrick Morrissette conducted a literature review of research pertaining to the experience of rural school counselors and later, in 2001, followed this with a qualitative study on the same topic. Likewise, Richard Pearson and John Sutton conducted studies in 1999 and 2002 in order to examine the roles and functions of school counselors in rural settings and to make suggestions for creating positive learning environments for all students. From these authors' findings, working in rural contexts can provide school counselors with a variety of both positive and negative experiences including the following:

Isolation. School counselors may experience a lack of support systems including fewer friendships, difficulties in connecting with peers and families, and feelings of loneliness. The sense of isolation or lack of connectedness may be one reason for turnover rates in school counseling jobs in rural settings.

"Organizational smallness." Coined by Pearson and Sutton in 1999, "organizational smallness" can refer to the physical size of the school and its ability to facilitate immediate connections among staff members. School counselors may find that due to the small size of the school, they have more direct access and control over what kinds of classes are offered, enrollment patterns, and the creation of different types of academic options for students. Immediate accessibility also facilitates communication between major stakeholders, including teachers, administrators, school board members and superintendents (Pearson & Sutton, 1999). However, "smallness" may also mean a lack of resources, which, when presented with students who require mental health counseling, can create an enormous stressor for school counselors (Morrissette, 1997). In this regard, school counselors may feel forced to practice beyond their scope of expertise while simultaneously having to think creatively about how to support students and families (Morrissette, 1997; Sutton & Pearson, 2002).

Role confusion. School counselors in rural settings may find themselves wearing unexpected hats, such as taking on administrative responsibilities. Although being understaffed may enable counselors to work with populations they may not have had traditionally been able to access, administrative tasks may blur the lines of professional identity (Pearson & Sutton, 1999). In some cases school counselors are perceived as more of an administrator (versus a colleague or counselor with a unique position) and thus are more likely to side with administration on certain issues against teachers (Pearson & Sutton, 1999). In other cases, role confusion may be the result of administrators not knowing or misunderstanding the role of the school counselor or school counselors' responsibilities regarding confidentiality and lack of it with the role of disciplinarian (Morrissette, 1997; Monteiro-Leitner, Asner-Self, & Milde, 2006). Multiple blurry roles can increase the likelihood of counselors' sense of isolation and burnout (Morrissette, 2000; Sutton & Pearson, 2002).

Autonomy. For some school counselors, the rural school has an advantage that other school contexts may not have: professional self-determination. These school counselors experience the freedom and opportunity to define their roles and to establish their school counseling program (Pearson & Sutton, 1999). At the same time, professional self-determination also means professional accountability; in essence, the school counselor *is* his or her program, and when issues arise the school counselor must be the one to solve them (Pearson & Sutton, 1999; Sutton & Pearson, 2002).

Privacy versus visibility. If the rural school counselor resides in the district in which they work, they will be immediately identified as the school counselor outside of the boundaries of the school (Morrissette, 2000). School counselors reported to both Morrissette (2000) and Sutton and Pearson (2002) that they experienced the sense of living in a "fishbowl," in which their behavior was consistently scrutinized, possibly for inappropriate professional behavior within the community. In Sutton and Pearson's study (2002), a school counselor reported being accosted by angry parents in the post office, while participants in Morrissette's study (2000) discussed students dropping by their place of residence unannounced. School counselors in these studies reported feeling guarded, cautious, and vulnerable, with sense of restricted personal space and privacy (Morrissette, 2000; Sutton & Pearson, 2002).

Restricted professional development and peer group. Depending on the context, school counselors may also have decreased accessibility to professional development, which can curtail their growth. School counselors may be the only helping professionals for miles, resulting in a lack of colleagues with which to brainstorm solutions and a lack of different perspectives on problems. Professional development for rural counselors can be restricted by limited budgets, time out of the building especially if the building is already understaffed, and a lack of available trainings and workshops that are easily accessible in terms of time and distance (Bardhoshi & Duncan, 2009).

Community pride/community trust. For many rural communities, it is the school which instills a source of pride and which can act as the hub of community enrichment (Morrissette, 2000). School counselors may experience the benefits of direct ties between the community and the school in terms of closer relationships with students and their families and generally stable student bodies (Morrissette, 2000). However, in order to gain credibility with the community, the school counselor must extend him or herself beyond the walls of the school and come to be seen as part of the community itself. Without trust, a school counselor's outreach to parents may be met with suspicion or the thought that the school counselor is "meddling" in family affairs that are not seen as the purview of the counselor. Community members must come to trust the school counselor as a dependable helping professional that sees the value of the community and in being a part of the rural context.

Gifted Students in Rural Schools

Studies examining the experiences of rural gifted students are scarce. Colangelo, Assouline, Baldus, and New (2003) stated that although research has been conducted on rural education and gifted education separately, few studies have explored how the two intersect. However, a body of literature is beginning to emerge from which ideas for prevention and intervention strategies can be derived.

First, in 1998, Cross and Dixon (1998) outlined what had been published on the topic of gifted rural students up until that point in time. These authors determined three primary themes in the literature, including: (a) the concept or misconceptualization of rural schools being "deficient" with regard to resources and facilities; (b) manuscripts that focused on specific subpopulations of gifted students, including young gifted women and American Indian students; and (c) the actual experiences of rural gifted students. The experiences of gifted women in rural settings was expanded upon by Janyce West in 1996 with the recommendations for counselors and educators, including: (a) identifying and building on womens' strengths while avoiding "antirural bias in language, attitudes, and judgments" (p. 79); (b) encouraging rural young women to maintain high goals while simultaneously helping them learn "urban strategies" to attain those goals (e.g., exposure to urban art and culture, connections to urban institutions); (c) urging gifted young women to read as much as possible; and (d) taking advantage, when possible, of technology in order to increase intellectual challenge as well as a means of facilitating friendships and support groups.

In 1999 and 2001, Colangelo and coauthors discussed their findings from the studies in *Gifted Education in Rural Schools: A National Assessment* and *Gifted Voices from Rural America*. Colangelo and coauthors relayed the many challenges facing gifted students in rural schools (Colangelo, et al., 1999; 2001; 2003). One of the most prominent challenges was the fact that although rural gifted students may be identified, often there was not appropriate programming available to assist them, an issue of mismatch also discussed by Shirley Aamidor (2007) in her report of findings from Projects SPRING I and II (Special Populations Rural Information Network for the Gifted). According to Colangelo and coauthors (1999, 2001), if programming did exist, the lessons did not necessarily enrich students' learning. Another common theme was that of access. Gifted students often lacked the time or resources to adequately enrich their learning; and for some, the only other option was classes at the community college because Advanced Placement courses were not available to them at the high school (Colangelo, et al., 2003). Lack of time for additional programming, lack of trained teachers, limited curricula, perceptions of elitism regarding gifted services and a sense of isolation for gifted advocates were all cited as challenges to gifted education in rural settings (Colangelo et al., 2003). Colangelo and coauthors provided additional depth to these issues in their 2006 *Gifted in Rural America: Faces of Diversity*, which provided detailed case studies of schools in four very different rural areas—Alabama, Iowa, Washington, and Hawaii—with unique demographics. These case studies frequently included the role of the school counselor in working with diversity, identification, and service support to gifted students (Colangelo et al., 2006).

Howley, Rhodes, and Beall (2009) discussed the following four major concerns in rural education and their consequences for gifted students, including: (a) declining population; (b) persistent poverty; (c) changing demographics; and (d) ongoing accountability requirements. These authors and others (Howley & Howley, 2012; Stambaugh, 2010) examined issues such as the community and family values, the "brain drain" of talent in rural areas, the lack of enrichment or accelerative options due to minimal district budgets, identification and service of diverse students in rural areas including ELL students, and the impact of accountability policies that do not always emphasize the academic growth of gifted or high-ability students. Chapter authors have woven these suggested best practices from these researchers into ideas school counselors can utilize in their work with gifted students in rural schools.

Perhaps the one study that can benefit the school counselor the most in planning prevention and interventions services for gifted rural youth was conducted by Cross and Burney in 2005. Their 3-year Project ASPIRE attempted to raise the number of low-income gifted students enrolled in Advanced Placement math and science classes at rural public high schools. During the study of this program, the researchers worked with faculty to increase the academic expectations of gifted low-income students and school counselors to understand better the needs of gifted, low-income, rural students. School counselors who participated in the study cited several challenges, many of which have also been identified by other authors (Colangelo et al., 2003; Colangelo et al., 2006; Howley et al., 2009; Howley & Howley, 2012; Stambaugh, 2010).

Small size. Because of the small size and isolated nature of rural schools, the number of gifted students in any given school will be small. Consequently, identified students may feel isolated and without a like-minded peer group or students with similar abilities.

Values. School counselors recognized that small, rural schools have both advantages and disadvantages for gifted students, but that educators still need to understand that these gifted students from poverty may have differing values than the school system they attend. Counselors also expressed that students and parents may not have seen why the advanced courses were applicable to the future of the student. The study also found that gifted students from poverty did not conform to middle-class norms (i.e., using Standard American English and appropriate language/behavior for a school setting). Gifted students from poverty were also more likely to be the first in their family considering college attendance, making the application, financial aid, and enrollment process more challenging (Cross & Burney, 2005).

Time and training. Participants mentioned there might not be teachers that are trained in curriculum planning for gifted students. Participants reported that they believed Advanced Placement courses had too much work or were too time consuming for students and that class expectations may interfere with other student responsibilities outside of school.

Limited local resources. The remoteness of some rural schools limits resources, such as museums and libraries, that gifted students can access to enrich their learning experience. In addition, gifted students from poverty may have gaps in their knowledge due to lack of resources, which may make advanced classes more difficult. This, in turn, may lead to frustration, with students eventually dropping out of these classes. The lack of educational opportunities is one reason for the lower psychological well-being of gifted low-income rural students, as reported by Cross and Burney (2005).

Relationships and role models. In a separate publication, Burney and Cross (2006) argued further that rural gifted students living in poverty may lack role models and feel confused and unprepared for exploring the options of college. This, in addition to issues previously mentioned, can lead to low self-esteem and low self-efficacy, which are cited as one of the main reasons that these students do not complete advanced coursework (Burney & Cross, 2006).

School Counselors and Gifted Students

Unfortunately, training and classwork pertaining to gifted students, including their unique needs and intervention and prevention strategies, are not generally provided in counselor education programs (Peterson & Wachter Morris, 2010), and the literature pertaining to how school counselors work with their gifted students is limited (Wood, 2010). The field of gifted education has developed several suggested best practices, models, and approaches for meeting the academic, personal, social, and career needs of gifted students (Cross & Cross,

2012; Mendaglio & Peterson, 2007), but these have not been empirically tested in order to ascertain their level of effectiveness.

What is known is that gifted students may actually be seeking the school counselor's help (Wood, 2009) for concerns such as career decision making, social acceptance, perfectionism, and fear of failing. But if school counselors are not trained, they may not be aware that gifted students can face a unique set of challenges during their K–12 schooling and into adulthood. This lack of awareness may explain why many gifted individuals as students learn that school counselors "are for the other kids" (Peterson, 2003, p. 64). Some recent studies suggest that school counselors' service is linked with their understanding and knowledge of gifted development and traits (Carlson, 2004; Wood, 2010). In addition, research shows school counselors can provide differentiated services to gifted students and feel they are more effective when doing so, even though they may also feel ill prepared to meet the needs of these students (Earle, 1998; Wood, 2010). School counselors who have a working knowledge of gifted issues and possess greater self-efficacy in advocacy will also have a greater level of advocacy activity with gifted students (Goldsmith, 2011). Last, there is a sense that gifted educators who work in buildings with school counselors would prefer to have the ability to collaborate more effectively with them in order to better meet needs of their gifted students (Wood, 2012).

Serving Gifted Students in Rural Settings Through a Comprehensive School Counseling Program

The American School Counselor Association (ASCA), the professional organization for school counselors, generates guidelines and best practices for the various roles and functions in which these professionals serve. ASCA's recently updated (2013a) position statement on gifted and talented programs charged the school counselor with the creation of an "environment in which the academic, career and personal/social development of all students, including gifted and talented students, is fostered" (p. 27). This statement also outlines several responsibilities in which the school counselor can engage, such as in (a) identifying gifted students through the use of multiple criteria and measurements; (b) working with gifted students and their families in college and career planning; (c) identifying opportunities for further academic achievement; (d) providing and advocating for needed counseling activities (e.g., individual, group, and classroom guidance) that address the unique needs of gifted students; (e) providing resources and materials to both student and family;(f) raising awareness of the needs of gifted students in schools; and (g) engaging in professional development activities in order to bolster their understanding of gifted students and how to serve them (ASCA, 2013a).

The school counselor can provide these services within the context of a comprehensive, development guidance program, which also supports "purposeful gifted and talented education programs" (ASCA, 2013a, p. 27). The following section discusses ways in which school counselors can enact these seven key responsibilities in rural school settings within the framework of a school counseling program based on specific ASCA (2012) National Model components. These components include service delivery in the three standard domain areas (academic, personal-social, and career), and the key skills of collaboration, advocacy, and leadership are woven through these topics as school counselors utilize them to facilitate their service delivery. Finally, authors discuss the incorporation of accountability measures in order for school counselors to determine if their gifted students are more successful as a result of the services the school counselor provides. Although there are varying definitions of success, authors suggest that school counselors might wish to consider if their gifted and talented students are sufficiently challenged academically, can identify and utilize positive peer support, have appropriate mentors and role models, and can articulate a plan for after high school graduation as possible indicators. Strategies that are suggested here are built upon and extended from the limited research on school counseling and gifted and talented students in rural settings (Colangelo et al., 2003; Cross & Burney, 2005; Howley & Howley, 2012; Stambaugh, 2010).

Awareness and Self-Reflection

We believe that services will be less effective without the school counselors' self-reflection upon issues pertaining to both gifted students and their thoughts about the rural context. Although current school counseling preparation programs seldom address the needs of gifted and talented students, all accredited programs address and incorporate throughout the program the need for multicultural competent professionals and their roles as social justice advocates (Council for Accreditation of Counseling and Related Educational Programs [CACREP], 2009). As suggested by the ASCA Position Statement, school counselors work as advocates in "promoting understanding and awareness of the unique issues that may affect gifted and talented students" (ASCA, 2013a, p. 27). In order to be effective, advocates for these students in rural environments may wish to pause and reflect on their own ideas and beliefs about gifted students and about rural schools. Wood and Peterson (2014) wrote that giftedness itself is a construct, and one that is not "defined similarly across cultures, and not resonating at all with some cultures. Awareness of this reality can help counselors advocate for services for high-ability students from nonmainstream cultures" (p. 640). Likewise, the concept of ruralness is also difficult to define, yet often there is an unspoken stigma attached to it as if to belong to or have come from a rural setting, a person is somehow deficient (Cross & Dixon, 1998; Howley & Howley, 2012). An antirural or middle-class bias (Howley & Howley, 2012; West, 1996) can affect the counseling process negatively as much as an anti-intellectual antigifted predisposition can (Schultz & Delisle, 2003; Colangelo & Wood, 2015). Wood and Peterson (2014) wrote that some cultures

> do not value placing anyone above others or displaying what one knows, instead valuing such elements as quietly serving one's community, being able to inspire others, listening, teaching, overcoming adversity, and having wisdom (rather than "book" knowledge). Counselors can encourage teachers to affirm those values in nonpatronizing ways, thereby helping adolescents from nondominant cultures to feel comfortable and respected in the individualistic, inherently competitive school environment. Confronting judgmental attitudes of dominant culture educators, which may reflect a belief that dominant culture values are the standard by which the values of other cultures should be measured, may also be warranted. (p.640)

Current authors echo this assessment for the need to reflect on giftedness as a possible subculture, ruralness as a cultural context, and how school counselors think and feel about them in order to ensure best practice in service delivery. Wood and Peterson (2014) suggested that school counselors and those educators with whom they collaborate utilize questioning as a form of self-reflection. Their suggested questions (Wood & Peterson, 2014, p. 641) are adapted here to include a specific focus on the intersection of giftedness and rural cultures. Also included are questions that arose from the Project Aspire research by Burney and Cross (2006). For school counselors and other educators who are interested in engaging in self-reflection regarding their approach to gifted students in their building, we encourage utilizing the questions in Table 24.1 in Wood and Peterson's (2014, p. 641) chapter of *The Handbook of Secondary Gifted Education*.

1. What are my thoughts regarding student achievement or underachievement? What emotions does the idea of a gifted student who is underachieving evoke? Do I believe specialized or differentiated programming and curriculum for gifted students is just as important for those who may be achieving versus those who appear to be underachieving? To what extent do I see gifted services as something gifted students "deserve" versus require for optimal learning?

2. Do I believe gifted programming (e.g., enrichment, honors, AP, pull-out, acceleration, or online learning) is appropriate for gifted students from diverse racial and ethnic groups, such as African American or Latino students? Gifted students living in poverty? If so, am I willing to allocate extra time to ensure these students have the necessary knowledge, study skills, and self-efficacy to be successful in these courses?

3. Does the gifted programming (e.g., enrichment, honors, AP, pull-out, acceleration) offered in my school district restrict access to students living in remote locations or living in poverty? If so, am I willing to find ways to accommodate the needs of those students or change the program in order for them to participate? Do I have the resources necessary to connect students via technology, including educators willing to asset students in online learning?

4. How willing am I to advocate for optimal programming for gifted students, including grouping, acceleration, or other forms of differentiated learning? Do I have the resources, contacts, and knowledge necessary to connect gifted students to talent searches, summer programming, or other enrichment opportunities? Do I have the relationships necessary with parents or families in order to discuss these topics and choices knowledgeably and empathically?

5. Am I prepared and willing to work with gifted students and their families to discuss sensitive topics—such as loss, change in family and peer dynamics, and possible desertion from the community—and provide emotional support should a student choose to leave the rural community to attend college? Am I adequately trained to assist the student in finding a college where she or he may be successful and reach her or his potential?

6. How do I conceptualize the idea of school "success" or school "failure"? Do I believe that the definition of success for any gifted student in this community is for her or him to go to college? Does the gifted student need to move away from the rural community in order to fulfill her or his potential?
7. How willing am I to advocate for additional resources, such as professional development, high-speed Internet, extracurricular opportunities, or afterschool transportation in order to facilitate the best learning environment and challenging programming for my gifted students? Even if it means rocking the proverbial boat in the school or community? What priority do I place on gifted students with regard to my energies, time, or personnel and budget in comparison to other student groups I must serve in a school with possible limited resources?

Service Delivery

Identification

Perhaps the most important role a school counselor can play is that of talent identifier. Depending on the specific building level, school counselors can complement gifted identification practices and programming matches in different ways. School counselors are trained to interpret tests, but they may need to consider expanding their repertoire with additional training in assessments used to identify gifted learners. Best practice in identification of gifted learners requires the use and interpretation of multiple assessments, including (but not limited to) behavioral checklists, portfolios, nonverbal tests of ability, tests of creativity, and performance-based measures (Stambaugh, 2010). School counselors and teachers working together can discuss how effective these measures are in terms of "recognizing disadvantaged gifted students based on their unique characteristics" who may demonstrate their talents in different ways, such as through creative or nontraditional outlets (Stambaugh, 2010, p. 67). As an example, portfolios are one way of allowing students to demonstrate the activities that they engage in within the context of the community including leadership, club participation, church functions, and agricultural projects (Stambaugh, 2010).

Academic Planning

Probably the most difficult task is ensuring that once a gifted student is identified that he or she receives the best match in terms of services that can provide academic rigor and personal support. School counselors must keep in mind that gifted and talented students who do not consistently demonstrate the use of proficient Standard American English, in writing or verbally, are often not identified for academically accelerated or enriched classes (Stambaugh, 2010). This may also be true of students with poor handwriting skills (Stambaugh, 2010). Unfortunately, students who wish to pursue a postsecondary education may encounter future barriers, as many colleges require both advanced courses and solid study/organizational skills for entrance and preparation for their own collegiate-level classwork (Stambaugh, 2010). In addition, rural students who are enrolled in enriched or accelerated coursework may find that this takes additional time in homework and project preparation, or more outside-of-school resources such as access to libraries or technology (Howley, Rhodes, & Beall, 2009). Cross and Burney (2005) recommended that school counselors collaborate with teachers to determine what exactly is required for completion of projects and homework and then to provide access to those resources. School counselors can also work with students to find a safe and quiet environment in which to focus on schoolwork, complete assignments (Cross & Burney, 2005), and brainstorm options for time allocation if students are needed for other duties at home, such as sibling care. Although school counselors may advocate for study halls or tutoring periods after school hours, they need to consider that some students may not be able to participate in these activities due to lack of transportation (Cross & Burney, 2005).

As fluent managers of data, school counselors can utilize their databases to examine pertinent issues such as enrollment, GPA, and absenteeism rates of students in advanced courses. Research suggests that gifted young women in rural settings may encounter challenges in pursuing advanced academics, including caring for family members (Cross & Burney, 2005; West, 1996); thus school counselors may wish to use data to examine enrollment patterns in identification for gifted services and advanced academic courses by demographic components (e.g., sex, free/reduced lunch, race, and ethnicity) to identify any educational barriers to access for subgroups of students. School counselors can consider examining student course selection for patterns and trends. Some students may choose not to "risk" a high grade point average by enrolling in honors or Advanced Placement classes. Along with this, school counselors may wish to dialogue with teachers and administrators about absenteeism and how it impacts deadlines and schoolwork; in many cases students may wish to complete assignments but may be unable to do so due to competing demands by family and work (Cross & Burney, 2005). In some instances schools have created radical changes to their semester or trimester scheduling in order to allow for students who have parents working as migrant laborers to complete classes (Colangelo et al., 2006).

One way in which "organizational smallness" (Pearson & Sutton, 1999) works in favor of a school counselors' service delivery is in their likelihood in being a part of teams and committees that select or plan for school curriculum or other academic considerations. School counselors may find their collaboration, coordination, and advocacy skills both shine and are stretched as they participate in these meetings. School counselors can act as advocates for the provision of advanced curriculum, including options for acceleration and differentiation and take a leadership position in vetting appropriate curriculum. Stambaugh (2010) and VanTassel-Baska and coauthors (2002) suggested that curriculum interventions should include provisions for critical thinking, encouraging student discussion, facilitating question asking, and metacognition (VanTassel-Baska & Stambaugh, 2007). School counselors may be in the position to consult with teachers about how to integrate these components into their current curriculum and to examine how they can incorporate them into their classroom guidance lessons.

However, school counselors may find their role is one of leader and systemic change agent in these teams as well (ACSA, 2013a). Research suggests that schools and communities may balk at providing differentiated curriculum due to time, budget, and human resource constraints (Cross & Burney, 2005). School counselors may find themselves working with competing values and mindsets about the provision of resources. Controversial topics in gifted education often pertain to acceleration and cluster grouping, despite the large body of research that supports these techniques as valid interventions, and specifically for gifted learners in rural settings, as "essential" to their success (Colangelo, Assouline & Gross, 2004; Stambaugh, 2010, p. 76).

Cross and Burney (2005) recommended that educators think creatively about how to offer cocurricular options and develop programming that does not take time away from family obligations. Montgomery (2004) suggested that educators begin with a needs assessment to identify potential services for gifted learners that may already be in place in the community. She offered a series of questions for educators to explore (Montgomery, 2004, p. 6) including:

> » Where is our fame (e.g., festivals, awards, harvests, tourism focus, historical points)?

» How can students be invited (e.g., electives, special interest groups, after school meetings, activity clubs)? and
» What do we have available (e.g., public library, historical society, music, artists, musicians, folk art and music, cultural dances)?

To her suggestions we would also add:
» Who are current allies that work with mental health concerns (including churches, agencies, or universities)?
» What technology is already in place that can extend and enhance both student learning and professional development (see Housand and Housand in this book for further information)?
» What have other rural schools done to increase partnerships with parents and community members (see Griffin's chapter in this book for more)?

As discussed previously, school counselors must invest in relationships in order to gain the trust of parents, families, and community members needed to create some of these unique opportunities. Conversations with families should also include their thoughts on what students are expected to do within the structure of the school day versus out-of-school time and what is feasible for students and families to do in terms of time and transportation (Cross & Burney, 2005; Stambaugh, 2010). In some cases, school counselors should be prepared to talk about why Advanced Placement courses are relevant to student learning and future planning, as well as the importance of ACT or SAT preparation time, especially for students who may be the first in their families to consider going to community or 4-year colleges (Cross & Burney, 2005; Stambaugh 2010). Howley, Rhodes, and Beall (2009) and school counselors in the Cross and Burney (2005) study suggested that educators, including school counselors, be prepared to discuss the advantages of students' pursuit of academically challenging classes and residential summer programs with parents and community members. School counselors can be important assets in community forums and can discuss the viability and rationale behind curricular decision making, including justification of time, personnel, money, and other resources such as computers, Internet, and other technology (Hines, 2002).

Online learning opportunities may be fiscally more feasible for some rural schools versus hiring an additional staff member to teach enrichment or accelerated classes (Cross & Burney, 2005; Stambaugh, 2010). Rural schools who have technological resources may wish to consider using Internet options for advanced coursework (Howley, Rhodes, & Beall, 2009); however, teams should evaluate possible curriculum for appropriateness and, hopefully, research-based demonstrated effectiveness (Stambaugh, 2010). Independent learning and organizational skills cannot be assumed for any student, including a gifted student; thus, programming and curriculum teams should also discuss how student work and motivation will be monitored, including pre- and posttesting (Howley, 2002; Stambaugh, 2010). School counselors may wish to support these learners with small groups dedicated to topics on independent learning, time management, organizational skills, and motivation. School counselors may also wish to reference the technology chapter in this book written by Housand and Housand for additional ideas and strategies.

College and Career Planning

Academic planning and college and career planning are integrally connected. The ASCA position statement on academic and college/career planning states that the focus of such planning is "threefold: to help students acquire the skills to achieve academic success, to make connections between school and life experiences and to acquire knowledge and skills to be college and career ready upon high school graduation" (ASCA, 2013b, p. 1). School counselors can engage students and parents in career and college planning in a variety of ways, many of which are suggested as best practices in working with rural gifted students, including:

Facilitate students' understanding that skills needed for school success may be similar to those needed for successful careers (ASCA, 2013b). Cross and Burney's (2005) school counselor participants suggested that rural gifted students could benefit from working on "soft skills," such as communication patterns that they would use with both teachers and future employers, including appropriate voice tone and curtailed use of familiar language. Similarly, school counselors can work with gifted students to review and edit résumés and college applications and role-play possible interview questions (Cross & Burney, 2005). Students can also develop portfolios that demonstrate their abilities, strengths, and interests (ASCA, 2013b; Stambaugh, 2010). Gifted students may resonate more with the experiences of adults who share similar interests, abilities, or career paths; hence, school counselors may wish to include mentorships through local businesses or community colleges so students can see how specific academic skills translate into the world of work (Clasen & Clasen, 2003; Cross & Burney, 2005; Stambaugh, 2010). Last, gifted students may enjoy the challenge of exploring or creating opportunities for employment like summer jobs and entrepreneurships in their local communities (Cross & Burney, 2005).

Assist students' understanding of the connection between coursework and life experiences, and identify and apply strategies to help students achieve future academic and career success (ASCA, 2013b). School counselors can facilitate rural students' self-reflection of their own personal skills and strengths, including those that have helped them overcome a variety of potential obstacles and facilitated academic success (Cross & Burney, 2005). Describing these skills in college applications or elaborating upon them in interviews may mean a greater awareness for gifted students and a better understanding of the students and their strengths from the perspectives of employers and college admissions officers (Cross & Burney, 2005). Students can also learn valuable question-asking and problem-solving skills by investigating co-op opportunities and starting salaries for different types of jobs, specifically those located in their communities (Cross & Burney, 2005). School counselors can provide technological resources including websites, such as "You Can Go!" sponsored by the College Board (http://youcango.collegeboard.org), ACT (http://www.actstudent.org/college/), and web-based applications such as Bridges (http://www.bridges.com) or the *Occupational Outlook Handbook* online (http://www.bls.gov/ooh) for students to explore career paths and steps to the college application process. Stambaugh (2010) suggested that school counselors could facilitate the exploration of dual enrollment options (e.g., community colleges) and the students' awareness of short-term versus long-term postsecondary academic planning and financial decision making. Last, school counselors and students can collaboratively discuss how students foresee their talents and abilities contributing to the growth and success of their community (Howley, Rhodes, & Beall, 2009).

Designing programming for college exposure. School counselors in rural contexts may have more flexibility in how they develop and implement their school counseling programs. Most comprehensive developmental guidance and counseling programs include an emphasis on career and college planning. Given the challenges of transportation, school counselors might have to think creatively and partner with multiple schools or businesses to host career fairs (Cross & Burney, 2005). Likewise, sending students home with videos or promotional materials for various colleges and utilizing websites that include "chat" abilities with college admissions counselors may be more feasible than arranging trips to colleges with groups of students. If local businesses are located close to the school, school counselors can organize career shadowing or apprenticeship opportunities (Cross & Burney, 2005; Stambaugh, 2010).

The most important thing school counselors can do is to be sensitive to the mores, beliefs, and values of their community and to their students and students' parents as they pertain to college and career preparation. School counselors should plan to address issues of finances in college planning with sensitivity, as research has suggested that parents may fear government scrutiny of their finances if students file a FAFSA form (Cross & Burney, 2005). Students and parents both may also feel fearful about students leaving home for residential summer programs or colleges that are located beyond a comfortable driving time especially if no other student from the community is attending (Cross & Burney, 2005). Thus, school counselors need to be prepared to address gifted students' personal and social concerns as they intersect with academics and career planning.

Personal-Social Counseling

By nature of being gifted, gifted students in rural contexts may experience specific issues tied to social interaction and friendships, emotional development, and other life issues in a unique way. School counselors can also assist with the emotional development of gifted students in their school. It is important to remember that gifted students experience some of the same issues as their nongifted peers, such as parental divorce, disagreements with friends or parents, or the death of a loved one; however, due to the overexcitabilities and sensitivities that help characterize giftedness, these students may experiences these events more strongly (Peterson, 2006). School counselors who are knowledgeable about the counseling needs of gifted individuals can anticipate these reactions from students and create individualized counseling strategies that take them into account. Although many gifted students tend to mask difficult personal issues (Peterson, 2006), a school counselor who is attune to the needs and characteristics of gifted students may be able to help these students normalize concerns and reactions in order to better cope.

In a rural district where the overall population is small, there are often fewer gifted students in each grade, limiting the number of intellectual peers for a gifted student (Colangelo et al., 2003). In addition, the smaller student population means that a few vocal students can have a great impact, positively or negatively, on the social life of a student who does not fit the norm, like a gifted student (Stambaugh, 2010). Gifted students may feel isolated and not able to fully embrace or share their idiosyncrasies with their same-age peers for fear of being seen as different (Assouline, Colangelo, & Heo, 2012). A school counselor who can facilitate programming or interventions to assist gifted students in the school should address these issues. For example, school counselors can reduce feelings of isolation by creating a small counseling or lunch group for gifted students, which would allow for connections to be made between gifted peers across age groups that may not have been facilitated by the students independently. School counselors can also advocate for teachers to also create small groups or pairings of gifted students for projects to assist with gifted peer interaction (Robinson & Bryant, 2012).

In addition, it is important that school counselors work with others in and outside the community to find adult mentors for gifted students (Peterson, 2006) in rural areas where there may not be many gifted role models. This is especially true for older, or more mature, students who are ready for an ongoing one-on-one relationship with a like-minded adult (Casey & Shore, 2000; Clasen & Clasen, 2003). With the use of technology, these role models can be located a few miles or a few thousand miles away. Seeking out mentors in a gifted student's area of interest can increase the interactions of the student with the mentor and "sustain the mentorship despite likely conflicts of interest" (Clasen & Clasen, 2003, p. 257). School counselors need to continue to be attuned to the needs of the student throughout the mentorship, especially if communication with the mentor becomes challenging for the student. If successful, mentorships have been shown to have great impact on students from disadvantaged backgrounds, including reducing negative attitudes about education and increasing the student's self-worth (Clasen & Clasen, 2003; Stambaugh, 2010).

One of the major concerns with counseling gifted students in rural settings in particular is the lack of privacy associated with seeking out help from the counselor. Because gifted students tend to mask their need for assistance to begin with, getting students to approach a counselor in a public space like the school can be more challenging. In the Pearson and Sutton (1999) study, school counselors shared that this "lack of privacy discourages some students from bringing their concerns to the counseling office" (p. 93). Counselors felt that not only did others in the school and community know that a student came in to see them, but that others also sought out information about the visit from the school counselor. Counseling office secretaries can either assist with this process by acting as a guide for the counselor providing valuable family information, or they can be a deterrent to students coming in if they inform others that a student has been in the office (Pearson & Sutton, 1999).

Collaboration

School counselors in rural environments are often placed in roles not listed within their job description. They are often asked to practice outside the scope of their training (Hann-Morrison, 2011) due to the lack of mental health counselors in the area that are accessible by their students and families. School counselors are trained as generalists and are not qualified to address serious mental health concerns or family counseling needs that may arise when counseling gifted students. However, in rural settings, school counselors may be the first and last line of defense, and they have to wrestle with the knowledge that if they do not work with the student or family, they will not get help (Morrissette, 2000). In addition, for many residents in small towns, mental health can be a taboo subject (Hann-Morrison, 2011), and the school counselor may be the only person they trust. Becoming better trained in mental health counseling or family therapy may be advantageous for school counselors in this more generalist role. This is especially true when working with gifted students, as few mental health practitioners have training in the needs of gifted individuals.

In general, residents in rural environments will need to travel significant distances to receive mental health services (Hann-Morrison, 2011; Hines, 2002). Cohn and Hastings (2013) also pointed to a distinct stigma in receiving mental health services, which may deter families from seeking out outside assistance. All of these are issues that school counselors in rural areas need to contend with when referring gifted students to outside mental health services. When transferring care is required, support for student and parents will be imperative given the culture and socioeconomic factors that may be deterrents for seeking outside assistance. School counselors should know all available resources in your general area and keep up to date on them, as they will constantly change. School counselors must also be prepared to find alternative transportation or find assistance to fund travel to and from an outside practitioner.

When seeking assistance for gifted individuals, however, the school counselor must carefully consider if receiving specialized counseling services from a mental health practitioner skilled in working with gifted students is more beneficial to that student. Because few mental health counselors are trained in the specific concerns of gifted students (Peterson, 2006), a school counselor could consider having a student video counsel with trained practitioner from across the state or country (Smalley et al., 2010). Another option would be for the school counselor to consult with gifted counseling specialists to provide more specific strategies to the student or to arrange for local mental health practitioners to work with specialists to better assist the student.

Professional Development

Given that school counselors may never have received accurate information about gifted and talented students in their preparation programs, let alone exposure to material that links the gifted experiences with rural contexts (Peterson & Wachter Morris, 2010), school counselors may find themselves in need of professional development (PD) in order to offer comprehensive programming and appropriate interventions for gifted students. Because school counselors in rural schools face additional barriers to engaging in PD (Bardhoshi & Duncan, 2009), organizations like ASCA are beginning to provide an increasing number of online PD, such as webinars and reading for continuing education credits. Given the obstacles that prevent school counselors from finding and receiving PD, making an argument to administration for in-services pertaining to gifted students and their needs can be challenging (Croft & Wood, 2015). However, school counselors to can refer to the ASCA position statement, which reads that school counselors "seek to keep current on the latest gifted and talented programming research and recommendations to employ best practices to meet the needs of identified students and collaborate with other school personnel to maximize opportunities for gifted and talented students" (ASCA, 2013a, p. 27).

Concluding Remarks

Working in rural schools provides professional school counselors with a wide range of opportunities and challenges when it comes to providing their gifted students with appropriate services in academic, career, and personal social counseling. Although there is little research on the experiences of school counselors in rural settings or their work with gifted students, there is little doubt that school counselors can play an important role in the positive talent development of their gifted students. We hope that the suggested strategies discussed will provide school counselors in developing their programs, collaborating with parents, business and agencies, and acting as an advocate for their gifted students. Chapter authors agree with what Cross and Dixon wrote in 1998 (p. 123), that although rural contexts may mean some limitations and challenges for gifted students, "perhaps the fact that small schools have generated a sizable number of society's leaders is a reflection of the character development that is often a byproduct of attending a rural school." We believe school counselors can be one of many key players in gifted students' development into leaders in their communities and in the nation.

References

Aamidor, S. (2007). Identification and intervention for rural, low-income gifted students: A follow-up study. *Gifted Children, 2*(1), 2–5.

American School Counselor Association. (2012). *The ASCA National Model: A framework for school counseling programs* (3rd ed.). Alexandria, VA: Author.

American School Counselor Association. (2013a). *The professional school counselor and gifted and talented programs*. Alexandria, VA: Author

American School Counselor Association. (2013b). *The professional school counselor and academic and college/career planning*. Alexandria, VA: Author.

Assouline, S. G., Colangelo, N., & Heo, N. (2012). Counseling needs and interventions for gifted students: Personality considerations and social-emotional development. In Cross, T. L., & Cross, J. (Eds.), *Handbook for counselors serving students with gifts and talents: Development, relationships, school issues, and counseling needs/interventions* (pp. 649–664). Waco, TX: Prufrock Press, Inc.

Bardhoshi, G., & Duncan, K. (2009). Rural school principal's perceptions of the school counselor's role. *The Rural Educator, 30*(3), 16–24.

Burney, V. H., & Cross, Tracy L. (2006). Impoverished students with academic promise in rural settings: 10 lessons from Project Aspire. *Gifted Child Today, 29*, 14–21.

Carlson, N. (2004) School counselors' knowledge, perceptions, and involvement concerning gifted and talented students. (Doctoral Dissertation, University of Maryland, College Park, 2004). Dissertation Abstracts International, 65(04), 04B. (UMI No. 3128875)

Casey, K. M., & Shore, B. M. (2000). Mentors' contributions to gifted adolescents' affective, social, and vocational development. *Roeper Review, 22*, 227–230.

Clasen, D. R. & Clasen, R. E. (2003). Mentoring the gifted and talented. In N. Colangelo & G. A. Davis (Eds.), *Handbook of gifted education* (3rd ed., pp. 254–67). Boston, MA: Allyn & Bacon.

Coh, T. J., & Hastings, S. L. (2013). Building a practice in rural settings: Special considerations. *Journal of Mental Health Counseling, 35*(3), 228–244.

Colangelo, N. (2003). Counseling gifted students. In N. Colangelo & G. A. Davis (Eds.), *Handbook of gifted education* (3rd ed., pp. 373–387). Boston, MA: Allyn & Bacon.

Colangelo, N., Assouline, S. G., Baldus, C., Ihrig, D. (2006). *Gifted in rural America: Faces of diversity.* Iowa City: University of Iowa.

Colangelo, N., Assouline, S., Baldus, C., & New, J. (2003). Gifted education in rural schools. In N. Colangelo & G. A. Davis (Eds.), *Handbook of gifted education* (3rd ed., pp. 572–581). Boston, MA: Allyn & Bacon.

Colangelo, N., Assouline, S. G., & Gross, M. U. M. (2004). *A nation deceived: How schools hold back America's brightest students.* Iowa City: The University of Iowa, The Connie Belin & Jacqueline N. Blank International Center for Gifted Education and Talent Development.

Colangelo, N., Assouline, S. G., & New, J. K. (1999). *Gifted education in rural schools.* Iowa City: University of Iowa.

Colangelo, N., Assouline, S. G., & New, J. K. (2001). *Gifted voices from rural America.* Iowa City: University of Iowa.

Colangelo, N., & Wood, S. (2015). Counseling the gifted: Past, present and future directions. *Journal of Counseling & Development, 93,* 133–142.

Council for Accreditation of Counseling and Related Educational Programs. (2009). *Council for Accreditation of Counseling and related educational programs 2009 standards.* Retrieved from http://www.cacrep.org/wp-content/uploads/2013/12/2009-Standards.pdf

Croft, L., & Wood, S. M. (2015). Profrssional development for teachers and school counselors: Empowering a change in perception and practice of acceleration. In S. Assouline, N. Colangelo, J. VanTassel-Baska, & A. Lupkowski-Shoplik (Eds.), *A nation empowered: Evidence trumps the excuses that hold back America's brightest students* (pp. 87–98). Iowa City: The University of Iowa, College of Education, Belin-Blank Center.

Cross, T., & Dixon, F. (1998). On gifted students in rural schools. *NASSP Bulletin, 82,* 119–124.

Cross, T. L., & Burney, V. H. (2005). High ability, rural and poor: Lessons from Project Aspire and implications for school counselors. *Journal of Secondary Gifted Education, 16*(4), 148–156.

Cross, T. L., & Cross, J. R. (Eds.). (2012). *The handbook for counselors serving students with gifts and talents: Development, relationships, school issues, and counseling needs/interventions.* Waco, TX: Prufrock Press.

Earle, S. (1998). A critical incident study of the school guidance counselor's interactions with gifted students. (Doctoral Dissertation, Kent State University). *Dissertation Abstracts International* 59, 07A. (UMI No. 9842490)

Goldsmith, S. K. (2011). An exploration of school counselors' self-efficacy for advocacy of gifted students. (Doctoral dissertation, University of Iowa). ProQuest Dissertations and Theses. (UMI No. 3494154)

Hann-Morrison, D. (2011). The varied roles of school counselors in rural settings. *Georgia School Counselors Association Journal*, 26–33.

Hines, P. L. (2002). Transforming the rural school counselor. *Theory into Practice, 41*(3), 192–201.

Howley, A. (2002). The progress of gifted students in a rural district that emphasized acceleration strategies. *Roeper Review, 24,* 158–160.

Howley, A. & Howley, C. (2012). Counseling the rural gifted. In T. L. Cross & J. R. Cross (Eds.), *Handbook for counselors serving students with gifts and talents: Development, relationships, school issues, and counseling needs/interventions* (pp. 121–136). Waco, TX: Prufrock Press

Howley, A., Rhodes, M., & Beall, J. (2009). Challenges facing rural schools: Implications for gifted students. *Journal for the Education of the Gifted, 32*(4), 515–536.

Mendaglio, S., & Peterson, J. S. (Eds.). (2007). *Models of counseling: Gifted children, adolescents and young adults.* Waco, TX: Prufrock Press.

Monteiro-Leitner, J., Asner-Self, K. K., & Milde, C. (2006). The role of rural school counselor: Counselor, counselor-in-training and principal perceptions. *Professional School Counseling, 9*(3), 248–251.

Morrisette, P. (1997). The rural school counselor: A review and synthesis of the literature. *Guidance & Counseling, 13*(1), 19–24.

Morrisette, P. J. (2000). The experiences of the rural school counselor. *Professional School Counseling, 3*(3), 197–208.

Pearson, R. E., & Sutton, J. M. (1999). Rural and small town school counselors. *Journal of Research in Rural Education, 15*(2), 90–100.

Peterson, J. S. (2003). An argument for proactive attention to affective concerns of gifted adolescents. *The Journal of Secondary Gifted Education, 14*(2), 62–70.

Peterson, J. S. (2006). Addressing counseling needs of gifted students. *Professional School Counseling, 10*(1), 43–51.

Peterson, J. S. (2009). Myth 17: Gifted and talented individuals do not have unique social and emotional needs. *Gifted Child Quarterly, 53*(4), 280–282.

Peterson, J. S., & Wachter Morris, C. (2010). Preparing school counselors to address concerns related to giftedness: A study of accredited counselor preparation programs. *Journal for the Education of the Gifted, 33*(3), 311–366.

Robinson, A., & Bryant, L. (2012). Gifted students and their teachers: Relationships that foster talent development. In T. L. Cross & J. R. Cross (Eds.), *Handbook for counselors serving students with gifts and talents: Development, relationships, school issues, and counseling needs/interventions* (pp. 427–442). Waco, TX: Prufrock Press.

Schultz, R. A., & Delisle, J. R. (2003). Gifted adolescents. In N. Colangelo & G. A. Davis (Eds.) *Handbook of gifted education* (3rd ed., pp. 483–492). Boston, MA: Allyn & Bacon.

Smalley, K. B., Yancey, C. T., Warren, J. C., Naufel, K., Ryan, R., & Pugh, J. L. (2010). Rural mental health and psychological treatment: A review for practitioners. *Journal of Clinical Psychology, 66*(5), 479–489.

Stambaugh, T. (2010). The education of promising students in rural areas: What do we know and what can we do? In VanTassel-Baska, J. (Ed), *Patterns and profiles from promising learners of poverty* (pp. 59–83). Waco, TX: Prufrock Press.

Sutton, J. M., & Pearson, R. (2002). The practice of school counseling and rural and small town schools. *Professional School Counseling, 5*(4), 266–277.

VanTassel-Baska, J., Johnson, D., & Avery, L. D. (2002). Using performance tasks in the identification of economically disadvantaged and minority gifted learners: Findings from Project STAR. *Gifted Child Quarterly, 46*, 110–123.

VanTassel-Baska, J., & Stambaugh, T. (Eds.). (2007). *Overlooked gems: A national perspective on low-income promising leaners*. Washington, D.C.: National Association for Gifted Children.

West, J. (1996). In God's country: Rural gifted women. In K. Arnold, K. Noble, & R. Subotnik (Eds.), *Remarkable women: Perspectives on female talent development* (pp. 69–80). New York, NY: Hampton Press.

Wood, S. (2009). Counseling concerns of gifted and talented adolescents: Implications for school counselors. *Journal of School Counseling, 7*(1). Retrieved from http://www.jsc.montana.edu/articles/v7n1.pdf

Wood, S. M. (2010). Nurturing a garden: A qualitative investigation into school counselors' experiences with gifted students. *Journal for the Education of the Gifted, 34*(2), 261–302.

Wood, S. M. (2012). Rivers' confluence: A qualitative investigation into gifted educators' experiences with collaboration with school counselors. Roeper Review, *34*(4), 261–274.

Wood, S. M., & Peterson. J. S. (2014). Superintendents, principals, and counselors: Facilitating secondary gifted education. In F. A. Dixon and S. M. Moon (Eds.). *The handbook of secondary gifted education* (pp. 627–649). Waco, TX: Prufrock Press.

CHAPTER 13

"Mommy, I'm Bored"
School-Family-Community Approaches to Working With Gifted, Rural Black Males

Dana Griffin, Ph.D., and Susannah M. Wood, Ph.D.

My son received an excellent preschool education. His school worked with him based on his abilities, the teachers held high expectations, and they continually engaged him in learning. When he continued to learn at a pace above his peers, the preschool director provided curriculum at higher, more engaging levels, so that my son would continue to be motivated and would continue to learn. He loved going to his "school" and loved learning. When he returned home each day, he always had more information for me about what he learned. My son was extremely excited to begin public school. In fact, it was all he could talk about since he was 3 years old. He could not wait to ride the yellow school bus as he had seen his big sister do for 6 years. I distinctly remember the night before his first day of school. He knew the rules: bath at 7 p.m., bed at 8 p.m., alarm set for 6:30 a.m. By the time I woke up at 6:30 the next morning, he was awake, fully dressed, and eating breakfast. He rushed me out the door so we could go to the bus stop. He had no worries, no anxieties, and no hesitations about going to school. We had attended the "Back to School" night and met his teacher and some other students who would be in his classroom. He had his Spider-Man backpack and Spider-Man lunchbox ready. On his feet were his new school sneakers, and although he was not wearing what I call appropriate school apparel, he was happily clothed in a Washington

Redskins football jersey and a pair of basketball shorts—his favorite outfit. His excitement and readiness for school continued for 2 weeks. On the third week of school, he told me he no longer needed to go to school because he already knew everything. I will never forget his words, "School is boring, Mom. I'm not learning anything new."

Introduction

The above paragraphs describe the first author's journey as a mother of a gifted African American young man. Dana does not consider herself well versed in the gifted literature, and she does not teach topics pertaining to gifted education in schools of education. However, she herself is a woman who has personal experience growing up in a rural community in the southeastern United States. Dana is exceptionally well versed in multicultural education policy and practice, family-school-community partnerships, and school counseling. She continues to be a fierce advocate for her son and for all African American students in K–12 education. To that end, she prefaces this chapter by citing the following points:

» African Americans make up 4.6 million, or 6.5%, of the country's rural population, and of those living in rural areas, 39% lived below the federal poverty line in 2008 (U.S. Census Bureau, 2008). Many low-income Black families live in rural areas, and when social class is added to racial bias, Black male students are further disadvantaged because higher SES students are more likely to be identified as gifted (Howley & Howley, 2012).

» Disproportionality patterns that exist in schools today continue to place Black and Latino males more at risk of academic failure than any other group (Bryan et al., 2012).

» Black male children who display above-average intellect are often not provided with a curriculum that matches their needs, which Ford (2010) called the stubborn problem of underrepresentation of Black and Hispanic students in gifted education and advanced placement courses.

» Problems that exist in high school for African American males (i.e., lower graduation rates, lower standardized test scores, higher suspension rates, higher placement rates in special education classes) begin in elementary school.

The statistics point to the great need for a fundamental change to occur, but the question is: Where should systemic change begin? Where does parent advocacy start? How can biases and preconceived notions be changed to truly see the intelligence and talents that Black males bring to the table? In counseling, when addressing multiple issues, we often search for the underlying issue that causes the presenting problem. When it comes to gifted education, the same philosophy needs to apply. What is the underlying problem, and what can schools, particularly rural schools, do to address it?

Susannah, the second author, is not a parent of a gifted student. She is White, and therefore a member of the dominant culture, one that has been traditionally identified with the stereotypical picture of "gifted." Although she describes herself as a daughter of a military family that frequently relocated, she never lived in a rural community. As a former school counselor and residential counselor for the gifted, she has frequently asked herself the same questions Dana relates above. These questions inspired her to connect the worlds, research, and training of gifted education and counselor education.

This chapter will interweave Dana's and her son's experiences with schools and an overview of what is known about parents' experiences with schools and advocacy for their gifted children. Each section will present themes and concepts that are derived from Dana's journey as a parent of a gifted African American young man, followed by both Dana and Susannah's exploration of these themes as they pertain to the literature. To provide a thorough exploration, the literature we provide is drawn from gifted education, multicultural and counseling literature, and family-school partnership literature. Themes include the following: (a) parents as talent identifiers and their role in the talent development process, (b) the experiences of parents with the gifted label and bias in the identification process, (c) helping parents wrestle with difficult and frequently emotional decisions regarding how best to provide for their gifted child in and outside of schools, (d) facilitating trust between families and schools, and (e) developing collaborative partnerships between the school and families of gifted students in rural settings.

We write this chapter as a dialectical experience; that is, the authors dialogue together about their stories, experiences, and what they know about the issues presented. Dialectical here does not mean we are providing opposing viewpoints and hoping to reconcile them. As we shift between first and third person, Dana and I work to write a discourse or an exchange of ideas and examine the relationships between these ideas, from which we hope to provide strategies for school personnel that can facilitate a safe, challenging, sensitive, and nurturing climate for gifted African American students—like Dana's son—in rural settings.

Parents and Families in the Talent Development Process

My son is extremely intelligent in math. I have been told by other professors that his reasoning and analytic skills are far above those in kindergarten or first grade. He laughs at me when I get a calculator to balance the checkbook, because he can do sums in his head. Yes, my son is intelligent, but I did not always think he was intelligent. In fact, he did not speak words until he was 13 months, causing me to have him tested for autism. The results of these tests showed developmental delays, but not autism. He did not answer questions he was supposed to know. Actually, he refused to interact with the test administrators at all. They spent 3 hours in our home administering tests to a 12-month-old who refused to communicate with them, either verbally or nonverbally. He never uttered a single word or sound. They left me with a list of resources for families with kids with developmental delays. I never had to use them. Within a month of that visit, my son began to speak. By age 2, he was reading stories of Dick and Jane. By the age of 3, he could do simple addition. At age 4, still in preschool, he completed a full year of kindergarten. By the time he was able to officially begin public school, he was reading and writing on a first-grade level.

Parents as Talent Identifiers

As Dana shared this with me (Susannah), I was initially jarred by my first connection between her story and what I know about parents and families of gifted students. Parents and family members are often accurate in their identification of their children's gifts (Silverman & Golon, 2008); however, some of those very characteristics that point to giftedness also can create anxiety in parents. Silverman and Golon (2008) wrote:

When children develop speech later than their siblings, parents often worry that the children are developmentally delayed, even if they display extraordinary facility with puzzles, construction toys, creating things from odds and ends, disassembly items and spatial memory . . . many are simply developing their right hemisphere before their left hemisphere. (p. 201)

Parents and family members play a pivotal role in a child's talent development. The family communicates values and beliefs from generation to generation, including how gifted children think about the following: (a) work and achievement; (b) education, money, status, and social standing; (c) creativity and curiosity; (d) finding meaning in careers and in recreation; (e) community, volunteerism, and service to others; and (f) locus of control, destiny, and perseverance (Olszewski-Kubilius, 2008; Robinson, Shore, & Enerson, 2007). Hard work, community pride, and the importance of the school in the community may become specific values communicated in families of rural gifted children. The concept of career as a value may be unique in these values because gifted students face difficult choices of staying and serving the community or leaving the community for other pursuits (see Howley and Howley's chapter, this volume).

Although Dana and her son may not see eye to eye on the use of calculators in balancing the family checkbook, Dana is helping her son develop his own unique talents and identity. Parents have to delicately balance closeness with their children along with the needed emotional and psychological space for the children to develop into their own unique person (Olszewski-Kubilius, 2002; 2008). Over time Dana may have challenged her son to work on the family budget and, by doing so, helped her son identify activities that match his talents and help facilitate them. I know finances can often play a role in family stress; however, stress can provide opportunities for problem solving, motivation, and persistence for gifted children. Parents can model how to cope with different types of stressors and how they identify and utilize healthy outlets for emotions (Olszewski-Kubilius, 2002; 2008). In rural contexts, problems posed within the community, such as the shutting down of a farm or factory, drought, the debate over wildlife protection, or the consequences of urban sprawl, may be a source of problem solving in families, schools, and the community itself.

Gifted Children's Development in the Family Context

Dana describes her son as a "sports-loving, athletic ball of energy"—a ball of energy that often requires Dana to be creative in ways to keep him on task and engaged. Raising a gifted child can be incredibly demanding and exhausting for parents. Divergent thinking coupled with high levels of energy can mean that gifted students require a stream of novel experiences, mental stimulation, hours needed to "play" with ideas and creative outlets, and less sleep (Lovecky, 1992; Silverman, 1993; Silverman & Golon, 2008). Asynchronous development, traditionally defined as the experience of having different rates of development (e.g., cognitive abilities develop more quickly than emotional coping), can be a source of stress and confusion to parents (Colangelo, 2003; Silverman, 2012; Silverman & Golon, 2008). Asynchronous development can cause parents to question: How can a child be so smart and yet not act his or her age? Silverman and Golon (2008) wrote:

> Gifted children are asynchronous. They can be both adult like and childlike, almost simultaneously. The same child who can communicate his love of dolphins by reciting the Latin names of virtually every species can be found moments later arguing over toys. (p. 205)

A gifted child's intellectual capacity may mean both advanced vocabulary and keen insight into family dynamics; parents may feel that at times they are talking to adults, which can lead to difficulty in establishing appropriate boundaries between parent and child, the child having more responsibilities at home, or children having more "power" in the home so that parents defer to them (Colangelo, 2003; Colangelo & Bower, 1987; Colangelo & Dettman, 1983; Keriouz, 1990; Moon, 2003; Moon & Thomas, 2003). Parents may be overwhelmed by persistent questions asked by children who display divergent thinking and whose communication style may come across as argumentative, defiant, or questioning of authority (Lovecky, 1992; Probst & Piechowski, 2012; Silverman, 1993; Silverman & Golon, 2008). However, these behaviors may simply be the child trying to understand family dynamics, making meaning of parental expectations, or exploring boundaries and his or her unique independence. Parents of more introverted children may be perplexed by their child's need for solitude and solo play.

Many of these characteristics and exchanges can occur, as in the case of Dana's son, before preschool. Thus, probably the first question that parents ask is, "Is my child gifted?" "Unfortunately by the time parents seek counseling to answer this question, they have often become frustrated. They want a simple answer and the answer is never simple" (Hertzog, 2012, p. 196).

Labels: Confusion, Bias, and Prejudice in the Identification Process

I believe my son is intelligent, even gifted, but our public school system has decided that students should be tested for Academically and Intellectually Gifted (AIG) programming beginning in third grade. However, I pushed to have him tested in first grade. He failed the test, which meant he was not gifted, and also not eligible to receive services that would engage him on his level. A few weeks after demanding my son be tested for the gifted program, I received a letter in the mail from the school system. The letter simply stated that my son did not meet requirements for placement in gifted education and I could try again next year. Not knowing the requirements for placement in gifted education, my next step was to schedule a meeting with the AIG coordinator, who administered the test to my son. At this meeting, she explained why my son did not qualify, which was, "He knew all the answers, but he could not explain them to me and one aspect of being gifted is to explain your answers." To make sure I understood correctly, I rephrased: "My son is not gifted because, although he had all the correct answers written down, he could not explain to you how he got the answers. So being able to read complex word problems and do the math in his head is not good enough?" As I am not a gifted educator, I did not have any resources to use in this conversation. Therefore, I set out to do my own research.

That same day, Dana visited the National Association for Gifted Children (NAGC; n.d.) website, a website that is supposed to be parent friendly, to see how they defined giftedness. The website stated that "there is no universal definition of giftedness" and that "nearly every state has its own definition of gifted and talented students . . . Not all states require that school districts follow the state definition" (para. 6). The website also provided a link that leads to the definition of giftedness by each state. By this definition listed next to Dana's home state, her son met the criteria. However, the gifted coordinator informed her that although the definition of gifted is broad, they have specific assessments to use and students must score a certain level to be identified as gifted, and her son fell just below the cutoff. She asked for a copy of the assessment, but privacy regulations precluded the coordinator from showing her the assessment. Dana wrote:

> *At this point I cannot help but wonder about the role that race and gender play in his lack of gifted identification. After all, racial and gender disparities exist in school practices, especially when it comes to suspension, placement in special education, dropout rates, Advanced Placement courses, and even gifted identification.* (Bryan, Day-Vines, Griffin, & Moore-Thomas, 2012; Ford, 2010)

Cultural Bias in the Identification Process

Dana is familiar with the study conducted by the Yale University Child Study Center, which showed higher rates of expulsion for 5–6-year-old students, African Americans, and males (Gilliam, 2005). Regarding her own experiences in the identification process, Dana wrote:

> *I have no doubt that if my son exhibited "problem" behaviors, there would be no hesitation in labeling him as disruptive or even trying to move forward with assigning a special education label to him. Indeed, when my son was acting out in class (exemplified by talking in line or during quiet time at lunch), I received emails and behavioral reports with suggestions for how to help curtail negative behavior and ways to teach him appropriate forms of behavior in school. If it is so easy to have Black male students referred (and accepted) as behavioral problems, why is it so difficult to have Black male students referred to (and accepted) as gifted?*

Ford (2010) described three major paradigms that lead to underrepresentation of African American and Latino males in gifted education:
1. deficit thinking: the belief that culturally different students are genetically and culturally inferior to White students;

2. colorblindness: intentionally or unintentionally suppressing the role of culture in learning, curriculum, assessment, and expectations; and
3. White privilege: unearned benefits that advantage Whites while systematically disadvantaging others.

Researchers and scholars believe that a deficit ideology is a main cause for the underrepresentation of Black males in gifted programming (Ford, 2010; Gorski, 2011; Henfield, 2013). Gorski (2011) asserted the deficit perspective that educators use when viewing students is the presenting problem, but the underlying issue is:

> a symptom of larger sociopolitical conditions and ideologies borne out of complex socialization processes. We can no more quash the deficit perspective without acknowledging, examining, and quashing these processes than we can eliminate racism without comprehending and battling white supremacist ideology. (p. 153)

Dana agrees with Gorski's perspective about the need to unlearn deficit ideologies, which is a focus on one's internal belief systems. Indeed, a plethora of research exists on the sociocultural impacts on students' academic achievement, from "acting White" and negative peer pressure (Ford, Grantham, & Whiting, 2008; Fordham & Ogbu, 1986), to the internalization of deficit thinking where one begins to believe he or she is not capable of producing high-quality educational work, and therefore does not try (Grantham, 2004).

As VanTassel-Baska and Johnsen (2007) believe, a procedural shift is needed among educators and other stakeholders in the nomination and identification process for gifted programs. Stambaugh (see her chapter in this volume) discusses best practices for identifying gifted students, and Ford (see chapter in this volume) provides a deep discussion of the importance of cultural competency in identification, recruitment, and retention, which can and should include professional development of staff (see the Croft chapter in this volume). Silverman and Golon (2008) specifically underscored the need for culturally competent examiners and test administrators who can both give and interpret tests and build relationships with students and families.

Requiring educators to involve parents in the identification and nomination process can be a way to address the cultural biases that some school educators have when it comes to viewing Black males as gifted students. Parent involvement is not a novel idea, as it has been used for years as a strategy for increasing academic achievement of all students. Parent involvement and its relationship to academic achievement is a central focus in educational research (Tillman, 2009). Requiring teachers and schools to work with parents can be the procedural shift in that the nomination and identification process must include meaningful involvement with parents.

The Role of the "Gifted" Label

As I read it, I am struck by how Dana's story illustrates how the concept and "gifted" definition has impacted her family over time and underscores the important, often undiscussed role of labels. Labels are mixed blessings. In Dana's experience, she knows that having her child appropriately identified will lead, should she choose to accept, to appropriate services, including the challenging curriculum a bright mind needs. However, the label of gifted can have negative connotations as well. It is, according to Colangelo (2003, p. 380) and Jenkins-Friedman (1992) the "reorganizer" of families.

The gifted label influences the parent/child system and the sibling system (Colangelo, 2003; Cornell, 1983; Moon & Hall, 1998). Having a gifted child may cause families to question how much time, energy and resources they put into their child's talent. This is a fine line to walk; on the one hand, parents and families are integral to their child's talent development, and on the other, overinvestment in one child may unbalance the family (Colangelo, 2003). The sibling relationship can be impacted by the label as the nonlabeled children may question what role and value they now have in the family, which can be further complicated if the sibling(s) miss the criterion cut-off scores for identification by one or two points (Jenkins-Friedman, 2002; Moon & Hall, 1998). When behaviors arise as a result of asynchronous development, parents must determine what they will do with a child who can at one moment be calculating sums in his or her head and the next fighting over crayons with their siblings. Colangelo (2003) wrote:

> In some families, behaviors are tolerated because the parents perceive that "this is how it is with a gifted child," or not tolerated because, "such behavior should not come from a gifted child." (p. 380)

Dana's gifted African American son has multiple labels now attached to him, creating a unique dynamic of being a "double minority" (Stambaugh & Ford, 2015). I am again challenged by these authors, who write:

> Because of these specific characteristics, gifted students in general and gifted students who are double minorities (i.e., gifted and of a different race/ethnicity or low-income status) do not fit into the traditional societal or school mold academically or socially. They must navigate their own cultural group norms and the expectations and socialization within the larger school context, while also coping with gifted characteristics and the social and cultural dilemmas accompanying each that contributes to and results in microaggressions. (p. 194)

These authors (Stambaugh & Ford, 2015) describe some of the negative reactions educators, students, and community members can have of gifted students of color. Examples of "'You are a credit to your race' (p. 196) and 'You are so articulate'" (p. 196) can be "viewed as degrading and illustrate inaccurate assumptions about race/ethnicity, cultural differences, and giftedness" (p. 193). Gifted students in rural settings may also be confronted by the additional conundrum of conflicting parental values, such as "Be all you can be, but don't leave your family home or community" (p. 195). These messages serve to shape and form student identity. In many ways, students must balance and integrate multiple identities stemming from the multiple cultures in which they reside. Rural is a culture and it influences perceptions, meaning, values and decision making. Rural culture shapes what parents and educators believe and do. Rural culture informs teaching and ways and means for challenging gifted students.

A Parent's Fear: Engagement and Challenge in and out of School

When I complained to my son's kindergarten teacher that the work she currently supplies for my son is below his academic ability, she let me know that she had to focus on the students who did not know their alphabet. With a kindergarten class size of 27 students, all with different levels of knowledge, I understood there were certain milestones the schools required and that she needed to make sure that all students reached those milestones. However, in doing so, students like my son were actually being left behind. So, yes, I am afraid when he says, "School is boring."

Dana's fear stems from knowing the research that demonstrates that although African American males are excited about starting school, they begin to lose interest by fourth grade (Hargrove & Seay, 2011; Harmon, 2002; Tyson, 2002). She is very familiar with the research that show the numerous factors leading to low academic achievement in Black males, such as peer influences, school discriminatory practices, and even negative teacher perceptions (Ford & Grantham, 2003; Hargrove & Seay, 2011). She is afraid because she knows that her son, with his energy and precocity, will be quick to be seen as aggressive and loud. She fears the negative possibilities that exist for her son because he is Black and male and *gifted*. Ford (2010) stated that a lack of a federal mandate for gifted education is part of the problem in terms of providing appropriate academic challenge for students like her son. For example, although the goal of No Child Left Behind is to improve the academic achievement of all students, the legislation ignores programs designed for gifted education, which leads to public schools focusing on improving the academic achievement of their low-performing students while ignoring enrichment programs for their high-performing students (Michael-Chadwell, 2010).

Dana writes that when her son is not intellectually or creatively engaged, he is engaged in using his energy in any type of sports activity. When Dana hears him say he's bored, she understands this to mean that he has disengaged himself from learning and engaged himself in other things. These other things may be the behaviors that teachers find problematic and lead to the labeling of students as "problem children." Indeed, Pedro Noguera (2008) asserted in his critical text on the issues with public education and Black males:

> The trouble with Black boys is that too often they are assumed to be at risk because they are so aggressive, too loud, too violent, too dumb, too hard to control, too streetwise, and too focused on sports. Such assumptions and projections have the effect of fostering the very behaviors and attitudes we find problematic and objectionable. The trouble with Black boys is that most never had a chance to be thought of as potentially smart and talented or to demonstrate talents in science, music, or literature. The trouble with Black boys is that too often they are placed in schools where their needs for nurturing, support, and loving discipline are not met. Instead, they are labeled, shunned, and treated in ways that create and reinforce an inevitable cycle of failure. (p. xi)

Although research with parents in rural areas show that parents have lower postsecondary educational attainment and educational expectations for their children than parents in urban or suburban areas (Provasnik et al., 2007), more recent research demonstrates that parents of students in rural areas actually do hold high expectations for their children (Griffin, Hutchins, & Meece, 2011). This is important, as parental expectations and support play an important role in the development in children's college and vocational aspirations (Bryan, Moore-Thomas, Day-Vines, Holcomb-McCoy, & Mitchell, 2009; Griffith, 1996; Simons-Morton & Crump, 2003). However, as college completion rates for adults tend to be lower in rural than urban areas, parents who have not attended college may lack important information that is needed to help children prepare for college (Griffin, Hutchins, & Meece, 2011; Provasnick et al., 2007; Saenz, Hurtado, Barrera, Wolf, & Yeung, 2007; Whitener & McGranahan, 2003). These parents, and thus, their children, may then turn to schools and to teachers for this information.

Decision Making and Service Options

If or when Dana's son is identified as gifted, she and her family will be faced with almost overwhelming decision-making, including whether or not to include her son in whatever special programming his school provides. Schader (2004, 2008) pointed to the fact that parents of gifted students want to ensure their child is challenged and supported in school, but making decisions about programming and services is difficult in light of contradictory information. Parents are often confronted with mixed messages from well-meaning entities including, school personnel, friends, community members, research in books and magazines, and the general media. As a result, "parents without experience evaluating research risk forming opinions and making decision based on unfounded information, misinformation or even disinformation" (Schader, 2008, p. 479).

Parents and guardians of gifted children in rural contexts may be even more frustrated if the school cannot provide for the child in terms of services or if the services are a mismatch with the child's talents. Children may require acceleration, which can range from single-subject to whole-grade to enrichment programming or even early entrance. When contemplating accelerative options, parents and schools should explore what will be required in terms of additional time in homework and project preparation, including safe and quiet environments, tutoring or study halls, sibling care and home duties, and how the students are to access out-of-school resources such as libraries or technology and transportation (Cross & Burney, 2005; Howley, Rhodes, & Beall, 2009). If both time and technology are available, parents can even consider homeschooling, which can provide for a more independent and individually tailored curriculum. Regardless of the type of programming gifted students require, curriculum that includes critical thinking, student discussion, question asking, and metacognition is needed (VanTassel-Baska & Stambaugh, 2007).

Rural schools are at a prime disadvantage when it comes to receiving funds for gifted education. Schools with lower enrollments receive less funding, which leads to fewer resources, which often means that special programs, such as gifted education, are not seen as a priority (Howley, Rhodes, & Beall, 2009). Indeed, all students in rural schools, especially in low-income rural communities, have limited access to a number of programs that can aid in higher educational achievement. In addition to access to gifted education, students in rural and low-income rural schools have less access in career counseling, college preparatory courses, career academies, and school-to-work programs (Provasnick et al., 2007). Without having specified gifted education coordinators or teachers, the burden of meeting the needs of gifted students most often falls to the regular classroom teacher whose first priority goes to students who are not demonstrating success. In Dana's son's school, the AIG coordinator's job was part of the budget cuts, meaning that the classroom teacher would have to be in charge of meeting his accelerated needs, in addition to meeting the needs of a number of other students in the classroom. Furthermore, if gifted educators are employed in rural school districts, they may be assigned to several small schools, which can lead to students receiving superficial gifted curricula (Howley, Rhodes, & Beall, 2009).

"I Stood Alone": Parental Advocacy for Gifted Services

Because my son is Black and because he is male, hearing him say he was bored were the scariest words I have ever heard. Not everyone will understand this statement. Certainly, school stakeholders and parents alike thought I was crazy, asking for too much for a kindergartner. As one parent said, "There is too much focus on learning. Kids this age should be focusing on learning social skills, not math and writing." This parent was upset about how much homework was sent home, while I was upset over the quality of homework that was sent home. I went to the teacher, to the principal, to other parents, to the gifted coordinator over the school district to discuss options for my son, to find solidarity in the disappointment of the school curriculum, to find support in my quest for a more developed curriculum for children who already knew how to read, knew how to count, and knew their colors. I stood alone. The ones who agreed with me had already taken their children out of public school and enrolled them in private schools, where they received higher quality curriculum, curricula that included learning a foreign language, learning complex math problems, and explorations in science and technology. Although this could be an option for me, I feel that public schools should also provide the same engaging curriculum for children. I believe that public schools should meet the needs of my son and others like him.

Parents like Dana have not always had the most positive experiences working with the entity of "the school." Raising a gifted child is a challenging prospect. Research suggests parents may seek support and guidance in a variety of areas concerning their gifted child, including (Colangelo, 2003; Moon, 2003; Hermann & Lawrence, 2012; Schader, 2008; Silverman & Golon, 2008): (a) effective parenting; (b) finding appropriate challenging resources and stimulation; (c) help with family dynamics including sibling relationships; (d) support in advocacy on behalf of the child with the school regarding identification and service; and (e) assistance in helping their child with friendship and peer interactions. Within rural communities, whom do parents turn to for support and information in order to best help their gifted child but the school? Nevertheless, experiences with support and help vary.

Colangelo and Dettmann (1982) developed a way of conceptualizing parent-school interactions involving gifted students. This interaction model includes four different ways families and schools interact based on the level (active or passive) that both the school and the family have. For example, Type IV interaction, "Natural Development" is described as an interaction based on a tacit agreement between parents and schools that the role of the school is passive (i.e., the typical school curriculum suffices) and a student's talent will develop on its own. This interaction assumes that if talent truly exists, then it will naturally develop (Colangelo, 2003).

Type III interaction, or "Interference," resonates with me (Susannah). Here, parents' main concern is the impact of the gifted label on the family and on the child's social relationships. Although the school may wish to provide services for the gifted child, parents may not want services or may be unsure if services are helpful or necessary. The fear is that the label separates the student via special programming in a way that will negatively impact his or her educational development (Colangelo, 2003). I believe my parents would have happily supported gifted services; however, I was the one to be afraid of being "different" and set apart from my peers in elementary school if I participated in a pull-out program. My parents honored my wishes. Although the label would have benefited me in other schools I moved to, this decision would be something I would come to reflect on years later.

Type II interaction, "Conflict", is what no parent wants to experience. I would hazard that no school would want to be described in this manner either. The conflict arises from parents who believe their student requires special programming, but the school believes that special programming is priority for students with special needs and that the regular curriculum is adequate for gifted students. Unfortunately, this interaction is characterized by blame, aggression, withdrawal, and undermining.

What Dana and her son hoped for is Type I, or the "Cooperation" interaction between families and schools. This interaction is illustrated by sharing of information, cooperation, and the belief that schools and families should be active participants in the students' talent development. Both parties believe that schools can provide for appropriate educational challenge through specific educational planning. Cooperation, however, is built on trust, not something easily established between parents and schools.

And, in the cases of many parents of color, trust is doubly hard to build with an entity that has historically marginalized and discriminated against its students, and with which parents have had negative experiences. Fornia and Frame (2001) wrote that trust is an issue that parents of gifted students find themselves challenged by through processes like identification (e.g., Do we trust our assessment of our child's abilities? Do we trust others to assess this fairly?), services (e.g., Do we trust the school to provide what is best for our child?), and even social and community interaction (e.g., Do we trust others to treat our child with respect if we communicate that he or she is gifted and in a special program?).

In rural settings, parents may receive conflicting messages about giftedness from their fellow parents or the schools. If in some community cultures, pursuing accelerated learning means "putting on airs" or "not knowing one's place," then parents can assume there will be a lack of trust between them, their student, and their community. However, many rural communities are close-knit. Parents may trust other parents and the school with their child's safety, such as driving them home after school or entrusting other families with their children for extended periods of time. Parents' trust in themselves would appear to be a theme in the literature, although it is not directly specified other than in Fornia and Frame's article (2001). Parents must trust that they are doing all that they can to advocate for their gifted sons and daughters.

Grantham, Frasier, Roberts, and Bridges (2005) wrote about the need for parental advocacy with culturally diverse gifted youth. In their article, they discuss an advocacy model for culturally diverse gifted students that concerned gifted program educators can use to work with parents to guide their advocacy efforts. However, as many schools still continue to struggle with working with African American parents, this advocacy model will be ineffective until gifted educators become aware of and are committed to increasing Black student enrollment in gifted programs.

Parents require advocates in the school who can speak to the resources in the community that can help support gifted students' learning (Silverman & Golon, 2008). These advocates should be knowledgeable about talent searches and weekend/summer enrichment options at local universities (see Olszewski-Kubilius and coauthors in this volume), Internet resources (see Housand and Housand's chapter in this volume), and other programming, such as special schools (see Lewis's chapter in this volume).

Research suggests that parents of gifted children frequently wrestle with their own efficacy in both providing the needed resources to keep their children engaged and in their ability to parent. Parents may struggle with feelings of inadequacy and anxiety as they contemplate if they are "smart enough" to guide their gifted child (Silverman & Golon, 2008, p. 205). In fact, research suggests that parents of gifted children are often disappointed in the lack of support they receive from schools and even friends and other family members (Alsop, 1997; Colangelo, 2003; Moon, 2003; Silverman & Golon, 2008). Thus, school advocates should help parents of gifted children find each other, a job that can become doubly challenging in rural settings when the number of potential parents is statistically smaller and geography can create difficulties in contact. However, within the school, school counselors can facilitate Supporting the Emotional Needs of Gifted (SENG) parent groups (http://sengifted.org/programs/seng-model-parent-groups), or provide parents with online forums (http://sengifted.org/programs/seng-online-parent-support-groups) and "blogs" to help them connect (http://www.hoagiesgifted.org/on-line_support.htm). Silverman and Golon (2008) suggested that one of the best types of support helping professionals can give parents of gifted students is working with them on advocacy skills. As the community plays a large role in how gifted students develop their talent in rural areas, a school-family-community approach focusing on parent involvement and community resources is of utmost importance when trying to overcome the problem of underrepresentation of Black males in gifted programs in rural environments.

Powerful Partnerships: Using Parent Involvement in Gifted Education

I have mentioned that I am not a gifted educator and I am not a researcher on gifted education. However, I do research with parents—specifically, parents of Black and Latino children in suburban and rural areas. My work with these populations tells me that parents can be a powerful resource for the schools, but in the cases of African American and Latino families, they are the most underused resource. Speaking generally, these groups of parents are ones that do not tend to be the visible ones in the schools. They are not known as the involved parents or the helicopter parents. Indeed, just as the negative stereotypes of Black males lead to underrepresentation in gifted education in the schools, schools' negative views of Black and Latino parents lead to underutilization of the strengths that parents can bring to the schools.

To this end, Dana proposes three main strategies for working with parents of Black males in rural schools as they continue to remain academically and socially marginalized in our public schools (Noguera, 2008). These include relationship-building, open communication, and community asset mapping. Susannah would add that professional development is a requirement if staff are to be trained to be culturally competent identifiers of talent (see Croft's chapter, this volume) and aware of positive practices in acceleration (see Assouline et al.'s chapter, this volume), in-school programming (see Lewis's chapter, this volume), and out-of-school enrichment opportunities (see Olszewski-Kubilius et al.'s chapter, this volume). Also, Dana and Susannah both know from experience that school counselors can play an integral role in identification, service provision, advocating for and with parents, and facilitating partnerships (see Wood and Lane's chapter, this volume).

Relationship Building

Even before the first day of kindergarten, schools should strive to establish strong, working relationships with parents. Indeed, Title I requires that schools involve parents and share information with parents on school programs, academic standards, and assessments to help parents be more knowledgeable regarding their children's academics (Epstein & Hollifield, 1996). Teachers should make time to talk with each parent before the first day of school. During this time, parents should be made aware of all educational opportunities available for their child, including the nomination and identification process for gifted education programs. This should be done in small group settings, with culturally diverse groups. It is important to not separate African American parents because at these meetings, they should receive the same information that other parents receive. In addition, they will be able to hear questions that other parents may ask, which can lead to information they may not have otherwise received.

Individual meetings should also be planned during which teachers should get to know the parents and begin to develop a trusting relationship with them. Getting to know parents and their children on a more personal level can lead to more collaborative relationships with parents that allow for mutual understanding between home and school and for educators to better understand the strengths and needs of parents (Griffin & Steen, 2010).

The creation of collaborative relationships with parents indicates a mutual respect and understanding of the parents and their families. One major outcome of focusing on relationship building moves the focus above and beyond academics and toward family support and developing parental efficacy, which is the parents' sense of ability to positively affect their children's achievement (Bower & Griffin, 2011). Building strong working relationships and partnerships with parents can also counteract the deficit approach that educators can hold against Black males and their families by allowing opportunities to get to know them on a deeper level and providing the opportunities to dispel biases and preconceived beliefs that teachers may hold.

Open Communication

Both a major requirement for relationship building and a natural outcome of relationship building, open communication is of utmost importance in all aspects of parental involvement, especially in the identification and nomination process for gifted males. When teachers talk to parents about gifted or advanced curricula, they need to be able to truly listen to how parents describe their children's attributes. Although teachers do need to share with parents the characteristics of gifted children, they also need to ask parents what they see from their child at home, as gifted attributes may be demonstrated differently. Although this may seem like an unnecessary step at early ages, parents from impoverished rural environments may be unaware of educational opportunities that occur in elementary school, which then may impact student placement and gifted identification at later stages.

When teachers begin to identify and nominate students for gifted education, they need to meet with all parents of students to share their rationale for nominating or not nominating students. Using open communication, teachers need to be prepared to share what factors went into their nomination. Teachers need to also let parents know they can nominate their own kids for gifted programming, as this is something of which they may be uninformed. Parents from my studies were unaware they could request certain things for their kids, believing that schools reserved the right to make all decisions concerning the education of their children. At this point, it may be helpful to begin to incorporate Grantham et al.'s (2005) advocacy model by providing parents with the knowledge needed to advocate on behalf of their kids.

Community Asset Mapping

Just as Black males, rural schools and communities can be viewed through a deficit perspective. Research on rural environments highlight higher rates of poverty, poorer school preparation, and lower parent expectations in rural areas (Byun, Meece, & Irvin, 2012). However, rural communities also have many resources, such as strong connections to families, schools, and religious organizations (Coleman, 1988; Howley, 2006; Elder & Conger, 2000). Community asset mapping is an approach that schools can use to find resources to help develop creative ways to engage Black male students in academics in early years, especially those who enter school well prepared for more advanced learning. Ensuring that Black males remain engaged in school is pivotal in the identification and nomination process.

Community asset mapping is a method to help people become more self-reliant and develop stronger social relationships with the community by engaging members of the school and surrounding neighborhoods in working together to identify the resources that are already readily available to them without having to rely on financial assistance (Jasek-Rysdahl, 2001). As parents and teachers in rural areas may be unaware of the resources available to them and lack knowledge on how to access those resources (Griffin & Galassi, 2010), community asset mapping can be used to find resources and opportunities to engage academically gifted Black male students in learning, when teachers may be overwhelmed with meeting the needs of the lowest performing students. Community asset mapping finds the locations of resources and programs without forcing schools to come up with the necessary funding for these programs. The use of community asset maps have been demonstrated to be effective in finding resources for schools and school counselors in working with kids with disabilities and with mental health disorders (Griffin & Farris, 2010).

Community asset mapping can provide parents with necessary information, empowering them to be more proactive in procuring resources for their children (Griffin & Farris, 2010), and can be especially helpful for working with gifted Black males students in rural areas. For example, schools can work with nearby businesses to teach students about any facet of their business, from the development, to the everyday organizations of the business; or schools can partner with farmers to learn about how to run a farm and how to grow fruits and vegetables. Community asset mapping is a proven strategy for securing resources in times when resources are hard to find. Using outside resources for gifted students can help students remained engaged in the learning process and continue their academic trajectory toward excellence.

Conclusion

This chapter shares Dana's fight for her son to receive quality education based on his level, not the level of the majority of the class. In fighting for her son, she is also fighting for high-quality education for all Black male children who are demonstrating high aptitude at early ages. Dana is an advocate of high-quality education for all children, regardless of their academic abilities, and fighting for her son has exposed her to the inaccessibility of gifted curriculum at young ages and the problems with the identification and nomination process. Susannah is also an advocate. She has seen the incredible blossoming of talent that occurs when gifted students finally find a home in challenging programs and with students like themselves. But how can we ensure gifted African American young men begin that path early? Trying to get Black males in gifted or Advanced Placement curriculum in middle or high school is simply too late.

As Dana's sister, a high school math teacher, said, "If students do not receive the math foundation early on in their educational career, it is difficult to suddenly catapult them to advanced levels later" (Marshall, personal communication, 2015). We both believe that parent involvement can be a starting point buffering against the sociopolitical culture that continues to place Black males at a disadvantage when it comes to educational opportunities in gifted education. However, we both know that this strategy is not the cure-all for the massive problem of underrepresentation of African American males in gifted education.

Schools need to change too, and rural schools have additional challenges. Teachers still need to be aware of cultural influences in their decision making regarding referrals for gifted education. We still need multicultural training for educators. We still need to address the current practice and policies related to gifted education referral and placement. And we still need to address the socio-emotional reasons that Black male students opt out of gifted or Advanced Placement courses (Ford, 2010). However, these issues are more long-term approaches to addressing the problems, while the strategies described in this chapter are changes that can occur now.

Using our personal experiences, we hope we have illustrated just how important families are to the talent development of all gifted children, specifically children like Dana's Black, intelligent, not yet identified as gifted, son. We offer an overview of what we know about the role of families in the lives of their gifted children; their experiences with schools, identification, and bias; and the impact of the gifted label. We have suggested ideas for schools and parents that can help them embrace the idea of working together and not against each other as they change the current cultural climate of gifted African American students in rural communities. We have done so in a dialectal exploration of issues, drawing on both our expertise and our experience and weaving our voices together so gifted children will never have to say, "Mommy, I'm bored."

References

Alsop, G. (1997). Coping or counseling: Families of intellectually gifted students. *Roeper Review, 20*(1), 28–35.

Bower, H. A., & Griffin, D. (2011). Can the Epstein model of parental involvement work in a high minority, high poverty elementary school? A case study. *Professional School Counseling, 15,* 77–87.

Bryan, J., Day-Vines, N. L., Griffin, D., & Moore-Thomas, C. (2012). The disproportionality dilemma: Patterns of teacher referrals to school counselors for disruptive behavior. *Journal of Counseling & Development, 90,* 177–190.

Bryan, J., Moore-Thomas, C., Day-Vines, N. L., Holcomb-McCoy, C., & Mitchell, N. (2009). Characteristics of students who receive school counseling services: Implications for practice and research. *Journal of School Counseling, 7*(21). Retrieved from http://www.jsc.montana.edu/articles/v7n21.pdf

Byun, S., Meece, J. L., & Irvin, M. J. (2012). Rural-nonrural disparities in postsecondary educational attainment revisited. *American Educational Research Journal, 49*(3), 412–437.

Colangelo, N. (2003). Counseling gifted students. In N. Colangelo, & G. A. Davis (Eds.), *Handbook of gifted education* (3rd ed., pp. 373–387). Needham Heights, MA: Allyn & Bacon.

Colangelo, N., & Bower, P. (1987). Label gifted youngsters: Long-term impact on families. *Gifted Child Quarterly, 31,* 75–78.

Colangelo, N., & Dettman, D. F. (1982). A conceptual model of four types of parent-school interactions. *Journal for the Education of the Gifted, 5,* 120–126.

Colangelo, N., & Dettman, D. F. (1983). A review of research on parents and families of gifted children. *Exceptional Children, 50*(1), 20–27.

Coleman, J. S. (1988). Social capital in the creation of human capital. *American Journal of Sociology, 94* (Suppl.), S95–S120.

Cornell, D.G. (1983). Gifted children: The impact of positive labeling on the family system. *American Orthopsychiatric Association, 53*(2), 322–335.

Cross, T. L., & Burney, V. H. (2005). High ability, rural and poor: Lessons from Project Aspire and implications for school counselors. *Journal of Secondary Gifted Education, 16*(4), 148–156.

Elder, G. H., & Conger, R. D. (2000). *Children of the land: Adversity and success in rural America.* Chicago, IL: University of Chicago Press.

Epstein, J. L., & Hollifield, J. H. (1996). Title I and school-family-community partnerships: Using research to realize the potential. *Journal of Education for Students Placed at Risk, 1,* 263–278.

Ford, D. Y. (2010). Underrepresentation of culturally different students in gifted education: Reflections about current problems and recommendations for the future. *Gifted Child Today, 33*(3), 31–35.

Ford, D. Y., & Grantham, T. C. (2003). Providing access for culturally diverse gifted students: From deficit to dynamic thinking. *Theory into Practice, 42*(3), 217–225.

Ford, D. Y., Grantham, T. C., & Whiting, G. W. (2008). Culturally and linguistically diverse students in gifted education: Recruitment and retention issues. *Exceptional Children, 74,* 289–308.

Fordham, S., & Ogbu, J. U. (1986). Black students' school success: Coping with the "burden of 'acting White.'" *The Urban Review, 18,* 176–203.

Fornia, G. L., & Frame, M. W. (2001). The social and emotional needs of gifted children: Implications for family counseling. *The family journal: Counseling and therapy for couples and families, 9*(4), 384–390.

Gilliam, W. S. (2005). *PreKindergarteners left behind: Expulsion rates in state preKindergarten systems.* Yale University Child Study Center, New Haven, CT.

Gorski, P. C. (2011). Unlearning deficit ideology and the scornful gaze: Thoughts on authenticating the class discourse in education. In R. Ahlquist, P. C. Gorski, & T. Montaño (Eds.), *Assault on kids: How hyper-accountability, corporatization, deficit ideologies, and Ruby Payne are destroying our schools* (pp. 15–176). Bern, Switzerland: Peter Lang.

Grantham, T. C. (2004). Multicultural mentoring to increase Black male representation in gifted programs. *Gifted Child Quarterly, 48,* 232–245.

Grantham, T. C., Frasier, M. M., Roberts, A. C., & Bridges, E. M. (2005). Parent advocacy for culturally diverse gifted students. *Theory Into Practice, 44*(2), 138–147.

Griffin, D., & Farris, A. (2010). School counselors and school-family-community collaboration: Finding resources through community asset mapping. *Professional School Counseling, 13,* 248–256.

Griffin, D., & Galassi, J. P. (2010). Exploring parental perceptions of barriers to academic success in a rural middle school: A case study. *Professional School Counseling, 14,* 87–100.

Griffin, D., Hutchins, B. C., & Meece, J. L. (2011). Where do rural high school students go to find information about their futures? *Journal of Counseling & Development, 89,* 172–181.

Griffin, D., & Steen, S. (2010). School-family-community partnerships: Applying Epstein's theory of the six types of involvement to school counselor practice. *Professional School Counseling, 13,* 218–226.

Griffith, J. (1996). Relation of parental involvement, empowerment, and school traits to student academic performance. *The Journal of Educational Research, 90,* 33–41.

Hargrove, B. H., & Seay, S. E. (2011). School teacher perceptions of barriers that limit the participation of African American males in public school gifted programs. *Journal for the Education of the Gifted, 34*(3), 434–467.

Harmon, D. (2002). They won't teach me: The voices of gifted African American inner-city students. *Roeper Review, 24,* 68–75.

Henfield, M. S. (2013). Special issue: Meeting the needs of gifted and high-achieving black males in urban schools. *Urban Review, 45,* 395–398.

Hermann, K. M., & Lawrence, C. (2008). Family relationships. In T. L. Cross & J. R. Cross (Eds.), *Handbook for counselors serving students with gifts and talents* (pp. 393–408). Waco, TX: Prufrock Press.

Hertzog, N. B. (2012). Counseling for young gifted children. In T. L. Cross & J. R. Cross (Eds.), *Handbook for counselors serving students with gifts and talents* (pp. 195–208). Waco, TX: Prufrock Press.

Howley C. W. (2006). Remote possibilities: Rural children's educational aspirations. *Peabody Journal of Education, 81*(2), 62–80.

Howley, A., & Howley, C. (2012). Counseling the rural gifted. In T. L. Cross & J. R. Cross (Eds.), *Handbook for counselors serving students with gifts and talents* (pp. 121–136). Waco, TX: Prufrock Press.

Howley, A., Rhodes, M., & Beall, J. (2009). Challenges facing rural schools: Implications for gifted students. *Journal for the Education of the Gifted, 32*(4), 515–536.

Jasek-Rysdahl, K. (2001). Applying Sen's capabilities framework to neighborhoods: Using local asset maps to deepen our understanding of well-being. *Review of Social Economy, 59,* 313–329.

Jenkins-Friedman, R. (1992). Families of gifted children and youth. In M. J. Fine & C. Carlson (Eds.), *Handbook of family school interventions: A systems perspective* (pp. 175–187). Boston, MA: Allyn & Bacon.

Keirouz, K. S. (1990). Concerns of parents of gifted children: A research review. *Gifted Child Quarterly, 34*(2), 56–63.

Lovecky, D. V. (1992). Exploring social and emotional aspects of giftedness in children. *Roeper Review, 15*(6), 18–25.

Michael-Chadwell, S. (2010). Examining the underrepresentation of underserved students in gifted programs from a transformational leadership vantage point. *Journal for the Education of the Gifted, 34*(1), 99–130.

Moon, S. (2003). Counseling families. In N. Colangelo, & G. A. Davis (Eds.), *Handbook of gifted education* (3rd ed., pp. 388–402). Needham Heights, MA: Allyn & Bacon.

Moon, S., & Hall, A. S. (1998). Family therapy with intellectually and creatively gifted children. *Journal of Marital and Family Therapy, 24*(1), 59–80.

Moon, S., & Thomas, V. (2003). Family therapy with gifted and talented adolescents. *Journal of Secondary Gifted Education, 14*(2), 107–113.

Olszewski-Kubilius, P. (2002). Parenting practices that promote talent development, creativity and positive adjustment. In M. Neihart, S. Reis, N. Robinson, & S. Moon (Eds.). *The social and emotional development of gifted children: What do we know?* (pp. 205–212). Waco, TX: Prufrock Press.

Olszewski-Kubilius, P. (2008). The role of the family in talent development. In S. Pfeiffer (Ed.), *Handbook of giftedness in children: Psychoeducational theory, research, and best practices* (pp. 53–70). New York, NY: Springer.

National Association for Gifted Children. (n.d.). Definitions of giftedness. Retrieved from http://www.nagc.org/resources-publications/resources/definitions-giftedness

Noguera, P. A. (2008). *The trouble with black boys . . . and other reflections on race, equity, and the future of public education.* San Francisco, CA: John Wiley & Sons.

Provasnick, S., KewalRamani, A., Coleman, M. M., Gilbertson, L., Herring, W., & Xie, Q. (2007). *Status of education in rural America* (NCES 2007–040). Washington, D.C.: National Center for Education Statistics, Institute of Education Sciences, U.S. Department of Education.

Probst, B., & Piechowski, M. (2012). Overexcitabilities and temperament. In T. L. Cross & J. R. Cross (Eds.), *Handbook for counselors serving students with gifts and talents* (pp. 53–74). Waco, TX: Prufrock Press.

Robinson, A., Shore, B., Enerson, D. (2007). Parent involvement. In A., Robinson. B. Shore, D. Enerson (Eds.), *Best practices in gifted education: An evidence-based guide* (pp. 7–14). Waco, TX: Prufrock Press.

Saenz, V. B., Hurtado, S., Barrera, D., Wolf, D., & Yeung, F. (2007). *First in my family: A profile of first-generation college students at four-year institutions since 1971.* Los Angeles, CA: Higher Education Research Institute.

Schader, R. M. (2004). Parent resource specialist report for the board of the National Association for Gifted Children. Unpublished manuscript.

Schader, R. M. (2008). Parenting. In Plucker, J. A. & Callahan C. M. (Eds). *Critical issues and practice in gifted education* (pp. 479–492). Waco, TX: Prufrock Press.

Silverman, L. (1993). The gifted individual. In L. Silverman (Ed.), *Counseling the gifted and talented* (pp. 1–28). Denver, CO: Love Publishing

Silverman, L. K. (2012). Asychronous development: A key to counseling the gifted. In T. L. Cross & J. R. Cross (Eds.). *Handbook for counselors serving students with gifts and talents* (pp. 261–280). Waco, TX: Prufrock Press.

Silverman, L. K., & Golon, A. S. (2008). Clinical practice with gifted families. In S. Pfeiffer (Ed.), *Handbook of giftedness in children: Psychoeducational theory, research, and best practices* (pp. 223–246). New York, NY: Springer.

Simons-Morton, B. G., & Crump, A. D. (2003). Association of parental involvement and social competence with school adjustment and engagement among sixth graders. *Journal of School Health, 73,* 121–131.

Stambaugh, T., & Ford, D. (in press). Microaggressions, multiculturalism, and gifted individuals who are Black, Hispanic, or low income. *Journal of Counseling & Development.*

Tillman, L. C. (2009). Facilitating African American parental involvement in urban schools: Opportunities for school leadership. In L. Foster & L. C. Tillman (Eds.), *African American perspectives on schools: Building a culture of empowerment* (pp. 75–94). Landham, MD: Rowman & Littlefield Education.

Tyson, K. (2002). Weighing in: Elementary-aged students and the debate on attitude toward school. *Social Forces, 80,* 1157–1189.

U.S. Census Bureau. (2008). *American community survey.* Retrieved from http://factfinder.census.gov

VanTassel-Baska, J., & Johnsen, S. (2007). Teacher education standards for the field of gifted education: A vision of coherence for personnel preparation in the 21st century. *Gifted Child Quarterly, 51,* 182–206.

VanTassel-Baska, J., & Stambaugh, T. (Eds.). (2007). *Overlooked gems: A national perspective on low-income promising leaners.* Washington, D.C.: National Association for Gifted Children.

Whitener, L., & McGranahan, D. (2003). *Rural America. Opportunities and challenges.* Washington, D.C.: Economic Research Service, U.S. Department of Agriculture.

CHAPTER 14

Leading Policy, Advocacy, and Relationship Building in Rural Schools

Elissa F. Brown, Ph.D.

Introduction

America's K–12 educational system has long been linked to the ideals of social mobility, improved opportunities for students, and society's commitment to the future of an educated workforce and informed citizenry. Public schools have a civic mission: They are expected to prepare young people to become citizens and to share in the responsibility of maintaining our society (Healy et al., 2014). It is worth noting that the reason public education was first established was to advance the common good of the community. Education began in small towns, where communities agreed that all of the children should be educated for the good of all and for the sake of the future (Ravitch, 2011).

Demographic projections around ethnicity, jobs, and a college-educated workforce reflect some interesting data for the future of the educational system in rural America (Johnson & Kasarda, 2011; Johnson, 2014; Young, 2013). Nationwide, rural school district enrollment grew by over 22% from 1999–2000 through 2008–2009. This compares with a 1.7% enrollment increase among all nonrural districts. From 2008 to 2009, more than 9.6 million students were enrolled in rural school districts, comprising 20% of all of the nation's total public school students. Another 1.8 million students were enrolled in rural schools where the school districts are not classified as rural

(Strange, Johnson, Showalter, & Klein, 2012). Together, these students comprised over 23% of public school students. Of those attending schools in a rural district, two in five lived in poverty (and that rate has increased by nearly a third in 9 years), one in four was a child of color, and one in eight had changed residence in the past 12 months. The projections of increasing minority populations, in particular Hispanic populations, indicated that by 2060, nearly 29% of the U.S. population will be Hispanic compared to 18% today (Johnson, 2014), and that the driving force behind the growth is natural increase (birth rates) and not immigration. Moreover, adult members of rural households are less likely to be college educated than their urban counterparts—49% compared with 63%, respectively (see Table 14.1). The homeownership rate for rural households in this same period was 83%, significantly higher than the homeownership rate of 63% for urban households. Rural households were more likely to own or lease a vehicle (93%) as compared with 87% of urban households.

The interplay of immigration, education, and social mobility has created a new reality for rural places and has implications for educational policy, advocacy, and relationships in rural schools for all students, including gifted learners. This section will describe what is known about current policy pertaining to both rural schools and gifted learners, as well as strategies for leading, advocating, policy making, and relationship building in rural America.

Challenges and Opportunities That Affect Policies in Rural Schools

The Overall Landscape

Rural schools and communities are quite diverse, therefore it is difficult to establish a set of generalizations to describe or define these communities. Rural America is not monolithic, so no single policy can address its varying challenges (Johnson, 2006). Each community is unique. Nonetheless, many rural places possess similar challenges and possibilities. These challenges or possibilities can serve as generalizations for educational policy, advocacy, leadership, and overall relationships. A sampling of the generalizations undergirding rural America's K–12 schools and the communities within which they reside that impact leadership, policy, and relationships are as follows.

TABLE 14.1
Selected Demographic Characteristics of Urban and Rural Households, Percent Distribution, 2011

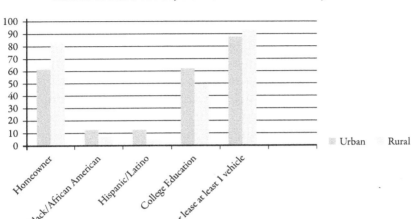

Note. Data from the Consumer Expenditure Survey (U.S. Bureau of Labor Statistics, 2011).

The transition from a natural resource-based economy to an economy based on trade and services. Farming, agriculture, and extractive industries such as mining, logging, and fishing are suffering economic hardships. Historically, they were the epicenters of a stable economy and a source of pride in rural communities. Today, with shifts in industry and the labor force, these communities have unemployment rates much higher than the national average of 5.8% (Chi & Leslie, 2015). Unemployment can range from 9%–17% or even greater.

Shift in education reform initiatives. The current focus of educational reform is on the promotion of national and global economies. Phrases such as "globally competitive" and "21st-century skills" have driven educational policymakers to enact policies and mandates that create an emphasis on content standards aimed at preparing students for college- and career-ready jobs. The invisibility of rural education persists in many states. Many rural students are largely invisible to state policy makers because they live in states where education policy is dominated by highly visible urban problems. All schools, including rural schools, face many pressures ranging from providing services to increasingly diverse student backgrounds, learning styles, and needs; new federal and state accountability requirements; and debates regarding the allocation and availability of education funding. These pressures are challenging in every

U.S. community, but rural schools face a unique set of challenges, largely due to their geographic isolation (Arnold, Newman, Gaddy, & Dean, 2005). For example, students are to graduate high school "college and career ready." Yet in many rural school districts, advanced courses in secondary schools may not be offered either because they do not have a teacher qualified to teach an advanced-level course such as biology or Advanced Placement (AP) calculus, or because there may not be a critical mass of students for whom a course could be offered. Schools can ill afford to offer an advanced course for the two or three students who may be ready for it. Although some rural schools have successfully met these challenges, many still struggle.

Changes in student demographics. Recently schools have been seen as sites of immigration-related conflict and inequality (Crosnoe & Turley, 2011). This is due to the rapid geographical and ethnic redistribution of the U.S. population driven by non-White population growth. Moreover, there's been an increase in interracial marriages. Research by the Pew Hispanic Center (Passel, Wang, & Taylor, 2010) revealed that since 1980, the rate of "out-marriage" individuals (marrying someone of a different race or ethnicity) has doubled. This has implications for rural schools because it may redefine "community." Does one associate with his or her ethnicity? Or in a rural district, is one's identity more closely aligned to place-bound or geographic location?

Student poverty. The high child poverty rate in rural areas is larger than those in urban areas for every ethnic and racial group (Johnson, 2006). Compounding this are issues such lack of access to health care services or centers that provide government support (Johnson, 2006). Approximately 51% of American workers living in rural areas in 2012 held middle-skill jobs that required either on-the-job training (e.g., apprenticeship model) or some post-secondary education, but no more than a 2-year degree. In urban households the national average of middle-skill jobs is 42% (Young, 2013). This trend reflects the migration of more highly skilled workers who leave small communities in search of higher paying jobs. Rural children continue to bear the brunt of economic difficulties. In schools, for example, if teachers are mobile, they may move to a larger urban or suburban area where the teacher pay scale is higher due to property taxes or other state and local incentives, thus leaving lower paid teachers in rural areas. Research supports pedagogical content knowledge as one way to improve student achievement (Huebner, 2009). Thus, if the teaching pay scale is based on credentials such as advanced degrees (e.g., master's degrees), urban or suburban locations have more higher education options and advanced programs and degrees for teachers than in rural areas. Children in rural areas therefore, may experience teachers who are less knowledgeable in a content area.

Leveraging Policies in a Way That Makes Sense in Rural America

The structure of rural schools provides a sense of connectedness that enhances academic achievement. Moreover, due to the overlapping roles between community activities and professional responsibilities, educational leaders in rural areas have a unique opportunity for leading change and implementing policies in a way that honors the intent of the policy yet ensures that the unique characteristics of the rural area are not lost.

One such characteristic to consider that is unique to rural settings is a strong sense of place (Budge, 2006). A variety of disciplines have confirmed that our point of view, behaviors, emotions, and dispositions are "indeed shaped not just by our genes, history, and relationships, but also by our surroundings" (Gallagher, 1993, p. 12). Geographical contexts and a critical sense of place are stronger in individuals from rural contexts because they enable people to cherish and celebrate local values, histories, culture, and the ecology of the place they inhabit. Tailoring these values, histories, and traditions into the school curriculum can enhance student engagement and cultivate a stronger connection between the student and the community.

Similarly, the concept of community has been central to the discourse of rural education for generations. In Budge's (2006) case study of a Northwest rural school community, comments such as "I have to be involved because there is no one else to do the work" or "You've got to be active. You're not just a number like in Seattle" were commonly voiced (p. 5). Leaders noted the privilege of living in a rural community because of the sense of community, people pulling together, and treating each other as family. This idea of collaboration and need for involvement can be cultivated by educational leaders to build a strong sense of community, more active engagement in schools, and unique relationships between school personnel and families that may not be as feasible in highly populated urban settings and may also positively impact student achievement. For example, Stracuzzi and Mills (2010) analyzed data on two groups of rural New Hampshire youth as part of a longitudinal study. They found that a sense of school connectedness is one of the most critical factors in promoting the socio-emotional development of students. The majority of rural students (63%) surveyed felt connected to their schools through the dimensions of social support, belonging, and engagement. The authors explained that students who feel connected are more likely to do well in school and show positive outcomes of academic performance. Furthermore, students reported higher self-esteem, decreased substance use, and fewer aggressive behaviors when they felt connected socially, had a place to belong, or were engaged in community-supported activities, such as 4-H clubs. Students in rural schools therefore, may have a stronger dimension of connectedness than their peers in urban or suburban school districts. Of course, with this collaboration and strong sense of place come the potential for competing and multiple roles of leaders, teacher quality and retention, and a reluctance to change.

Competing Priorities and Multiple Roles of Educational Leaders

Because there are few, if any, centralized formal educational roles, such as an assistant superintendent for curriculum, school principals often have teaching or central office leadership responsibilities in addition to their other roles. As such, rural schools leaders have to be generalists and may not be able to focus on a single role or project. In essence, leaders wear many hats (Anderson, 2008) with mutual and reciprocal relationships between teacher leaders, principals, and curriculum directors.

Employing a distributive leadership model (Spillane, 2005) in a rural school district is one leadership model that would work well because rather than leadership being a traditional top-down linear model, distributive leadership employs a horizontal approach or shared leadership model. This could look different depending upon the needs of each community. In some districts, a leadership council makes decisions consensually and members of the council rotate. In other districts, teachers are teacher leaders and conduct professional development or write curriculum for the district based on the expertise of the individuals involved. Leadership is reciprocal, less formal, and highly interactive. In many instances, the main vehicle for exchanging ideas and sharing decision making is through teachers because they are not afraid to act independently and voice their opinions due to their already well-established relationships in the small community. "Everybody has their say; everybody usually looks at the problem and comes to a consensus of what should be done" (Anderson, 2008, p. 12).

Attracting and Retaining Highly Qualified Teachers

The need to attract and retain highly qualified teachers to implement mandated initiatives is another concern that is especially pronounced in rural schools (Powell, Higgins, Aram, & Freed, 2009). Given the demonstrated link between teacher quality and student achievement, the need for evidence-based guidance concerning teacher recruitment, preparation, and professional development is even more critical for teachers, superintendents, and principals in rural communities (Powell, Higgins, Aram, & Freed, 2009). Rural school leaders also are eager for information about research-based interventions and strategies that enhance student success and graduation rates that are feasible within the context of their geographic setting (Strange, Johnson, Showalter, & Klein, 2012).

Readiness to Change

In rural America, the pace of life is slower and localities with significant natural amenities, such as recreational opportunities, scenic landscapes, mild climates, or retirement opportunities, are less likely to change or adopt new practices and policies (Johnson, 2006). Additionally, if families are from a particular location for generations and have a strong sense of place (Budge, 2006), the influence of rurality is stronger than the need to change. We have heard the saying "out of sight, out of mind," and for rural America, the sense of urgency to change policies and practices may not exist. There is a strong sense of independence and therefore, geographic isolation from global markets is not only real, but for many communities, preferred. "We have generational connections and a pride in taking care of one's own" (Budge, 2006, p. 4).

Policy as Necessary Infrastructure for Gifted Learners

Now that issues impacting policy for rural schools has been discussed, what does this mean for gifted learners? In terms of policy development, state regulations regarding programming, services, and curriculum options for gifted learners are less documented in policy language and are not evident in many states (Brown, Avery, VanTassel-Baska, Worley, & Stambaugh, 2006). Approximately half of the states have a mandate or partial mandate for servicing gifted learners (Shaunessy, 2003). In a recent report by the National Association of Gifted Children (NAGC) and the Council of State Directors Programs for the Gifted's (2013) State of the State report, 26 states reported having mandates that require services for gifted and talented students. Many states systematically define and identify gifted students, but how these identification policies link to programming and curriculum options is less obvious. Curriculum policy should extend standards-based regular curriculum and should be designed to meet the learning needs of gifted students (VanTassel-Baska, 2006).

There are explicit state policies in gifted education as well as broader educational policies that encompass gifted. Explicit state policies that focus directly on gifted students may include identification, service delivery models, grouping, acceleration, and contact time. Detailed descriptions of these strategies and implications for rural gifted learners are included in Part II of this book. Policy language specifying contact time is another example of explicit policy language that ensures that gifted students have guaranteed time together, typically linked to a service option. Some states, which have policies addressing placement arrangements and/or contact time, are predominately rural or have geographically isolated areas. These include, but are not limited to, Alabama, Arkansas, Georgia, Guam, Mississippi, Missouri, Ohio, South Carolina, Utah, and West Virginia.

Perhaps more importantly, there are broader educational policies emerging from state and national educational reform initiatives that impact gifted students and programs. These broader educational policies are built on several assumptions. These assumptions undergird the necessity of supporting policies that are not necessarily targeted specifically for gifted education but whose outcomes can benefit gifted students and programs. They are as follows:

» Gifted students are part of the overall Pre-K–12 educational landscape and therefore are impacted by local and state policies. Policies are designed to be broadly applied. They are, by nature, more inclusive than exclusive.
» Policies are part of the infrastructure providing the foundation for educational practices. For gifted students, leveraging this tool is critical. As infrastructure, policies assist in safeguarding against scarce educational resources, teacher and administrator turnover, and political agendas.
» Gifted education stands to benefit from ensuring that general education policies imply gifted students. When policies use language such as "All, Each, Every," when referring to students, or "Will or must," when referring to implementation, it implies gifted students, as well.

» Gifted students are diverse. Supplemental educational policies may serve some populations of gifted that gifted policies leave out. For example, if the gifted policy specifies a particular type of service delivery or programming, it may unintentionally preclude some gifted students from accessing alternative modes of learning.

These broader policies in curricula and instruction, teacher evaluation, or other K–12 initiatives, although not explicitly directed at gifted learners, have positive implications for gifted students, as well as teachers and administrators. The field of gifted must leverage these policy opportunities in order to ensure and scale effective and coherent systems for identifying, serving, and assessing gifted learners.

Gallagher (2006) noted that one of the only ways to create support systems for gifted students is through policy changes. These general education policies support gifted education by using phrases such as "all students will" and help mitigate marginalizing gifted programs. For example, a broader policy initiative such as Race to the Top (RttT; U.S. Department of Education, 2010), a federal education stimulus program, provides funding to states and local school systems that meet certain requirements and expectations. A prerequisite for states to receive RttT funding was the adoption of the Common Core State Standards (CCSS). To date, 43 states have adopted the CCSS, which are curriculum frameworks in the content areas of English language arts and mathematics (NAGC, 2014). Even though RttT does not explicitly mention gifted students, it is implied in its intent to have all students "college and career ready." In states where the majority of students are in rural school districts, state policies that are inclusive of gifted students hold promise as long as the intent of "all" is explicitly communicated to include gifted learners. Other examples of more generalized policies at state and local levels that have implications for gifted students may include the following:

» policies on virtual courses;
» emphasis on science, technology, engineering, and mathematics (STEM) initiatives;
» links to teacher evaluation;
» flexible graduation requirements;
» off-level testing to demonstrate scope of abilities; and
» waivers from state accountability measures of growth.

Leveraging a General Policy for Gifted: One State's Example

The waiver process for relief from the No Child Left Behind Act (NCLB; 2001) requires states to adopt and assess college and career ready standards, thereby increasing the number of states focusing on this reform effort. Any state receiving a waiver must also provide a measure of student growth on a teacher evaluation instrument. By focusing on the growth of *each* student, states and local education agencies have data to determine if students performing at high levels of proficiency are also making strides in their learning. The new assessments are designed to provide sufficient ceiling for performance at high levels, providing an opportunity for the brightest students to demonstrate growth. The waiver in the accountability standards in North Carolina through policy passed by the North Carolina State Board of Education (NCSBE; 2014) lists "Academically and/or Intellectually Gifted" students as a subgroup, thus creating a requirement for public reporting on the achievement of gifted students against goals listed in the waiver for NCLB. Other states could follow suit.

But, what does this have to do with rural gifted learners? In this next section, rural and gifted are linked with practical applications.

What Is the Same or Different for Rural Gifted Learners?

There are several reasons why exploring these issues is relevant to gifted learners, specifically in rural contexts. First, each child deserves the right to access opportunities that challenge his or her abilities and in doing so maximize his or her potential. Rural communities cannot afford to lose the contributions gifted students can make to their community, culture, and economy. Rural places and ways of life are under extreme pressure from urbanization—not only from immigration and out-migration but also from the extension of media and technology into homes, no matter how isolated geographically (Lawrence, 2009). To nurture and sustain rural ways of living, rural communities need articulate leaders who understand and love rural places—people who are visionary and deeply rooted in rural life and who will create new businesses and products, stories, music, art, and responsible ways to develop resources (Lawrence, 2004).

In addition, many gifted students from rural places want to stay in their communities instead of leaving to find suitable work or an academic environment better matched to their cognitive needs (Gentry, Rizza, & Gable, 2001). But for gifted learners, staying requires enormous courage and self-knowledge because it goes against the assumption of mainstream society that happiness requires mobility, acquisitiveness, and status. Moreover, gifted learners internalize cognitive and affective dissonance at a deeper level (Daniels & Piechowski, 2009). They experience the emotional pull between staying home in their community versus the compelling pull of higher education or a financially more lucrative career if they leave their community and family.

Third, many rural communities do not offer higher level courses in high school such as Advanced Placement (AP) or specialized coursework either due to insufficient enrollment numbers or lack of teacher capacity and advanced training (Greenberg & Teixeira, 1998). Without substantive high school coursework, gifted students are at a disadvantage in terms of prerequisite knowledge when they enter a competitive 4-year institution of higher education with peers from urban or suburban areas.

Lastly, school, district, and state leaders need to pay attention to these broader educational policies that augment, not supplant, gifted education, especially within an educational context of tight budget constraints. By leveraging and maximizing other policies, we can ensure that educational opportunities, customization of learning, and supporting structures are in place for gifted students from rural areas.

Specific Strategies for Policy Makers and Educators in Rural Areas

Researchers suggest that rural schools confront some special challenges when it comes to meeting the needs of gifted learners, but also offer some unusual opportunities (Howley, Howley, & Pendarvis, 2003). Table 14.2 provides an overview of some suggested strategies and the implications for increasing leadership, advocacy, and relationship building for gifted students living in rural areas. Following Table 14.2 is a more descriptive narrative on each strategy and the rationale for its importance in gifted education.

TABLE 14.2
Suggested Strategies and Implications for Gifted Education

Suggested Strategy	Implications for Gifted Education
Opportunity to learn	» Create and sustain mechanisms (e.g., online delivery systems, summer programs, etc.) to increase opportunities, options, and coursework for gifted students to receive an education commensurate with their abilities and increase ways for gifted learners to be with other like-ability peers. » Deliberately interface with the community to create learning options for gifted students broader than what's provided within a school and match to their area of interest(s). » Develop specific strategies for college and career counseling.
Recruit and retain educational leaders	» Provide professional development for rural administrators that can highlight the benefits of integrating school-community relationships with high academic standards for all students, especially those with gifts and talents. » Build upon personnel knowledge and relationships between administrators and community priorities.
Adopt flexible leadership and school models	» Strategically use a distributive leadership model (Spillane, 2005) rather than a hierarchical, linear model of leadership in order to build upon individuals' strengths and allow for shared and fluid leadership.
Advocate for flexible funding models	» Consider ways to be flexible with teacher pay, not just based on credentials (e.g., degrees). » Use other money, such as 21st-century learning communities to augment the operational budget.
Embrace positive rural attributes	» Use a talent development framework as a lens to increase and accelerate a student's trajectory. Personalized and customization of instruction is easier in a rural school because of the strong relationships among students and teachers. » Employ flexible grouping, acceleration, and other curricular and instructional models, which are empirically supported and less resource intensive. Other strategies, such as mixed-age classrooms, schools-within-schools, and community service, can serve gifted students well. » Rural schools offer benefits of trust building and security and emotional benefits that larger, more urbanized schools do not.
Community and parent aspirations and expectations	» The role of "place" is critical in rural students' identities, and yet they have to come to grips with the future and viability of a theory of action for their own and others' expectations (Budge, 2006). » Community members and parents should overtly have conversations, discourse, and strategies around the separation of schooling from the context most known to students—their community. Allow students to stay connected while simultaneously encouraging autonomy and risk taking. » Encourage a climate of success and reach out to those role models who can serve as professionals in a field or domain.
Tailor policy implementation	» Leverage existing policies or create new ones that will serve all students and at the same time benefit gifted students, such as seat time waivers, credit by demonstrating mastery, early entrance and exit policies, access to alternative modes of learning, etc. » Consider policies that allow for rural consortia to be developed. » Implement policies that allow for models of mentoring (e.g., medical model) gifted students and provide credit for community service.

Opportunity to Learn: Embed Policy Mandates Within the Community Context

If the No Child Left Behind Act (2009) holds schools and districts accountable for ensuring that all students reach the proficient performance level for identified standards, students must have the opportunity to learn the knowledge and skills embedded in those standards. Opportunity to learn is the notion that students have access to a viable curriculum and to effective instruction. Of the school-level factors examined in a meta-analysis of student achievement (Marzano, 2000), opportunity to learn was found to have the strongest relationship to student achievement. Therefore, one of the most effective strategies for increasing student achievement is to ensure that students have the opportunity to learn content identified in district and state content standards. Standardized test scores suggest that rural schools have done a good job of teaching the basics. Rural students have been shown to hold their own against their urban counterparts on standardized tests (Gibbs, 2001; Economic Research Service, 2003).

But rural schools typically offer fewer advanced and college preparatory courses, and lower proportions of rural students take advanced classes, such as physics and calculus (Greenberg & Teixeira, 1998). In a study that drew from a large sample of diverse students from 24 schools in seven states equally distributed among rural, urban, and suburban, data analysis revealed that rural gifted students reported that they had "fewer opportunities for challenge than their suburban peers" (Gentry et al., 2001, p. 124). Gifted rural children and their parents often find that there are insufficient services and options for them. According to the researchers, student perceptions around lack of challenge may be attributed to a variety of reasons, including limited funding, isolation, less access to a well-developed variety of programs, fewer chances to be identified as gifted, and fewer peers with whom to work. Their perceptions of less challenge indicated how important gifted programming is in rural schools.

There are, however, ways in which rural communities could extend gifted programming through the use of capitalizing on the ideas celebrated in the community. For example, if a student is mathematically precocious and does not have access to high-end mathematics curriculum within the school, a school district could have the student learn about applying math through mentoring with local craftsmen, artisans, or professionals (e.g., doctors). A gifted student could explore his or her interest area by extending the learning and connecting it throughout the community. In Alabama, an elementary student created a child's guide to the local history as a way to build upon her strengths and interests in an in-depth independent research project (Reis & Renzulli, 2014).

Recruit and Retain Educational Leaders Who Know Rural Schools

Similar to the issue of teacher quality is the problem of recruiting and retaining administrators who are adequately prepared to create and sustain high-performing learning systems that ensure that all students meet high standards. This problem begins in university administrator preparation programs that are geared primarily for training urban and suburban school leaders. Rural education literature points to a shortage of information about the professional development of rural administrators. Rural school districts face a different set of challenges in recruiting administrators than do their urban and suburban counterparts. Rural administrators have to assume more responsibilities in small districts (e.g., instructional leader, athletic director, bus driver) because there are fewer administrators in the district and they therefore must wear more hats. They also receive less compensation than their urban/suburban counterparts (Johnson, 2007) and have greater visibility in their communities. Preston, Jakubiec, and Kooymans (2013) found that administrators who were raised in the community where they were the current administrator had a greater understanding of and deep appreciation for the values, priorities, and culture of the community. Possessing this personal-historical link to the school community is particularly helpful when administrators have to deal with tensions that sometimes spill into the school from stakeholder community groups. In contrast, research also highlights that rural administrators who do not share social, political, historical, cultural, or ethnic familiarity with the school or community they lead are often viewed with suspicion by community members (Browne-Ferrigno & Allen, 2006; Keddie & Niesche, 2012). In rural school districts, teachers' sense of efficacy and worth as contributing members of the district and community increase their motivation to be involved (Budge, 2006). "You've got to be active in your community because there's no one else to do it," explained one teacher (Budge, 2006, p. 5). Another teacher shared, "I think in a bigger district, I wouldn't take on the challenges, or I wouldn't feel the need to continually be getting better. In a larger district, I would defer to others because there would be people that I could just be mentored by. Here, I'm taking more of a leadership role" (Budge, 2006, p. 6).

Administrators can increase the retention of teacher leaders by managing the social aspects of rural teaching, both within and outside of school (Goodpaster, Adedokun, & Weaver, 2012). For example, there's an intersection between life and work. Within the school, benefits of school structures, including availability of teaching resources, safety, flexibility, and maintaining close relationships among teachers, administrators, and students, are all key in retaining quality teachers. Outside of school, incorporating less conventional teaching activities that promote student interest and potential career paths are areas that influence the positive aspects of teaching in a rural area.

Adopt Flexible Leadership Models That Work Best in Rural Schools

The conceptualization of leading an educational organization has typically been a top-down approach, with a superintendent and a principal. In rural districts, employing a nontraditional leadership model that is less top-down and more dynamic and shared is a better match to the rural context. Sometimes known as distributive leadership (Spillane, 2005), this model employs shared responsibility and mutual accountability toward a common goal or goals for the good of an organization. Distributive leadership is a potential solution for easing the burden on rural school administrators because it involves a school improvement model that is fluid, can easily change over time, and honors capacity and expertise from many individuals, not just one (Anderson, 2008). Moreover, the idea of building leadership capacity from within the educational context may be an additional strategy in order for community acceptance. In today's educational environment that focuses on the merits of standardized academic achievement, the rural principal walks a fine line between successfully leading this age of accountability and centralized policy, while simultaneously serving the local community and its needs, wants, and identity.

Policies that support a distributive leadership model would include models such as a rural consortium of leaders, forging partnerships with outside organizations, or operating community services from the school. For example, a rural school district could house the local community cable channel and in exchange allow students to receive credit for broadcast journalism. The idea of decision making in rural schools thereby is inventive and mutual versus bureaucratic and static.

Advocate for Flexible Funding Formulas

Rural schools and districts need the internal capacity to successfully reach the goals of increasing student achievement. When test scores coincide with additional state and federal funding incentives, studies have documented that rural schools play "catch-up" (Powell, Higgins, Aram, & Freed, 2009). Typically, the external funding mechanism takes into account the numbers of students (e.g., Average Daily Membership or ADM), and rural schools have fewer students, thus leading to fewer state or federal additional revenues. One must examine whether rural schools and districts have adequate resources and the infrastructure to implement programmatic innovation. Professional isolation can lead to weak professional communities that perpetuate ineffective practices. Such organizations may lack leaders who know how to build internal capacity, such as systems that facilitate ongoing improvement of practices. Additionally, rural schools face significant resource limitations, particularly in terms of economic and human resources. There are also social, cultural, and political forces that can influence the capacity of rural schools to improve. Therefore, priority should be given to developing and testing strategies that build school and district capacity to improve student achievement. Rural schools serve almost 20% of the nation's students, so ensuring that rural districts receive formula funds as well as expanding the flexibility of funding to support their schools is critical. For example, in the U.S. Department of Education's (2010) *A Blueprint for Reform*, one proposal is to make it easier for teachers in rural areas to teach multiple subjects by defining teacher quality not exclusively by credentials but taking into consideration multiple factors. Another idea posited in the report is to provide additional money for school and community collaboration under strengthening the 21st-Century Community Learning Centers program (U.S. Department of Education, 2010).

Embrace the Positive Attributes of a Rural Community to Develop Talent

Because rural schools are often small, educators in such schools are better able than educators in larger schools to learn about the talents of their students (Budge, 2006). Talent-development models have emerged from retrospective studies of highly accomplished learners, creators, and performers in ways that might be useful for research and practice (Olszewski-Kubilius, 2000; Sternberg & Davidson, 2005). A talent development model, just as the name implies, aims to delineate the trajectory from childhood precocity to adult accomplishment in specific domains. Although families set the stage for the development of elite talent, most of the models focus on variables associated with expert teachers or mentors, individual abilities, and psychosocial factors. One of the suggested strategies to foster gifted students' growth over time, along of path of potential to performance, is to employ capitalizing on one's developed strengths to achieve desired, culturally relevant goals while shoring up weaknesses.

In a talent development trajectory model for students in rural areas, this could translate to students conducting an interdisciplinary unit of study involving the community and community members. Gifted students could be placed in multiage classrooms with opportunities for informal acceleration in their content areas of strength. Policies could be set up to allow students to earn a myriad of credits through community service options, online courses, and even work-study options, where students work locally and receive course credit for the work, as it aligns with school goals and community aspirations.

Understand and Work Within Community and Parent Aspirations and Expectations

Rural community aspirations and expectations can influence the success of school improvement efforts, both positively and negatively. For many years, the conventional wisdom has been that rural economic development should be based on attracting businesses that offer these lower wage/lower skill jobs (Hobbs, 1998). Thus, academically talented rural youth often have been encouraged by their parents and teachers to stay in school, go to college, and move to the city to find higher paying jobs. As a result, there has been a steady migration of the most successful graduates away from rural areas (Jischke, 2000).

A related issue is parent expectations, which are an important factor in improving student achievement. In fact, as Marzano (2003) noted, "high expectations communicated to students are associated with enhanced achievement" (p. 129). Thus, schools can boost student achievement by encouraging parents and other community members to recognize the potential of higher aspirations and expectations and provide opportunities within the community for growth and development instead of assuming the brightest students should leave if this is not what they want.

Tailor Policy Implementation for Rural Communities

Educational policies, whether state or local, can fit the community context while still honoring the intent of the policy. For example, if there is a mandate for gifted services, it may be that multiage opportunities allow a more maximum benefit than one grade level. Student busing to support grouping opportunities in one school to create a critical mass may be a better option than a teacher traveling to multiple schools and having less time with each student. What works in urban schools may not work in rural ones, so rural schools should craft their own ways for thinking about grouping, dual enrollment, or other policies to serve gifted students. Policies do not have to be limiting. Partner with neighboring rural districts or urban districts to provide services and create a larger critical mass are all appropriate.

There are examples of gifted students attending cross-county centers or specialized schools. In Virginia for example, there are academic year Governor's schools, where students from multiple counties attend a cross-county Governor's school. These students meet initial entrance criteria and are recommended from their home schools, then travel to a particular site and are in classes either part time or full time with like-ability peers. This serves a dual purpose of both meeting their academic needs while simultaneously creating a community of learners (e.g., friends) from across county lines. Additionally, this type of model is similar to what students will ultimately face when they attend college.

Policy to Practice

Policy represents our commitment for ensuring gifted children access to a quality education. Legislative mandates, components of mandates, and state aid to local districts contribute to a more equitable and more social economic standard-neutral distribution of opportunities. Thus, the presence of state mandates for gifted education is a significant equalizer of opportunities. If changes in the education of gifted and talented learners are to occur, existing rules, regulations, and standards must change (Ambrose, VanTassel-Baska, Coleman, & Cross, 2010; Gallagher, 2012). Gifted education stands to benefit from leveraging general education policies that imply gifted students. When policies use language such as "All, each, every," when referring to students, or "Will or must," when referring to implementation, it implies gifted students, as well.

Leading Policy, Advocacy, and Relationship Building

Implementing educational policies is complex, critical, and provides the infrastructure for program implementation. In the absence of policy, educational practices are person dependent; it is the "devil in the details." Professionals such as school administrators, teachers, or district coordinators are not usually the individuals who wrote the policy, so frequently, they may not be sure of the policy intent. Additionally, policy is written in such a way as to be broadly applied to large groups of students so the nuances of each community or school context are not addressed.

Policy to practice is intent to implementation. Sometimes the inverse is true. Implementation can lead to policy development. In education, there are many examples when educational practice outpaces policies. In other words, new initiatives such as e-learning opportunities frequently begin at local levels, and as these initiatives scale, a policy around their access and use may ultimately get written. Therefore, administrators have to pay attention to both policy and practices and determine the degree to which gifted students would benefit. Policy to practice and practice to policy requires leadership, communication, advocacy, and strategic, intentional efforts to maximize the benefits to gifted students and programs. Gifted education is determined at state and local levels (Brown, Avery, VanTassel-Baska, Worley, & Stambaugh, 2006; Baker & Friedman-Nimz, 2004).

State directors of gifted, state advocacy organizations, parents, local program coordinators, and other professionals need to find ways to safeguard gifted students and programs, either implicitly or explicitly. Gifted education leaders need to constantly scan the environment and look for opportunities that may coalesce into policy. The most effective gifted education leaders seize the opportunity to be proactive and leverage policy opportunities. Gallagher (2006) noted that one of the only ways to create support systems for gifted students is through changes in policy. Leveraging these general education policies to support gifted education will mitigate marginalizing gifted programs. School, district, and state leaders must pay close and ongoing attention to broader educational policies which augment, not supplant, gifted education, especially within an educational context of tight budget constraints. By leveraging and maximizing other policies, we can ensure that educational opportunities, customization of learning, and supporting structures are in place for gifted students from all geographic areas.

Conclusion

Growth in rural school enrollment is outpacing nonrural enrollment growth in the United States, and rural schools are becoming more complex with increasing rates of poverty, diversity, and special needs students. Moreover, these trends, while widespread, are most intense in the South, Southwest, and parts of Appalachia (Johnson, 2006). As with many components of education, if one teacher, administrator, or small group of teachers support a method of teaching or realize that a student or small group of students need something different, than that pocket of students will be well served. This is more likely to occur in a rural context than in an urban or suburban context. More funding does not necessarily translate directly to increased services and opportunities. Sometimes additional funding adds extra layers of bureaucracy and "red tape." Teachers and administrators in rural areas—just like teachers anywhere else—need training, time, and support for the needs of gifted students, whether its learning how to differentiate and develop curricula, planning community experiences, and meeting social-emotional needs, but it may be easier to accomplish these things in a rural school than in a larger, more complex educational context. Small enrollment can translate to greater opportunity for students for discussion, interaction, relationship building, activity in clubs and events, and a higher degree of interaction with children in other grades (Colangelo, Assouline, & New, 1999). Teachers in rural schools are more apt to compare notes and collaborate about specific students, thus becoming advocates.

References

Ambrose, D., VanTassel-Baska, J., Coleman, L., & Cross, T. (2010). Unified, insular, firmly policed, or fractured, porous, contested, gifted education? *Journal for the Education of the Gifted. 33*(4), 453–476.

Anderson, K. D. (2008). Transformational teacher leadership in rural schools. *The Rural Educator, 29*(3), 8–17.

Arnold, M. L., Newman, J. H., Gaddy, B. B., & Dean, C. B. (2005). A look at the condition of rural education research: Setting a direction for future research. *Research in Rural Education, 20*(6),1–25.

Baker, B. D., & Friedman-Nimz, R. (2004). State policy influences governing equal opportunity: The example of gifted education. *Educational Evaluation and Policy Analysis, 26,* 39–64.

Brown, E., Avery, L., VanTassel-Baska, J., Worley, B., & Stambaugh, T. (2006). A five-state analysis of gifted education policies. *Roeper Review, 29*(1), 11–23.

Browne-Ferrigno, T., & Allen, L. W. (2006). Preparing principals for high-need rural schools: A central office perspective about collaborative efforts to transform school leadership. *Journal of Research in Rural Education, 21*(1), 1–16.

Budge, K. (2006). Rural leaders, rural places: Problem, privilege and possibility. *Journal of Research in Rural Education, 21*(13), 1–10.

Chi, J., & Leslie, K. (2015). Analysis of the current employment statistics program using customer outreach survey results. *Monthly Labor Review.* Retrieved from http://www.bls.gov/opub/mlr/2015/article/analysis-of-the-current-employment-statistics-program-using-customer-outreach-survey-results.htm

Colangelo, N., Assouline, S., & New, J. (1999). *Gifted education in rural schools. A national assessment.* Iowa City: The University of Iowa, The Connie Belin & Jacqueline N. Blank International Center for Gifted Education and Talent Development.

Crosnoe, R., & Turley, R. N. (2011). K–12 educational outcomes of immigrant youth. *Future of Children, 21*(1), 129–152.

Daniels, S., & Piechowski, M. (2009). *Living with intensity: Understanding the sensitivity, excitability, and the emotional development of gifted children.* Scottsdale, AZ: Great Potential Press.

Economic Research Service. (2003). *Measuring rurality: Rural-urban continuum codes.* Retrieved from http://www.ers.usda.gov/briefing/rurality/RuralUrbCon

Gallagher, J. J. (2006, April). *Future prospects for gifted education.* Presented at the Javits Grantee meeting. Hartford, CT.

Gallagher, J. J. (2012). Political issues in gifted education. In C. M. Callahan & H. L. Hertberg-Davis (Eds.), *Fundamentals of Gifted Education: Considering Multiple Perspectives* (pp. 458–469). New York, NY: Routledge.

Gallagher, W. (1993). *The power of place.* New York, NY: HarperCollins.

Gentry, M., Rizza, M. G., & Gable, R. K. (2001). Gifted students' perceptions of their class activities: Differences among rural, urban, and southern student attitudes. *Gifted Child Quarterly, 45,* 115–129.

Gibbs, R. (2001). The challenge ahead for rural schools. *FORUM for Applied Research and Public Policy, 15*(1), 82–87.

Goodpaster, K., Adedokun, O., & Weaver, G. (2012). Teachers' perceptions of rural STEM teaching: Implications for rural teacher retention. *Rural Educator, 33*(3), 9–22.

Greenberg, E. J., & Teixeira, R. (1998). Educational achievement in rural schools. In R. M. Gibbs, P. L. Swaim, & R. Teixeira (Eds.), *Rural education and training in the new rural economy: The myth of the rural skills gap* (pp. 33–39). Ames: Iowa State University Press.

Healy, S., Dobson, D., Kyser, J., Herczog, M., & Genzer, D. (2014). Civic learning success stories: State initiatives to restore the civic mission of schools. *Social Education, 78*(6), 286-292.

Hobbs, D. (1998). Forward. In R. M. Gibbs, P. L. Swaim, & R. Teixeira (Eds.), *Rural education and training in the new rural economy: The myth of the rural skills gap* (pp. vii–viii). Ames: Iowa State University Press.

Howley, A., Howley, C., & Pendarvis, E. (2003). The possible good gifted programs in rural schools and communities might do. In J. Borland (Ed.), *Rethinking gifted education: Contemporary approaches to understanding giftedness* (pp. 80–104). New York, NY: Teachers College Press.

Huebner, T. (2009). The continuum of teacher learning. *Educational Leadership, 66*(5), 88–91.

Jischke, M. C. (2000). Boosting rural human capital. In M. Drabenstott (Ed.), *Beyond agriculture: New policies for rural America* (pp. 93–101). Kansas City, MO: Center for the Study of Rural America, Federal Reserve Bank of Kansas City.

Johnson, J. H. (2007). Shaping the business leaders of tomorrow: America's K–12 education crisis is a higher education problem. *Sustainable Enterprise Quarterly, 3*(3), 1–2.

Johnson, J. H. & Kasarda, J. D. (2011). *Six disruptive demographic trends: What census 2010 will reveal.* Chapel Hill: University of North Carolina at Chapel Hill, Frank Hawkins Kenan Institute of Private Enterprise, Kenan-Flagler Business School.

Johnson, K. M. (2006). Demographic trends in rural and small town America. Retrieved from http://scholars.unh.edu/cgi/viewcontent.cgi?article=1004&context=carsey

Johnson, K. M. (2014). New populations projections reflect slower growth and increasing diversity. The Carsey Institute at the Scholar's Repository. Paper 232. Retrieved from http://scholars.unh.edu/carsey/232

Keddie, A., & Niesche, R. (2012). "It's almost like a white school now:" Racialised complexities, indigenous representation and school leadership. *Critical Studies in Education, 53*(2), 169–182.

Lawrence, B. K. (2004). *The hermit crab solution: Creative alternatives for improving rural school facilities and keeping them close to home.* Charleston, WV: ERIC Clearinghouse on Rural Education and Small Schools.

Lawrence, B. K. (2009). Rural gifted education: A comprehensive literature review. *Journal for the Education of the Gifted, 32*(4), 461–494.

Marzano, R. J. (2000). *A new era of school reform: Going where the research takes us.* Aurora, CO: Mid-continent Research for Education and Learning.

Marzano. R. J. (2003). *What works in schools.* Alexandria, VA: Association for Supervision and Curriculum Development.

National Association for Gifted Children. (2014). *Common Core and Next Generation Science Standards for gifted and talented students* (Position paper). Retrieved from http://www.nagc.org/index2.aspx?id=11370

National Association for Gifted Children, & Council of State Directors of Programs for the Gifted. (2013). *State of the states: A report by the National Association for Gifted Children and the Council of State Directors of Programs for the Gifted.* Washington, D.C.: Author.

No Child Left Behind Act of 2001, Pub. L. No. 107-110, § 115, Stat. 1425 (2002).

North Carolina State Board of Education. (2014). GCS-A-016, Policy delineating use of state-designated assessments for the North Carolina teacher evaluation process. Retrieved from http://sbepolicy.dpi.state.nc.us/

Olszewski-Kubilius, P. (2000). The transition from childhood giftedness to adult creative productiveness: Psychological characteristics and social supports. *Roeper Review, 23,* 65–71.

Passel, J., Wang, W., & Taylor, P. (2010). *Marrying out.* Washington, D.C.: Pew Research Center Publications. Retrieved from http://pewresearch.org/pubs/1616/american-marriage-interracial-interethnic

Powell, D., Higgins, H. J., Aram, R., & Freed, A. (2009). Impact of No Child Left Behind on curriculum and instruction in rural schools. *Rural Educator, 31*(1), 19–28.

Preston, J. P., Jakubiec, B. A., & Kooymans, R. (2013). Common challenges faced by rural principals: A review of the literature. *Rural Educator, 35*(1), 1–12.

Ravitch, D. (2011). American schools in crisis. *Saturday Evening Post*, September/October. Retrieved from http://www.saturdayeveningpost.

com/2011/08/16/in-the-magazine/trends-and-opinions/american-schools-crisis.html

Reis, S., & Renzulli, J. (2014). The Schoolwide Enrichment Model: A focus on student strengths and interests. In S. Reis & J. Renzulli *The Schoolwide Enrichment Model: How-to guide for talent development* (3rd ed., pp 323–352). Waco, TX: Prufrock Press.

Shaunessy, E. (2003). State policies regarding gifted education. *Gifted Child Today, 26*(3), 16–21.

Spillane, J. (2005). Distributed leadership. *The Educational Forum, 69* (Winter), 143–150.

Stracuzzi, N. F., & Mills, M. L. (2010). Teachers matter: Feelings of school connectedness and positive youth development among Coos County youth. Retrieved from http://scholars.unh.edu/carsey/122

Strange, M., Johnson, J., Showalter, D., & Klein, R. (2012). *Why rural matters 2011–12: The condition of rural education in the 50 states. A Report of the Rural School and Community Trust Policy Program*. Washington, D.C.: Author.

Sternberg, R. J., & Davidson, J. E. (Eds.). (2005). *Conceptions of giftedness* (2nd ed.). New York, NY: Cambridge University Press.

U.S. Bureau of Labor Statistics. (2011). Consumer expenditure survey. Retrieved from http://www.bls.gov/cex/csxstnd.htm#2011

U.S. Department of Education. (2010). *A blueprint for reform: The reauthorization of the Elementary and Secondary Education Act*. Washington, D.C.: Author. Retrieved from http://www2.ed.gov/policy/elsec/leg/blueprint

VanTassel-Baska, J. (2006). State policies in gifted education. In J. H. Purcell & R. D. Eckert (Eds). *Designing services and program for high-ability learners*. Thousand Oaks, CA: Corwin Press.

Young, J. R. (2013). Middle-skill jobs remain common among rural workers. Retrieved from http://scholars.unh.edu/carsey/196

CHAPTER 15

Rural Teachers of the Gifted
The Importance of Professional Development

Laurie Croft, Ph.D.

Rural Teachers of the Gifted: The Importance of Professional Learning

On July 15, Mrs. Graham learned she had an offer to teach for the following year. She had moved to the new community with her 12-year-old twins and her husband, a minister, who had answered a call from a local church. With her K–12 certification and 3 years of experience as an art teacher, she had hoped she could find a similar position in the rural district. The offer included teaching art at two different elementary schools for 40 percent of her time, as well as teaching remedial reading classes at each school for 10% of her time; the offer also included a position as the half-time gifted education teacher at the elementary schools, plus the middle school.

Mrs. Graham was told she would need a provisional endorsement in gifted education. The superintendent explained that she needed to develop a Plan of Study to earn the required hours of coursework in the field so that the district could submit the required paperwork, but the district did not reimburse teachers for the cost of the university tuition. Mrs. Graham would have 2 years to complete her coursework.

Although Mrs. Graham felt apprehensive about working in areas beyond her previous experience and certification, at least the Grahams' twins had been identi-

fied for the gifted program in fourth grade at home. Mrs. Graham had some sense of what elementary students did in a gifted program but no idea what options were appropriate for middle school students. Of greater concern, Mrs. Graham learned that she would need to expand the identification process to the program as soon as the school year began, trying to find more of the district's diverse learners. Unfortunately, Mrs. Graham couldn't find any records about the identification process the district had used the previous year, and the teacher who had launched that process had moved out of state. Mrs. Graham knew she needed to look for answers.

Rural Schools and Gifted Education

There are a number of natural ties between gifted education and rural education. Both have borne the brunt of educational fads, both have received low priority in terms of funding, and both have received minimal national attention. (Colangelo, Assouline, Baldus, Ihrig, & New, 2006, p. 2)

The description of Mrs. Graham is based not on one particular teacher but on queries from dozens of teachers who learn each year that they will have new responsibilities in their rural schools. Because preservice teachers receive little information about gifted education or strategies to effectively differentiate curriculum for high-ability learners (Dixon, Yssel, McConnell, & Hardin, 2014; Troxclair, 2013), most of these teachers have no background in working with gifted children. With over nine million students in rural schools throughout the United States (Johnson, Showalter, Klein, & Lester, 2014), as many as 900,000 academically gifted students could benefit from professionals who understand their unique needs (e.g., the top 10% of natural abilities described in *Differentiating Model of Giftedness and Talent*, Gagné, 2013). Although districts in states that do not mandate services for gifted learners might not provide programs or hire gifted education specialists, 25 states do require the identification of and services for gifted students (National Association for Gifted Children [NAGC] & Council of State Directors of Programs for the Gifted [CSDPG], 2013). Of these states, 12 also mandate that those professionals working directly in gifted programs hold credentials in the field (NAGC & CSDPG, 2013). Of the 14 states with half or more of all public schools defined as rural, however, only six mandate the identification of and services for gifted students; of those

14 states, only four also mandate that educators working in gifted programs hold professional credentials (Johnson et al., 2014; NAGC & CSDPG, 2013).

Challenges to Rural Gifted Education

Rural schools face challenges that make the provision of services for gifted students difficult. More than 40 percent of rural students also live in poverty, a situation that more often correlates with special education services than with identification for gifted programs, yet low rates of rural students identified for special education "reflect the unwillingness and lack of capacity to deliver the services more than the incidence of need for the service" (Johnson et al. 2014, p. 14). Gifted education is not mandated by the federal government; teachers of the gifted can be perceived as unnecessary to districts that have difficulties meeting state and federal mandates (Azano, Callahan, Missett, & Brunner, 2014). Communities can also question investments in gifted education that encourage students to leave for college and careers in other places (Howley, Rhodes, & Beall, 2009; Lawrence, 2009; Roscigno, Tomaskovic-Devey, & Crowley, 2006). Although rural communities vary significantly across the country, 45% of adults in chronically poor rural areas have a high school degree or less, and the lack of educational opportunities spans generations (Ulrich, 2011).

Rural schools deal with a host of financial constraints, from limited school funding to the financial challenges of high costs for building repair, updating educational resources, and for the expenses related to transportation for students who travel as much as 2 hours each day (Azano et al., 2014; Davalos & Griffin, 1999; Gentry, Rizza, & Gable, 2001; Howley, 1989; Howley et al., 2009; Williams, 2010). Students may not be able to easily access academic materials, libraries, consistent Internet connections, computers, printers, and copy machines. Travel for gifted services can be an issue, especially to extracurricular or university programs or to academic competitions that provide high-ability students with rare opportunities to interact with others of similar ability (Burney & Cross, 2006; Colangelo, Assouline, & New, 1999; Howley et al., 2009; Pendarvis, 2009). Rural schools pay teachers less, contributing to difficulties recruiting and retaining experienced and qualified teachers (Barton, 2012; Beesley, 2011; Howley et al., 2009; Jimerson, 2004). "Rural schools have a below-average share of highly trained teachers . . . and they struggle to provide specialized services" (Witte, Coutts, Holmes, & Sheridan, 2013, p. 3).

Challenges for Rural Teachers of the Gifted

Teachers in rural schools have complex teaching loads, and they face demanding expectations, filling multiple roles in the district and teaching a variety of classes (Azano et al., 2014; Howley et al., 2009). Just as teachers receive almost no preservice education in working with gifted and talented learners, those who do not grow up in rural areas are given little programming specific to rural needs, leaving them unprepared for their new settings (Barton, 2012; Simmons, 2005; White & Kline, 2012). Teachers of the gifted often teach in multiple schools, losing instructional time driving from place to place. They may perceive a lack of access to resources and may feel both personal and professional isolation in rural communities (Azano et al., 2014; Seltzer & Himley, 1995; Simmons, 2005). Teachers of the gifted may encounter traditional values and beliefs that fail to encourage creativity, academic curiosity, and educational aspirations. Adults may not value gifted programming that conflicts with family responsibilities such as chores, caring for younger siblings, or earning money through a job after school or on the weekends (Howley et al., 2009; Lawrence, 2009). Some parents may be reluctant to allow a child to be identified as different from others his or her age (Sheridan et al., 2014). Faced with demands to comply with high-stakes accountability measures, some schools have reduced the number of more challenging academic offerings, emphasizing direct instruction to enhance the achievement of those whose scores could increase enough to suggest schoolwide improvement (Howley et al., 2009). Teachers of the gifted are often "sole advocates for gifted students in their districts without a cadre of peers or supervisors providing professional support" (Azano et al., 2014, p. 96).

Catalysts for Talent Development in Rural Schools

In spite of the varied and complex factors that inhibit services for gifted and talented learners in some rural areas, rural schools possess characteristics that are recognized as important for student success. The smallness of the schools is associated with a sense a belonging. Rural schools often are characterized by a sense of social cohesion, with strong teacher-parent connections, close relationships between teachers and students, high levels of mutual trust, and high levels of school-community interaction (Barton, 2012; Burney & Cross, 2006; Colangelo et al., 1999; Seltzer & Himley, 1995). Smaller class sizes, stable communities with a higher percentage of two-parent families, and community support are all correlated with better attendance, fewer disciplinary incidents, and lower dropout rates (Barton, 2012; Burney & Cross, 2006; Gentry et al., 2001; Colangelo et al., 1999; Roscigno et al., 2006; Smink & Reimer, 2009). Hallmarks of rural schooling have included multigrade or mixed-age classrooms, interdisciplinary learning, a more individualized focus, community service, and high levels of student participation in a wide variety of extracurricular activities (Seltzer & Himley, 1995; Colangelo et al., 1999; Robinson, Blaine, & Pace, 2004). Teachers in rural schools have greater autonomy than many teachers in other geographic settings (Barton, 2012; Gentry et al., 2001); they often have the flexibility to engage in spontaneous planning to meet the needs of their students (Colangelo et al., 1999). Rural teachers use "ingenuity to address the educational challenges of their environment" (Beesley, 2011), and many express enthusiasm toward the professional development (PD) that will provide them with new ideas (Gentry & Keilty, 2004; Glover, Ihlo, Nugent, Trainin, & Shapiro, 2014).

The Need for Professional Development

"In reality, teaching and learning are not activities that can be perfected but are processes that continually grow and change." (Kragler, Martin, & Sylvester, 2014, p. 490)

Effective teachers are the "most important school-related factor influencing student achievement" (Rice, 2003, p. v), and professional development provides the opportunities for teachers to enhance the knowledge and skills they need to support learners (Reutzel & Clark, 2014). Effective professional learning "reconnects [professionals] to the goals and ideas that brought them into teaching" (Matthews, Foster, Gladstone, Schieck, & Meiners, 2009). For decades, PD has been recognized as the way to improve teacher interaction with students and strategies for teaching that lead to more successful student learning (Desimone, Porter, Garet, Yoon, & Birman, 2002; Borko, 2004; Caena, 2011; Guskey, 2002; Organization for Economic Cooperation and Development [OECD], 2009; Penuel, Fishman, Yamaguchi, & Gallagher, 2007; Yoon, Duncan, Lee, Scarloss, & Shapley, 2007; Yuen, 2012).

The Evolution of Professional Development

The conceptualization of PD has changed significantly over the years. Elements of earlier models of PD are incorporated in newer models, but the evolution of PD has helped to define teachers as professionals, responsible for their own learning. For several decades, "teacher training" consisted of short in-service workshops. Experts instructed teachers on the implementation of a new strategy. In-service goals were to change teacher behaviors by introducing scripted materials. Although scripted curriculum has been re-introduced as a response to high-stakes accountability measures, in-service sessions have been evaluated as largely ineffective (Dettmer & Landrum, 1998; Gubbins, 2013; Kragler et al., 2014).

As theories of adult learning emerged in the 1960s, many schools replaced in-service workshops with staff development that more effectively engaged teachers in learning. Staff development was conceptualized as a long-term process, giving teachers greater responsibility for planning and implementation; teachers were encouraged to collaborate in order to address goals. Staff development, however, still focused on an implicit deficit model, trying to change specific teacher behaviors to achieve better results for students (Dettmer & Landrum, 1998; Kragler et al., 2014).

In the early years of the 21st century, the importance of constructivism as a critical approach to student learning fueled a reconceptualization for teacher learning that resulted in the phrase and philosophy of professional development (Kragler et al., 2014). Recent studies have defined effective PD, noting that the learning experience should be determined by the participants, situated in their professional setting, and characterized by longer periods of PD engagement, as well as active collaboration by school faculty (e.g., Caena, 2011; Darling-Hammond, Wei, Andree, Richardson, Ophanos, & The School Redesign Network at Stanford University, 2009; Desimone et al., 2002; Garet, Porter Desimone, Birman, & Yoon, 2001; Penuel et al., 2007; Pedder & Opfer, 2013; Yates, 2007).

Importance of PD in Gifted Education

In order to fully develop the talents of academically gifted students, PD in gifted and talented education is equally essential (Croft, 2003; Dettmer & Landrum, 1998; Dettmer, Landrum, & Miller, 2006; Gallagher, 2001; Karnes, Stephens, & Whorton, 2000; Reis & Westberg, 1994; Tomlinson, Tomchin,

Callahan, Adams, Pizzat-Tinnin, Cunningham, & Imbeau, 1994; VanTassel-Baska et al., 2008). Teachers today, however, confront expectations that they will prepare the next generation to succeed and thrive in a technologically complex global economy. Simultaneously, they must comply with local, state, and national mandates aimed at raising student achievement, and schools that had differentiated the learning experiences of high-ability learners eliminated successful practices in order to help more students achieve proficiency (Valli & Buese, 2007). PD has been defined as key to overall school improvement and achieving educational reforms (Jones & Dexter, 2014), and PD literature emphasizes strengthening the collective teaching capacity of a school faculty in order to close the achievement gap (Education Resource Strategies, 2013). The emphasis on closing the achievement gap, however, has been linked to inhibiting the academic growth and development of talent among gifted students (Xiang, Dahlin, Cronin, Theaker, & Durant, 2011). The nature and needs of the gifted, and strategies to meet those needs, rarely emerge as topics for PD (Little & Housand, 2011).

The 2012–2013 *State of the States in Gifted Education* (NAGC & CSDPG, 2013) reported that only two states require professional learning related to gifted education for general education teachers. In surveys specifically focused on the status of gifted programs, PD about the gifted ranged from 15 minutes to 4 days per year at the elementary level (Callahan, Moon, & Oh, 2013a). Almost 80% of middle schools reported fewer than 5 hours of PD about gifted education each year (Callahan, Moon, & Oh, 2013b), and almost 60% of high schools reported fewer than 5 hours per year (Callahan, Moon, & Oh, 2013c). The lack of PD dedicated to gifted and talented education is a serious disservice—to both the students and the nation—to the development of the abilities of some of the nation's most capable students.

Standards for Learning

The field of gifted education has not neglected to outline the body of specialized knowledge essential for professionals working with high-ability learners (Coleman, Gallagher, & Job, 2012). In 2006, NAGC and The Council for Exceptional Children, The Association for the Gifted (CEC-TAG) collaborated on knowledge and skill standards necessary for teachers working with gifted children (Johnsen, 2012); the organizations updated these standards in 2013 (NAGC & CEC-TAG). Each of the seven standards elaborates on the understandings essential for gifted education professionals, including the following:

- » *Standard 1: Learner Development and Individual Learning Differences*: emphasizing the variations in cognitive and affective development, even among those identified as gifted, and recognizing how culture, language, economic status, or disability can impact the development of talent;
- » *Standard 2: Learning Environments*: stressing the importance of safe, inclusive, and culturally responsive environments for gifted learners;
- » *Standard 3: Curricular Content Knowledge*: highlighting the importance of pedagogical content knowledge, as well as familiarity with differentiation strategies;
- » *Standard 4: Assessment*: including the identification of children from traditionally underrepresented groups for gifted and talented programs, as well as the use of assessments to facilitate plans for ongoing learning;
- » *Standard 5: Instructional Planning and Strategies*: elaborating on the knowledge of and ability to implement evidence-based practices, including both acceleration and enrichment, to enhance cognitive and affective development;
- » *Standard 6: Professional Learning and Ethical Practice*: encouraging reflection on the multiple and complex roles necessary for gifted education professionals; and
- » *Standard 7: Collaboration*: outlining the contemporary significance of collaborative teams, including educators, families, and gifted children, in order to maximize individual development.

Pre-K–Grade 12 Gifted Programming Standards

The field also provides Pre-K–Grade 12 Gifted Programming Standards (NAGC, 2010) to provide comprehensive guidelines for professionals who endeavor to develop, improve, and/or evaluate programs that nurture high-ability learners. The standards, outlining both student outcomes and evidence-based practices recommended to facilitate the achievement of outcomes, include:

- » *Standard 1: Learning and Development*: promoting student self-understanding, student and family/community awareness of needs, and cognitive and affective growth;
- » *Standard 2: Assessment*: highlighting identification outcomes, as well as learning progress and evaluation of programming;

- » *Standard 3: Curriculum Planning and Instruction*: elaborating on curriculum planning, talent development, instructional strategies, culturally relevant curriculum, and resources appropriate for gifted and talented learners;
- » *Standard 4: Learning Environments*: outlining outcomes and practices related to the gifted student's personal competence, social competence, leadership, cultural competence, and communication competence;
- » *Standard 5: Programming*: exploring the variety of evidence-based programming, coordinated services, collaboration, adequate funding for appropriate resources, comprehensive and aligned services, clear policies and procedures that provide for advanced learning needs, and exploration of career pathways for gifted learners; and
- » *Standard 6: Professional Development*: emphasizing the need for ongoing PD that facilitates effective talent development for high-ability students, as well as socio-emotional development, and promotes lifelong learning.

Surveys of gifted programming, however, suggest that approximately 50% of elementary programs, barely 30% of middle schools, and only 35% of high school programs were using the standards in any way (Callahan et al., 2013a, 2013b, 2013c).

From Professional Development to Professional Learning: Rural Realities

Professional development on behalf of place, community, a land ethic, and sustainability would depend on a different view of what the education of educators entails. (Howley & Howley, 2005)

If PD, understood in the context of school improvement (Evans, 2014), only infrequently addresses the needs of gifted learners, an educator such as Mrs. Graham, a teacher new to her rural school who is assigned to the role of gifted and talented educator, has the professional learning paradigm as an alternative. Especially in rural schools, where individuals dedicated to gifted education are often lone practitioners (Purcell & Eckert, 2006), "they must become learners, and they must be *self*-developing" (Easton, 2008, p. 756). Professional learning is predicated on reflective teacher inquiry and is based on specific needs embedded in specific schools.

Independent Teacher Learning

Teaching has evolved into a profession in which educators can identify the issues that affect their schools and organize and implement solutions, and the outcome will be not only a more productive learning environment for children but also an environment that inspires teachers' learning. (Kragler et al., 2014, p. 495).

Independent teacher learning is one type of professional learning that facilitates strategies for mastering national standards in gifted education that are critical to the talent development process (Jones & Dexter, 2014; Yates, 2007). Although school-based collaborative PD has been recommended as effective, "collaborative professional learning in professional communities is not the only valuable form of professional development" (Hargreaves, 2014, p. xvii). Joyce and Calhoun (2010) suggested that independent learning has great potential for professionals. Formal independent learning in gifted education includes the pursuit of credentials in the field, such as an endorsement or even a degree in gifted and talented learning. Credentials in gifted education are required in some states for those who work directly with children identified for gifted and talented programs; the formal coursework that results in professional certification suggests that educators have developed the knowledge and skills that are valued by the field (Ingvarson, 2014).

Alternatively, independent learning can be an informal process, with a teacher finding resources as necessary. Independent learning can be interactive, taking advantage of opportunities to connect with others either in person or online. Technological options, from listservs to social media, such as Facebook or LinkedIn groups, can develop a sense of connectivism—that is, a cycle of independent personal learning, followed by interactive learning (Jones & Dexter, 2014). Technology minimizes the effects of geographical challenges faced by rural schools (Belecastro, 2002), and online learning is recognized as an increasingly effective option for professional growth, allowing teachers access to lesson plans and even videos of exemplary practice (Hargreaves, 2014; Little & Housand, 2011). When several educators perceive a similar need for their students, they may develop informal learning communities, identifying their goals and necessary resources, collaborating as needed, and constructing understandings that inform practice (Borko, 2004).

Professional Learning Communities

The professional learning community (PLC) has evolved as a more formal or organized process, allowing teachers to collaborate with others who share their interests to develop their practice. Members of a PLC assume responsibility for their own learning, as well as shared responsibility for the collective learning of the group; they reflect on their beliefs and attitudes about teaching, exploring their craft in careful and systematic ways (Caena, 2011; Caskey & Carpenter, 2012). The Critical Friends Group is one example of the PLC that revolves around reflective inquiry, examining student work as a way to better understand pedagogical theory and translate research into practice (Caskey & Carpenter, 2012; Howley & Howley, 2005).

Personal Action Research

"Professional learning is an ongoing and messy process," (Kragler et al., 2014, p. 497), but honest personal reflection on beliefs and practice leads to the cognitive dissonance that allows for the transformation of practice. Personal action research is an effective professional learning option for rural educators who want to not only better understand the requisite knowledge and skills outlined in the national standards in gifted education but also to improve the educational experiences and outcomes of the gifted learners in their programs. Action research reflects the complexity of teaching itself (Willis & Edwards, 2014) and has a simple but effective implementation cycle. The teacher reflects on classroom challenges or experience with students in the rural setting. With national standards in gifted education in mind as another part of the relevant context, the teacher explores ideas and strategies to improve the outcomes for students. Reviewing research-based strategies, possibly consulting with colleagues and experts, the teacher implements the new practice and monitors student outcomes, both cognitive and socio-affective. The cycle ends—and begins again—with reflection on the experience (Walker-Floyd, 2014).

Resources for Professional Learning

> Rural communities cannot afford to lose the contributions gifted students can make to rural community, culture, and economy. (Lawrence, 2009, p. 462)

A variety of online resources provide information about gifted and talented students that can support independent professional learning goals.

Online Resources Focused on Gifted and Talented Education

The Connie Belin & Jacqueline N. Blank International Center for Gifted Education and Talent Development (http://www.belinblank.org). The Belin Blank Center, located in Iowa—a state with more than one-third of its public schools designated as rural, and at least half of those rural districts having fewer than the national rural median of 533 students (Johnson et al., 2014)—offered its first professional development opportunity, the Connie Belin & Jacqueline N. Blank Fellowship Program in Gifted Education, in 1980. The annual fellowship has provided hundreds of educators with an overview of gifted education. The Center now offers multiple professional development opportunities throughout the year, including webinars, online and in-person courses, and summer programs, all of which facilitate the completion of an endorsement in gifted and talented education. The current schedule of professional learning opportunities is available by following the link to "Educators" from the Homepage menu. The "gifted-teachers listserv" provides an online community that includes hundreds of rural educators. The Center is also home to the Acceleration Institute (http://www.accelerationinstitute.org), with links to the publications that explore the strong research basis for acceleration options for high-ability learners.

The Belin-Blank Center provides links to important information about students characterized by twice-exceptionality—that is, giftedness as well as learning disabilities. The Center also published three reports about gifted education in rural America: *Gifted Education in Rural Schools, Gifted Voices from Rural America,* and *Gifted in Rural America: Faces of Diversity* are available at http://www2.education.uiowa.edu/belinblank/researchers/.

The Davidson Institute (http://www.davidsongifted.org/). The Davidson Institute was established by Jan and Bob Davidson in 1999 to support profoundly intelligent young people and to provide opportunities for them to develop their talents to make a positive difference. Rural students have benefited from the Davidson Young Scholars and Davidson Fellows Scholarship programs. The Institute hosts the Educators Guild, an online community, for teachers committed to serving the needs of highly gifted youth. The website has a link to the Davidson Database, a collection of resources. Materials are organized by topic (resources and articles). Additionally, users can perform an advanced search if seeking information about a particular topic.

The Jack Kent Cooke Foundation (http://www.jkcf.org). The Jack Kent Cooke Foundation was established in 2000 to support exceptional students from elementary school to graduate school through scholarships, grants, direct service, knowledge creation, and knowledge dissemination. Significant funding has supported rural students and programs. In collaboration with the National Association of Gifted Children (NAGC), the Jack Kent Cooke Foundation sponsored the National Leadership Conference on Low-Income Promising Learners in 2006, resulting in the publication, *Overlooked Gems: A National Perspective on Low-Income Promising Learners*, as well as the National Summit on Low-Income, High-Ability Learners in 2012, resulting in the publication, *Unlocking Emergent Talent: Supporting High Achievement of Low-Income, High-Ability Students.*

Supporting Emotional Needs of the Gifted (SENG; http://www.sengifted.org). SENG was founded in 1981 to emphasize the importance of the unique emotional needs of gifted children. Their website provides a resource library, which includes articles, media, and reading recommendations for individuals interested in learning more about how best to support gifted students. In addition, they have webinars (called SENGinars) with experts who share information about social and emotional needs of the gifted.

Online Resources Focused on Rural Education

Other online resources emphasize rural students, including gifted and talented learners, and their educators.

The Institute of Education Sciences' National Center for Education Statistics (NCES; http://nces.ed.gov/surveys/ruraled/resources.asp). The NCES, a federal entity dedicated to collecting and analyzing data about education in the United States and other nations, has developed publications about issues and professional development in rural America. The website provides information on professional development strategies for instructional improvement in rural settings, as well as current research programs that target rural populations. A search of their website for "gifted" yields useful information.

The National Center for Research on Rural Education (http://r2ed.unl.edu/resources_organizations.shtml). The National Center for Research on Rural Education, founded in 2009 and housed at the University of Nebraska-Lincoln, is committed to research that will enhance the education of rural students. The website provides a list of rural organizations that may be of interest to educators. Additionally, resources regarding funding sources, journals, and special topics are also provided.

The Rural Education Resource Center (http://www.ed.gov/rural-education). The U.S. Department of Education supports the Rural Education Resource Center, which provides information about various resources (including grants) that may be useful in rural communities.

Resources for Schoolwide Professional Development

Although independent professional learning is an important option for many educators in rural districts, valuable resources are available that can provide guidance for PD involving groups of teachers. It is important to acknowledge, however, that "no solid empirical work on effective rural professional development exists" (Howley & Howley, 2005, p. 2), and any plans for PD need to be modified for the needs of the specific rural school.

Imbeau, M. (2006) Designing a professional development plan. In J. H. Purcell & R. D. Eckert (Eds.), *Designing Services and Programs for High Ability Learners: A Guidebook for Gifted Education* (pp. 183–194). Thousand Oaks, CA: Corwin Press and the National Association of Gifted Children.

Slade, M. L., Dettmer, P. A., & Miller, T. N. (2015). Professional development for the education of secondary gifted students. In F. A. Dixon & S. M. Moon (Eds.), *The Handbook of Secondary Gifted Education* (2nd ed., pp. 605–626). Waco, TX: Prufrock.

Gubbins, J. (2013). Professional development for novice and experienced teachers. In J. A. Plucker & C. M. Callahan (Eds.), *Critical issues and practices in gifted education: What the research says* (2nd ed.; pp. 505–517). Waco, TX: Prufrock.

Dettmer, P., & Landrum, M. (Eds.) (1997). *Staff development: The key to effective gifted education programs.* Waco, TX: Prufrock.

Conclusion

As many as 900,000 academically gifted children attend rural schools in the United States. Many of these students receive limited services designed to match their unique needs; some have no access to any accelerated or enriched curricular options. Professional development has been acknowledged as a critical factor in improving the overall quality of schools as well as student success, but local, state, and federal mandates to ensure that increasing numbers of students achieve a level of academic proficiency has minimized professional development oriented to the needs of gifted and talented learners.

Teachers committed to the learner outcomes in the Pre-K–Grade 12 Programming Standards for Gifted Programs (NAGC, 2010), as well as the Teacher Preparation Standards in Gifted and Talented Education (NAGC & CEC-TAG, 2013), can develop effective personal professional learning experiences. These independent learning experiences, formal or informal, encourage educators to systematically reflect on and update their practice. When implemented as personal action research, teachers enact a reiterative cycle of reflection on the teaching-learning experience in their rural classroom, exploration and selection of evidence-based strategies to enhance student outcomes, implementation of new strategies, and reflection on outcomes. Professional learning has the potential to facilitate effective talent development programs for academically gifted students, as well as strengthen the sense of professionalism among rural teachers.

References

Azano, A. P., Callahan, C. M., Missett, J. C., & Bruner, M. (2014). Understanding the experiences of gifted education teachers and fidelity of implementation in rural schools. *Journal of Advanced Academics, 25*(2), 88–100.

Barton, R. (2012). Recruiting and retaining rural educators: Challenges and strategies. *Principal's Research Review, 7*(6), 1–6.

Beesley, A. (2011). Keeping rural schools up to speed. *Technological Horizons in Education (THE) Journal, 38*(9), 26–27. Retrieved from thejournal.com/Articles/2011/10/04/ruralresearch.aspx?Page=2

Belecastro, F.P. (2002). Electronic technology and its use with rural gifted students. *Roeper Review, 25*(1), 14–16.

Borko, H. (2004). Professional development and teacher learning: Mapping the terrain. *Educational Researcher, 33*(8), 3–15.

Burney, V. H., & Cross, T. L. (2006). Impoverished students with academic promise in rural settings: 10 lessons from Project Aspire. *Gifted Child Today, 29*(2), 14–21.

Caena, F. (2011). *Literature review: Quality in teachers' continuing professional development.* Luxembourg: European Commission.

Callahan, C. M., Moon, T. R., & Oh, S. (2013a). *Status of elementary gifted programs.* Charlottesville, VA: National Research Center on the Gifted and Talented/University of Virginia.

Callahan, C. M., Moon, T. R., & Oh, S. (2013b). *Status of middle school gifted programs.* Charlottesville, VA: National Research Center on the Gifted and Talented/University of Virginia.

Callahan, C. M., Moon, T. R., & Oh, S. (2013c). *Status of middle school gifted programs.* Charlottesville, VA: National Research Center on the Gifted and Talented/University of Virginia.

Caskey, M. M., & Carpenter, J. (2012). Organizational models for teacher learning. *Middle School Journal, 43*(5), 52–62.

Colangelo, N., Assouline, S. G., Baldus, C. M., Ihrig, D., & New, J. (2006). *Gifted in Rural America: Faces of Diversity.* Iowa City: The University of Iowa, The Connie Belin & Jacqueline N. Blank International Center for Gifted Education and Talent Development.

Colangelo, N., Assouline, S. G., & New, J. (1999). *Gifted Education in Rural Schools: A National Assessment.* Iowa City: The University of Iowa, The Connie Belin & Jacqueline N. Blank International Center for Gifted Education and Talent Development.

Coleman, M. R., Gallagher, J. J., & Job, J. (2012). Developing and sustaining professionalism within gifted education. *Gifted Child Today, 35*(1), 27–36.

Croft, L. J. (2003). Teachers of the gifted: Gifted teachers. In N. Colangelo & G. A. Davis (Eds.), *Handbook of Gifted Education.* (3rd ed.; pp. 558–571). Boston, MA: Allyn & Bacon.

Darling-Hammond, L., Wei, R. C., Andree, A., Richardson, N., Ophanos, S., & The School Redesign Network at Stanford University. (2009). *Professional learning in the learning profession: A status report on teacher development in the United States and abroad*. Dallas, TX: National Staff Development Council.

Davalos, R., & Griffin, G. (1999). The impact of teachers' individualized practices on gifted students in rural, heterogeneous classrooms. *Roeper Review, 21*(4), 308–314.

Desimone, L. M., Porter, A. C., Garet, M. S., Yoon, R. S., & Birman, B. F. (2002). Effects of professional development on teachers' instruction: Results from a three-year longitudinal study. *Educational Evaluation and Policy Analysis, 24*(2), 81–112.

Dettmer, P., & Landrum, M. (Eds.). (1997). *Staff development: The key to effective gifted education programs*. Waco, TX: Prufrock.

Dettmer, P. A., Landrum, M. S., & Miller, T. N. (2006). Professional development for the education of secondary gifted students. In F. A. Dixon & S. M. Moon (Eds.). *The Handbook of Secondary Gifted Education* (pp. 611–648). Waco, TX: Prufrock.

Dixon, F. A., Yssel, N., McConnell, J. M., & Hardin, T. (2014). Differentiated instruction, professional development and teacher efficacy. *Journal for the Education of the Gifted, 37*(2), 111–127.

Easton, L. B. (2008). From professional development to professional learning. *Phi Delta Kappan, 89*(10), 755–759.

Education Resource Strategies. (2013). *A new vision for teacher professional growth and support: Six steps to a more powerful school system strategy*. Waterstown, MA: Education Resource Strategies. Retrieved from http://www.erstrategies.org/library/a_new_vision_for_pgs

Evans, L. (2014). Leadership for professional development and learning: Enhancing our understanding of how teachers develop. *Cambridge Journal of Education, 44*(2), 179–198.

Gagné, F. (2013). The DMGT: Changes within, beneath, and beyond. *Talent Development and Exellence, 5*(1), 5–19.

Gallagher, J. J. (2001). Personnel preparation and secondary education programs for gifted students. *Journal for the Education of the Gifted, 12*(3), 133–138.

Garet, M. S., Porter, A. C., Desimone, L., Birman, B. F., & Yoon, K. S. (2001). What makes professional development effective? Results from a national sample of teachers. *American Educational Research Journal, 38*(4), 915–945.

Gentry, M., & Keilty, B. (2004). Rural and suburban cluster grouping: Reflections on staff development as a component of program success. *Roeper Review, 26*(3), 147–155.

Gentry, M., Rizza, M. G., & Gable, R. K. (2001). Gifted students' perceptions of their class activities: Differences among rural, urban, and suburban student attitudes. *Gifted Child Quarterly, 45*(2), 115–129.

Glover, T. A., Ihlo, T., Nugent, G. C., Trainin, G., & Shapiro, E. S. (2014). The influence of rural professional development characteristics on teacher perceived knowledge and practice (R²Ed Working Paper No. 2014-2). Retrieved from http://r2ed.unl.edu

Gubbins, E. J. (2013). Professional development for novice and experienced teachers. In J. A. Plucker & C. M. Callahan (Eds.), *Critical issues and practices in gifted education: What the research says* (2nd ed., pp. 505–517). Waco, TX: Prufrock Press.

Guskey, T. R. (2002). Professional development and teacher change. *Teachers and Teaching: Theory and Practice, 8*(3/4), 381–391.

Hargreaves, A. (2014). Foreword: Six sources of change in professional development. In L. E. Martin, S. Kragler, D. J. Quatroche, & K. L. Bauserman (Eds.), *Handbook of Professional Development in Education.* (pp. x–xix). New York, NY: Guilford.

Howley, A. (1989). The progress of gifted students in a rural district that emphasized acceleration strategies. *Roeper Review, 11*(4), 205–207.

Howley, A. & Howley, C. B. (2005). High-quality teaching: Providing for rural teachers' professional development. *Rural Educator, 26*(2), 1–5.

Howley, A., Rhodes, M., & Beall, J. (2009). Challenges facing rural schools: Implications for gifted students. *Journal for the Education of the Gifted, 32*(4), 515–536.

Ingvarson, L. (2014). Standards-based professional learning and certification: By the profession, for the profession. In L. E. Martin, S. Kragler, D. J. Quatroche, & K. L. Bauserman (Eds.), *Handbook of Professional Development in Education.* (pp. 385–411). New York, NY: Guilford.

Jimerson, L. (2004). *Teachers and teaching conditions in rural New Mexico.* Arlington, VA: Rural School and Community Trust. Retrieved from http://www.ruraledu.org

Johnsen, S. K. (2012). Standards in gifted education and their effects of professional competence. *Gifted Child Today, 35*(1), 49–57.

Johnson, J., Showalter, D., Klein, R., & Lester, C. (2014). *Why rural matters 2013–14: The condition of rural education in the 50 states.* Washington, D.C.: Rural School and Community Trust. Retrieved from http://www.ruraledu.org/articles.php?id=3181

Jones, W. M., & Dexter, S. (2014). How teachers learn: The roles of formal, informal, and independent learning. *Education Technology and Research Development, 62*(3), 367–384.

Joyce, B., & Calhoun, E. (2010). *Models of professional development: A celebration of educators.* Thousand Oaks, CA: Corwin.

Karnes, F. A., Stephens, K. R. & Whorton, J. E. (2000). Certification and specialized competencies for teachers in gifted education program. *Roeper Review, 22*(3), 201–202.

Kragler, S., Martin, L. E., & Sylvester, R. (2014). Lessons learned: What our history and research tell us about teachers' professional learning. In L. E. Martin, S. Kragler, D. J. Quatroche, & K. L. Bauserman (Eds.), *Handbook of Professional Development in Education.* (pp. 483–505). New York, NY: Guilford.

Lawrence, B. K. (2009). Rural gifted education: A comprehensive literature review. *Journal for the Education of the Gifted, 32*(4), 461–494.

Little, C. A., & Housand, B. C. (2011). Avenues to professional learning online: Technology tips and tools for professional development in gifted education. *Gifted Child Today, 34*(4), 18–27.

Matthews, D., Foster, J., Gladstone, D., Schiek, J., & Meiners, J. (2009). Supporting professionalism, diversity, and context within a collaborative approach to gifted education. *Journal of Educational and Psychological Consultation, 17*(4), 315–345.

National Association for Gifted Children. (2010). *2010 Pre-K–grade 12 gifted programming standards.* Washington, D.C.: Author. Retrieved from http://www.nagc.org/resources-publications/resources/national-standards-gifted-and-talented-education/pre-k-grade-12

National Association for Gifted Children, & the Council of State Directors of Programs for the Gifted. (2013). *State of the states in gifted education: National policy and practice data 2012-2013.* Washington, D.C.: Author.

National Association for Gifted Children, & Council for Exceptional Children, The Association for the Gifted. (2013). *NAGC-CEC teacher preparation standards in gifted and talented education.* Washington, D.C.: Author. Retrieved from http://www.nagc.org/resources-publications/resources/national-standards-gifted-and-talented-education/nagc-cec-teacher

Organization for Economic Cooperation and Development. (2009). *Creating effective teaching and learning environments: First results from TALIS.* Paris, France: OECD Publishing. Retrieved from http://www.oecd-ilibrary.org/education/creating-effective-teaching-and-learning-environments_9789264068780-en

Pedder, D., & Opfer, V. D. (2013). Professional learning orientations: Patterns of dissonance and alignment between teachers' values and practices. *Research Papers in Education, 28*(5), 539–570.

Pendarvis, E. (2009). Eligibility of historically underrepresented students referred for gifted education in a rural school district: A case study. *Journal for the Education of the Gifted, 32*(4), 495–514.

Penuel, W. R., Fishman, B., Yamaguchi, R., & Gallagher, L. P. (2007). What makes professional development effective? Strategies that foster curricular implementation. *American Educational Research Journal, 44*(4), 921–958.

Purcell, J. H., & Eckert, R. D. (Eds.). (2006). *Designing services and programs for high-ability learners: A guidebook for gifted education.* Thousand Oaks, CA: Corwin and the National Association for Gifted Children.

Reis, S. M., & Westberg, K. L. (1994). The impact of staff development on teachers' ability to modify curriculum for gifted and talented students. *Gifted Child Quarterly, 38*(3), 127–135.

Reutzel, D. R., & Clark, S. K. (2014). Shaping the contours of professional development, PreK–12: Successful models and practices. In L. E. Martin, S. Kragler, D. J. Quatroche, & K. L. Bauserman (Eds.), *Handbook of Professional Development in Education.* (pp. 67–81). New York, NY: Guilford.

Rice, J. K. (2003). *Teacher quality: Understanding the effectiveness of teacher attributes.* Washington, D.C.: Economic Policy Institute.

Robinson, V., Blaine, T., & Pace, N. J. (2004). Voices in the hallway: Three rural Iowa schools. *Rural Educator, 25*(3), 1–4.

Roscigno, V. J., Tomaskovic-Devey, D., & Crowley, M. L. (2006). Education and the inequalities of place. *Social Forces, 84*(4), 2121–2145.

Seltzer, D. A., & Himley, O. T. (1995). A model for professional development and school improvement in rural schools. *Journal of Research in Rural Education, 11*(1), 36–44.

Sheridan, S. M., Kunz, G. M., Witte, A., Holmes, S., & Coutts, M. (2014). Rural parents and teachers as partners: Preliminary results of a randomized trial (R²Ed Working Paper No. 2014-4). Retrieved from the National Center for Research on Rural Education: http://r2ed.unl.edu

Simmons, B. J. (2005). Recruiting teachers for rural schools. *Principal Leadership, 5*(5), 48–52.

Smink, J., & Reimer, M. (2009). *Rural school dropout issues: Implications for dropout prevention—Strategies and programs.* Clemson, SC: National Dropout Prevention Center/Network. Retrieved from http://www.dropoutprevention.org/major-research-reports

Tomlinson, C. A., Tomchin, E. M., Callahan, C. M., Adams, C. M., Pizzat-Tinnin, P., Cunningham, C. M., & Imbeau, M. (1994). Practices of preservice teachers related to gifted and other academically diverse learners. *Gifted Child Quarterly, 38*(3), 106–114.

Troxclair, D. A. (2013). Preservice teacher attitude toward giftedness. *Roeper Review, 35*(1), 58–64.

Ulrich, J. D. (2011). Education in chronically poor rural areas lags across generations. *The Carsey Institute at the Scholars' Repository.* Paper 132. Retrieved from http://scholars.unh.edu/carsey/132

Valli, L., & Buese, D. (2007). The changing roles of teachers in an era of high-states accountability. *American Educational Research Journal, 44*(3), 519–558.

VanTassel-Baska, J., Feng, A. X., Brown, E., Bracken, B., Stambaugh, T., French, H., McGowan, S., Worley, B., Quek, C., & Bai, W. (2008). A study of differentiated instructional change over 3 years. *Gifted Child Quarterly, 52*(4), 297–312.

Walker-Floyd, L-K. K. (2014). Individual action research. In J. W. Willis & C. L. Edwards (Eds.), *Action Research: Models, Methods, and Examples* (pp. 95–109). Charlotte, NC: Information Age Publishing.

White, S., & Kline, J. (2012). Developing a rural teacher education curriculum package. *Rural Educator, 33*(2), 36–42.

Williams, D. T. (2010). *The rural solution: How community schools can reinvigorate education.* Washington, D.C.: Center for American Progress.

Willis, J., & Edwards, C. L. (2014). Varieties of action research. In J. W. Willis & C. L. Edwards (Eds.), *Action Research: Models, Methods, and Examples* (pp. 45–84). Charlotte, NC: Information Age Publishing.

Witte, A. L., Coutts, M. J., Holmes, S. R., & Sheridan, S. M. (2013). *The impact of teacher motivation for intervention on rural student behavioral outcomes* (R²Ed Working Paper No. 2013-4). Retrieved from http://r2ed.unl.edu

Xiang, Y, Dahlin, M., Cronin, J., Theaker, R., & Durant, S. (2011). *Do high flyers maintain their altitude? Performance trends of top students.* Washington, D.C.: Thomas B. Fordham Institute. Retrieved from http://edexcellence.net/publications/high-flyers.html

Yates, S. M. (2007). Teachers' perceptions of their professional learning activities. *International Educator Journal, 8*(2), 213–221.

Yoon, K .S., Duncan, T., Lee, S. W.-Y., Scarloss, B., & Shapley, K. (2007). *Reviewing the evidence on how teacher professional development affects student achievement* (Issues & Answers Report, REL 2007–No. 033). Washington, D.C.: U.S. Department of Education, Institute of Education

Sciences, National Center for Education Evaluation and Regional Assistance, Regional Educational Laboratory Southwest. Retrieved from http://ies.ed.gov/ncee/edlabs

Yuen, L. H. (2012). The impact of continuing professional development on a novice teacher. *Teacher Development, 16*(3), 387–398.

CHAPTER 16

Concluding Thoughts and Voices From Gifted Individuals in Rural Areas

Tamra Stambaugh, Ph.D.

Throughout this book, authors have shared research, or lamented a lack thereof, on a variety of strategies found effective when educating rural gifted learners. They have also shed light on the benefits and struggles of living in a rural area. In this final chapter we will examine the common themes surrounding rural education through the eyes of rural gifted students, adults, their educators, and their school counselors. Many of these voices come from chapter authors or those they have learned from when crafting their own research agenda in this area of inquiry. Although this chapter is not a formal qualitative study, it adds real-world experiences to many of the concepts that have emerged from this book. These concepts include sense of place and the benefits of rural areas, the impact of rural poverty, the struggle between staying and leaving a rural area, and the impact of educational access and support systems/strategies for developing talent.

The Rural Life and Sense of Place

A rural lifestyle matters. There is a natural pull to living in a rural area, typically dubbed as "sense of place." Although rural areas differ greatly, the critical role of family, spirituality, and the value of relationships are coupled with varying and competing definitions of success that shape the lives of rural gifted students in different ways. The appeal to a rural area can be nostalgic. The countryside, freedom to run, and the draw of nature are important aspects for many who live in rural areas. As one gifted student who just graduated from an elite university explained:

> There are both positive and negative aspects of my experiences growing up in rural [state]. Considering the bright side of things, I feel that unlike a majority of people of my generation, I was able to play in an environment surrounded by nature. My babysitter and grandparents live in wooded areas, and some of my best childhood memories are my friends and my explorations through these areas. I also grew up on a farm, which means that cows, chickens, and ducks were plentiful. For a young child, these are exciting things.

Another individual recalled the benefits of living off the land:

> You learn to love what situation you are in as a kid. I love blackberries and blackberry pie. We'd pick them and eat them. A lot of kids in the city don't get that.

The draw to rural areas and a rural way of life is something that is not outgrown. A grandfather, reflecting back on his life in rural Appalachia, said:

> I lived in the city part of the time when in second and third grade but rural was just second nature. That's where we lived. That's where I was from. I love rural and have lived rural all my life. I feel free; there's a cool wind a blowing, without the smog. The sense of owning land of your own out where you control your own environment is important. Sitting on the porch and letting the wind blow is nice. Rural [state] is tremendously favorable to me. I'd live there right now if not for the grandkids.

Community is another important aspect of the rural life for many. There is security in being known within a community. A recent college graduate explained it this way:

I benefitted from finding myself in a close-knit community. As I grew, a larger and larger fraction of my hometown learned my name. I rarely encounter strangers when I'm at home, and if I ever find myself introducing myself, I can usually reference who my grandparents are to give the other person an idea of who I am.

Another individual, who returned to a rural community for work, continued the sentiment of support experienced while growing up in a small town, as well as the role of family that pushes him toward meeting future goals:

I did feel fully supported emotionally by my family and community and enjoyed growing up in my rural community; I think indirectly, my engagement with the community, particularly in the form of many leadership opportunities, paved the foundation for me to feel confident about disciplining myself to reach any goal that I set... I dropped out of university after my third year, with no intention to return. My grades were fine, and the academics weren't challenging, but my career path (engineering, at the time) didn't seem to be fulfilling much of a "purpose of life" for me. I eventually finished up my bachelor's degree, but only for the sake of my mom, because I knew it meant so much to her—it gave her a sense of closure, I think, to some of her maternal duties to have me reach that point. It wasn't until several years later that I realized how valuable her push turned out to be.

Another individual recalled a sense of overall friendless in rural areas that he feels cannot be found elsewhere:

The people of a rural area are better natured, friendlier. You can speak to someone in a city and they just look at you and won't even speak back. In a rural area, they will stop and talk with you. They will answer you and say "hi" back. That's the way it was when I was small. We'd go to town on Saturday just to meet people and have a good time.

Differing values from the mainstream, common in many rural areas, are also an important part of sense of place. A college professor in a rural area explained:

Rural is in my blood, to the point where I (often subconsciously) view rural places as valuing relationships as opposed to urban and suburban places valuing money and power. In other words, I think I make a generalized value judgment on locale, with rural coming out on the moral high ground. I'm not saying I'm proud of this fact, but I'm acknowledging it as a prejudice that I have. But even "prejudice" isn't the right word, because I've lived in large cities for a reasonable portion of my life, 4 or 5 years. In terms of shaping me, growing up in a rural area has made me appreciate nature and even crave it; during the times when I have lived in cities, some of my most poignant memories were the times I spent at the parks, which was my connection with nature, and with rural areas. I've also developed a strong sense of spirituality and of spiritual things being more valuable than material things; I think all of this stems from the community in which I was raised.

"Outsiders" also notice this draw to the community, sense of place, and pride as a valuable part of rural life. As a school counselor observed:

I began my school counseling position as an outsider in a small town. Many of the teachers, staff, and administration in the district had lived in the area for most of their lives. Many had graduated from the consolidated high school for which I worked. From these individuals and others in the community, I learned a great deal about pride and support. I watched parades and ceremonies honoring multiple generations. I listened as parents shared the accolades of their gifted students, their eyes beaming. These small communities were willing to provide as much as possible to give their gifted students what they needed to be successful through high school.

She continued:

I learned quickly that in order to fully engage the students and help them work through their career, academic, or personal concerns, I had to connect with more than just the student; I had to include the entire family. My students considered their college and career decisions by the impact it would have on their family. Almost all of my students either chose career paths that kept them close to home or chose colleges that were within a couple of hours of their homes, but the students maintain strong relationships with their families and will enhance the future of their communities.

Brain Drain and the Push/Pull of Living in or Leaving Rural Areas

The positive draw to remain home conflicts with the pull to urban and suburban areas where many jobs and opportunities are located—especially for gifted learners. Brain drain in dwindling rural communities causes conflict in our gifted students, who feel a push toward an urban lifestyle with a pull toward home. With that come expectations of family and friends and a rural versus urban lifestyle. Competing priorities and definitions of success contribute to this conflict. A recent college graduate reflected on moving away and stated the following:

> When I was accepted to [an elite university] in my senior year, there were both encouraging and discouraging reactions. My family was excited that I had been accepted to a good school close to home for a reasonable cost. Guidance counselors, though, urged me to reconsider attending. They discussed its distance as being far from home, even though it's only an hour's drive. They encouraged me to go to a school with a less reputable academic reputation, all in the name of a negligible difference in funding. Some teachers were proud of my accomplishments and actively encouraged me to attend [this elite school]. Others viewed my decision with skepticism and accused my motivations of pretentiousness . . . Some friends are excited about my future plans. Others remark how my leaving will place serious strain on our possibilities of maintaining the strength of our bonds. It's a mixed bag of responses; so making a decision for my future has not been easy. I have responded by developing a fierce resolve to succeed in light of such praise and criticism.

This conflict was also noted by a first-generation college student who discusses how friends and family have responded to her pursuit of higher education and moving two states away for college:

> At first, my family couldn't have been more proud that I was going to do big things. But as the time for me to leave came nearer, they got less and less excited for me. In the recent event of the death of a family member, I chose not to go home because of things I needed to do at school, which was very upsetting to my family. They often have a nega-

tive attitude toward me because they feel as if I am choosing the world over them, as if I have gotten too good for them. It's a heartbreaking experience, but once I realized that it was for the best, it gets easier.

She further explained that:

Being a first-generation college student can mean many things to many people. Some people I have encountered have been ecstatic for me, and others have wished me luck and turned away. Not only being the first one to go to college, but choosing to go to a college far away from home poses a whole new set of challenges. Family values are a large part of rural life: family over everything. When living for your family is what you have been raised for and all you have ever known, it is hard to see them struggle as you continue to do your own thing away from them. I find myself in situations where I am torn between my family and my schooling. Having "high family morals" is something that is very engrained in those coming from small towns, so I often feel as though I am abandoning my family just by leaving.

A grandfather and businessman who grew up in a high poverty area in rural Appalachia explained his choices for not going to college after an invitation to try out for an athletic scholarship at an out-of-state university:

I didn't grow up going to a one-room schoolhouse but my mom and dad did. I was part of the first generation that went to high school and graduated. I guess I didn't have the courage to think outside of Appalachia. I knew that I had something special and had already showed that by excelling in high school track. I set records that are still not broken. I was given an invitation to try our for the track team at Wake Forest. I wasn't adventurous enough. People like me, from Eastern Kentucky, don't go to places like Wake Forest. Plus, if I went there, I wouldn't have married [my wife].

While some choose to stay rural, for others, the lure to the city is more enticing and a better fit, but not without conflict:

As it seems to me now, I will not be returning to my rural community anytime soon. I genuinely find myself happier in urban areas. The jobs I want for my future are not found in rural communities. This decision is not without reservations, and there are still many ties to my rural community I want to maintain. I still have a network of family and friends living at home. While I love life in the city, there is a certain pristine and peaceful quality about living surrounded by nature in the countryside. Perhaps I will return to my rural home later in life, after I have experienced the urban lifestyle I have always wanted, but for the immediate future, the life I desire is not on the farm.

The first-generation college student, who chose a different path than her rural family preferred, noted the impact on her relationships with them and her friends, as a result:

I have seen so many things and met people that not going away to college could never have been allowed to happen. I have changed a lot since going away to college. When I go home, it's like a different place. It's almost like I am a guest in my own home. I don't relate to my family and old friends as well as before I left. My family and I have grown separately and have had different influences on our lives, and we aren't the same people anymore. While it is a happy time to see my family, it is also slightly sad to see them and not feel connected to them any longer.

Moreover, many rural areas do not have the infrastructure to support the types of jobs that interest many gifted students. As an educator lamented:

Growing up in a rural area, I understand the benefits and liabilities. It can be a great lifestyle but also somewhat suffocating with decreasing opportunities for some gifted students. This is especially true when the main industry in the town is closing and unemployment is at a record high. I have always had a difficult time advising my gifted students. I saw their potential and wanted them to enjoy a life of happiness where they could pursue their interests. Many times this meant encouraging them to leave the community for education and career opportunities, as there was nothing left in the community for them—especially if they were interested in the hard sciences or obscure humanities.

Poverty in Rural Areas

Rural poverty is a real and persistent problem that prohibits talent development. As many authors in this book have explained, high poverty rates in rural areas, as well as a lack of access to appropriate opportunities are a growing problem. Poverty comes with lower education rates, excessive drug abuse, and lower paying jobs or unemployment.

One student who recently graduated from an elite university described his poverty-stricken hometown:

> The negative aspects of growing up in a rural town, in my opinion, are just as bad as the positive aspects are good. Over a quarter of residents in my hometown live below the poverty line. This situation festered in its residents. Teenage pregnancy is not uncommon and drug abuse runs rampant for a town of my size. Both of these issues stemming from poverty have had a profound impact on my life. My mother had me 2 months after turning 18 while still in high school and I have never met my biological father. The first 5 years of my life were filled with drug and physical abuse in my home that led to multiple broken arms and a broken thumb. These things can happen anywhere, but I attribute my situation to forces stemming from issues of rural poverty. Thankfully though, the possibility of a stable home life presented itself when my grandparent's took custody of me instead of allowing me to fall into the foster care system. These experiences led me to my desire to leave my rural hometown. I have always known that I wanted to be in the legal profession because of the powerful role it played in securing my future. Legal jobs are not abundant in my hometown and if I expect to realize my morally invested dreams, I must move on.

Poverty causes chasms between the haves and the have-nots and has the potential to negatively impact intrapersonal skills that contribute to talent development such as motivation, self-esteem, and social connections. As someone raised by a single mother in a rural area reflected:

> I was a "have-not" child. This is how adults in my community viewed me, how teachers viewed me, and how the kids named me. I was poor, raised by a single mother, I didn't speak properly, didn't wear the right clothes, and didn't display the proper behaviors. Being Black was not

Concluding Thoughts

an issue in my community, because we all were Black. I was set apart by my family makeup and social class. My mom didn't care, or didn't let me know that she cared. She was always blunt with me when I got off the school bus, crying after being teased and picked on the entire hour-long bus ride from school. "People are mean. Get over it," or "You don't go to school for friends, you go to get your education."

Children of poverty are also less likely to be identified or recognized as gifted, especially if they are also minority. Stereotypes are difficult to overcome—especially in small communities. We learn from someone who grew up in a rural, Black community and who was poorer than others in the area, that stereotypes abound for those who are poor and it is difficult to gain access to appropriate educational opportunities:

> I do not see myself as smart or gifted or talented. My teachers never said I was smart. I was never identified for gifted programs. In sixth grade, when planning for middle school, I overheard a group of classmates saying they would be in gifted classes for seventh grade because of their grades. As I had the same grades, I thought I should be in this "gifted" class, too. However, unlike my classmates, who were automatically scheduled for these courses, I had to ask the teacher to select these courses for me. "I don't know if you qualify," she told me. I could go on and on with stories of my experiences in school growing up poor and Black in rural Virginia. People viewed me through a stereotyped lens of being a poor, Black child of a single mom. Based on their expectations, I was supposed to be a high school dropout raising six kids of my own by the age of 18 (someone actually told me that was what they thought would happen to me). People were surprised I was so smart, or as it was often said, then, that I had "book learning." Because I didn't really have much of anything else, I focused my energy on school. School, specifically fiction books, math, and science, became my best friends. In these, I could leave reality and be another person. Computing complex math problems and understanding science meant I wasn't thinking about what I didn't have. And of course, reading took me to another world.

A teacher also reflected on her students' situations, living in a high-poverty area in rural Appalachia:

I had a student who came to school and was made fun of because of his body odor. I later learned he had been living in a chicken coop. I was also surprised to learn that running water was not common in many homes outside the town and was not a required amenity for foster care services. When I hosted one of the first parent meetings for students identified as gifted, I was surprised that only a few parents came. I later learned that most did not have the gas money to attend something as luxurious as a parent meeting. Instead, they had to conserve their gas money for the necessities of work and had just enough gas to get to work and back for the week, sometimes having to call off because they didn't have gas money. It was a vicious cycle. Many students were bright but lacked the social networks and access to develop their talent. They had to work second and third jobs and could not take advantage of extracurricular or summer enrichment opportunities because they needed to support their family or babysit younger siblings while their families worked.

Being from a rural area of poverty and moving to an elite university can also cause some culture shock. Students of poverty have to figure out how to navigate their own path as they adapt to a different economic and social culture. A student who attended an elite university explained this transition from rural poverty:

The differences were more abundant than the similarities between my hometown and [my new university]. My freshman year, one of my hallmates discussed his family's yacht in New York. His type wasn't the overwhelming majority, but it certainly wasn't uncommon either. I visited a friend's family for Thanksgiving in a gated community on Long Island. Their house was like nothing I had ever seen in real life. Before moving in at [my university], these kinds of people were fictitious—things off television shows and movie screens. I had never really noticed my family's means as limiting until I was in the presence of my peers at [my elite university]. This forced me to situate myself somewhere in between where I grew up and where I now found myself. I wanted to fit in, but I wanted the same when I went back home. This was an art difficult to master.

And another student, from a lower socio-economic rural area, reflected on his transition from school to a top-tier college:

One of my hardest challenges that I have experienced in my life was transitioning from a rural school to a top-tier university. I was given more opportunities than anyone else in my school—special schedules, taking classes early, and squeezing every academic class I possibly could out of my high school of 600 students. Even with all of that, moving to a top-tier university was a sobering experience. For the first time in my life, my defining characteristic—how I learned, my ability to take great amounts of information and apply it—was not unique. It forced me to re-evaluate myself, and figure out what my defining characteristic would be in a world where I am academically not superior. I had to learn who I was at the core of my person, while also dealing with issues from back home and meeting and experiencing so many new kinds of people that I had never encountered before. No matter how many extra classes I would have taken, I think that I still wouldn't have been prepared for college. My school pushed to make sure students graduated, not go to great schools. Once again, the top was sacrificed, allowed to get lazy and complacent, for the good of the overall body. I believe that my high school needed a fundamental change in the way that my school functioned in order to for me to have been ready for the culture change, the culture shock that I encountered.

Education and Access for Rural Gifted Students

Educators and school counselors need to be creative in finding ways to connect rural gifted learners to appropriate educational opportunities. The role of mentor, accelerated curriculum, and overall access to enriched and accelerated curriculum are important components of talent development. The following voices of rural gifted students and their educators explain issues of access, the importance of a mentor or teacher in talent identification, and an increased need for accelerated opportunities to be offered in rural areas.

Acceleration

As previously discussed by Assouline et al. in this book, acceleration is a viable option for many rural gifted students. However, it is not commonly embraced. One rural student, now attending a top-tier university, reflected on his accelerated experiences of skipping first grade and continuing with additional acceleration and personalized mathematics opportunities:

> What I know is that being accelerated is what kept me from finding school to be a completely boring waste of time. Advancing a grade, personalized math, and other various opportunities allowed me to really thrive. In the classroom, I was actually pushed, at times even challenged in my growth. And spending time in other subjects with other students a year older allowed me to grow and develop socially, learning to know people who didn't learn the same way I did.

. . . but it was not without a struggle within the system for this to happen:

> In my time as a student growing up in a rural area, going to school in a town of 800, I often came across a double standard when it came to my academic options; while I was applauded, awarded, and told that I was a once-in-a-generation student, things changed quickly when my family and those educators around me pushed for additional opportunities and resources. The institution resisted change; we were told that skipping a grade would be bad for me. As a 5-year-old kindergartener, you don't know all these things; I went to school every day, destroyed my schoolwork, and spent my time reading or playing teacher with the other students. The reasons why I was told I couldn't do things were numerous and varied. I couldn't skip a grade because my motor skills were too poor. I would get behind in art, and I would physically be miles away. Socially I would be a hermit, rejected by my classmates as the nerd. Rather than push me to be my absolute best, I was told to succeed via their rules, rules that would pull me back down to the crowd.

He continued:

> They said I would never play sports. I wasn't great, but I lettered in two varsity sports. They said I would be a hermit. As I write this, my best friend, the high school starting quarterback, is visiting me from his school, and we are as close as ever. I have a wonderful, loving girlfriend whom I love very much. They said I would never improve my handwriting. Well . . . they were right about something.

Support systems for advanced educational opportunities are needed, and there are rural educators and school counselors who rally around students to find creative ways within the community to make sure rural students have the opportunities necessary for growth. A school counselor in a rural area described how she found ways to support her students through accelerated and enriched opportunities via technology:

> Technology was essential to my work with these rural gifted students. I used the Internet and social media sites to help students connect to outside resources. For example, we accessed additional AP courses through online companies, we researched new ideas and concepts the student or I had seen on Twitter or other media, and we made connections with professors or professionals across the country and the world to give students new perspectives.

When these support systems are in place for gifted students, the results can be life changing. As the student who was accelerated reflected:

> Rural schools are trapped in a bit of fear, a fear of change. They are afraid of what happens when they let students deviate from a formula that more or less works. When they embrace that change, though, I believe that students are allowed to strive, to challenge themselves, to grow into their fullest potential, and become great examples of success of rural schooling. That's my experience.

Role of Mentors and Significant Individuals

The need for guidance and support of rural gifted students is critical. Many gifted students in general reflect on the role of mentors or supportive educators as major contributors to their life trajectory and life choices, especially for career planning. The mentor role is even more critical for students of poverty. A first-generation college student from a rural area explained her need for a mentor and other support networks as she pioneers a new path in pursuing a college education:

> My support structure coming from home is not the best, while my support system at school is phenomenal. One of many positive experiences I have had as a freshman is that I have met many amazing people along

the way that are willing to help me. It's a great feeling to be told by someone that you are doing the right thing, even when you think you aren't. I feel that having some kind of support structure is very important, and if it doesn't come from family, it could come where you least expect it.

A now college professor from a single-parent home and a high-poverty rural area described how a special educator impacted her life simply by recognizing potential and providing access to an opportunity:

My teachers didn't talk to me about my future. The school counselor never talked to me about my options after high school. Because I was unaware of what I could do, I made plans for what I knew I could do, and that was working, same as my mom. College was not something to which I could aspire as a poor, Black, student of a single mother; no matter that my GPA has me ranked fourth in my junior class. If it were not for an African American special education teacher at my school—a teacher who had never taught me but who for some reason walked up to me in the hallway one day, put a college application in my hand and said, "you should apply to this program,"—I know my entire adult life would have been different. I was a "have-not" child and I am a "have-not" adult. I cannot erase my childhood educational experiences. Instead, I now embrace my "have-not" status and use it to fuel my advocacy efforts for other poor kids, kids of single moms, kids who are not seen for their potential, but instead are viewed through stereotypes, stereotypes that discount one's aptitude for learning just because they are poor and Black.

And another individual recalled his scolding from his teacher about his early career choice:

I do remember an interesting incident that occurred. I had received my bachelor's degree already and had moved back to my hometown where I was substitute teaching in the school I had attended K–12. I was in a grocery store one day and I saw my eighth-grade English teacher. She asked me what I was up to and, when I told her I was substitute teaching with no particular plans beyond that, she let me have it. I remember it vividly—it was in between the soup and the snacks aisle, and she raised her voice to scold me, saying that it would be such a waste of potential if I never aspired further than substitute teaching. She was clearly emotionally invested and even mentioned something about her career being meaningless if students "like me" didn't go on and do "something great."

Educators and parents can be strong supports in students' lives. As noted from a college student who, in elementary school, was one of the first students ever accelerated in his rural school, a strong support system of people who rallied around him to provide the services necessary for him to thrive was instrumental in his future:

> I was very, very lucky in my support system. I had parents who knew I needed more, a gifted teacher who would do anything to help me, and administrators from an educational service center who spent many, many hours fighting for me to have the chance to do my best. These people weren't going to let me fall through the cracks; they saw my potential and they made sure I would be able to show it.

Lack of Awareness and Access

Although mentors have played an influential role in the lives of rural gifted individuals, mentors seem to be few and far between. Rural gifted students note a lack of access, lack of awareness of possible career choices, and inappropriate preparations for succeeding in college, if they choose to attend. When asked about influential factors or supports in his talent trajectory, a professor from a rural area reflected on his path:

> I certainly didn't know anything about graduate school when I was in high school, even though I was valedictorian. My graduating class had 65 students and was located in a small, primarily agrarian community. The first time I remember even hearing about graduate school as an option for me was from my academic advisor in college. So, I can't say that there were any direct supports, and the only direct detractor was a lack of awareness.

Educators and school counselors try to find opportunities for their students but have some difficulty locating appropriate resources, as a school counselor explained:

There were many things the community could not provide to their gifted students. As a school counselor, I struggled to find appropriate and accessible mental health providers for referrals to my gifted students and their families. Though many of the gifted students in the rural communities had a strong work ethic, time and energy to take on a full load of challenging courses was limited. Many of the students were engaged in a large number of school extracurricular activities, as well as multiple church and family work commitments that made it difficult for them to commit the extra amounts of time necessary to take on several Advanced Placement courses each semester. When exploring career options, students were sometimes reluctant to consider paths that were unknown and finding appropriate mentors or role models in the area was difficult.

If students do decide to attend college, they may not feel as prepared, especially if pioneering a path. A first generation college freshman from a high-poverty rural area described her first semester at college:

> My experiences at home did not at all prepare me for college. I never learned anything outside of what my mother knew, who was born and raised in the same town as I was. Education was never stressed in my house, confined solely to my time in the school building. Where I was raised, nobody really leaves. I was one of the few who made the decision to go out of state. It is a very work-oriented area where college is not something that is expected. Academically, I was not prepared for the work. Socially, I was not ready for the diversity. Financially, I was not expecting the issues I have encountered paying for school on my own. The high school I attended was not geared towards preparation for college, but more for graduation. The classes I took had little bearing on my choice or acceptance to college. I have chosen to take on a completely different demographic than where I came from, and I have had to figure out a lot of it on my own.

Conclusion

Rural areas have many positive aspects that make them a great place to live. The strong sense of community—of being known, opportunities for leadership, and the beauty of the outdoors are part of rural culture that many celebrate. However, rural poverty is prevalent and prohibits talent identification and development. Moreover, educational opportunities are teacher dependent and rural gifted students need access to mentors, accelerated educational experiences, and specialized opportunities to develop their talents. They also need supportive educators and parents to help them understand their college and career choices within their rural area as well as outside their town, should they choose. Of course, infrastructures of schools and the viability of the rural community play a large part in how talent in rural areas is or is not developed. There are many talent development opportunities for rural students to embrace within a rural community if rural educators are creative, work to understand the needs of gifted students, embrace flexibility and change, and maximize the uniqueness of the community to benefit and connect students to appropriate learning opportunities.

About the Editors

Tamra Stambaugh, Ph.D., is an assistant research professor in special education and executive director of Programs for Talented Youth at Vanderbilt University Peabody College. She received her Ph.D. in Educational Policy, Planning, and Leadership with an emphasis in gifted education from the College of William and Mary. She is the co-author/editor of several books including *Comprehensive Curriculum for Gifted Learners* (with Joyce VanTassel-Baska), *Overlooked Gems: A National Perspective on Low-Income Promising Students* (with Joyce VanTassel-Baska), *Leading Change in Gifted Education* (with Bronwny MacFarlane), the *Jacob's Ladder Reading Comprehension Program Series* (with Joyce VanTassel-Baska), and *Practical Solutions for Underrepresented Gifted Students: Effective curriculum* (with Kim Chandler), as well as numerous book chapters and research articles. Stambaugh's research interests focus on talent development support structures for gifted students and key curriculum and instructional interventions that support gifted learners—especially those students from rural backgrounds and those from poverty.

Susannah M. Wood, Ph.D., is an associate professor at the University of Iowa where she teaches both doctoral students and students who are pursing their master's in school counseling with an emphasis in gifted education in partnership with The Connie Belin and Jacqueline N. Blank International Center for Gifted Education and Talented Development. Susannah received her M.Ed.

in School Counseling and Ph.D. in Counselor Education and Supervision from the College of William and Mary. She was a middle school counselor working with 6th and 7th grade students in Newport News, VA during the academic year, and spent summers as a residential counselor for programs such as Johns Hopkins' Center for Talented Youth and the Virginia Governor's School for the Visual and Performing Arts and Humanities. Her research interests encompass preparing school counselors for their practice with a focus on serving the gifted population in collaboration with other educators and professionals.

About the Authors

Susan G. Assouline, Ph.D., is the director of the University of Iowa's Belin-Blank Center for Gifted Education and Talent Development and a professor of school psychology. She is especially interested in the identification of academic talent in elementary students and is coauthor (with Ann Lupkowski-Shoplik) of both editions of *Developing Math Talent: A Comprehensive Guide to Math Education for Gifted Students in Elementary and Middle School*. As well, she is codeveloper of the *Iowa Acceleration Scale*, a tool designed to guide educators and parents through decisions about grade-skipping students; she has consulted on hundreds of decisions concerning acceleration. She has also developed, with Megan Foley-Nicpon, a research agenda on twice-exceptionality that has resulted in receiving the MENSA Research Award from the MENSA Education & Research Foundation. In 2004, she coauthored and coedited, with Nicholas Colangelo and Miraca U. M. Gross, the ground-breaking two-volume publication, *A Nation Deceived: How Schools Hold Back America's Brightest Students.*

Elissa F. Brown, Ph.D., is the Statewide Director of Secondary Projects at the North Carolina Department of Public Instruction, where she facilitates coordination of large-scale state initiatives for middle and high schools. In addition, she serves as a Regional Lead for the Statewide System of Support model as part of Race to the Top. She came to the state agency in 2007 as State

Consultant for Academically/Intellectually Gifted. Prior to her move to North Carolina, she was the Director of the Center for Gifted Education at the College of William and Mary in Williamsburg, VA. She has taught undergraduate and graduate courses in education at several universities and is an adjunct professor at Duke University. She received her bachelor's degree from the University of Georgia and a master's from Western Carolina University. She received her Ph.D. in Educational Planning, Policy, and Leadership from the College of William and Mary. She is a published author and presents widely. She is president-elect of the North Carolina Association for Research in Education. She has been a high school principal, USED grant manager, central office administrator, and teacher.

Eric Calvert, Ph.D., is an associate director at the Center for Talent Development at Northwestern University, where he oversees the Gifted LearningLinks online program and teaches graduate courses in gifted education and facilitates professional development on gifted education topics for K–12 educators. Previously, he served as Assistant Director for Gifted Education at the Ohio Department of Education and taught in the Learning Design program at Bowling Green State University. Dr. Calvert is actively involved in gifted education and educational technology organizations and serves on the governing board of the Ohio Association for Gifted Children.

Nicholas Colangelo, Ph.D., is the Dean of the College of Education at the University of Iowa. He is also the Myron & Jacqueline Blank Professor of Gifted Education and Director Emeritus of The Connie Belin & Jacqueline N. Blank International Center for Gifted Education and Talent Development. He is author of numerous articles on counseling gifted students and the affective development of gifted and acceleration. Dr. Colangelo has edited three editions of *Handbook of Gifted Education* (with Gary Davis). He has coauthored *A Nation Deceived: How Schools Hold Back America's Brightest Students* (with Susan Assouline and Miraca Gross) and *Gifted Education in Rural Schools: A National Assessment* (with Susan Assouline and Jennifer New). He has presented a number of research papers at national and international conferences and has been a keynote speaker on numerous occasions. His work has been recognized by several prestigious organizations both nationally and internationally.

Susan Corwith, Ph.D., is an associate director at the Center for Talent Development at Northwestern University. Dr. Corwith received her Ph.D. from the University of Wisconsin-Madison in educational leadership and policy analysis with an emphasis on attributes of high-quality programs for gifted students. She has been active in the field of gifted education for over 20 years as a K–12 educator, gifted program coordinator, and researcher. Prior to joining

About the Authors

CTD, she was president of the Wisconsin Center for Academically Talented Youth.

Laurie Croft, Ph.D., is a clinical associate professor in the Department of Teaching and Learning at the University of Iowa College of Education and is the associate director for professional development at The Connie Belin & Jacqueline N. Blank International Center for Gifted Education and Talent Development. She received her bachelor's and master's in history from Oklahoma State University and the University of Oklahoma, respectively. She earned her Ph.D. in educational leadership at the University of Tulsa, with an emphasis in gifted programming. Research interests include the conceptual foundations of gifted education and professional development for teachers of the gifted. Croft has made presentations at various state, national, and international conferences, and to parent groups, teachers, and school boards. She also has experience facilitating professional learning in gifted education for educators from around the world. Croft is responsible for coordinating the comprehensive program of classes and workshops in gifted education that enable educators to earn an endorsement in gifted education, and she supervises practicum experiences in gifted education. She has developed new courses in curriculum concepts and in program models in gifted education. Croft serves as the honors advisor for the College of Education Honors Opportunity Program, and she encourages undergraduates in the Teacher Education Program to complete coursework in gifted education, a shortage area in Iowa, as well as other states.

Megan Foley-Nicpon, Ph.D., is an associate professor of counseling psychology and Associate Director for Research and Clinic at the Belin-Blank Center for Gifted Education and Talent Development, both at the University of Iowa. Dr. Foley-Nicpon's research and clinical interests include assessment and intervention with twice-exceptional students—particularly gifted students with autism spectrum disorder, ADHD, and emotional/learning difficulties—and the social and emotional development of talented and diverse students. She has more than 35 referred articles and book chapters in the areas of gifted, counseling psychology, and twice-exceptionality, and more than 60 presentations at international, national, and state professional meetings. Dr. Foley-Nicpon provides clinical and research supervision to doctoral students in counseling psychology, many of whom focus on twice-exceptionality and talent development. Awards include the NAGC Early Scholar Award, AERA Research on Giftedness, Creativity and Talent Path Breaker Award, AERA Division E Outstanding Research Award in Human Development, and, twice, the MENSA Research Award from the MENSA Education & Research Foundation.

Donna Y. Ford, Ph.D., is a professor in the Peabody College of Education and Human Development at Vanderbilt University. She holds an appointment in the Department of Special Education and the Department of Teaching and Learning. Ford has been a professor of special education at the Ohio State University, an associate professor of educational psychology at the University of Virginia, and a researcher with the National Research Center on the Gifted and Talented. She also taught at the University of Kentucky. Ford earned her doctoral degree in urban education (educational psychology), master's degree (counseling), and bachelor's degree in communications and Spanish from Cleveland State University. Dr. Ford conducts research primarily in gifted education and multicultural/urban education. She is highly published and has a extensive line of scholarship. Specifically, her work focuses on closing the achievement gap in five major ways: (a) recruiting and retaining culturally different students in gifted education, (b) developing multicultural curriculum and instruction, (c), reversing underachievement among gifted Black students, (d) increasing Black family involvement, and (e) developing culturally competent educators. She consults with school districts and educational organizations nationally, and serves in several leadership roles in both gifted and urban education.

Kristin Flanary is the administrator for the Iowa Online AP Academy and the director of the AP Teacher Training Institute at the University of Iowa's Belin-Blank Center for Gifted Education and Talent Development. Through these avenues, Kristin works to bring access to Advanced Placement and above-level courses to high-ability students in rural schools across Iowa and beyond. She brings personal experience to this area, as she grew up as a gifted education student in a small, rural school. Kristin has also worked at the Texas Tech University Honors College as a mentor to first-year honor students. There, she was named Honors Student of the Year when she graduated *summa cum laude* with a B.A. in psychology and Spanish. She then studied social and cognitive neuroscience at Dartmouth College, where she received a M.A. in experimental psychology.

Marcia Gentry, Ph.D., is a professor of educational studies and directs the Gifted Education Resource Institute at Purdue University. She has received multiple grants worth several million dollars in support of her work with programming practices and underrepresented populations in gifted education. Dr. Gentry's research interests include student attitudes toward school and the connection of these attitudes toward learning and motivation; the use of cluster-grouping and differentiation to meet the needs of students with gifts and talents while helping all students achieve at high levels; the use of nontraditional settings for talent development; the development and recognition of talent among underserved populations, including students with diverse cultural backgrounds such as Native American youth; and children who live in poverty. She actively participates in the National Association for Gifted Children, serving two terms on its Board of Directors; serves on the American Educational Research Association's Special Interest Group for research on gifted, creativity, and talent; frequently contributes to the gifted education literature (with more than 100 publications); and regularly serves as a speaker and consultant. She has collaborative projects across the country (15 states) and around the world. Prior to her work in higher education, she spent 12 years as a teacher and administrator in K–12 settings. She enjoys spending time with family and friends, gardening, hanging out in the horse barn, collecting contemporary Navajo weavings, spending time at her a cabin on Whitefish Bay (Lake Superior), and working with her doctoral students. She was the 2014 recipient of the prestigious National Association for Gifted Children's Distinguished Scholar Award.

Dana Griffin, Ph.D., is an associate professor at The University of North Carolina at Chapel Hill. A former school counselor, Dr. Griffin now teaches in the School Counseling program in the School of Education. Dr. Griffin researches best practices for schools and school counselors working with culturally diverse parents and communities, specifically African American and Latino populations. Further, she is committed to social justice and advocacy, and believes that school counselors are in pivotal roles to pave the way for bridging the gap between families, schools, and communities. She is committed to the multicultural training of preservice and professional counselors in hopes that it may lead to better relationships, collaboration, and increased effectiveness when working with culturally diverse families and students.

Angela M. Housand, Ph.D., is an associate professor at the University of North Carolina Wilmington and a national consultant. As a former teacher, Dr. Housand brings an applied focus to her instructional programs for teachers, as well as her research testing the effectiveness of the FutureCasting digital life skills program. Over the years, her work has been presented internationally and published in top journals. Her efforts directly support teachers as they challenge students to achieve advanced levels of performance while becoming productive citizens in a global society. For more, visit http://www.angelahousand.com.

Brian C. Housand, Ph.D., is an associate professor and co-coordinator of the Academically and Intellectually Gifted Program at East Carolina University. In 2014, he received the Max Ray Joyner Award for Outstanding Teaching in Distance Education at ECU. Dr. Housand earned a Ph.D. in educational psychology at the University of Connecticut's Neag Center for Gifted Education and Talent Development with an emphasis in both gifted education and instructional technology. He currently serves on the National Association for Gifted Children Board of Directors as a Member-at-Large. Brian frequently presents and works as an educational consultant on the integration of technology and enrichment into the curriculum. He researches ways in which technology can enhance the learning environment and is striving to define creative-productive giftedness in a digital age. His website is http://www.brianhousand.com.

Aimee Howley, Ph.D., founder and lead researcher for WordFarmers Associates, has a broad background in educational research, evaluation, and policy studies. She is also professor emerita at Ohio University, where she served as a faculty member in the Educational Studies Department and as Senior Associate Dean of the Patton College of Education. Dr. Howley's research explores the intersection between social context and educational practice, and she has used both quantitative and qualitative methods to investigate a wide range of questions relating to rural education, educational reform, school leadership, and education for diverse learners. Dr. Howley has authored or coauthored five books, numerous book chapters, and more than 60 refereed journal articles.

Craig Howley, Ed.D., has studied educational scale, rural education, intellect and talent development, mathematics education, and the relationship between culture, political economy, and schooling. Retired from Ohio University, he currently does evaluation and research for WordFarmers Associates. At the university he taught courses on rural education and directed dissertations as an adjunct faculty member. His undergraduate degree is in comparative literature, his master's degree in gifted education, and his Ed.D. in school administration (from West Virginia University). He has authored or coauthored 27 books or book chapters and 57 peer-reviewed research articles. He lives with his family on a small farm in rural Ohio.

Gail Fischer Hubbard served as Supervisor of Gifted Education for Prince William County Public Schools in Virginia for 26 years. Before she entered administration, she was a high school gifted education resource teacher for a decade. Mrs. Hubbard has served as the President of the Virginia Association for the Gifted, as Chairperson of the Virginia Consortium of Administrators of Gifted Programs, and as Chairperson of the Virginia Advisory Committee for the Education of the Gifted. Mrs. Hubbard received her A.B. from Bryn Mawr College and her Masters of Arts in Teaching from Harvard University. She taught in Washington, D.C., in Niagara Falls, NY, and in Ithaca, NY, before moving to Virginia. She was raised in a rural community and began first grade in a two-room schoolhouse.

Erin Lane is a doctoral student in counselor education and supervision at the University of Iowa. Upon entry, she was awarded a Presidential Fellowship

About the Authors

from the Graduate College. As part of that award, Erin assists with the planning and implementation of the STEM Excellence program, an afterschool STEM acceleration course for gifted students in rural schools provided by their schools through support from the Belin-Blank Center for Gifted Education and Talent Development. Prior to her doctoral work, Erin served as the Gifted Education Counselor for 9th–12th-grade students in Pleasant Hill, IA. Erin received her M.A. in School Counseling from the University of Iowa after 5 years as a teacher and administrator in private education. Ms. Lane's research interests include the counseling experiences of gifted students in K–12 education, college and career readiness factors for gifted students, and school counselor advocacy.

Joan D. Lewis, Ph.D., is a professor emeritus of teacher education at the University of Nebraska at Kearney. Until her retirement, she directed the graduate program in gifted and talented education for the University of Nebraska System, developing and teaching the six endorsement classes, including for distance transmission and interactive online delivery. Dr. Lewis has published widely and speaks frequently at local, state, national, and international conferences in the areas of alternative assessment, gifted girls, the role of school principals in supporting quality education for gifted learners, public relations and advocacy, use of RtI for identifying and serving gifted and talented learners, rural gifted education, social and emotional needs of gifted learners, and uses of technology in education. Dr. Lewis has coauthored a book chapter on public relations, as well as books on advocacy and educating rural gifted students. Her work with local and state associations in gifted education has spanned more than 30 years.

Marybeth J. Mattingly, Ph.D., is Director of Research on Vulnerable Families at the Carsey School of Public Policy and a research assistant professor of sociology at the University of New Hampshire. Her work examines how child poverty and policies affect rural, suburban, and urban families and how growing up poor influences life outcomes. Beth has been published in several academic journals, including *Social Forces and Journal of Marriage and Family*, and in edited volumes. Her work has been featured in *Time* magazine, *Real Simple* magazine, *USA Today*, and other media outlets. Beth received her master's and doctoral degrees from the University of Maryland. She has an undergraduate degree in geography from Dartmouth College.

Paula Olszewski-Kubilius, Ph.D., is the director of the Center for Talent Development at Northwestern University and a professor in the School of Education and Social Policy. Over the past 30 years, she has created programs for all kinds of gifted learners and written extensively on issues of talent development. She has served as the editor of *Gifted Child Quarterly*, coeditor of the

Journal of Secondary Gifted Education, and on the editorial review boards of *Gifted and Talented International*, *The Roeper Review*, and *Gifted Child Today*. Dr. Olszewski-Kubilius is Past-President of the National Association for Gifted Children and received the Distinguished Scholar Award in 2009 from NAGC.

Zachary J. Richards grew up on his family's cattle farm in Scottsville, KY in the south central region of the state. He graduated in 2014 from Vanderbilt University with a Bachelor of Arts in the history of art and philosophy, with highest honors for his senior thesis, "My Rural Life: Inheritance, Race, Morality, and Education." In addition to his studies, Zachary also served as a grant assistant for Vanderbilt Programs for Talented Youth's Jack Kent Cooke Foundation Grant, helping to provide access to the organization's summer programs for gifted learners to students of poverty. He is currently pursuing his Juris Doctorate at the Georgetown University Law Center as a member of the class of 2018.

Andrew Schaefer is a Vulnerable Families Research Associate at the Carsey School of Public Policy and a doctoral candidate in Sociology at the University of New Hampshire with a concentration in religion, family, and work. His work at Carsey focuses on poverty, the social safety net, and women and work, including policies and programs that support low-income and other working families. He is currently working on projects exploring the gender gap in leisure time and children's access to public health insurance during and after the Great Recession.

Kristen Seward has over 17 years in public schools as a teacher, at-risk counselor, and guidance director. She teaches undergraduate and graduate classes and coordinates Purdue University's Gifted Education Resource Institute's Summer Residential programs for students in grades 5–12. She assists parents, students, and K–12 educators with various issues related to educating gifted students. Her research interests include the affective needs of gifted students, gifted education in rural contexts, gifted education teaching and learning for all students, and professional development.

Daniel Showalter, Ph.D., received an M.S. in mathematics from Ohio University and a Ph.D. in mathematics education from Ohio University. He teaches mathematics, mathematics education, and research methods courses at Eastern Mennonite University. Dr. Showalter has published on the intersection of mathematics and fields such as rural education, place-based education, adult basic education, music, and East Asia. He works as a quantitative analyst for the Rural School and Community Trust, a nonprofit organization focusing on rural schools.

About the Authors

Joyce VanTassel-Baska, Ph.D., is the Jody and Layton Smith Professor Emerita of Education and former Executive Director of the Center for Gifted Education at The College of William and Mary in Virginia, where she developed a graduate program and a research and development center in gifted education. She also initiated and directed the Center for Talent Development at Northwestern University. She has worked as a consultant on gifted education projects in all 50 states, as well as internationally, and served as the president of the National Association for Gifted Children. Dr. VanTassel-Baska has published 29 books and over 550 refereed journal articles, book chapters, and scholarly reports and has received over $15 million in grants to explore curriculum interventions for gifted learners.